An eminent physician and consultant in Bombay for well over four decades, Dr. R.H. Dastur has participated in and presented papers at several national and international seminars and has lectured extensively on health problems. He has been interested in the health of the manager as well as the worker. He has all along been involved in educating the lay people on various aspects of health and has been a regular columnist on health topics in the Sunday Review of the *Times of India*. He has advised numerous industrial organisations and workers' unions on preventive health. He has spent more than two decades in evolving the concept that the diseases of modern civilisation depend upon how we respond to stress: how to neutralise its ill-effects and how to use stress to prevent diseases and lead a full life. He is an approved Fellow in sex education of the International Council of Sex Education and Parenthood of the American University, Washington, and a Member of the Indian Society of Health Administrators. In February 1990, International Council of Sex Education and Parenthood (ICSEP) honoured Dr. R. H. Dastur for his leadership and contribution in the field of sexuality. He is a recipient of a special decoration from the Bombay Hospitality Committee as 'A Distinguished Author'. He is also a winner of the Escorts Book Award presented by the Delhi Management Association.

By the same author :

Rock Around the Clock
Are You Killing Yourself Mr.Executive?
Sex and Diseases
What the Doctor Says...

SEX POWER

The Conquest of Sexual Inadequacy

Dr. R.H. DASTUR

Cover Illustration
R.K. Laxman.

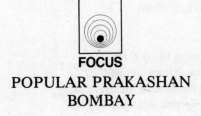

FOCUS
POPULAR PRAKASHAN
BOMBAY

Illustrated by
S. G. Kamat

First published 1983
Reprinted 1983, 1985, 1987, 1989, 1990,
Reprinted 1992, 1993, 1994, 1998, 2000

(4001)

ISBN 81-7154-126-7

Phototypeset by the Type Shop
52, Mittal Court, 'C' Wing, 5th Floor
Nariman Point, Mumbai 400 021

PRINTED IN INDIA
By Tarun Enterprises, Delhi

Published by Ramdas Bhatkal for
Popular Prakashan Private Limited
35-C, Pandit Madan Mohan Malaviya Marg,
Opp. Crossroad, Tardeo, Mumbai 400 034.

THIS BOOK IS DEDICATED TO YOU:

Dear Parents: The seed of impotency or frigidity is often sown in the cradle. You can teach your children healthy sexuality and prevent sexual inadequacies, when they grow up.

The space century male: You can have the latest information on sexual responses to improve your performance.

The prematurely ejaculating or impotent male: You feel 'there is no light anywhere and you cannot take it anymore'. This book will 'lead you out of the darkness' and restore your normal sexual responses.

The inhibited female: The book shows you how to respond spontaneously in sex; how to cope with frigidity and have the sublime satisfaction of 'putting together once again' your impotent or prematurely ejaculating partner.

The knowledge-seeking family physician: You are the backbone of the medical profession yet you know not where to turn for 'light'.

The virile Casanova: You don't need to read this book, Sir.

FOREWORD

As a practising gynaecologist and reproductive endocrinologist specialising in sterility and conversant with sexual dysfunction in both sexes, it gives me great pleasure to introduce this up-to-date, eminently readable and illustrated book to the reader. During the last two decades the West has been suffering from over-exposure to 'sex' in the media, resulting in lack of interest and loss of desire. On the other hand, an abysmal ignorance, myths and misconceptions about sex prevail in our country. Sex is still taboo, not to be written or talked about. The so-called evils of masturbation, night discharges, spermatorrhoea and orgasmic difficulties are still major causes of sexual dysfunction in our country.

In *Sex Power,* Dr. Dastur has not only given modern methods of treating sexual dysfunction but also shows the way to its prevention. 'The seed of sexual inadequacy,' he rightly says, 'is sown in the cradle.' The stress on the preventive aspect of sexual dysfunction from the cradle to old age is a unique feature of this book, which I do not recollect having seen in other works on sex. The detailed case histories lend authenticity to the text.

Another striking feature is Dr. Dastur's tremendous concern and knowledge about the art of arousing and gratifying the female partner. *Sex Power* is a harmonious blend of the East and the West in sexuality. The book will be of immense help to every man and woman seeking sexual enlightenment. It will also serve as a useful guide to family physicians, eager to help their patients overcome common sexual problems.

In conclusion, I would say that Dr. Dastur in his constant endeavour to promote public health education through medical articles and books has filled an important lacuna in our knowledge about sexuality and sex.

Dr. Geeta N. Pandya
M.B.B.S., D. (Obst.) R.C.O.G. Fellow of the Royal College of Obst. and Gynace.
Honorary Consultant, Gynace Endocrinologist,
Jaslok and Breach Candy Hospitals.

ACKNOWLEDGEMENTS

It was possible to complete my third book because of the help and cooperation of many people, in spite of a very busy office schedule. First and foremost, I must thank Dr. D.R. Sanjana for looking after routine work at the office. Miss Coomi Chinoy for so painstakingly editing the manuscript. A researcher who prefers to remain anonymous for her invaluable help. Miss Veena Peswani and Mrs. Surekha Prabhu for typing the manuscript. I am indeed grateful to my wife for sparing me from social engagements.

Last but not the least, I am grateful to all the readers of my articles on 'Preventive Health' in the *Times of India* who have expressed a keen desire for a comprehensive book on 'Sexual Inadequacies' so prevalent in our country.

I sincerely regret the inconvenience caused to all the readers due to the non-availability of my books originally published by India Book House.

I am happy that Popular Prakashan will henceforth publish my books under the banner — Focus on Health

R. H. DASTUR

'Shanti Kuteer'
Netaji Subhas Road
BOMBAY-400 020.
1st May 1987

CONTENTS

therapeutic concepts — Basic principles of sex therapy —
Therapy programme — Do it yourself technique — Solo
erotic experiences (single partner) — Handling a female
partner — Exercises with a partner — Other modes of
treatment: Aphrodisiacs — Drugs — Sex hormone
therapy — Sex aids — Internal devices — How to get what
you want in sex without an erection — Temporary loss of
erection — Permanent loss of erection — How to make a
limp penis enter a vagina.

INTRODUCTION

When you can't take any more
When you feel your life is over
Put down your tablets and pick up your pen
And I'll put you together again.

If your faith withers away
If God can't bring you your answer
Write me a letter and I'll read it and then
I'll put you together again.

If there's no light anywhere
And you've got no one to turn to
I'll lead you out of the darkness and then
I'll put you together again.

Put us together together again
Put us together again
When things look hopeless just write me and then
I'll put you together again.

HOT CHOCOLATE

SEX IS the element force in life. Nature's mighty urge is stronger than hunger and fear. Life without the spice of sex is like an insipid Goa curry without coconut or condiments! Success in sex comes from vibrant health— a state of complete physical, mental, emotional and sexual well-being.

My two earlier books, *Are You Killing Yourself, Mr. Executive?*

and *Rock Around The Clock* and the articles on health in the *Times of India, Sunday Review* show you the way to be physically fit, mentally alert and emotionally well-balanced. This book, *Sex Power,* is an attempt at providing much-needed knowledge on how to conquer sexual inadequacies and lifts the veil of doubt, disillusion and depression which haunts so many unfortunate men and women. It aims 'to put you together again' to experience the joys of sexual fulfilment.

Many readers suggested the urgent necessity for a scientific book on normal sex and sexual disorders based on our culture and conditions. A pathetic, pleading letter from a 14-year-old Delhi schoolboy spurred me to a quick decision. It said, 'I am desperate and cannot sleep. I am now becoming a man and if I practise self-abuse, I get instant relief from the restlessness but our cook told me that I would not only lose my manhood but also become mad. I have been very worried and not sleeping since then. My parents feel I am too young to know anything about sex. My Daddy says he will talk to me when I am eighteen, but what do I do till then? Please, doctor, reply immediately, otherwise I will become more mad.'

Sexual inadequacy, premature ejaculation and impotency are increasing rapidly in our country. The unfortunate victim is miserable and keeps thinking why 'manliness' has eluded him. He is convinced that he will never be a 'man' again. He does not know where to turn for help.

Sexual myths, ignorance of the basic elements of sex and false sense of modesty prevail even amongst a large section of the educated population. To name a few—masturbation is harmful, frequent sex saps the vitality, forty drops of blood make one drop of semen, the bigger the size of the male organ, the better.

You may legitimately ask why such a book has become necessary in India—the land where Vatsyayana wrote his memorable *Kama Sutra* and Kalyanamalla the *Ananga Ranga.* Vatsyayana was the world's pioneer sexologist who, as early as 400 A.D., advocated sex education and recognised the art of eroticism. He also believed that sexual satisfaction was important in the female and that without it she might become physically and mentally unbalanced. Our country had a tremendous depth of sexual understanding in those early days, unlike the West which woke up 1500 years later. However, with the imprint of law-giver Manu's Code, and later the influence of British culture on our society, we gradually gave up the rich sexual heritage of Vatsyayana.

Sex became a closed chapter, not to be talked or written about. As a consequence, young people often pick up wrong information about sex from the media, or from schools and colleges or from ignorant parents and friends. The Delhi student got the information from his cook! Even in medical colleges until recently, teachers did not touch sex with a barge-pole. For instance, when I was a house surgeon at Bombay's Sir J.J. Hospital, a professor who wanted to lecture on masturbation was not given permission. When all the students protested and insisted that they wanted the lecture, the Dean reluctantly agreed. The lecturer concluded with the statement, 'Ninety-nine per cent of young men masturbate and the remaining one per cent are liars.' The Dean looked shocked and asked, 'Do you suggest that even I masturbate?'

This was, dear readers, the state of knowledge up to 1944 in one of the premier medical colleges of India. The lecture, however, inspired me to study the neglected subject of sex and sexuality in great detail and it has been a very rewarding experience, as sexual inadequacy is increasing at an alarming rate in the Stress Century. Even today our medical schools and colleges turn out doctors whose teachers never taught them anything about sexuality or sex. Is it any wonder that the unfortunate family physician has no knowledge of treating sexual dysfunction, leaving the field wide open for quacks and charlatans to make a fortune? The incidence of psychogenic impotence and sexual inadequacy is directly proportional to the increasing prevalence of stress disorders such as heart attacks, bronchial asthma, high blood pressure and emotionally induced illnesses.

In the West, after the Second World War, two important events resulted in the creation of a sexual explosion and the permissive society. Firstly, during the War, women worked side by side with men. After the War, they were no longer content to be second-class citizens but demanded equality with men. The result: the liberated female of today. Secondly, with the advent of the female contraceptive 'pill', the fear of pregnancy disappeared. Like her male counterpart, the modern eve was at liberty to indulge in free sex. Virginity and the intact hymen were laughed upon as relics of a conservative Victorian era.

The impact of these violent changes in Western societies have had a marginal impact on our sexual norms. Recently, some schools have started teaching the anatomy of the sexual organs in their biology classes. A few magazines have articles on sex and a handful amongst the 'in crowd' have pre-marital sex. The intact hymen, considered of no consequence by Western girls, is still eagerly sought after by almost all Indian bridegrooms as an erroneous proof of his bride's virginity. In other words, the intact hymen has no value in Western societies but in our culture it is as precious as guinea-gold—a sign of sexual purity!

The concept of sex and sexuality in books published in the West and available in India, is based on Western culture which is different from ours. Let me clarify with a few examples from both Western and Indian cultures. In the permissive societies prevalent in the West, especially in the USA, if a young man invites a young lady to dinner, it implies in most cases after-dinner sex as part of the 'menu'!

A few years ago, I heard a radio programme in the USA on modern sexuality, where a boy who had had a sexual experience, was interviewed. I recapitulate from memory. The interviewer asked the boy, 'How long have you known the girl?' He replied, 'I met her the same evening. We had dinner, then I went to bed with her.' The boy enjoyed the love-making very much and had an orgasm but when questioned, 'Did she have one?' the young man coldly replied, 'I don't know.' Finally, when asked, 'What was the name of the girl?' he replied unconcernedly, 'I did not bother to ask!' In the sex-crazy West, it is easier to take a woman to bed than know her name! Although many mod young Indian ladies especially in the cities, like to ape the West—and some do—still, deep down they are conservative and when it comes to the 'nuts and bolts' they have pangs of conscience!

In the West, experienced surrogate partners (not prostitutes) are available to sexologists for the treatment of impotency and premature ejaculation. In our conservative society, one cannot dream of using such sexual partners for treatment. Occasionally, the poor male has to take permission from his mother, even after marriage, to sleep with his wife!

A just-married lady clerk sobbed as she told me, 'We live in a one-bedroom flat, doctor. My husband sleeps on a bed, his parents on a double-bed, and I, on the floor. He has to ask his mother whenever he wants to sleep with me. Often the old lady refuses, "Not today, Daddy is not well".' That was the end of the story.

The epoch-making researches of Dr. William H. Masters and Mrs. Virginia E. Johnson, sixteen centuries after Vatsyayana, spurred tremendous interest in human sexual behaviour when they announced the sexual reactions during foreplay and orgasm of 382 women and 312 men, who were studied in their sex laboratory for the first time. This book draws heavily from the researches of these modern pioneers in sex.

Dr. Masters observes that a woman is capable of many orgasms during masturbation (auto-manipulation). The lay press and medical writers on sex jumped to the erroneous conclusion that women can also be multi-orgasmic in sex. The result of this research, which was only during auto-manipulation, has led to tremendous sexual strains and stresses on the unfortunate male. He thinks he is inadequate if he cannot produce an orgasm, or preferably many, in his partner. Similarly, the woman thinks that there is something wrong with her if she is incapable of being multi-orgasmic.

Society, film-makers, novelists and journalists have all portrayed orgasm in the female as the most important event in her life. The result: the modern woman spends her valuable time and energy in its pursuit, often without success. She believes that she is sexually inadequate, and that 'If I don't come, my partner will go elsewhere.' The subject of female orgasm is dealt with in depth in this book and doubts and fears clarified. However, lady readers will naturally ask why, in these days of equality of the sexes, more attention is paid to the male of the species and many chapters devoted to him? My answer: it is only Almighty Man, conqueror of the moon, who suffers from impotency. The male must have an erection to penetrate the female, be potent and preserve the race. The female partner, on the other hand, can remain passive and does not have to carry the eternal burden of potency. However, improved male performance will help his partner considerably.

Sex is a learning process and does not, as is popularly believed, come naturally. Learning is replacing ignorance with knowledge.

This book shows you the way. It is written in simple English, is easy to understand and is illustrated with case histories and diagrams. It is based on our culture and is the complete answer to your sexual problems in the twentieth century. Do not hide it from your female partner—who may at first shout at you for reading a book on sex at your age! My advice to male readers is to quietly leave the book where your female partner may find it. Her innate curiosity will compel her to digest it thoroughly from cover to cover! Moreover, if she knows the physiology of the male sexual response, she will be more happy and fulfilled in sex.

The book is divided into four parts. Part 1, 'Know Thyself', informs you about normal sexual functioning. Part 2 is devoted to the prevention of impotency and frigidity in adult life. Impotency is a preventable disorder. Its seed is sown in the cradle, nurtured through ignorance in boyhood and blossoms in manhood, on the manure of folklore from the 'Fantasyland' of sex. Strange as it may seem its prevention, therefore, begins in the cradle. None of the books on impotency in the male or frigidity in the female, stress the importance of their prevention. I have attempted to fill this deficiency in our literature on sex. As Dr. William Mayo says, 'The aim of medicine is to prevent disease and prolong life; the ideal of medicine is to eliminate the need of a physician.' Part 3 deals with the causes and treatment of impotency, premature ejaculation and frigidity. Part 4 enlightens you on how to 'put yourself together' again with your new knowledge.

As I shall repeat time and again in the book, the power of erection is present in the male from the cradle to the grave. It is nature's gift to man, but is unfortunately not under the control of the will. A man can never 'will' an erection nor can a woman 'will' herself to arousal. Yet you can learn to respond naturally as nature intended. The knowledge is yours. You only have to read and digest the contents of this book—even if it gives you mild indigestion! Read on and instantaneously feel the difference—the new you, the sexy you, responding to the right male or female stimulus.

Part I

Know Thyself

Chapter 1

SEX IS NOT FOR ME

O say what is that thing call'd Potency,
Which I must ne'er enjoy,
What are the blessings of sexual intimacy,
O tell your poor impotent boy.

WITH APOLOGIES TO COLLEY CIBBER

IT IS STRANGE but true that these poignant, pathetic lines are applicable to a large number of men in the twentieth century. Sexual inadequacy is spreading like wild-fire, affecting innumerable men in the West and even in our country. They do not know what to do and where to turn for help. The unfortunate male buries his sexuality in shame and solitude.

I will illustrate with a few case histories:

—The anxious adolescent, Atul, tortured himself mentally in order not to succumb to masturbation but his will power was swept away by his torrential sexual urge. He could not resist any more. Guilt-ridden, he summoned his obedient right hand to obtain sweet release. Later he feared he had no manhood left and would be impotent forever.

—The dejected denim-donning Derek tells me, 'Doctor, I am finished! I wanted to do the "in thing" with Gloria, but on that fateful evening the damn thing just would not go in! Is it the end of the sex game forever?'

—The goody-goody groom Ghanshyam was anxiously waiting to deflower his bride but, alas, he was too quick on the trigger and ejaculated on her thighs. He lay awake the whole night wondering what went wrong.

—Middle-aged Kapil who suffered from the seven-year itch said, 'I paid a lot of attention to the willowy Wandana at the cocktail party. With endless flattery and boundless enthusiasm I at last succeeded in seducing her.' Kapil wiped the perspiration on his forehead and continued, 'I had high hopes of launching my rocket into space. But I am ashamed to tell you, Doctor, at the critical count-down my blooming rocket did not get off the ground.' He took a deep breath and blurted out, 'Will I be potent again?'

—Then there was the three-score-and-one who had been told that sex after fifty strains the heart and hence he had become a 'brahmachari' for the last ten years;

—Finally, the female partners of these unfortunate males who deserted the burning ship without extinguishing the fire, started wondering as they lay awake, unfulfilled, 'Is something wrong with me? Does my partner find me sexually unattractive?'

Potency and Impotency

In the space age of rockets and missiles, of hydrogen and neutron bombs, of libbers and liberators, man is the only animal who, though born potent, suffers from impotency. Potency depends upon normal erection of the penis, the sexual male organ. The capacity for erection is present from the cradle to the grave. Erections are possible in newly-born infants and I have known many old men, aged 70 to 80, who are potent and are capable of having sexual intercourse.

Impotency, on the other hand, is a condition where a male cannot attain or maintain sufficient erection for intercourse. He is, therefore, unable to obtain or give gratification in the sexual act. Man is the only animal who though born potent develops impotence in later life. All the other lower animals like leopards and lions, dogs and deer, horses and hares are permanently potent. Impotence is a disorder of modern civilization. It is not found in primitive societies.

Technological revolution

Man's genius has produced the technological revolution. Life has been evolving on our planet for about 2,750 million years. All living organisms, from the ant to the antelope and from the monkey to man, are products of this evolution. Man is the latest and yet is undoubtedly the monarch of all he surveys. There is none to dispute or deny his right on this planet—except the modern woman! The unchallenged supremacy of man has been made possible by modern science.

In fact, the last hundred years of civilisation have been a glorious era of scientific revolution. It has given man longevity, better health, perfect contraceptives—and increased impotence. Why is it so? Let us examine this paradox, to ascertain why man instead of being ever potent has become impotent in the Stress Century.

LONGEVITY: Prehistoric man lived only about 18 years. With the Romans, life expectancy increased to 22 years. In the Middle Ages it was about 35 years. In 1900, life expectancy in the USA was 47 years but it has increased today to over 70 years. In 80 years the life span has increased by 23 years. In 1940, longevity in India was 26 years and in 1966 it has increased to 50 years. It is now 50 plus.

It is modern science which has prolonged life, because it has considerably cut down on infant mortality as well as controlled infections. Tetanus, diphtheria and small-pox have been almost eradicated in many countries. It is quite on the cards that the high mortality caused by heart disease and cancer will be controlled in the next few years.

A better understanding of nutrition has resulted in more healthy human beings. Control of infections and improved treatment of diseases have also helped to promote general health. We will soon have healthy old men who would like to enjoy normal sex.

MODERN CONTRACEPTIVES: With the perfection of contraceptives, women can have babies only when they want them. In other words, the reproductive function and sexual intercourse have become two different things altogether. Till a few years ago, when contraception was not perfect, there was always the fear of pregnancy during intercourse, which inhibited many women. The perfection of the pill and the loop as safe and foolproof methods of birth control, has removed this fear in women. They are therefore no longer inhibited in their demand for sex.

Impotence is a disorder of modern civilization seen in the stress and strain of the space age. Almost all cases of impotence are psychological in origin. Organic impotency may be caused by hormonal imbalances like deficiency of the male hormone

testosterone, metabolic disorders like diabetes and diseases affecting
the nervous and vascular systems, injuries and surgery where the nerve
supply of the genital organs is affected (see Chapter 14).

Civilised man is a tired man. He suffers perpetually from emotional
and physical fatigue. This is due to boredom at work, and artificial
life, the keen competition he has to face for survival in the modern
economy, and unhealthy emotions like hate, jealousy and frustration.
The machine does most of the work, giving him little scope during
working hours to do anything creative or stimulating. He is thus bored
by routine. His leisure hours are spent idly in the house reading a
novel or magazine, watching television or listening to the
radio—which tires him further. A tired man cannot function sexually
because sex needs a lot of energy.

Modern man also leads an unnatural life where most of his time and
efforts are devoted to acquiring power and worldly goods like a car, a
radio, a flat and furniture. Part of the sexual drive is therefore
diverted into this channel. At work, he faces keen competition from
colleagues. He feels others are getting ahead while he is left behind,
which leads to unhealthy emotions like frustration, rivalry, fear,
anxiety and self-pity. These unhealthy emotions further deprive the
individual of nervous energy and result in diminished potency.

Fear of failure is the commonest cause of impotency in the younger
age group. A man has to produce an erection during coitus (intercourse) and doubts in his mind that he may not succeed, results in
impotence. Fear is due to lack of confidence in oneself about the
power of erection. It acts as a brake and healthy sex cannot thrive
where there are inhibitions or brakes. Thus, modern civilization,
which is supposed to contribute to man's happiness and well-being,
has led to increased sexual inadequacy and impotency.

Loss of potency is one of the worst catastrophes that can befall a
man. He suffers such unimaginable anguish that it permeates every
minute of every hour of every day of his unhappy life. It is a negation
of life and living. He rarely complains openly and like the ostrich
buries his head in shame. Unlike most infectious or degenerative
diseases for which there is specific treatment, he runs from pillar to
post vainly searching for the magic pill which can cure him overnight.
He is 'alone and palely loitering' in the vast jungle of quacks who give

him potency potions and deprive him of a sizeable portion of cash. He feels dejected and depressed that all the pills and potions he has been secretly swallowing show no results.

He has even tried the magic cream and the potency spray (he tells his wife he has bought a special after-shave from Frankfurt!), but his impotency continues. His friends have recommended the famous *palangtod-paan,* powders of precious pearls, diamonds and extracts of Spanish fly to improve his performance, but nothing happens. He remains sexually inadequate. His family physician has given him male hormones. He feels better mentally when the hormone which produces erection of the penis is pumped into him. He gets strong early morning erections, but at the sight of the naked female form, that obstinate mule, his penis, remains lifeless and limp. At last he believes in the old proverb that you can take a mule to the pond but cannot make it drink. He is like Humpty Dumpty who had a great fall but, alas, all the medications could not put him together again.

The effect of most of these pills and potions is psychological, except in cases where there is a genuine glandular deficiency which can be corrected by administration of the male hormone. The cure lies with you. It lies in a change of mental attitude towards your sexual power—replacing fear of performance with confidence and not concentrating on your penis and watching to see if it gets hard. Erection is a natural process when you are turned on—you never get an erection by becoming tense and telling yourself, 'I must get hard.'

I will narrate the case of Dorab, a sales manager, who told me, 'Doctor, my job involves a lot of touring, about twenty days in a month away from my family. You know, doc, men are polygamous by nature and during these tours I have a fling or two to relieve boredom. During one of my trips to Pune, I succeeded in seducing Diana, a voluptuous 40-year-old widow. With my mastery of the art of foreplay and skilful use of the index finger, I set her on fire but was a little diffident of extinguishing the whirlwinds of tempestuous storm I had aroused in her. As I was about to enter her, she moaned, "Oh, darling, pierce me like an arrow, keep on piercing me till I moan, groan and die in your arms." As soon as she said, "Darling, pierce me like an arrow", I grew limp and could do nothing. I tried very hard to get an erection but nothing happened. She turned over to her left side, lay there for a few minutes, then getting up angrily threw a pillow at me and went to the bathroom. When she returned, I could still see the unquenched sexual fire in her. Dejected and humiliated, I hurriedly dressed and looked at her with imploring eyes to give me a chance another time. But she kissed my cheek with affectionate indifference, put her hand on my shoulder and said sarcastically, "It does not matter, Dorab, but I want performance from a man. We will be good friends but no sex." I bade her goodbye and it has been goodbye to sex ever since. Doctor, please help me, I have been impotent for the last four years.'

Dorab's story illustrates brilliantly the delicate nature of the erection response. Like a burning matchstick, it can be quickly and easily extinguished. Diana's sexual demand, 'pierce me like an arrow', instantaneously shattered Dorab's 'bow'. He became self-conscious, seized by lingering doubts about his erection and lost it. He did what any modern man does today. He tried to 'will' an erection. Will power conquers all except erection, for it is not under the conscious control of the will.

When I ask patients about their sex life in my clinic, at least half of them are dissatisfied and one-third suffer from actual sexual difficulties like premature or weak ejaculation, or rapidly losing an erection and loss of interest in the sex act. It is strange but true that when one meets these men socially they are all 'Casanovas' narrating to friends tales of their sexual conquests. In a small survey conducted at my clinic during 1970-77 on 2860 males, aged 35 to 55 years, only 17 per cent were fully satisfied with their sex life, whilst 83 per cent confessed that they were not happy with it.

Psychology Today conducted an extensive investigation of the sex life of 52,000 American males. The findings revealed that 55 per cent of the men were dissatisfied with their sex life and 39 per cent suffered from sexual disorders. The staggering figures of sexual inadequacy and dissatisfaction suggest that most men are not happy with their performance. They want a more potent model with greater horse-power!

Why is this so? From the cradle to the grave our culture projects man as a sexual giant. The poet Schiller brilliantly portrays this consciousness of masculinity in *Dignity of Man*:

Upon God's image I impress
My manhood's royal seal;
And on love's fountain I possess
A claim without repeal.

I am a man! this potent spell
Inspires with trembling fear
A princess in a lonely dell,
Though ragged I appear.

Newspapers, television, movies, poets, writers and folklore have all projected this overrated sexual profile of the sawdust Caesar—the modern male and his manliness. For instance, the James Bond movies show Sean Connery as a he-man, mating and dating by the hour and living dangerously.

We are gullible by nature and unconsciously want to ape the non-existent superman against whom we measure our sexuality. We are jealous of Sean Connery and Amitabh Bachchan who make women tremble with longings. Alas, in real life, things are entirely different and we become resigned to our inadequate sexual existence. Though men talk freely about women and the number they have subdued in bed, most men secretly think the other chap is better. This inferiority makes them very reticent about their sexuality and sex life. They are reluctant to talk about it even to their doctors. Detailed questioning by the physician embarrasses them and therefore I do not ask a patient about it unless I know him intimately and have his complete confidence.

Ignorance about sex
I remember that as a medical student, apart from the basic teaching of the anatomy and physiology of the male and female sex organs, no other training on sex was imparted. Whilst a lot of time and money is spent on eradicating infectious diseases, controlling heart ailments and trying to conquer cancer, very little is done to prevent impotency. It is imperative that immediate attention is given to this problem. With increased longevity and better health, the aim of medicine should be not merely healthy old men but healthy potent old men. A female

patient of mine commented, 'What is the good of "Feminine Forever" females who can enjoy sex all their lives? Where are the men to satisfy them?'

This book is an attempt to provide the answer—the potent partner for the evergreen woman. The twentieth-century male wants to know up to what age he can be potent. The answer is: *as long as he lives!*

Chapter 2

THE MYTHOLOGY OF SEX

We had fed our hearts on fantasies.

W.B. YEATS

BHARAT IS a land of saints, sadhus and snake-charmers, the *Ramayana* and the *Mahabharata*, and, last but not the least, the Land of Sexual Myths. Sex is taboo and talking about it is shunned in our society. There is a lack of scientific education and knowledge about sex, resulting in sexual ignorance and the prevalence of sexual myths. Our ancient saints, pundits and philosophers decreed what was good or bad, according to their personal whims and fancies in the folklore of sex. In the tradition-bound Indian society, our forefathers unquestioningly accepted the preachings of these men and passed them on to their children. Myths are responsible for most of the sexual disorders prevalent in our society today which prevent normal sexual functioning. Let us examine a few of these sexual myths in both sexes and 'cremate' or 'bury' them forever, so as to restore normality in sex.

MALE MYTHS

Sexual myths about the male are different from those about the female. They vary from culture to culture depending upon ancient traditions and knowledge of sexuality. In the permissive Western societies, where the physiology of sex is well-known, the Western male is not usually worried about night discharges, masturbation or spermatorrhoea. In our culture, repression of these normal and harmless sexual releases are responsible for producing ailments like impotency, loss of vitality and memory, feelings of guilt and insomnia. The size of the penis plays a dominant role in the fantasies of all cultures.

Fantasies about the Penis

Let us examine a few common fantasies about the penis, the King of Kings in the Kingdom of Sex—the bigger the better; becomes erect instantaneously; hard as steel; when erect it is a battering ram of muscle engorged with blood; 'sprang out at her like an angry lion from its cage'; once erect it never gets exhausted; like a machine-gun it can 'shoot' semen all night without being loaded.

THE BIGGER THE BETTER: Sex is the domninant urge in life. The urge for sex is stronger than hunger, stronger than fear. The male organ is the symbol of manliness. According to the noted author of *Impotence in the Male,* Wilhelm Stekel, 'A man is like his penis. The penis is an image of the entire man.' Is it any wonder that in the fantasyland of sex which the poets and authors of erotic novels, the *hakims* and the *vaidyas* portray, the size of the penis is the centre of attraction?

In the *Kama Sutra* Vatsyayana has classified the erect penis (*lingam*) according to its size into three different varieties: the Horse is the longest and thickest, about 22 centimetres; the Bull is of medium dimensions, about 15 centimetres; and the Rabbit is the shortest, about 11 centimetres. Ancient Indian erotic art has many statues with oversized male genital organs.

Our society admires tall men. 'How handsome and tall he is!' we say. We do not respect the short man unless he is a commanding politician like Napoleon. Largeness is respected in our affluent culture from childhood—a jumbo doll, a jumbo cake, a jumbo sandwich, a jumbo ice-cream, and now the jumbo jet.

In schools, colleges and in the shower-rooms of clubs, the size of the penis matters. It is natural, therefore, that men are extremely conscious of their sexual dimensions right from childhood and later, as young men, feel inferior to the man with a bigger organ. If this inferiority complex persists, it might result in impotency.

Having described the size-consciousness in our society, let us examine objectively the facts about sexual ability and the size of the male organ. Biologically, it is true that during evolution, nature tried to evolve huge monsters—but they could not survive. Creatures like the dinosaurs are extinct today. One, therefore, needs to take a second look at our concept of jumbos. A world-famous gynaecologist once observed that the most perfect women are short women. They usually go through pregnancy and labour like a shot, while tall women, in spite of their roomy pelvis, have problems. The same applies to short men.

Let me tell you about Charlie. He always worried about the small size of his organ and blamed nature for it. 'Doctor, if only primitive man had protested loudly when the Almighty distributed the male organs, individuals like me would not be left with such miniatures,' he said. 'Look at the horse, the donkey or the zebra. They all have what they wanted!' I listened attentively as Charlie continued, 'They say Sunder has been gifted with the longest and biggest organ in our Company. Can a big penis be transplanted on me? I think it would be a simple operation compared to one on the heart, kidney or liver. Yet in fairness to my wife and girl friends, they have never complained about my size.' It was impressed on Charlie that it is not the length of the barrel but the magazine behind it that counts!

Hakims, vaidyas and quacks advertise and give drugs, massages and electrotherapy for increasing the size of the organ. The physical stimulation of the penis temporarily makes it semi-erect or erect and its unfortunate owner believes that it has grown longer and stronger. However, disappointment is in store for him after a few hours, when the congestion of blood disappears and the organ becomes smaller, making him feel more dejected and depressed.

Size of the penis and the female partner: Does a female partner really need a 'horse' size penis as catalogued by Vatsyayana for her sexual fulfilment and enjoyment in sex? The answer is a definite 'no' for most women. Your huge organ may be a showpiece in male dressing-rooms and give a tremendous boost to your ego but you will be surprised to know that when it come to sex, the majority of women are least concerned about the size of your penis or testes. At the height of her passion, a woman is so self-centred that she is not bothered whether it is ten or twenty centimetres long. Undoubtedly, there are a few women who because of the propaganda by the media believe that the bigger it is, the better. A huge battering ram can be a source of discomfort and pain to the woman, if she is not well-lubricated. In fact, some of her most enjoyable moments occur when the male has ejaculated and the erection has partially died down. It is not generally realised that, in satisfying a woman completely, it is not the penis alone but the tongue and the index finger which play a dominant role. I have known cases where individuals with a huge penis have left women dissatisfied.

BECOMES ERECT INSTANTANEOUSLY: Modern science has given us gadgets like the electric light, fan, heater, radio, TV, which usually respond instantaneously on pressing a button. Our culture has made us believe that a man should also respond immediately with push-button frequency! Unfortunately it is not so. Your tube-light, after some use, does not light immediately if the starter is defective. Your radio does not work if one of the valves has burnt out or there is a loose contact in the circuit. Your car can conk out on the road because of a faulty condenser. You accept all these philosophically. After all, something can always go wrong with gadgets sometimes. What about your own gadget? Can't something go wrong with it occasionally? Why become anxious if an erection does not come on? The world has not come to an end! You were perhaps tired, preoccupied or worried about the office.

As age advances, and particularly after the mid-thirties, the erective response does not take place through excitement alone, as in youth. You may require direct physical stimulation by your female partner. Accept it as a normal physiological process of ageing. Don't pull the alarm chain of anxiety and think that you have become old and impotent. On the other hand, Nature has given you a sexual bonus. You may be slow to 'rise' but you will take longer to 'come'. Do you know that your partner is not interested in an immediate erection but is likely to be disturbed by instantaneous discharge, the quick-on-the trigger mechanism of youth, which leaves her high and dry and unsatisfied?

HARD AS STEEL: Our culture makes all men believe that their penis when erect should be as hard as steel or like a rock. Men are deeply conscious about the hardness of their organ. They usually hold the erect penis in their hand and feel anxious if the hardness is not to their satisfaction and the penis becomes soft as the erection dies down. The penis is not meant for drilling holes into steel columns—it has merely to enter the vaginal cavity. It may surprise you to know that even a semi-erect or a soft penis can get into a vagina of a woman. (See Chapter 14, 'Impotence'.) A certain degree of hardness, however, is necessary to deflorate a virgin. Otherwise women do not relish rods of steel or ramming machines during intercourse. In fact, many find it uncomfortable or even painful. Stephen Vizinczey vividly brings out this theme in *In Praise of Older Women:* 'Don't leave' she said when we first came, 'I like to feel him small.'

IT IS A BATTERING RAM OF MUSCLES: Even medical writers and novelists have fallen into this trap! Dr. R.P. Sethi, in his *Increase Your Sexual Power and Efficiency,* says this about the penis: 'It is a specialised item in medical science and is made up of muscles.' The penis is not 'made' of voluntary muscular tissue. If it were so, we could have contracted the penis and made it erect with our will power as we contract the biceps in our arms. There would then be no impotency and not the slightest necessity for this book! In her eternal wisdom, Nature has made the penis of hollow spongy tissue which is not under the direct control of our will. There are no muscles in the penis, except the pelvic muscles at its base which with correct exercises improve sexual performance in both sexes (see Chapter 5).

'SPRANG OUT AT HER LIKE AN ANGRY LION FROM ITS CAGE': The sober, shy Sunil sowed his wild oats during his sojourn at the Harvard Business School in the USA—the ultimate Mecca for the sons of affluent Indians. His innate shyness attracted a lot of female curiosity and attention and many women wanted to 'bed' this virgin lad from India. Sunil graduated into a master of sex, but his happiness was short-lived. He suddenly lost his manhood.

When he was in Bombay, during his holidays, he came to see me about his impotence. 'My sex life in America was good,' said Sunil, 'except that until my partner fondled me, I could not get an erection for the first three or four times I had sex. I was fine afterwards.' After a brief pause, he continued hesitatingly, 'My partner gave me Harold Robbins' best-selling novel *The Betsy.* I read the book and became impotent.' 'Why do you think the book made you impotent?' I asked.

Sunil blurted out, 'Why can't my organ spring out like an angry lion?' I impressed on Sunil that *The Betsy* was fiction and not reality. The Fantasyland sexual encounters described there did not exist in reality. Sunil was so taken in by this fiction that he believed it to be the gospel truth! He worried, became anxious and impotent, when his penis did not 'spring out from his trousers, like an angry lion'. The case vividly illustrates the impact of Fantasyland sexual culture on a young impressionable mind.

ONCE ERECT IT NEVER GETS EXHAUSTED: All male Casanovas secretly long to have a 'beat-the-clock battering ram' which can go on thrusting back and forth in the vagina endlessly. You believe that this would make you qualify with flying colours and win a medal as a great lover and that your partner will admire your staying power! I am sorry to disappoint you, Mr. Casanova, for harbouring such a fantasy. Your partner will have to consult a sexologist as she still feels inadequate after your marathon session. The vagina is relatively insensitive compared to the clitoris and the vulva and therefore prolonged penetration is not for many women an enjoyable experience and does not necessarily result in orgasm. In fact, prolonged sex can be uncomfortable and painful if the vagina has become dry.

PROMINENT VEINS ON THE PENIS: The veins on the penis are a source of worry and anxiety to many individuals as during the flaccid or lax state, they appear tortuous and enlarged. The individual thinks that there is something wrong with his circulation and the quacks are ever alert to take advantage of their unfortunate victim. They give all sorts of treatment including blister-forming chemicals which cause ulcers which can turn septic and take a long time to heal. They are ultimately replaced by scar tissue with loss of sensation.

Veins are present all over our body and as the mechanism of erection works by filling up the penis with blood, nature has endowed the male organ with an ample supply of veins and arteries. If you look at the back of your hands, there are prominent veins. Similarly, there are veins on the legs which are visible and can become varicose. You are not worried about them. Why then worry about the veins on your organ, which nature has provided?

SIZE OF THE TESTES: Like the size of the penis, the size of the testes is a source of perpetual worry to penis/testes-conscious men. They perpetually keep looking in the mirror at the size of their organs and the smallness of their testes. It is popularly believed that the male with small-sized testes is at disadvantage sexually. Similarly, if the scrotum is not tight but hangs loosely, it is believed to be a sign of diminished potency. The adolescent should be told that the size of the testes or the elasticity of the scrotal skin has nothing to do with sexuality. Only in cases where both testes are removed after an injury or severe infection or cancer can impotency result. Even in such cases, the use of the male hormone can restore potency. I repeat once again that the size of the testes, whether they are small, medium or large, has no relation with potency at all and matters little where intercourse is concerned.

POSITION OF THE TESTES: Nature's anatomical arrangement of the left testis being one centimetre lower than the right testis causes sexual anxiety to many laymen. They feel that their left gland has lost its elasticity and hangs loosely. Persistent worry along such lines may obsess a person so much that he may even become impotent.

FORTY TO FOUR HUNDRED DROPS OF BLOOD MAKE ONE DROP OF SEMEN: The ancients were mystified by the life-producing white fluid from the male and thus evolved the popular myth that 40 to 400 drops of blood (the figure varies from culture to culture), were necessary to manufacture just one drop of semen. Even today, innumerable males believe that life-giving semen is as precious as gold, silver or platinum. Production of semen is a normal physiological process like the saliva in our mouth or the acid in our stomach.

LOSS OF SEMEN IS LOSS OF VITALITY: Many individuals still believe they feel weak and limp after ejaculation as precious fluid, semen, is lost. The loss can occur in three ways: through masturbation, nocturnal emissions, or intercourse. I will consider each of them separately, as they play an important role in causing all the imaginary ills that the male flesh is heir to.

(1) Masturbation: This is the commonest sexual outlet in the adolescent (also see Chapter 12). Most young men have masturbated at some time or other. It has been conclusively proved that masturbation by itself produces no harmful effects. It is the guilt or fear about

masturbation which damages a teenager's sensitive nervous system. However, if masturbation is practised in preference to heterosexual contact, then it is anti-social: the individual wishes to masturbate in private and is not prepared to risk a sexual situation with a female partner. Masturbation is a normal phenomenon at all ages in both sexes, when they are unable to obtain, for some reason, sexual gratification during intercourse. However, all the ailments under the sun from insomnia, impotency, lack of concentration and loss of vitality to insanity, have been attributed to masturbation.

I shall illustrate with a case history. Seventeen-year-old anxious, introverted Jamshed was brought to me by his mother for behaving like a child, unable to concentrate and being backward in his studies. 'Look at him!' she exclaimed, 'he should be a man by now but he behaves like a sissy at seventeen.' The docile boy was crest-fallen and looked down whilst the mother catalogued his complaints and finally ended by saying, 'He needs male hormones. Give him a few shots!'

I asked the mother to wait outside whilst I interrogated the boy. Jamshed sobbed as he narrated his story. I discovered that the stern parents had deprived him of all touching and sensuality in childhood and his mother had repeatedly impressed on him, 'Boys should be boys. Women are dirty, you should have nothing to do with them,' reflecting perhaps her own marital unhappiness. Masturbation was denied to him as a sexual outlet. His eagle-eyed mother kept a stern watch on him during the night and he was made to sleep next to her. He masturbated in solitude in the school toilet, whenever he got a chance. He excused himself during class by saying that he was suffering from diarrhoea and trembled with fear as he did it. If his mother ever discovered that he was masturbating secretly, he would never be forgiven for his sins against nature! Is it any wonder that his personality, at this young age, was warped by his over-protective yet misinformed mother? Jamshed was a sitting duck for the development of impotency.

(2) Noctural emissions or night discharges: This is another sexual outlet. It is most common in single males between adolescence and marriage. Physical stimulation can produce erection and orgasm. During sleep the individual is not so inhibited and therefore an erection and orgasm can occur, though I have known a few male patients

who have never had a nocturnal emission in their life. The sexual urge is overpowering and intercourse provides a natural release. However, when there is no opportunity for it and if the sexual urge is denied, nature takes the initiative in her own hands by producing wet-dreams or noctural emissions.

I shall reproduce my conversation with 19-year-old John.

John:	Doctor, please give me a sleeping tablet. I cannot sleep at night. I lie awake for hours and I feel I will become mad.
Dr. RHD:	Is something bothering you? You must be in love!
John:	Nothing, absolutely nothing! I have a girl friend and I am afraid even to touch her.
Dr. RHD:	Do you know that masturbation is harmless and you can masturbate whenever sexual tension builds up? (One can, with years of medical practice, find out what is really bothering a patient. I felt John was not sleeping because of sexual tension.)
John:	(Obviously relieved and relaxed) Is masturbation not harmful? I was taught that it is a sin. What about night discharges? Are they harmful? I feel so weak and run down every time I have one.
Dr. RHD:	Night discharge is an absolutely normal and natural process during an erotic dream, if you deny yourself masturbation.
John:	I lie awake at night tormented and tortured for hours by an erection. The harder I try not to masturbate, the worse it gets. When at last I fall off to sleep, I wake up suddenly with wet pyjamas and a strong sense of shame.

I impressed on John that he would never win in his fight against the all-powerful sexual urge. It would be advisable to obtain relief by masturbation.

(3) Sexual intercourse: This is the third outlet for relieving tension (see Chapter 9).

Myths about semen

SPERMATORRHOEA or Semenuria is the involuntary discharge of semen in the urine. In the tradition-bound Indian culture, life-producing semen is thought of as the priceless white fluid to be conserved by men. Loss of semen is equivalent to loss of vitality and energy, and a slight white discharge from the penis is an alarm signal for its unfortunate victim. Quacks have called it a dreadful disease—spermatorrhoea, meaning loss of vital semen. Having frightened the unfortunate victim out of his wits, they treat it with every conceivable medicine which he faithfully swallows morning, noon and night. He is even given electrotherapy to fix the leakage.

PHOSPHATURIA: This is a harmless condition where the urine contains a high percentage of phosphates. It is common in vegetarians whose diet tends to produce an alkaline urine loaded with crystals of phosphates which give it a whitish appearance. Many adolescents mistake it for spermatorrhoea and worry that the continuous loss of vital semen will ultimately make them impotent. A simple microscopic examination of the urine will show that it is loaded with phosphate crystals.

SEX RESULTS IN LOSS OF VITALITY: Individuals who have lived in a culture where sex for the male means ejaculation of 'vital' semen complain of feeling low after intercourse. 'I feel so tired after sex, it takes days for me to recover the lost vitality,' complained Shankar. A typical story of many male patients is, 'If I do not discharge I do not feel weak and run-down. It is much better this way.' I explained to Shankar that his feeling was psychological. Sex is rejuvenating and normally one should feel full of vitality.

Sex is nature's safe antibiotic against stress. William Osler, the eminent Canadian physician and writer, says, 'The natural man has only two primal passions—to get and to beget.' In other words, there are two main instincts in man—the aggressive drive to be the monarch of his environment and the sexual drive through which he not only reproduces the species but also gets immense sexual gratification. Primitive man exercised his instincts freely, without any inhibitions, whenever he wished. His emotions were primitive and he was not fettered by the conventions of modern civilisation.

ABSTINENCE FROM SEXUAL INDULGENCE: Saints, sadhus and politicians have been advocating for centuries that for spiritual uplift man must refrain from earthly pleasure like sex, which saps his vitality and weakens his soul. Mahatma Gandhi, the Father of our Nation, and Shri Morarji Desai, the former Prime Minister, have preached abstinence and practised it themselves for the greater part of their lives.

Is refraining from sex healthy or does it harm the body due to suppression of the powerful sexual instinct? Dr. Wilhelm Stekel, one of the greatest psychotherapists, states in *Impotence in the Male,* 'Impotent men are the main support of various abstinence movements which are so plentiful, whereas the really great man, even in respect to his sexuality, can only think and feel with greatness.'

Albert Ellis in his book *Sex and Liberated Man* believes that 'voluntary abstinence remains an unnecessary evil. Accept that misery and you seem off your rocker. You'd better see a psychologist, fast, than keep affecting yourself with that kind of nonsense.'

In my experience, many of my patients and friends have temporarily refrained from sexual activity for varying reasons, such as a form of spiritual discipline or an involvement in prolonged activity such as preparing for examinations. Healthy human beings are adaptable to their environment and many found the experience helpful. They could understand themselves better and there were no detrimental effects on their health. Some found initial difficulty when starting sexual activity again but after some time they started functioning normally.

FREQUENCY OF SEX: Men often worry about how often they can have sex without harming themselves. Everyone has his own theory about the frequency of sex. I shall begin by quoting Luther's famous maxim on the frequency of sexual intercourse, 'Twice a week injures neither you nor I and makes in a year a hundred and four.' According to Wilhelm Stekel, 'The injuriousness of successively repeated copulation is exaggerated. I am acquainted with men who visited their mistress once each week for twenty years, cohabited in succession without sustaining the slightest injury to health. Bachelors become seemingly impotent.'

In males, intercourse in dependent on erection. In other words, when satiety is reached erection does not take place. The amount of sexual activity is generally much more in the younger age groups than after fifty. The decline in frequency is due to the false belief, still prevalent, that man is old and becomes impotent at fifty.

FEMALE MYTHS

The myths regarding the female are basically different from those about the male. In general, age and appearance are mainly responsible for them—the younger the better. The attractive female has more sex appeal than the plain Jane. Women are also worried about the size, appearance and elasticity of their breasts, whether they are firm or loose and sagging after childbirth. Fantasies about sex and orgasm are also prevalent in the female. The media have projected that the rougher the sex, the better for her, and innumerable women accept it as a part of their lives though they suffer pain and anguish and crave for gentleness in love. But the emancipated Indian female expects to be orgasmic during sex—in fact, wants multiple orgasms.

AGE: In all cultures, and more so in our country, age plays an important part in the choice of a female partner. A 60-year-old male would be happy to have a 16-year-old partner. This fantasy about young women is also brought out in Kalyanamalla's *Ananga Ranga* published in the fifteenth or sixteenth century. A *bala* is a young girl up to her sixteenth year; from sixteen to thirty, she is known as *taruni,* a young woman. From thirty to fifty-five, she is a *praddha* or a fully grown-up woman. An old woman is called *vradha*. Kalyanamalla recommends that after a man has sex with a *bala,* he gains in strength and vigour, whilst intercourse with a *taruni* makes him lose his strength. Finally, any sex with a *praddha* would make a man old. He is only supposed to talk to her about the moon! Is it any wonder that in India old men still run after young girls? So do their Western counterparts, but they have now found that older and experienced women are better and more responsive during sex than the inexperienced *balas.*

FIGURE AND APPEARANCE: Manufacturers of cosmetics and rainbow-coloured saris, designers of innumerable types of brassieres, beauticians and masseurs have one aim—to give woman a sleek, slender, sexy look which would enhance her appeal to men. Whether at school or college, while applying for a job or husband-hunting in the matrimonial market, undue importance is given to her complexion and appearance. Is she fair or dark? Is she thin or fat? These factors have all put a premium on appearance and the plain Janes feel self-conscious and inadequate. But it is the experience of many men that sexually many plain Janes are more responsive than the so-called neutron bombs in whom sex oozes from every pore—but that is as far as it goes!

BREASTS: The size of the breasts bothers many young ladies and having heard of plastic surgery, innumerable young women want to improve on their size. This is due to the erroneous belief that men like 'a handful' or 'a palmful'. Similarly, women who have oversized breasts are self-conscious about them and go in for plastic surgery to make them smaller. Lack of firmness, loss of elasticity or sagging breasts, especially when breast-feeding has been done, is another source of immense worry to women. Let me assure such women that the response of the breasts during sex does not depend upon their size or elasticity. Some women with small breasts respond instantaneously, whereas in many women with large breasts, the response is not so spontaneous.

ORGASM: The Indian woman never worried about orgasm, being brought up to believe that her role was to gratify the male and ensure his pleasure in sex. Her role was passive. However, with emancipation of our women, especially in the cities, and with the Masters-Johnson Sexual Revolution, women now believe that they should reach an orgasm during sex. Formerly, it was 'what you did not know you did not grieve for', but now with her new knowledge, she is unduly worried and thinks that something is wrong with her if she is unable to reach an orgasm with her partner, though she can easily reach it during automanipulation (see Chapter 11, 'Orgasm in the Female').

CLITORAL AND VAGINAL ORGASMS ARE DIFFERENT: The myth that women have two different types of orgasm has been exploded by the pioneering work of Masters and Johnson. They have conclusively proved that all orgasms originate in the clitoris and then spread to the vagina. There is nothing like a pure clitoral or pure vaginal orgasm—only a sexual orgasm.

WOMEN LIKE IT ROUGH: The media have projected the idea that the modern woman likes it rough during sex. The rougher the better. Males somehow have been indoctrinated into this culture and women have also started believing it. It is essential to know that most women like their partners to be gentle, at least in the early stages of foreplay and coitus till they get used to their partner. The great sexologist, Vatsyayana, has recommended gentleness on the part of a male when wooing the female.

A WOMAN'S 'NO' MEANS 'YES': Someone has said that if only stupid man realised that when a woman says 'No' she means 'Yes', ninety per cent of the trouble in the world would not be there! The message, 'Never take a woman's "No" seriously', has been portrayed in our novels, movies, plays and magazines. The unfortunate male is therefore at his wit's end. Does she or doesn't she want sex? Should he go ahead, irrespective of her 'No'? Do women like to be taken in spite of their protestations? It is part of our culture to take women despite their protestations. It is also part of our culture for women to be shy and coy and resist initially male sexual advances.

WOMEN WANT SEX ALL THE TIME: 'What do I do with my wife?' Anil asked me in exasperation. 'She wants sex all the time! I come home tired and she expects me to perform. Can't I give her a tranquilliser? Doctor, I will be sending her to you on some pretext. Please speak to her.'

As married men frequently do, Anil had got the message from Meera wrong. The sex act for her was secondary and not as important. All that she craved for was a kiss, a hug, a little tenderness and being together. Anil now knows that when he kisses or hugs Meera, it does not mean that he has to go all out to have sex with her, though many males erroneously think that to be great lovers all that they have to do is to have intercourse and prolong it as long as possible.

I repeat that for most women sex is secondary and the technique does not matter much. A woman admires a gentle and understanding male who makes her feel very special as a woman, sexually and non-sexually as well. Here is Amita talking of Charles, 'He is the most magnificent lover, well-mannered, kind and courteous. Time seems infinite with him. As soon as he enters my room he is so warm, tender, affectionate and appreciative. The world can wait when he is with me. I know he has a roving eye; but why should I worry about others as long as he gives me all that I want from a great lover?'

SEX IS DIRTY: 'How can people read such books?', exclaimed one of my shocked secretaries as she saw some pictures on sexual anatomy. '*Shi! Shi!* Sex is dirty', she said and covered her face with both hands while peeping at the pictures through her fingers, her innate curiosity getting the better of her sexual inhibitions! It was not the fault of the young lady that her mother had drilled into her from childhood false notions about sexuality. Emancipated women are more knowledgeable about sex than their orthodox sisters, but one has only to remove their liberated mask to reveal their innate puritan make-up.

GUILT ABOUT SEX: In the West, after the sexual revolution in the mid-sixties, women have become quite used to going to bed with a man without a sense of guilt. Women believed that it was for them a great emancipation—the freedom to say 'Yes' to sex whenever they wanted it. Many women, however, found that indulgence in merely physical sex without loving their partner was not a satisfying experience. The clock has turned full circle and many Western women now feel that a period of celibacy is a healthy experience. Frequent promiscuity in the past had left them anxious and unsatisfied in sex.

Free sex, except in a few high-society girls, is not so prevalent in India. The vast majority of women prefer to remain celibate till they marry. However, even after marriage a sense of guilt about sex still prevails in some women due to their stern upbringing. They have been indoctrinated that not only is sex dirty but it is a sin to indulge in it for pleasure. Sex is only for reproduction. This childhood indoctrination persists throughout their lives and unless treated, makes many women unresponsive in their sex life as they develop a guilt complex. The foundation of frigidity is often laid during childhood in such cases.

SEX DURING MENSTRUATION IS HARMFUL: Until recently, almost all cultures considered menstruation as something unclean and a curse on women. Even today innumerable women in our country are segregated during those days till they have a ritual bath. It is now accepted that the period is a normal physiological phenomenon of the female reproductive cycle. Sex during a period is not harmful, apart from being messy. Many female patients have told me that they enjoy sex more during a period. However, male prejudices die hard and a lot of men are still averse to it.

WOMEN DO NOT MASTURBATE NOR DO THEY GET NOCTURNAL ORGASMS: Whilst boys are prone to masturbate in company and compare notes with each other, girls are much more reticent about it. Masturbation is not as common in girls as in boys but as they get enlightened about sex, a number of them are resorting to it. The same applies to nocturnal orgasms in the female; they are not as frequent as in males.

WOMEN ALSO EJACULATE: The ancient authorities on the science of love, Audalaki and Vatsyayana, have a very ingenious explanation about the sexual desire in a woman. Audalaki states that there are countless parasites in the vagina of women causing an itching sensation. During coitus, the rhythmic penile friction is supposed to relieve the itching. Vatsyayana disagrees with the theory of 'relief of itching'. He rightly argues that the female is comparatively tranquil initially during coitus and is aroused more and more as the intercourse progresses. She desires to disengage after she has reached an orgasm and emits the seminal fluid. The ancients had mistaken the normal vaginal lubrication and mucus from the Bartholin's glands for seminal fluid. The myth persists. Some women still use the word ejaculation for an orgasm, and males still delight in fixing the 'itching' of their partners—a term often used after a satisfactory sexual encounter. To conclude, unlike men, women do not ejaculate after their orgasm.

Chapter 3

CREMATE THE MYTHS

A man loses his illusions first, his teeth second, and his follies last.

HELEN ROWLAND

THE PREVIOUS chapter, 'The Mythology of Sex', outlined the commonest sexual myths prevalent in our culture. Many believe that the 'super sex image' described therein exists in reality. We compare ourselves with these 'insatiable sexual creatures' and find to our horror that we are hopelessly inadequate. We are convinced that nature has been unkind and given us miniature equipment. The Casanovas, on the other hand, as portrayed by the erotic novelists and the media are generously endowed and are only available in the 'extra-large size' (like a tube of toothpaste or shaving cream)! Besides, like a longplaying record these sexual stereos can play the music of love at any time! We lose interest in sex when our high expectation does not match the media image.

Men and their sexual exploits

When men get together, one loudmouth usually brags about his sexual acrobatics, the number of women he has driven to ecstasy bordering on madness! You should always take such talk of sexual exploits with a pinch of salt. The wife of one so-called Casanova came to see me a few days later for a medical problem. As she was leaving, she said casually, 'Doctor, why don't you do something for Manu? He can't do a thing for the last six months. He just comes home, reads a book till dinner and then goes off to sleep.' That is the low-down on Manu.

Most men who boast have some inferiority about their sexual performance. The real sexual giants who are confident about their sexual prowess are usually not prone to cataloguing their achievements in company. The erotic woman in 'Fantasyland' is supposed to respond with push-button frequency to volcanic, earthquake-like orgasms. One would imagine the seismograph would record shocks of great intensity when she is orgasmic! In actual practice, she is completely disillusioned after imagining that sex is sublime and nothing sensational happened. No doubt, orgasm is a very pleasurable experience, but it is not what she imagined. Is there something wrong or lacking in her, she wonders?

Women by nature are not used to talking about their sexual exploits. They are always more reticent and discreet, unlike the male who after a drink in him, catalogues his sexual conquests as if he has been decorated with a *Vir Chakra* for his services to the cause of women in India!

The other basic difference is that a man in general is performance-oriented in every walk of life, especially sex. His erect penis is the yardstick by which he judges results. He takes any deviation from his ideal model very badly and thinks that he is impotent. A woman, on the other hand, is not usually performance-oriented and even if she does not reach the mind-shattering orgasm, it is not the end of the world for her. The whole sexual experience is enjoyable for her and not just its termination—the orgasm; while for the male, the end-point of intercourse, ejaculation, is the most sought-after moment.

Myths are part of you

It is not easy to bury sexual myths, as they have become a part of yourself and your family traditions. You may have a few hang-ups not mentioned here. You have to read Chapter 2 again and again. Isolate the different myths you think you are suffering from. Convince yourself that they are myths. It is only when you are genuinely convinced that they are fantasy that you will win the first round in your war against inadequacy.

The next step is to regroup your forces for an all-out assault on the impregnable citadel of impotency, premature ejaculation and frigidity, not by your will power but by natural normal arousal. Let your expectations be related to the new realities and not to the fantasyland sex to which you aspired without success all along.

Dr. Hans Selyle, Director of the Institute of Experimental Medicine and Surgery, University of Montreal, Canada, rightly observes, 'fight for your highest attainable aim, but never put up resistance in vain.' In other words, strive for what is really worthwhile and attainable in sex. Reality should be your guiding star. Strive sexually for what you can achieve without frustration and the humiliation of failure for whatever is within your innate abilities.

Everyone has his own limits—in eating, drinking, working and in mating. Do not feel discouraged that you are sexually limited. It is really not so. Nature has lavishly endowed all of us and you will be amazed at your normal sexual potential. However, you can be in trouble if you are over-ambitious to scale unattainable sexual heights by aping the media. For example, you have seen Jeetendra and Sean Connery in the movies coveting women by the hour. You say to yourself, 'I must be like them'. But deep down you have lingering doubts about your sexual horse-power. Can your two-litre engine match sexually the four-litre performance of the stars on the silver screen? The result: undue stress, producing sexual inadequacy. *Stress is the deadly enemy of sex.* In fact, as stress increases, performance diminishes, except for a very small minority of individuals whose sexual power is not affected by stress. You will argue that you were under severe stress in your office as you climbed the executive ladder, yet you have not got a heart attack or a peptic ulcer. Stress is certainly produced in both cases but your organs react differently. Your heart, your stomach and your arteries are very tolerant and give you a long rope before they hang you. Not so your penis. Your penis is a no-nonsense organ and its response when there is fear or anxiety is swift and definite: immediate impotency.

You will ask: how does one know the limits of one's sexual performance? The first rule is to indulge in sex when you are really turned on or when you want it. You will automatically know that you have reached satiety, when you are not interested in sex or do not have an erection. The fantasyland model thinks that he has become impotent. But not the new you. You know that your penis is on a 'short holiday', and will soon start functioning with renewed vigour. You also know that your penis is as temperamental and obstinate as a mule. It will go on a sit-down strike if you pressurize it to perform. The fantasyland model thinks that it is the end of the world for him. The model based on reality does not shout from the housetops and does not register a complaint against the penis in the Supreme Court of Sexuality. He gives it the benefit of the doubt. If something can go wrong with your lungs or heart or kidneys, why not your penis? Left to itself for a little while, it will soon start functioning normally.

The fantasy model voltage
You have lived up to now in the Fantasyland of Sex, where only Casanovas exist. You were born with a clean sexual slate; all the myths about sex have been learnt from parents, teachers, school friends and from books. If you have unfortunately picked up wrong information, it is not your fault but the fault of your teachers who knew no better and themselves need to be taught. An electric iron which works on 220 volts gets fused if it is plugged on 440 volts. Similarly with your faulty training. You have used the high voltage (440 volts) fantasyland current for your sexual equipment which is only meant for 220 volts. The result is that the equipment is, so to say, short-circuited and you suffer from sexual inadequacies, premature ejaculation, impotency, or frigidity. Your electric iron has to be rewired before it can function. Similarly, although you have realised your mistake of using the wrong voltage, you cannot immediately function normally. You have to relearn. This book shows you how. It will take some time for you to function effectively on the voltage which nature has provided you, but with perseverance success will ultimately be yours.

Let me illustrate the fantasy model voltage with the case history of a 37-year-old bachelor. Vivek told me, 'I did not marry as I cannot be faithful to one woman, doctor. As the old saying goes, when milk is available, why keep a cow? I can have any number of girl-friends but unfortunately my virility has disappeared. At the moment I am sticking to just three of them. I see them every week and build visions of finishing them off. But, when it comes to actual performance, I am a miserable failure.'

Vivek's hero on the silver screen was Sean Connery. He honestly believed that like him he could also jump in and out of bed with different women. Vivek was a typical example of an individual wanting sex on the 440-volts fantasy model. Naturally, he was a hopeless failure.

Vivek was made to realise that only when he learnt to use his sexuality properly and dropped his voltage would he be a successful lover. It took a long time for Vivek to be convinced that loving a single partner and knowing her well is more rewarding than flitting like a butterfly. I am happy to say that Vivek has finally settled down to just one partner and has become potent again.

Sex is a learning process
Sex, like walking, talking and bowel control in an infant, is a learning process in all of us. It is not, as is popularly believed, 'doing what comes naturally'. Learning is replacing ignorance with knowledge. The sexual instinct is the strongest instinct in animals and man. Yet, between the sexual instinct and sex with a woman there is a wide, wide gulf that is bridged only by learning. Let me clarify with a case history. 'Oh doctor, Zeenat Aman does something to my chemistry,' teenager Neville excitedly told me. 'I am aroused as soon as I see her on the screen. I go "nuts" with a burning desire to bed her, but, alas, beggars can't be choosers in this world.' The instantaneous sexual response in Neville did not come naturally but was the result of long years of indoctrination to respond sexually on seeing a 'sex-bomb'.

Sex even in the lower animals does not depend entirely on instinct. They learn it before they function normally. The young ones of animals kept in solitary confinement miss their mark sexually when they grow up. Harry Harlow has studied in great depth the importance of the early-learning process in monkeys, which he describes in *Learning to Love*. He isolated young monkeys, so as to prevent them from having early childhood experiences like being touched and fondled by their mothers or playing with other baby monkeys and watching adult monkeys have sex. When the secluded monkeys grew up and attempted sex, they were very clumsy. They had the natural sexual instinct and drive but since they had not learnt the know-how they were unable to have sex with female monkeys. Similar experiments have been done by other researchers as well.

Fortunately in animals the fantasy model does not exist. Sex is based on reality and for generations the young ones learn the right way from their parents, unlike human beings who are influenced in their outlook by societal norms and by saints, preachers and teachers who themselves need to be taught.

Animals are driven to sex by their powerful instinct
In animals, sex is basically a mechanical process to propagate the species. They only indulge in it periodically, especially mammals when the female is in heat. Human beings, apart from having sex for reproduction, find it an extremely pleasurable experience. Unlike animals, they can indulge in sex at any time—even when they are not turned on.

Sex often provides much-needed relief, especially for the male in this Stress Century, provided it is carefree and not performance-oriented. Such sex is like a well-tailored suit—made to measure—and when you wear it, you carry it off naturally. Similarly, after gratifying sex, you feel rejuvenated and relaxed, and automatically switch off the sympathetic system. Nothing stimulates your entire body as much as carefree, gratifying sex. You feel on top of the world, physically, mentally and emotionally. It revitalises every cell of your body. It is nature's great gift to you.

KNOW THYSELF

On the ashes of yesterday,
Let us plant the oaks of tomorrow.

ANON

Sex in tomorrow-land is going to be exciting and invigorating. You will enjoy it, as it is based on reality and not on make-believe myths. Up to now you were so overwhelmed by the abnormal fantasyland sexual model that you believed it to be the norm. You must remove the distorted debris of sexual myths you have harboured in your mind over the years by realigning your sexual beliefs to the new reality. Our ancient culture recognised that the most important but also the most difficult mental exercise is 'Know Thyself'. Knowing yourself includes not only knowing your mind but also your body and particularly the genital organs for adequate performance. You will be amazed to find that knowing your body has a great curative value. To give you an example: the 50-year-old worries that he is turning impotent when he does not get an instantaneous erection. He needs reassurance that the erection response after 35 is not instantaneous but takes some time, and is a normal physiological process. His potency is immediately restored and he functions normally when he knows that innumerable men after fifty take some time to get a 'hard-on'.

Know your genitals

The first ground rule for both sexes is knowledge about your genital organs and their functions. A lot of ignorance about sexual anatomy still prevails. Let me give you the example of Shilpa, a lady architect, who told me, 'We went on our honeymoon with marriage manuals on sex, as both of us did not have any knowledge about it. I was the baby of the family and therefore my parents and my elder sister kept me away from sexual information.' One can multiply such cases many times. Know your own as well as your partner's anatomy thoroughly. You can always tell her that you would like to look at her 'down there'. She may initially resist but on repeated pleadings she will ultimately permit you. The anatomy and physiology of the male and female genital organs are outlined in Chapters 4 and 5 respectively. Read on and realise the curative effect of your newly acquired knowledge. You are now on the way to win your 'war' against sexual inadequacy with the most potent and powerful weapon—knowledge.

Chapter 4

THE MALE SEXUAL ORGANS

A million million spermatozoa,
All of them alive:
Out of their cataclysm but one poor Noah
Dare hope to survive,
And among that billion minus one
Might have chanced to be
Shakespeare, another Newton, a New Donne—
But the one was Me.

ALDOUS LEONARD HUXLEY

THE MALE genital organs consist of the (1) Testes, (2) Scrotum, (3) Epididymis, (4) Ductus Deferens or Seminal Ducts, (5) Seminal Vesicles, (6) Ejaculatory Ducts, (7) Prostate, (8) Bulbourethral Glands, and (9) Penis (Fig. 4-1).

The TESTES or TESTICLES are the male reproductive glands. They are enclosed in a pouch called the SCROTUM and are suspended by the SPERMATIC CORDS, the left testis hanging a little lower than the right. Each testis is oval in shape, about 4 to 5 centimetres long, 2.5 centimetres wide, 3 centimetres in diameter from front to back, and weighs 13 grammes. The testis consists of two groups of cells. One group of cells secretes the hormone TESTOSTERONE, which is responsible for the secondary sexual characteristics in the male—manliness. The other group, the TESTICULAR TUBULES, produce the SPERMATOZOA, the male seeds of life. When seen under a microscope, they resemble tadpoles swimming merrily in the 'Seminal Sea'. The champion swimmer amongst them makes it to the female uterine tube before the others. If

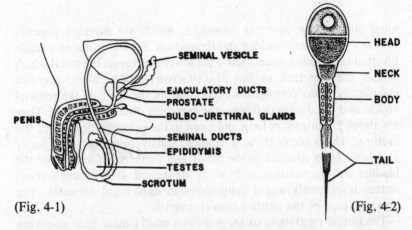

SEMINAL VESICLE

EJACULATORY DUCTS
PROSTATE
BULBO-URETHRAL GLANDS
PENIS
SEMINAL DUCTS
EPIDIDYMIS
TESTES
SCROTUM

HEAD

NECK

BODY

TAIL

(Fig. 4-1)   (Fig. 4-2)

a female cell (ovum) is waiting at the finishing line, they embrace each other and unite to start a new life. If not, the disappointed spermatozoon gets lost along with his millions of brothers. In each ejaculation there are 60 to 120 million sperms. What a colossal waste, to ensure reproduction, on the part of nature!

The scrotum is a skin pouch in which are suspended the testis and part of the SPERMATIC CORDS. The skin of the scrotum is thin and wrinkled, brown or darker than normal skin, and covered with hair. In colder climates and the younger age groups the scrotum is tight but in warm climates and older males it loses its elasticity and hangs loosely. The testes contain nearly a thousand thread-like tubes, each 65 to 90 centimetres long. The male cells are manufactured in this sophisticated sexo-chemical factory—about 50 million a day. They are then transferred to the warehouse called the EPIDIDYMES, a pair of 7-metre-long, tortuous canals that lie on the upper part of the testes. They consist of 15 to 20 tubules which eventually open into a single channel. In the storage tube the sperms attain motility and greater fertility.

The convoluted epididymis can be felt by the fingers through the scrotum. The DUCTUS DEFERENS is a continuation of the tail of the epididymis and is a twisted tube in the first part which gradually becomes straighter. It is situated behind the testis and continues as the SPERMATIC CORD. It runs along the groin and enters the pelvis through a small opening called the inguinal ring. In the pelvis it lies on the inner side of the SEMINAL VESICLES, which are inverted pouches between the urinary bladder and the rectum. Each consists of a single inverted tube coiled upon itself—the lower end forms the canal which carries the secretion to the EJACULATORY DUCT. There are two ejaculatory ducts formed on either side by the duct of the seminal vesicle and the ductus deferens, the excretory duct of the testis. They are about 2 centimetres long and open in the prostatic portion of the urethra. The PROSTATE is a conical, partly muscular and partly glandular body situated in the pelvis and surrounds the neck of the bladder and the urethra, in front of the rectum. It measures 4 centimetres transversely and 2 centimetres in its vertical diameter. The prostatic part of the urethra runs through it.

The BULBO-URETHRAL GLANDS are two small glands, each about the size of a pea, situated on the outer side of the membranous urethra. Each gland has a duct about 3 centimetres long opening in the membranous portion of the urethra (the prostatic urethra becomes the membranous portion; see Fig. 4-1). The prostate, the seminal vesicles and the bulbo-urethral glands secrete the milky white alkaline fluid which blends with the semen and nourishes the sperms. The sperms need fuel for their motility which is supplied by the fructose present in the semen. The sperms from the testes are stored in the epididymis.

The SEMEN, a thick, whitish liquid, consists of the products of the tubules in the testes, the sperms and the epididymis. The prostate and the seminal vesicles supply the fluid part. The total quantity of semen at an ejaculation is 4 to 7 millilitres and contains on an average about 60 to 120 million sperms, of which only one fertilizes the ovum. All the other sperms disintegrate. The sperms retain their motility for sixty days and their fertilizing power for thirty days. If a seminal ejaculation does not take place, the sperms ultimately degenerate by a process of liquefaction. Fertility in the male is reduced if the sperm count is below 60 million or if more than 20 per cent of the sperms have abnormal heads or the motility of the sperms is reduced.

Consistency of the semen and potency
The fantasyland culture has ingrained in the male that the semen should be thick like honey. A thin and watery semen is supposed to signify lack of potency and procreating power. First and foremost, the

semen has nothing to do with potency, but is concerned with reproduction (the spermatozoa produced by the testicular tubules and mixed with various secretions from the seminal vesicles and prostate). Erection and ejaculation are entirely different mechanisms which are outlined in Chapter 15. A male may be potent, that is have normal erection and ejaculation, but if the semen does not contain spermatozoa (it is called azoospermia), he will be sterile and unable to reproduce.

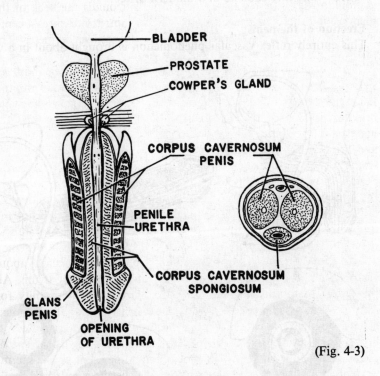

(Fig. 4-3)

The PENIS is the male organ of copulation. Its average dimensions—length and diameter in flaccid and erect states—are intentionally omitted as size-conscious males will immediately measure themselves and feel inadequate if they happen to be smaller than the average size (see Chapter 2). The penis consists of three cylinders of erectile tissue, the two CORPORA CAVERNOSA which lie adjacent to each other and a third mass, the CORPUS SPONGIOSUM which lies beneath them (Fig. 4-3). The corpus spongiosum contains the urethra and is enlarged to form the tip or GLANS PENIS. At the root of the penis, the two corpora cavernosa are attached to the pelvic bones. All the three cylinders are enclosed in a fibrous covering, which is surrounded by the skin of the penis. Nature has partitioned off the cavernous cylinders into innumerable small compartments—cavernous spaces—like tiny cubicles in a modern office.

Erection of the penis

This entirely reflex vascular phenomenon is brought about in a very

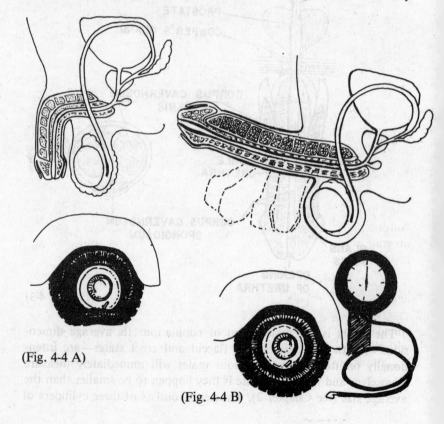

(Fig. 4-4 A)

(Fig. 4-4 B)

simple yet ingenious way. Let us see how this marvel of nature takes place.

Each cavernous space resembles a small rubber balloon containing blood, not air. The arteries bring oxygenated blood to the penis, whilst the veins return the blood to the heart. Normally the small arteries entering the rubber balloons (cavernous spaces) remain partially contracted to limit the amount of blood to the penis. But when they dilate for erection, the balloons are filled with blood and get inflated. The veins have valves which prevent the blood from leaving the penis. Just as when air is pumped into a tube, the outer wall of the tyre prevents the tube from over-distending and makes it hard, similarly the cavernous spaces fill up with blood and make the penis hard and erect with the fibrous covering acting like the outer wall of the tyre.

Nerve supply of the penis

The penis is richly supplied with nerves which control the blood vessels. It is necessary that you should be familiar with the working of the nervous system before learning about the nerve supply of the penis and how it produces a normal erection and how an imbalance of the nervous mechanism can result in sexual inadequacy.

The vast, uncharted and unknown kingdom of the human body (you probably know more about your car than your body!) is ruled and regulated by two ministers: the External Affairs Minister—the Central Nervous System (CNS), which responds and regulates the body to the external environment, and the Home Minister—the Autonomic Nervous System (ANS), which looks after law and order in your body, that is, taking care of all the vital functions like regulating heart rate, circulation, digestion and glandular secretions, and, last but very important, erection of the penis and the mechanism of ejaculation.

CENTRAL NERVOUS SYSTEM: The CNS consists of the brain and the spinal cord which have an intimate dual connection through the nerves with the rest of the body and particularly with the genital organs. The brain receives sensory signals and transmits messages to the muscles, for appropriate action. The sensory signals initially play a very important role in sexual arousal (see Chapter 6).

AUTONOMIC NERVOUS SYSTEM: The ANS is outside the control of the will, and regulates your internal environment. It is also responsible for producing erection of the penis and ejaculation. It functions quietly day after day, whether you are awake or asleep. Normally you are not conscious of your heart beats or the digestion going on in your alimentary tract. The ANS maintains law and order in your body through its own intelligence agencies. Every organ is under its surveillance. The moment it misbehaves (for example, indigestion or a heart attack), it is promptly reported to the boss—the central nervous system, for the necessary corrective action. For instance, when an individual suffers from a heart attack, the pain in the chest alerts the CNS to take appropriate action—take a sedative or lie in bed or consult a doctor.

The ANS consists of two components, the sympathetic and the parasympathetic.

THE SYMPATHETIC NERVOUS SYSTEM is the accelerator of the human engine, like the accelerator of a car. It is concerned with the instantaneous preparation of the body for defence against external threats. The caveman or the wild beast, when attacked, had two alternatives, depending upon the type of threat visualised by the thinking brain. The animal or man may decide that it is better to run away (he who runs away lives to fight another day), or he may decide to fight it out and perhaps be killed. This is called the FIGHT OR FLIGHT RESPONSE. The body, when mobilised by the sympathetic nervous system, resembles a boxing champion ready for a fight. The muscles become tense and alerted, the heart beats faster to supply more blood to the muscles and the brain, and the breathing becomes more rapid to supply increased oxygen to the blood. (Extra glucose is burnt by the muscles to produce extra energy to fight the opponent or run away). The overheated body combustion is cooled down by excessive sweating.

Modern man stimulates the sympathetic nerve to produce stress. (This subject is dealt with in detail in my book *Rock around the Clock*). During the stress of a life-and-death situation, obviously the mechanism of sex is kept in abeyance, as the man has either to fight or run away. It is fitting, therefore, that the sympathetic nerve which produces stress is also responsible for contracting the small arteries in the penis, resulting in blood returning to the body and loss of erection. The sympathetic nerve is also the motor nerve for producing ejaculation.

THE PARASYMPATHETIC NERVOUS SYSTEM brings the body back to its normal relaxed condition and restores vital energy. It is like the brake of a car that brings to a halt the accelerating automobile—the human engine. The accelerator and brake of a car are under the conscious control of the driver but, unfortunately, in human beings the autonomic nervous system is not under our conscious control.

The parasympathetic nerves bring about rest, relaxation and recuperation. They are the nerves of pleasure, erection and copulation. The parasympathetic fibres originate in the second and third sacral vertebrae of the spinal cord to form a single nerve on each side—called the NERVIERIGENTES. Stimulation of the nervierigentes leads to dilation of arterioles (minute arteries) and filling up of the cavernous spaces with blood, producing erection of the penis.

The penis receives a double nerve supply from the spinal nerves as well as from the autonomic nervous system. The spinal supply conveys the sensations of touch, pain and heat from the skin of the penis to the sensory centre in the brain (thalamus). The pleasant sensations produced by arousal and erection of your penis when your partner caresses your organ are conveyed by the spinal nerves to the brain via the spinal cord. If brief, while stimulation of the parasympathetic (nervi erigentes) causes erection, stimulation of the sympathetic nerves (hypogastric) causes ejaculation and subsequent loss of erection, due to contraction of the arterioles and decrease in the blood supply to the penis.

Nervous mechanism of ejaculation

The process of ejaculation is a highly complex mechanism—more intricate than erection—involving not only the accessory sexual organs (epididymis, ductus deferens, seminal vesicles and prostate), but also the pelvic muscles to propel the semen into the vagina. The sympathetic nerve, where stimulation causes stress and loss of erection, is also responsible for ejaculation (see Fig. 4-5).

Let us analyse the complicated process of ejaculation. Imagine that

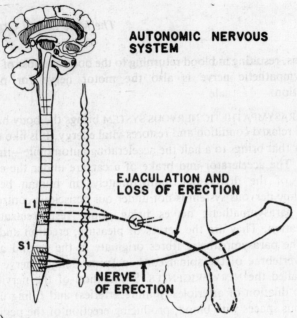

AUTONOMIC NERVOUS SYSTEM

EJACULATION AND
LOSS OF ERECTION

L1

S1

NERVE
OF ERECTION

(Fig. 4-5)

Explorer XY is on the launching pad ready for a voyage to the planet Venus—the vagina of your partner. The countdown now begins...

Explorer XY is launched into (her) space. As it zooms to and fro it becomes a beehive of activity, sending innumerable messages to the control tower (the brain) from the vagina—the resistance offered by it, the humidity and the temperature. If we now imagine a situation where due to metal fatigue or a short circuit, the rocket blows up, similarly ejaculation is an explosive end to intercourse, a means of propelling the semen into the vagina. The process of ejaculation begins by contractions of the muscular coat of the epididymis, ductus deferens, seminal vesicles and the prostate to propel the semen into the prostatic part of the urethra. The internal urethral orifice is sealed off to prevent voiding of urine or flowing of the semen into the urinary bladder. Powerful contractions of the prostate aided by the pelvic muscles expel the semen into the vagina in six to eight strong squirts. Erection soon dies down and the penis is limp and lifeless for some time and then the process starts all over again.

To recapitulate
The male organs of reproduction consist of the two testes suspended

by the spermatic cord in the scrotum—a wrinkled skin pouch. The testes produce the spermatazoa—the male seeds of life, and testosterone—the male hormone. The union of a spermatozoon and an ovum starts a new life. The epididymis are a pair of long convoluted tubes connecting each testis to the ductus deferens, which is a continuation of the epididymis. Both the epididymis and the ductus deferens act as a storehouse for sperms. The ductus deferens carry the sperms from the scrotum via the groin into the pelvic cavity where it eventually joins the duct of the seminal vesicles to form the ejaculatory duct. The seminal vesicles are two small pouches located between the urinary bladder and the rectum. They provide additives to the semen like fructose, amino acids and vitamins—the semen now becomes vitaminised! The lower end of the seminal vesicles unite with the ductus deferens on each side to form the short ejaculatory ducts—one on each side—opening into the urethra which serves the dual function of evacuating the urine or the semen. The bulbo-urethral glands are two small glands, situated on either side of the urethra below the prostate gland. Each has a duct which pours its viscid secretion into the urethra to provide lubrication of the penis during intercourse.

The penis is the male organ of sexual expression. It consists of three hollow cylinders of erectile tissue, with the urethra traversing through one of them. All the three cylinders are enclosed in a fibrous covering from which various partitions divide the cylinders into innumerable spaces containing blood. The penis is richly supplied with arteries and veins.

Erection of the penis is produced in an ingenious way. Normally the tiny arteries entering the cavernous spaces are partially contracted to limit the amount of blood to the penis. However, when they dilate for erection, the balloons are filled with blood and get inflated. The veins have valves which prevent the blood from leaving the penis. Just as when air is pumped into a tube, the outer wall of the tyre prevents the tube from over-distending and makes it hard, similarly the cavernous spaces fill up with blood and make the penis hard and erect with the fibrous covering acting like the outer wall of the tyre.

The penis is governed by the autonomic nervous system which is not under your conscious control. You can therefore never 'will' an erection. Erection just happens when you are sexually turned on. The parasympathetic nerve from sacral 2 and 3 (nervi erigentes) is responsible for erection. The sympathetic nerve is responsible for loss of erection and also for producing ejaculation—a complicated process where on receiving signals from the nervous system, the accessory organs of reproduction penetrate the seminal vesicles and the ductus deferens contract, aided by the pelvic muscles, to produce ejaculation. The semen is squirted into the vagina in six to eight strong jets. After ejaculation the erection soon dies down till the sexual batteries are recharged once again.

Chapter 5

THE FEMALE GENITAL ORGANS

Full many a gem of purest ray serene
The dark unfathom'd caves of ocean bear:
Full many a flower is born to blush unseen
And waste its sweetness on the desert air.

THOMAS GRAY

UNLIKE A man's sex organs, the genital organs of the woman are largely concealed within her body, and guarded by two fleshy gates called the LABIA MAJORA. They swing apart to permit 'traffic', usually one way. Urine, the menstrual flow and the baby reach out, whilst the fingers during love-play and the penis during intercourse penetrate in.

Ignorance about female sex organs

The ignorance even today about female sexual organs in both sexes is appalling. A successful lady executive once told me, 'Until I got married I didn't know if babies came from the mouth or stomach.' The ignorance is due to lack of sex education, though a few enlightened schools have recently begun teaching sex physiology.

Men seem to be equally ignorant and not at all bothered about female anatomy and the physiological functions of the sexual organs. Farida's husband, Akbar, is a typical example. After telling me about her headaches, backaches, frustrations and tensions, Farida suddenly blurted out, 'Doctor, I have been married for seven years, have had three children, yet I have never reached an orgasm. Akbar leaves me high and dry without any preliminary love-play. Like an animal! he just jumps on me and, after finishing, turns over and snores. He never touches my inside. He considers me dirty there and will not even look that way.'

A few days later, at my request, Farida brought her husband Akbar, a dental surgeon, to see me. I tactfully broached the subject of foreplay and the erotic zones in a woman—her whole body in general and the breasts and the clitoris in particular. Akbar asked, 'Where is the clitoris?' and continued after a brief pause, 'Doctor-Saheb, do animals have love-play? Their females are quite satisfied. I can make Farida pregnant every time I have sex. I am potent and have produced three children. Why do I have to touch there and hunt for the clitoris? I have better things to do!' He got up angrily, left the room and played hell with his wife who was in the waiting-room. 'Why have you brought me here and not only wasted the doctor's but my time also?' he snapped at his wife. As they left quarrelling, I thought about man's inhumanity to woman in sex and felt sorry for Farida. Because of the ignorance of their partners, the clitoris in innumerable women is like a flower 'born to blush unseen and waste its sweetness on the desert air'.

THE FEMALE GENITAL ORGANS

The female genital organs consist of an external group, also called

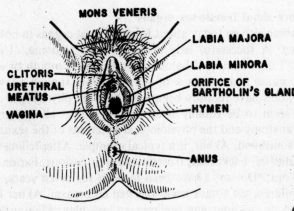

(Fig. 5-1)

the VULVA, comprising the (1) MONS VENERIS, (2) LABIA MAJORA, (3) LABIA MINORA, (4) BARTHOLIN'S GLANDS, (5) HYMEN and (6) CLITORIS.

The internal group which is enclosed and protected in the pelvic cavity consists of the (1) VAGINA, (2) UTERUS, (3) UTERINE TUBES and (4) OVARIES (see Fig. 5-1).

The genitalia vary in size from women to women.

External Genital Organs

The MONS VENERIS, a term derived from the Latin 'Mount of Venus' (goddess of love) is a rounded mass of fat at the lower end of the abdomen, above the VULVA in front of the SYMPHYSIS PUBIS or the junction of the two bones of the pelvis.

The LABIA MAJORA or large lips are two visible longitudinal folds which begin at the mons veneris and extend backwards to within 2 centimetres of the anus. The labia majora protect the perineum and contain large sweat glands like the scrotum.

The LABIA MINORA or small lips are two small folds 25 to 35 millimetres long, 8 to 14 millimetres high and 3 to 5 millimetres thick and are devoid of fat. They become visible when the labia majora are separated. The two small lips are united to form the hood or foreskin of the CLITORAL GLANS. At the back, the two labia are joined together behind the vaginal entrance to form a rim called the FRENULUM (small fold of skin), which disappears after frequent intercourse. BARTHOLIN'S GLANDS are situated in the labia minora. Their ducts open on the inner surface of the labia minora and lubricate the vaginal entrance with a transparent and slippery mucus secretion and thus help the introduction of the penis. The main lubrication during intercourse is provided by the walls of the vagina.

The HYMEN or the virginal membrane is a thin fold situated at the entrance of the vagina and is supposed to guard the abode of Venus. It does not completely cover the vaginal entrance, to permit the menstrual discharge to flow out. The hymen, as I have pointed out in the Introduction, has been considered the hall-mark of chastity and purity in a female. All races and cultures since primitive times have erroneously exaggerated its importance.

The hymen's defloration is a must for the male ego. It is supposed not only to flatter the penetrating power of his erect penis but also to prove his manliness. It is therefore eagerly sought after on the wedding night.

The hymen varies in size, shape and thickness from individual to individual. It may be crescent-shaped, ring-shaped, or scalloped at the edges. During the first act of intercourse, the hymen is torn or perforated, causing a loss of blood, which may be slight or considerable. The male penetration may cause pain depending on the thickness of the hymenal membrane, the mental make-up of the individual, and the skill with which he does it.

Occasionally, a woman's hymen is exceptionally tough and fleshy and the husband in spite of repeated efforts fails to penetrate her. The wife suffers a lot of pain during these attempts at forcible entry. The erection in the husband dies down after a time, and he starts wondering whether there is something wrong with his potency.

Countless women in our country have suffered humiliation and agony on their wedding night when their husbands have doubted their purity and accused them of having had pre-marital sex. Let me recount Shanti's pathetic story in her own words. 'Doctor, my trouble started on my honeymoon night. I had carefully preserved my virginity for the man of my dreams—Ratan. I was the happiest woman on earth and suffered agonising pain as Ratan, whom nature has generously endowed, forcibly entered me. It was a shocking experience in itself, but more shocks were in store for me. He left me high and dry and to top it all accused me of not being a virgin.'

The mascara from her eyes rolled on to her cheeks as she sobbed and continued, 'Something in me grew dead instantaneously. I became frigid. Though my husband apologised profusely afterwards, I have never enjoyed sex with him and have never had an orgasm in my life. I have two lovely children whom I adore. But do you think my headaches are due to this accumulated tension of not being orgasmic?'

I would sincerely advise my male readers not to overrate this bit of tissue, and not to jump to wrong and unjust conclusions about a woman's chastity. Its presence does not mean that your partner is a virgin, as there are innumerable women who have had countless sexual encounters and their hymen is not ruptured as it is so elastic it is merely pushed away or dilates as the penis goes past it. On the other hand, its absence does not mean that the woman has had sex. It can rupture in innumerable ways—during an accident, or in athletic events, or during masturbation, and in girls using tampons the hymen can gradually rupture.

The CLITORIS is situated just above the vaginal entrance at the upper end of the labia majora and is partially hidden by the labia minora. The clitoris is homologous or similar to the penis in the male and consists of a small erectile shaft and a glans which is highly sensitive. Like the penis it is composed of erectile tissue which hardens on physical or psychic stimulation. As stated earlier, the glans of the clitoris is covered by the hood or prepuce formed by the union of the upper part of the two small lips.

POSITION AND SIZE OF THE CLITORIS: The shaft of the clitoris may be as thick as a lead pencil and about two centimetres long or it may be longer and thinner. The size varies considerably from female to female. The glans is usually a little smaller than a green-pea. However, the glans increases appreciably in size in women who masturbate frequently. The position of the clitoris on the front of the symphysis pubis is variable. In the past, sexologists erroneously believed that the clitoris came in direct contact with the penis during coitus. The lower the position of the clitoris on the symphysis pubis and the longer its size, the better would be its contact with the penis and the greater the response in the female.

MUTILATION OF THE CLITORIS: No organ in the human body has been subjected to such unimaginable mutilation as the unfortunate clitoris. It is a classical example of ignorance about the normal physiology of the most voluptuous organ in the human female. Ignorance on the part of a layman one can forgive; but what does one say about the learned medical men who, until forty years ago, chopped off the clitoris, just as they excised tonsils and appendixes! For removing the latter organs, there was some justification—an infected tonsil could impair health by acting as a septic focus, causing rheumatic fever which might affect the heart and the joints. An acutely inflamed appendix could cause death, if not operated upon in time. But what reason was there to cut off the clitoris? It was supposed to prevent madness, masturbation and nymphomania in women, the motto of the medical men being 'When in doubt, cut in out'.

In the 19th century Dr. Isaac Baker in London excised the clitoris as a cure for various conditions like sleeplessness, sterility and other ills that his unfortunate victim was supposed to suffer from. In 1859, Dr. Charles Maigs advised a concentrated silver nitrate solution to be applied to the clitoris to prevent masturbation. And in the USA, surgical societies were conducting classes to educate surgeons in clitoridectomy until 1925. The wise men pronounced that 'it saves women a lot of sickness and suffering.' Far from alleviating suffering, it increased it in the unfortunate women. According to *Ms Magazine* of March 1980, the wife of a US Congressman states, 'My friend, a contemporary who must be in her sixties now, when she was four to five years old, her family was enlightened and well-to-do, but they accepted this as a treatment for masturbation.'

The medical evidence that the operation saved the women from innumerable ills is nil. In fact, there are reports that they grew worse after the mutilating surgery. The immediate complications were haemorrhage and infection. Later they developed frigidity, sterility, pain during sex and a number of psychosomatic illnesses like headaches, backaches and abdominal pains. The male perpetrators of these crimes did not shed a single tear, for after all a woman was not supposed to enjoy sex! In fact, they argued that they had done a good turn to the females because their continuous masturbation would have resulted in sexual promiscuity, perversion and madness.

It is estimated that 30 million women in the world are suffering from genital mutilation. The different types of mutilation are: (1) Sunna or Circumcision, where the tip of the clitoris is removed; (2) Clitoridectomy, where the entire clitoris, the prepuce, the glans and the adjoining part of the labia minora are removed; and (3) Infibulation (from the Latin word *fibula* meaning 'clasp'), where the entire clitoris, the labia minora and labia majora are removed and the scraped vulva is sewn across the vagina. A small opening is left by inserting a thin matchstick or a wooden or metal rod for urine and menstrual flow. The poor infibulated woman is opened up before marriage to permit intercourse.

Clitoral mutilation is common even today in parts of Africa, the Arabian Peninsula, Pakistan and Malaysia. According to a United

Nations report, clitoridectomy is practised in more than 26 countries in Africa.

Fortunately for us, the Indian culture which is influenced to a great extent by the teachings of Vatsyayana and Kalyanamalla, never took to clitoridectomy. Indian sexologists even in those days knew about the role played by the clitoris in sex. Kokaka has given a beautifully graphic description of this organ which he called *kamatapatra*. He describes the clitoris as hidden in the folds of the labia minora and labia majora and compares it to the unfolded and folded petals of the lotus flower. Normally, the petals of the lotus are folded but during sex they become unfolded.

FUNCTIONS OF THE CLITORIS: Never has Mother Nature packed so much voluptuous sensation in so little space as the clitoris because it is richly supplied by nerves. Its stimulation is the master-key to unlock a woman. Unfortunately, during sexual intercourse, the clitoris does not come into direct contact with the penis except in certain positions. You need to stimulate it with your fingers. If you want a Bachelor's degree in 'Love Making', you must be a master at stimulating the clitoris. Know its location, and how and when to stimulate it in order to levitate your partner into ecstatic climaxes.

The clitoris is a unique organ which has no other function except to give pleasure during intercourse. The penis, its male equivalent, provides pleasure, but also deposits sperms in the vagina and voids urine. According to Masters and Johnson, the clitoris has two important functions. It is a Receptor and a Transformer of sensations it receives when a woman is sexually aroused.

Let us examine and understand both these functions in depth as the clitoris is the focal point of sexual response in the female.

THE RECEPTOR FUNCTION is similar to the receiving station of a power-house. Just as electricity is generated at the power-house and then transmitted to the receiving station, in the same way the sexual power-house is in the hypothalamus, the part of the brain situated at the base of the skull. It is the seat of our emotions and the head-quarters of the autonomic nervous system (ANS). The hypothalamus is intimately connected with the pituitary, a tiny gland about the size of a large pea, situated at the base of the brain and located inside the skull. The pituitary is the most important gland in our body and is rightly termed the leader of the 'endocrine orchestra'.

The pituitary is the master regulator of our body and is also the self-starter of the sexual machinery. Just as the car engine starts when you press the self-starter, similarly the pituitary gland is the starter of the sexual motor—you are 'turned on'. The receiving station of the female sexual power-house is the clitoris. It receives messages from the breasts when the male partner is fondling them or when the finger is stimulating it or during indirect stimulation of the clitoris in sexual intercourse. As seen in Fig. 5-1, the vaginal opening is far from the clitoris. In the normal man-on-top position, obviously the penis cannot directly stimulate the clitoris. The method of indirect stimulation was first observed by Dr. Masters and Mrs. Johnson in their sex laboratory. The vagina is like a barrel and the penis moves to and fro in it like a piston during intercourse. The labia minora can be compared to a crank-shaft moving up and down at right angles to the penis. When the penis is thrust in, the labia minora are pulled down resulting is sliding of the prepuce over the glans. When the penis withdraws, the labia minora move up and so does the prepuce, uncovering the clitoral glans.

STEP-UP TRANSFORMER FUNCTION: The response of the clitoris is unique. It is easy to understand by comparing it to a step-up transformer which can convert a 110 volt current into 220 volts. Similarly, the clitoris increases sexual tension (like the higher voltage of a step-up transformer), ultimately producing sexual release and orgasm, when the voltage cannot be stepped up further.

Internal genital organs

The VAGINA is a fibro-muscular tube 7.5 to 10 centimetres in length extending from the vulva to the cervix or neck of the uterus, and directed upwards and backwards from the vulva. It is situated behind the urinary bladder and urethra and in front of the rectum and anal canal. The vagina performs a dual role—as an organ of copulation it accommodates the erect penis, and during childbirth it functions as the exit for the infant. The CERVIX projects into the vagina forming four recesses or fornices—in front, back and on the sides. The recess at the back, called the posterior fornice, forms a receptacle for the

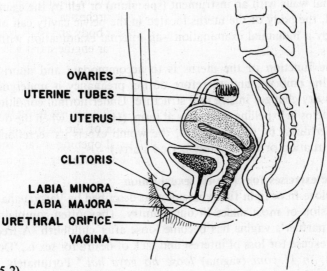

OVARIES
UTERINE TUBES
UTERUS
CLITORIS
LABIA MINORA
LABIA MAJORA
URETHRAL ORIFICE
VAGINA

(Fig. 5-2)

seminal discharge during ejaculation. Normally the walls of the vagina are in contact, but during coitus or childbirth they separate to form a canal or passage. The vagina is surrounded by a band of striped muscular fibres termed the BULBO-SPONGIOSIS.

The vagina is the means of sexual expression for the female just as the penis is for the male. Unlike the clitoris, it is not supplied with nerves; only the lower third has sensations. The response of the vagina during the various phases of the sexual cycle is described in Chapters 7 and 11.

The UTERUS or WOMB is a thick-walled, hollow muscular organ about 7 centimetres long, suspended in the pelvic cavity behind the urinary bladder and in front of the rectum. It is supported by ligaments and muscles. The uterus is pear-shaped and consists of a body or corpus uteri. Its upper expanded portion called the fundus extends above the opening of the uterine tubes while the lower part or cervix surrounds the cervical canal and projects into the vaginal cavity. The cervical canal is about 2.5 centimetres long and extends from the internal orifice of the uterus to the external orifice of the cervix in the vagina. While the cervix can be seen on separating the vaginal walls with an instrument (speculum) or felt by the examining hand, the body of the uterus located in the pelvic cavity can only be felt by a bimanual examination—an internal examination with both hands.

The function of the uterus is to accommodate and nourish the growing embryo, and therefore during pregnancy it undergoes the necessary changes in size and structure. Under normal conditions, it also helps in expelling the foetus at term. (However, when the ovum is not fertilized by a male sperm, the womb expels its secretions and menstruation or the monthly period starts.)

Pelvic exercises for close-fit sexual union

The close-fit or tight-fit sexual union as described by Vatsyayana is the obsession of most males in our country. They often complain that their partner's vagina has become loose after childbirth. A frequent male excuse for loss of interest and lack of desire for sex is, 'Doctor-saheb, *in ki yoni* (vagina) *loose ho gaya hai.'* Fortunately, such women need not despair for there is a very simple home remedy to enhance their as well as their partner's sexual pleasure—pelvic exercises.

A chance remark or an observation by patients to their doctors, has

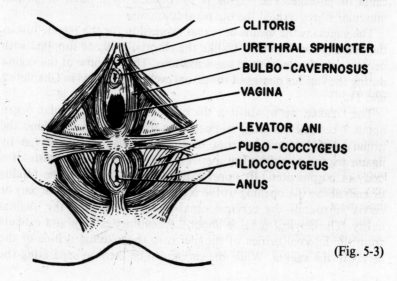

- CLITORIS
- URETHRAL SPHINCTER
- BULBO-CAVERNOSUS
- VAGINA
- LEVATOR ANI
- PUBO-COCCYGEUS
- ILIOCOCCYGEUS
- ANUS

(Fig. 5-3)

often resulted in important medical advances. Pelvic exercises are one amongst the many such contributions. Dr. Arnold Kegel, Los Angeles gynaecologist, was routinely prescribing pelvic exercises for women who had problems after child-birth with holding their urine; whenever they laughed or coughed or sneezed, they passed a drop or two of urine which distressed them considerably. The exercises improved their bladder control, and some women told Dr. Kegel that they noticed an improvement in their sexual pleasure as well. Dr. Kegel reported this improved sexual performance in an article entitled, 'Sexual Function of the Pubococcygeus Muscle' in the *Western Journal of Surgery.*

Pelvic exercises are helpful to both sexes. In the male, as I shall describe later, they are particularly beneficial to patients like Ghanshyam, who are quick on the trigger and discharge prematurely.

In order to do these exercises, it is necessary to understand the anatomy of the pelvic musculature. In the female, the vagina is held in position by powerful muscles during penile thrusting in intercourse and also during childbirth. There are two groups of pelvic muscles which can be exercised by conscious thought control. The first group consists of the VAGINAL SPHINCTER OR BULBOCAVERNOSUS whose two halves, like the upper and lower lips of the mouth, surround the vagina and contract to close the vaginal opening. During relaxation, the vaginal orifice opens up once again. The powerful contraction of this muscle, called vaginismus, can even prevent the penis from entering the vagina.

The other muscle, the URETHRAL SPHINCTER, stops the urine at the end of urination. It is situated a little inside the vagina and can be contracted with a simple exercise.

The second group of muscles, anatomically named the LEVATOR ANI (which means 'raising the anus'), comprises the PUBOCOCCYGEUS, ILLIOCOCCYGEUS and PUBORECTALIS and extend from the anus to the pubis. These muscles surround the deeper part of the vagina and are very powerful. They are exercised when one holds back a bowel movement.

You will naturally ask, 'How do I locate the pelvic muscles?' You can feel their contraction in two ways. First, imagine that you have a strong desire to pass a stool and cannot do so immediately as there is no bathroom and you have therefore to hold it for some time. The muscles you contract to hold the bowel movement for some time are the levator ani. Secondly, start and stop the stream of urine while you are urinating. The muscles you use to stop the urine are the ones you have to train. Having located them, here is how you do the Kegel exercises.

(a) The easiest way to do this exercise is to pass a little urine, then stop it and later urinate again. Do this stop-start exercise at least 15 to 20 times at a stretch three times a day.

(b) In order to do the second exercise, attempt to hold back a bowel movement by contracting the muscles 15 to 20 times 3 to 4 times a day. Gradually the tone of this muscle will also improve.

You should not feel sore or have aching pelvic muscles after the exercise. It is best to increase the number of contractions gradually. For instance, if you are exercising 20 times today, do it 25 times the next day and so on. After a fortnight try this variant. Contract the muscles while you count up to three, then relax. Repeat 10 times. After some time, this will become a daily routine, not requiring any special attention. The exercises will improve the sexual performance of both partners and enhance pleasure even in normal individuals. For instance, the contraction of the external sphincter muscle by the female, grips the penis and makes the erection more powerful. Vatsyayana was aware that some women in India, especially from Andhra, knew how to contract these muscles and increase the pleasure of their male partners. Similarly, contraction of the levator ani is felt by the glans penis and tremendously increases sexual pleasure.

HELPS MEN ALSO: These exercises done by men help to improve their holding power and make erection more powerful. They form the basis of the treatment for premature ejaculation (see Chapter 15).

The FALLOPIAN or UTERINE TUBES are two in number, very slender and supple. One end of each tube is joined to the side of the uterus, while the other end opens into the abdominal cavity. Each fallopian tube is about 10 centimetres long. Its interior has numerous folds and tiny hair or cilia which move and flicker all the time and thus bring together the ovum and the male sperm in the uterine cavity and later transport the female egg to the womb.

The two OVARIES are homologous with the testes in the male. They are situated one on either side of the uterus in a depression called the ovarian fossa.

Each ovary is about 4 centimetres long, 2.5 centimetres wide, a little over one centimetre thick, and is a marvel of nature's packaging, containing at birth 500,000 fully formed eggs of which about 400 mature from puberty till menopause.

A FOLLICLE consists of the female egg surrounded by a layer of hormone-secreting cells and is enclosed in a thin outer-covering. Every month one follicle becomes bigger owing to hormonal secretion and ultimately the outer membrane bursts, discharging the egg into the funnel of the fallopian (uterine) tubes. The remnant of the ruptured follicle is converted into a yellow gland called CORPUS LUTEUM which secretes a hormone called progesterone. If pregnancy takes place, the corpus luteum is responsible for continuing the pregnancy and cessation of periods and ovulation.

If the egg remains unfertilized, the corpus luteum withers away after a period of 12 to 14 days, thus cutting off its hormone supply. The womb which has made all the preparation for an oncoming pregnancy now discards a part of its inner lining. This breakdown is the monthly period—menstruation—characterised by bleeding and shedding of the inner lining and lasts for four to five days.

FEMALE HORMONES AND MENSTRUATION

Oh, menstruating woman, thou'st a fiend
From whom all nature must be screened!

Menstrual myths

The nature of the menstrual flow was not understood until recently and almost all races and religions considered this normal physiological process not only unclean but a curse on woman. She was not supposed to touch food or a human being from its onset till she had the 'ritual bath' at its end. As late as 1878, the *British Medical Journal* said, 'It is an undoubted fact that meat spoils when touched by menstruating women.' It is now accepted that the period is a normal phenomenon of the female reproductive cycle, though many women themselves continue to believe in the monthly pollution and purification.

Periods last from puberty till menopause, when owing to deficiency of the hormone oestrogen, the periods cease, resulting in menopause when the woman is about 50 years old. Menopause, appropriately termed 'change of life', is a psychological landmark in a woman's life. It causes unpleasant symptoms in some women which can usually be corrected. Women, however, feel dejected that it is the end of their sex appeal, which is not so. The absence of ovulation prevents pregnancy taking place but, contrary to prevalent belief, sex can be enjoyed better without the tensions of an unwanted pregnancy.

Oestrogen and Progesterone

Till about sixty years ago, scientists believed that the only function of the ovaries was to act as a storehouse for eggs and mature one every 28 days. In 1923, Dr. D. A. Doisy discovered that the ovaries also produce hormones. Further research led to the isolation of the two hormones—oestrogen and progesterone. The menstrual cycle of a woman is governed by these two hormones—the oestrogen in the first half, and the progesterone in the latter half.

Oestrogen promotes the growth of the womb, the vagina, the external female organs, the breasts and the hair in the armpits and the pubis, which occurs at puberty. Oestrogen is the hormone of 'feminine attraction and well-being'. It keeps a woman sexually active, emotionally healthy, protects the bones and prevents high blood pressure, heart attacks and strokes. Till menopause women are much less susceptible to heart attacks, high blood pressure and strokes than men. Progesterone is the hormone which keeps pregnancy going, stops the periods and is responsible for the development of the placenta. Progesterone also inhibits ovulation during pregnancy.

INHIBITION OF OVULATION: During pregnancy, ovulation and menstruation do not take place. This is due to the continuous secretion of progesterone.

The administration of progesterone inhibits ovulation.

A number of synthetic compounds (progestogens) have an action similar to progesterone in inhibiting ovulation. These compounds, such as norethindrane and norethindral, inhibit ovulation and are therefore used as contraceptive agents, administered from the 15th to the 26th days of the period. To prevent bleeding during their administration and to permit normal menstrual cycles, the synthetic progesterones are combined with small doses of oestrogen.

Composition of the Pill

Oral contraceptives contain the female sex hormones oestrogen and progestogen. The composition of the Pill varies. Some contain sex hormones extracted from natural sources, while most contain hormones manufactured synthetically. The ratio of oestrogen to progestogen also varies slightly in different brands.

MODE OF ACTION: The Pill, if taken regularly and according to instructions, prevents the ripening and release of the egg from the ovaries during the menstrual cycle. The proportion of oestrogen and progestogen in the Pill closely resembles the proportion of these hormones in the second half of the menstrual cycle in a woman (from the 14th to the 28th day after ovulation). The Pill thus postpones ovulation, so long as it is taken, and the ripening and release of the egg, thus preventing pregnancy.

Do's and Don'ts during a Period

(1) DIET: The period is a normal physiological process in a healthy woman. It has no side-effects. However, some women suffer from pain, uneasiness and lassitude before and during the first two days of the period. During each menstrual cycle 30 to 60ml. of blood is lost; this involves a monthly loss of 15-30 mg. of iron, which is equivalent to three weeks of the iron ingested by her in food. She thus has only one week during which she must absorb and store enough iron from the food to maintain a positive iron balance, so that she does not become anaemic. As long as she has her normal periods, it would be advisable to ingest foods rich in iron like liver and kidney, egg yolk, black currants, dried figs, prunes and dates, wholewheat bread and *chapatis, gur* and molasses, and vegetables like spinach, carrots, potatoes, cauliflower and beans. Iron is, however, in a form which cannot be readily used by the body. If her diet is deficient in iron or the bleeding is excessive, she may suffer from iron deficiency anaemia. This can be corrected by taking iron tablets or, in extreme cases, injec-

tions but it is advisable to consult a gynaecologist if excessive monthly flow persists.

(2) PHYSICAL EXERCISES: Some women have won world champion-ships during a period, but many tend to feel lethargic and uneasy and should refrain from excessive physical activity. However, there is no need to refrain from your normal daily routine during a period.

(3) SEX: Contrary to popular belief, sex is not barred medically during a period, but if the bleeding is excessive, it is messy. Some women enjoy sex more just before and during the first two days of a period.

(4) PRONENESS TO INFECTION: As the inner lining of the uterus is discarded it leaves an open wound. Married women especially are more prone to vaginal infections and irritations during periods, if their toilet hygiene is defective or if they fail to clean themselves pro-perly after passing stools or urine.

(5) PADS AND TAMPONS: A vast majority of Indian women use pads during menstruation. These should be sterile and frequently changed as the menstrual discharge emanates an unpleasant odour and irritates the delicate skin. Some married women find tampons more conve-nient. However, a recent report on tampons from the USA states that they can cause a severe bacterial infection in the vagina called 'Toxic Shock Syndrome', and since January 1980, 334 cases and 29 deaths have been reported.

To RECAPITULATE

You should be thoroughly conversant with the anatomy of the female sex organs, which are largely concealed within the body. They are shown in Figure 5-1. You should be able to locate the 'sex bomb'—the clitoris, just above the vaginal entrance. Its correct stimulation is the master-key to unlock a woman's sexuality. As it is located away from the vaginal entrance, it does not come in direct contact with the penis in the usual 'man-on-top' position and so should be manually stimulated with the fingers. The clitoris has a dual function—receiving messages from the brain and also acting as a step-up transformer, increasing sexual voltage and ultimately producing release and orgasm. No other organ in the human body has been subjected to so much mutilation as the clitoris. Even today, clitoral mutilation continues in some African and West Asian countries.

The hymen guards the vaginal entrance. It serves no purpose but men erroneously regard it as a sign of purity and its defloration is an ego-booster. Its presence does not mean that its owner is a virgin and its absence does not denote that the bride has had pre-marital sex.

The vagina is a fibro-muscular tube, designed to accommodate ideally the erect penis. Like the penis, though not richly supplied with nerves, it is the organ of sexual expression for the female.

The uterus is a hollow muscular organ designed to house and nourish the growing embryo. It also helps to expel the foetus during childbirth. The ovaries produce the ovum—the female egg cell—which is picked up by the hairlike cilia of the fallopian tubes. Fertilisation usually takes place in the outer third portion of the tube. After childbirth, the vaginal wall loses some of its elasticity which diminishes sexual pleasure. The importance of exercising the pelvic muscles to improve sexual performance in both sexes is highlighted. The Kegel exercises are given to improve vaginal tone and enhance enjoyment during sex.

The physiology of a normal menstrual cycle and the ovarian hormones are given. The hormones are oestrogen and progesterone. Oestrogen is the hormone of feminine attraction. It keeps a woman sexually active, emotionally healthy, protects the bones and prevents high blood pressure, heart attacks and strokes until the menopause. Progesterone is the hormone of pregnancy. It keeps it going, stops the periods, prevents ovulation and is responsible for the development of the placenta.

Chapter 6

SEXUAL AROUSAL AND RESPONSE
IN THE MALE

*No sooner met but they look'd; no sooner look'd but
they lov'd; no sooner lov'd but they sigh'd; no sooner
sigh'd but they ask'd one another the reason; no
sooner knew the reason but they sought the remedy.*

WILLIAM SHAKESPEARE

THE SEXUAL DRIVE depends upon sexual instinct and cultural conditioning. All organisms have physiological needs which are necessities of life—food, water, warmth and sex. These urges are inborn and part of our biological heritage. They drive the organism to activity which persists till the need is satisfied. The internal conditions responsible for our behaviour are called physiological drives, for example, the hunger drive or the sex drive. It is the hormones secreted by our sex glands which are responsible for sexual motivation and drive. Male sex hormones—androgens—are secreted by the testes and also by the adrenal glands. If the testes are cut off before puberty, there is no sex drive and no erection. If they are excised after puberty, sexual drive and erection may be absent, though there are many recorded cases of the sexual performance remaining unimpaired for life because the sexual reflex activity once established carries on even without testosterone.

One ovarian hormone is named oestrogen. If the ovary is removed in an experimental animal before puberty, the typical female characteristics like periodic heat fail to appear. In an experiment, mature female rats were placed in cages attached with revolving drums. It was observed that they spent a great deal of time running.

The activity reached its peak every fourth or fifth day with the animal running the equivalent of 24 kilometres. This activity period was followed by a relatively inactive day, followed by a day of great activity when the rat was very receptive to mating. However, the periodic activity never developed and mating did not take place in rats whose ovaries were removed before puberty. Similarly, when the ovaries were removed in a mature female rat, the activity cycle and mating ceased. This proves the importance of the sex hormones in these animals. However, in an adult male or female, hormones do not play such an important role.

An instinct comprises unlearned responses which are characteristic of a species. For example, physiological needs like eating and mating in mammals such as dogs or cats are satisfied through their characteristic instincts which come to them naturally and the process automatically repeats itself in successive generations. But as we go higher up the scale of evolution, mating ceases to be a stereotyped process as in the cat or the dog. For example, copulation is a learning process in the chimpanzee, despite the sexual instinct. The young chimpanzee develops adult mating patterns through trial and error by play behaviour with the adult monkeys. Like the chimpanzee, sex in human beings is mainly a learning process beginning in the cradle. We are not born with the sexual know-how: the human sexual drive depends mainly on cultural conditioning. We are born with a normal sexual instinct and a clean slate of sexuality upon which, through the learning process, we imprint our sexual norms.

Growth of sexual awareness
The genital region even in babies is an important erotic centre and playing with the genitals always produces pleasure. During childhood and growth the stirrings of sexuality are ever present, the sexual longings becoming suddenly more pronounced during the transition from childhood to puberty. Puberty is an important landmark when the foundation of future sexuality and lifelong sexual attitudes is laid. It is therefore essential that at the onset of puberty, objective and factual information about sex is imparted to adolescent boys and girls. Puberty in the Stress Century comes on at a much younger age than before. The onset of puberty is very apparent in young girls between

nine and 13 years. The hormones from the pituitary gland produce the secondary sex characteristics, namely, the sudden change in the hips with the deposition of fat, giving them a feminine appearance. The nipples and breasts enlarge and more hair appears on the pubis and in the armpits. A little later, menstruation begins in young girls.

Puberty in boys appears at a much later age and is variable between 11 and 16 years. The penis enlarges at the age of 12 to 13 years and so do the testicles. A beard develops on the face and the voice becomes hoarse.

Puberty is a period of considerable emotional and physical strain. The pituitary gland, the leader of the endocrine orchestra, is as small as a pea but has a finger in almost every pie of human living. It is responsible for switching on the sex glands—the ovaries in the females and the testes in the males. The switched-on sex glands at puberty start producing three hormones, namely *testosterone, oestrogen* and *progesterone*, which are responsible for turning us on.

Sexual arousal and erection in the male

It is important to understand the normal mechanism of sexual arousal and response, for only then can we pinpoint the feelings which result in sexual inadequacy. Sexual arousal or desire or excitement is a feeling of being turned on. You have a strong desire to have sex with your partner. It is described differently by individuals as tension, a surge of blood, a warmth suffusing the body, especially the penis, or a gnawing feeling demanding release. The sexual arousal results in erection of the penis and can be triggered off even by imagination; for instance, by thinking of a movie star of just seeing her picture. The sense organs in the normal male are a source of sexually stimulating impulses. Looking at a lovely face, hearing a woman's voice, inhaling her perfume or natural body odour can turn on the male.

The brain is like an electric gadget which responds only to the proper voltage. A 220-volt electric shaver does not work on a 110-volt plug. Similarly, the 'voltage' of the sensory messages must be adequate to arouse you sexually and produce an erection. Such a response is called the 'all or none' phenomenon and is the only way our nervous system responds to a stimulus. Either the brain responds to a proper stimulus and turns you on or, if the impulse is weak, it

es not respond. The sensory pathways, especially those from the
ve special senses—touch, sight, hearing, smell and taste—play an
important role in sexual arousal as well as inadequacy. When they
function normally, the sexual mechanism is in top-gear, but if the
sensory input is blocked or inhibited sexual inadequacy results. I shall
later refer in detail to the sensory pathways in the prevention and
treatment of sexual disorders.

Male sexual behaviour is a complex process in which are involved
the sex hormones, both male and female, the brain, especially the
hypothalamus and the pituitary glands, the spinal cord, the long
pathways of nerves carrying sensations from the special senses to the
brain and the neuro-motor fibres which carry the impulses from the
brain to the erection centre situated in the sacral region of the spinal
cord and finally to the penis.

Carlos Beyer of the Metropolitian University in Mexico, speaking at
a symposium on 'Reproduction Endocrinology', stated that three
reflex mechanisms are involved in copulatory behaviour. They are the
Arousal Mechanism (AM) which turns us on, a separate mechanism
for having intercourse called the Copulatory Mechanism (CM), and a
Modulatory or Regulating Mechanism (MM) which is responsible for
the control of sexual behaviour in man. The three mechanisms are
schematically shown in Fig. 6.1

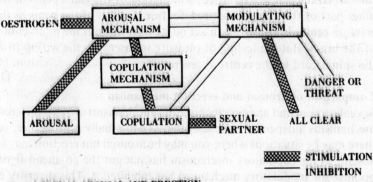

Fig. 6-1 SEXUAL AROUSAL AND ERECTION

Male sexual behaviour: [1]arousal, [2]copulation and [3]modulating mechanisms. The female
hormone oestrogen stimulates arousal in men. The Modulating Mechanism receives two kinds
of messages — all-clear and danger or threat in the environment to the animal or man. Its brakes
are off when it is all clear and therefore arousal and erection can take place.

The Arousal Mechanism is stimulated in males by the female hormones and is located in the hypothalamus and preoptic area of the brain. It has been found that lesions in this area suppress male sexual behaviour. The Arousal Mechanism arouses you sexually, gets you in the mood for mating and directs the Copulatory Mechanism, 'On your mark, get set, go!' It fires the shot that sets the pace for the Olympic race (intercourse), of which the erect penis is the torch-bearer.

Copulation is a complex process involving the brain, the spinal cord and the motor pathways in the nervous system. Its headquarters are probably situated in the brain near the Arousal Mechanism. It is responsible for co-ordinating the complicated act of intercourse, involving the erection of the penis and all the muscular and vascular changes in the body, preparatory to and during intercourse. The Arousal Mechanism, as I have stated before, stimulates the Copulatory Mechanism. No arousal, no erection, no copulation.

Erection and ejaculation are reflex phenomena—not under the direct control of the brain—and can take place even in the 'spinal' man. During the Second World War there were cases of wounded men whose spinal cords were injured by a fracture of the spinal column or cut due to gunshot injuries. The individual became completely paralysed below the level of the cord injury (spinal man). After some time when the reflexes returned, stimulation of the glans penis or the inner part of the thighs produced a reflex erection of the penis as the erection centre in the cord can act on its own without the intervention of the brain. But the feeling of pleasure is absent, as the wiring from the spinal cord to the centre is severed.

Comparison of arousal and erection mechanism

Sexual arousal and erection (copulatory mechanism) are two different mechanisms independent of each other. They usually act together, yet there may be situations where you may be aroused but erection may be absent, as the copulatory mechanism has not got the go-ahead signal because the modulatory mechanism has inhibited it. This diversity of action is only found in man; in animals the two mechanisms always act in unison. Thinking and feeling aroused are two entirely different things. Men often 'think' that they are aroused but they just mechanically want to get aroused. Under such circumstances there is no erection response. On the other hand, when a man sees a beautiful thigh, he 'feels' aroused, a natural process resulting in an erection. Thinking yourself to arousal involves the central nervous system, while feeling yourself aroused is the natural process mediated by the autonomic nervous system.

Regulatory or Modulatory Mechanism

The Modulatory or the Regulatory Mechanism (MM) is an emergency brake to inhibit sex when there is sudden danger or threat. Just as the alarm chain in a train when pulled brings the train to a grinding halt, similarly, the Modulatory Mechanism is an emergency mechanism to stop the sexual activity of the Arousal and Copulatory Mechanisms.

I will explain in detail how this mechanism regulates sexual activity in animals and man. Let us study animals first. The Modulatory Mechanism has an up to date feedback from the environment—what is happening in the jungle. A monkey may be driven by the sexual urge to copulate. The modulatory mechanism has given the green signal to the Arousal and Copulatory Mechanisms to go ahead. Its brakes are off! Imagine for a moment that a tiger appears on the scene. The Modulatory Mechanism as soon as it gets the information about the tiger from its sensory feedback, instantaneously jams the brake on the Arousal and Copulatory Mechanisms. Sexual activity stops as the monkey runs for its life. The preservation of life is more important at the moment than its propagation.

In man the Modulatory Mechanism acts as an inhibiting mechanism of sexual arousal and erection. Let me illustrate with the case history of Ravi who had been invited by his girl-friend Chitra to spend a quiet evening in her cosy apartment. 'Doctor, she looked dazzling in her slinky blue sari,' Ravi told me as we sat down. 'I couldn't take my eyes off her as she played with her sari; it kept sliding off her shoulder and uncovering her breasts. A gentle breeze blew her favourite perfume, "Joy", on to me.' Ravi breathed rapidly and continued, 'I was aroused and could not wait a second longer. An overpowering desire consumed me as I kissed and hugged her passionately.' The brakes of Ravi's Modulatory Mechanism were off. They had given the go-ahead signal.

'Things could not be better for a sizzling sexual encounter,' the Modulatory Mechanism told its two buddies—AM and CM. Ravi went on, 'I was about to mount my sweetheart when the doorbell rang loudly. My erection died down instantaneously, as I hurriedly got up to dress and answer the doorbell.' He paused, played with the pincushion on my table and hesitatingly asked, 'Doctor, the incident happened 15 days ago, yet whenever I am with Chitra, although I am aroused and on fire, nothing happens. Even after her office colleague left the other night, I could do nothing.' I reassured Ravi that the erection response is very sensitive. The slightest disturbance can make his MM send alarm messages to his AM and CM to stop temporarily. A few months later, I met the couple at a party, where as soon as I entered, Ravi told me, 'Remember, doctor, my penis went to sleep on hearing the doorbell? It is now functioning fine.'

When an animal faces real danger, the Arousal and Copulatory Mechanisms are immediately inhibited. Unfortunately, civilized man is inhibited not only by real threats, as in the case of Ravi, but also by symbolic threats, such as fear of performance. Let me explain. If owing to some reason like extreme tiredness, a man fails to get an erection, his confidence is shaken and he is afraid that he may not be able to perform again. Fear of performance is a symbolic threat. The inhibitory factors are explained below:

(1) FEAR OF FAILURE: Fear, anxiety and doubt are the greatest enemies of erection. A sexually inadequate male often wonders before intercourse, whether he will get an erection or sustain it during intercourse. In such cases the penis remains limp and lifeless. If for some reason erection is absent, there is always a fear of failure the next time the person attempts sex. Sex should be spontaneous and carefree and never performance-oriented. You can certainly perform better in your office by conscious effort but in sex you should never say to yourself, 'I must have a strong erection.' The result is no erection.

(2) WATCHING WHETHER AN ERECTION TAKES PLACE: Dr. Masters has called it 'Spectator Role'. During foreplay, instead of letting go with his partner, a man keeps 'thinking' how his penis will perform. His attention is on his penis and not on his partner.

(3) TRYING TO 'WILL' AN ERECTION: I have repeated time and again,

that a man cannot force an erection by using his will power. It never works.

(4) PREOCCUPATION: Whenever one is worried or preoccupied with office work or problems one cannot have satisfactory sex.

(5) STRESS: As stated earlier, stress stimulates the sympathetic nervous system. As the sympathetic is the nerve which inhibits erection when stimulated, any erection present is lost.

(6) WHEN THE PREREQUISITES OF SEX ARE NOT MET: The fantasyland culture attributes a unique power to the penis to respond instantaneously like a flash camera, whether one is aroused or not, whether one is in the mood for sex or not. It assumes that your penis should respond and get hard instantaneously as already described in the games the penis plays in Chapter 2. The penis is a very temperamental and obstinate organ and does exactly the reverse of what is expected of it. It can get erect at odd times or cause a man a sleepless night, or stay mulishly limp when he desperately wants it to be erect! There is not a thing in the world a person can do to make it erect. This happens because most individuals have some prerequisites for erection which are described in detail in Chapter 9, under the section on Foreplay. In some cases the female partner may have to caress it. A man may think that he is abnormal because his organ needs his partner's help. I repeat the penis is not a push-button mechanism and there is nothing wrong for a man to have his prerequisites met.

(7) ALCOHOL: Alcohol is a depressant of the central nervous system and impairs sexual functioning. The seed of impotency in innumerable cases is laid when the male partner has had too many drinks. However, in cases of anxiety or nervousness, a little alcohol removes inhibitions, making the individual carefree and hence improves sexual performance.

(8) GUILT: Individuals who have been indoctrinated by their parents that sex is sinful suffer from a guilt complex which seriously impairs their sexual performance. Similarly, males having an illicit affair may suffer from guilt and become impotent despite their longing to prove their 'manliness'.

(9) FATIGUE is a great enemy of sex. Top physical fitness is necessary to be tops in sex. A tired man cannot perform satisfactorily, as he does not have the physical and nervous energy.

(10) LACK OF PHYSICAL FITNESS: Sexual performance depends on good health. In order to be sexually efficient for life, a person should ensure vibrant health by living sensibly.

(11) ORGANIC DISEASES like uncorrected diabetes, impair sexual performance.

(12) DEFICIENCY OF MALE HORMONES: Psychologists and sexologists have led us to believe that erection is in the head, and nót in the penis, and that impotency is psychological in most cases. But endocrinologist Richard Spark of Boston's Beth Israel Hospital reports in the *Journal of the American Medical Association* that in as many as 35 per cent of cases, the impotency is not mental but due to deficiency of the hormone, testosterone. Dr. Spark's study is based on 105 impotent men between the ages of 18 to 75 years. Using modern radio immuno-assay techniques which can detect even very minute quantities of deficiency, he also found that over-active thyroids produce an endocrine imbalance and impotency. By administering the male hormone and correcting the over-activity of the thyroid gland, the potency of these experimental subjects was soon restored.

(13) LACK OF DESIRE is one of the commonest causes of sexual impairment and is due to loss of interest resulting from lack of variety of sex with one's partner, or having too many partners.

Sexual response

Masters and Johnson have divided the sexual cycle in males and females into four separate stages. They are: (1) Excitement Phase, (2) Plateau Phase, (3) Orgasmic Phase, and (4) Resolution Phase. The male sexual response is comparatively simple, though there are variations in duration during which a male can perform, but basically the intensity is the same.

STAGE 1: The immediate male response during sexual arousal is erection of the penis. It occurs instantaneously in young adults, but takes some time in middle-aged and elderly males. In some cases, the partner may have to stimulate the penis manually.

It is a popular notion amongst both sexes that males do not need any foreplay. Many men, however, need a bit of love-play to turn them on. An erotic female in the mood for sex should know how to entice her partner when he returns home tired after a day's hard work. She must use her subtle charm to turn him on by titillating all his senses, except touch (it may produce a premature ejaculation if employed too early). It is well known that when one sense is aroused, the other senses are automatically switched on. For instance, the way to a man's heart is through his taste buds and the tastier and more 'aphrodisiacal' the meal the better. Once his taste buds are stimulated, he sees better, hears better and has a strong desire to touch her. Perfume also has a stimulating effect on the nervous system. Similarly, sound can arouse him. A tender love song by Lata Mangeshkar or a sexy one sung by her sister Asha turns on millions of men. This preliminary love phase removes the feeling of fatigue and diverts his attention to the erotic woman and nature does the rest. Some women have even mentioned to me the tremendous turn-on-effect of a soothing massage. In general, the erotic areas of the male are around the body opening and near nerve endings like the buttocks, the thighs, the stomach, the insides of the elbow, the navel and the pubis just below the hairline.

STAGE 2: During the Plateau Phase, the penis undergoes further vaso-congestion and becomes bigger. The glans penis turns reddish purple in colour in fair males but this is not noticeable in dark skins.

STAGE 3 is the Orgasmic Phase when the ejaculation takes place. It results from contractions of the various muscles in the perineal region, the urethra, and the bulbospongiosus. The corpora cavernosa and the corpus spongiosum are hollow cylinders which contain no muscles, but merely fill up with blood to permit erection of the penis. The base of the penis is securely anchored into the pelvic bone by strong muscles, the ischio-cavernosus and the bulbospongiosus, whose contractions permit the ejaculation of semen. During these contractions, the semen is forced out from the prostatic, membranous and penile urethra. (For easy identification the portion of the urethra which passes through the prostate is called prostatic urethra, the succeeding portion is membranous and the segment through the penis is called the penile urethra.) The contractions of the penis during ejaculation resemble the contractions of the female during orgasm.

STAGE 4 OR RESOLUTION: The penis after ejaculation soon resumes its flaccid state. Unlike the female who can respond immediately if restimulated during the Plateau Phase, the male has a refractory period which varies from individual to individual during which time he does not get an erection.

GENERAL RESPONSES: The general body response is characterized by increased muscle tension due to contraction of the muscles and vaso-congestion (increased blood supply). The response is identical in males and females. The breathing is faster, the heart rate increases as the tension rises and so does the blood pressure. Dr. Masters observed in his study that the systolic blood pressure was elevated 40 to 100 millimetres of mercury (mm. of Hg.) and the diastolic 20 to 50 mm. of Hg. To illustrate, if the systolic blood pressure is 130 mm. of Hg., it can shoot up before ejaculation to over 230 mm. of Hg. and if the diastolic is 80, it can rise to 130 mm. of Hg. A skin rash, noticed in fair skins, and sweating are additional features of the general response during sexual stimulation.

The Male Response Cycle is simple and straightforward compared to the intricate and innumerable changes that take place in the female genital organs during arousal.

Chapter 7

SEXUAL AROUSAL AND RESPONSE
IN THE FEMALE

We know for how brief while
In woman's heart the fire of love can burn,
If eye and hand plenish it not, afresh.

DANTE

S EXUAL AROUSAL in women is far more complex than in men, and its mechanism is difficult to describe. Until recently our knowledge was limited and derived mostly from guess work, as only male sexologists were describing a process about which they knew little. Fortunately, in the last twenty years, female sexologists have helped fill the gaps in our knowledge of the sex drive and the factors which influence it.

Arousal in the male and the female differ

There are important differences in the pattern of arousal in both sexes. The flag-pole of male arousal is the erect penis flying the flag of his potency, easily visible to himself and sexually stimulating to his partner. It is an infallible proof of his arousal. On the other hand, women can only rely on the amount of vaginal lubrication; a less convincing and more invisible indicator than the erect penis.

Erection in the male depends upon his age and physical fitness. In normally healthy males, it is instantaneous in youth, takes a few seconds in middle age, and longer in the elderly. However, after ejaculation, the erection dies down and it takes some time before a man can have an erection again. This time interval is called the refrac-

e extent of the refractory period—shorter in youth and longer in the elderly—varies from a few minutes to a few days.

Arousal in the female takes much longer—from ten to fifteen minutes to an hour, though there are some highly passionate women who respond rapidly and do not need prolonged foreplay.

Unlike the male, if the female is restimulated after her orgasm, she can be multi-orgasmic, that is, she can have many orgasms. Her orgasmic potential—single or multiple—is not stamped on her; in fact, she herself is unaware of her capability. For instance, the so-called sex-bomb with a sexy walk, a husky voice and inviting lips may be only mildly orgasmic or not at all. In spite of all her sex appeal, she just peters out at the finishing line. On the other hand, some of the plain Janes who all walk, talk, and look alike can be extremely sensual. There is a torrent of pent-up passion in these not-sexy-to-look-at types waiting to be unlocked by the right male—the sensuous male who restimulates her after she has had the first orgasm until she responds again and has a second one. After a pause of a few seconds, keep on rekindling her passions until she has reached satiety and calls it a day. You will earn her eternal gratitude for having fulfilled her completely. If you have already ejaculated and cannot continue with penile stimulation, your faithful and obedient ally—your index finger—is always at your command for any length of time. Unlike the penis, you can use your will power to make it perform at any time, anywhere, for as long as you want.

The female responds more promptly as she grows older and has acquired sexual experience, unlike the male in whom arousal and erection are delayed with advancing age. Repeated sexual exposure makes her respond more quickly, whereas a virgin inexperienced in the intricacies of arousal is naturally slow and clumsy. In the West, where sex is free, older and sexually mature women are more eagerly sought after than raw virgins. In his book *In Praise of Older Women*, Stephen Vizinczey says, 'I've found nothing more pathetic than the universal misery of young boys trying to charm young girls. There were luckier times, of course, when the girls kept their dates and even permitted themselves to neck with me. It was like being on a plane that zooms back and forth along the runway and never takes off. I began to feel unattractive, unwanted and helpless.'

In our country, virgins are prized for their inexperience in bed. They are eagerly sought after in marriage and in extra-marital sex. This is because most men go to bed only to satisfy their sexual lust. They do not expect performance from their partners, nor do they take the trouble to arouse them. For them, sex is for self-gratification or procreation. However, women are no longer prepared to be passive partners in such one-sided sexual enjoyment; they want men to arouse them sexually. Nowadays, the male in order to get more in sex, must give more.

Sex is the central game of life in both partners, yet a woman has to invest much more of her energy and time as a result of sex, than a man. She is like a core industry where she has to invest heavily, there is a long gestation period, and the returns are slow. She has to invest nine months of her precious time before her first dividend—the infant—is born, and has to spend additional time in nurturing it. In sharp contrast, the male has only to invest one sperm and fifteen to twenty minutes of his time in intercourse to procure dividends. Man is like a consumer industry—a small investment in terms of time, a large turnover and quick profits. As a result, he is more readily aroused than the female and is trigger-happy about sex. Like a butterfly he flits from the pursuit of love to the love of status symbols—position, power, wealth and worldly goods. The poet Byron has vividly described the difference between a man and a woman's love:

'Man's love is of man's life a thing apart,
'Tis woman's whole existence.'

Arousal in the female
Arousal depends on the woman's (1) anatomy and physiology; (2) mental and emotional make-up; (3) environmental factors; (4) cultural conditioning; and (5) partner.

ANATOMY AND PHYSIOLOGY: The highly sensitive and sensuous clitoris is the primary organ for sexual pleasure in the female. Other erotic zones which arouse a woman sexually are the lips, the ears, the side of the neck, and the breasts (see Chapter 8).

MENTAL AND EMOTIONAL MAKE-UP: 'It's all in your mind,' a lady remarked while talking to me about sexual arousal and response, adding, 'There should be no mental blocks about sex. Take my sister's case. She has some aversion in her mind ever since she broke off her engagement.' If a woman has a mental block about sex due to an unpleasant episode like a man forcibly trying to possess her, or the boss at the office pestering her about a date, she may not be aroused fully.

Men are more erotically aroused than women by psychic stimuli like reading about a torrid love episode, seeing a nude picture or a shapely female. Women are aroused more by touch than by sight.

ENVIRONMENTAL FACTORS: These play an important part in turning on a female, unlike the male who can usually perform anywhere, as long as he is not disturbed. A woman on the other hand is turned on by the right 'atmosphere'—moonlight, a rainy or cloudy day, soft music, enchanting scenery, the sound of the sea, dancing with her partner or even by a situation of extreme grief or danger, such as bombing during a war. She likes to be protected from danger by the male. Strange as it may seem, the secret desire of *some* women is to be raped and they often dream about being sexually molested!

CULTURAL CONDITIONING: This shapes the sexuality of a woman. She is usually guided by society mores. If she has lived in a society where free sex is practised, she will indulge in it when she grows up without any pangs of conscience. On the other hand, if she has grown up in a culture where sex is taboo and even touching a male is not permitted before marriage, she may ultimately develop a guilt complex which may affect her arousal.

HER PARTNER: Monica, an advertising executive, said to me, 'Very few Indian men know the art of arousing a female. Most of them fumble, are clumsy, heavy-handed and just want to grab the breasts. They think they are peeling mangoes!' She hesitated, played with the pin-cushion on my table and ruefully remarked, 'As for intercourse, most of them are what the Americans call 'Slam-Bam-Thank-You-Ma'am' and discharge in a few minutes. There are classes for short-hand, typing, elocution, advanced management, but there is nothing for teaching males how to turn on their partners and for females how to respond sexually.' Monica is right. 'The Tragedy of the Bedroom', as Tolstoy calls it, could be easily avoided with a little knowledge of how to arouse a woman.

Different women look for different attributes in men. Some want intelligence, social status, wealth, power, while others are attracted by an ability to converse, wit, or skill in sports. Sunil Gavaskar makes the heart of many females throb, and so does the handsome Nawab of Pataudi with his polished batting and impeccable behaviour. Being handsome, is, however, low down on the list of most women.

One frequently finds positively ugly-looking men being ardently pursued and loved by very beautiful and attractive females. 'I don't know what she sees in him!' say the jealous onlookers who have lost the race. The answer: **a sensuous man.**

A sexually knowledgeable and experienced male once told me, 'Doctor, contrary to whatever you read in the books, an extra inch of male anatomy makes all the difference to some women. A few become orgasmic just looking at a generously endowed male, whilst others reach many orgasms with such males.' However, with the majority of women, the size of the penis is low down on their list of priorities. Most women enjoy sex best if they love their partners, rather than have it with someone for whom they have no emotional attachment. What they want most is gentleness, tenderness, a man who cares for them and desires them. Many women get aroused quickly not only because their partner wants sex but because he desires them and appreciates them.

SEX AND THE MENSTRUAL CYCLE: Sexual desire is highest just before the onset of the period and for the first two days of the period. The woman is easily aroused and responds more intensely during this time.

FEMALE SEXUAL BEHAVIOUR: Fortunately the female, unlike the male, does not have to produce an erection for sexual intercourse. However, any lack of hormones, particularly testosterone, lessens her sexual desire and interferes with her enjoyment of sex. It is strange but true that the male sex hormone is responsible for arousal in the female, and the female sex hormones in the male. The female sex hormones, oestrogen and progesterone, are responsible for a woman's feminity and the normal changes in her sexual apparatus during menstruation, sex and pregnancy. Similarly, testosterone in the male is responsible for his manliness and for the development of his sexual organs including the penis. The hormones keep their respective sexual machinery in trim to respond to a stimulus from the arousal centre. Hence both sexes need male and female hormones for effective sexual responsiveness. The same three reflex mechanisms as in men, (see Chapter 6), Arousal (AM), Copulatory (CM), and Regulating Mechanism (RM), are involved in female sexual behaviour.

Arousal inhibitors

The factors which inhibit female arousal are:

FEAR OF PERFORMANCE: Only the male has to perform during sex as he must produce an erection. Hence there is always a nagging fear in the male mind that he might fail the sexual test one day. There is no corresponding fear in the female. She need not perform and can lie passive during sex, if she so wishes. However, with Masters and Johnson's finding that women can be orgasmic or multi-orgasmic in auto-manipulation, many females have become performance-oriented like males. They think they must be orgasmic every time they have sex!

FEAR OF PREGNANCY: It is said that if males were to become pregnant, the problem of the population explosion on our planet would be solved! Though there are many contraceptive devices like the pill, the loop, the vaginal cap and the condom, many women are averse to using them because of cultural conditioning and religious beliefs. Besides, the pill and the loop have general and local side-effects respectively. The most important side-effects of the pill observed in a few women are loss of sexual drive, thrombo-embolic phenomenon (clotting in a leg vein which detaches and settles in the lungs), raised blood pressure and cancer of the uterus. The loop causes a certain amount of bleeding and irregular periods in the first few months.

'IT IS NOT A MALE CONCERN': Sorry, gentlemen, but pregnancy is as much your responsibility as hers. 'To have or not to have' a baby should be a joint decision. It's up to the two of you together to decide on what form of contraception to use. Of course, this is particularly important in the case of pre-marital or extra-marital sex. If by chance your girl-friend becomes pregnant, do not desert her at this trying time in her life. Give her the mental, moral, emotional and financial support she needs. Be by her side when she has to have an abortion. Here is what Rakesh said when he came to see me with his sweet seventeen. 'How do I know, Doctor, that it is not someone else? I am prepared to pay the expenses. You can send her somewhere and get her fixed.' His bewildered partner started crying at Rakesh's callous attitude. 'You can cry your heart out, but I cannot accompany you. I have my family honour to protect,' he told her indignantly.

His partner, whom the Romeo must have promised the moon, burst out sobbing loudly. Rakesh got up and told her in parting, 'Wait in the doctor's waiting-room for 15 minutes. I do not want to be seen leaving the doctor's office with you.' 'Goodbye doctor,' he called out to me as he left, and added, 'Don't take any notice of this little twerp!'

The distraught, two-months-pregnant girl continued to sob hysterically till she recovered from the shock, then burst out angrily, 'Doctor, I could shoot that bastard if I had a gun! Thank you for letting me stay in your consulting-room while you made the arrangements for me.'

The other inhibitory factors are outlined in Chapter 18, 'Do You Manhandle Your Partner?'

Sexual response
The female, like the male, when sexually aroused goes through four stages: (1) Excitement Phase, (2) Plateau Phase, (3) Orgasmic Phase, and (4) Resolution Phase.

STAGE 1 is the onset of sexual excitement. The first sign of sexual arousal in the female is the secretion of the lubricating fluid by the vagina. The vaginal lubrication occurs within 10 to 30 seconds after sexual stimulation in normal women. (The first sign of arousal in the male is erection of the penis.) Dr. Masters calls it 'the sweating reaction of the vagina'. Just as beads of perspiration appear on the face, in the same way beads of moisture appear on the inner vaginal wall and coalesce (unite) to form the lubricating fluid. However, if the sexual stimulation by the male is not of the right kind, the vagina remains dry and the usual moistening is absent. Innumerable impatient males try to enter a woman's dry vagina. Not only is such an entry difficult for him but it causes the woman intense physical pain and emotional disturbances. It is essential for the male to stimulate her mons area with the finger until she is moist before he enters her.

Changes in the clitoris: As stated in Chapter 5, the clitoris is the master-key to unlock the female orgasm. The male partner must be well aware of its location and thoroughly familiar with its anatomy. It is situated just above the vaginal opening and below the mons area and consists of a body and the glans. The smaller-than-pea-size glans is packed with nerves and is so highly sensitive that most women cannot bear it being touched directly by the finger.

The two small lips unite above to form a hood or prepuce to cover the glans. During the Excitement Phase, the first change is enlargement of the clitoris and swelling of the clitoral glans due to engorgement of blood vessels inside it; in some women it doubles in size. The size of the clitoral glans like that of the penis bears no relationship to orgasmic responsiveness. The clitoral response during the Excitement Phase is prompt if the area around the mons and the clitoral shaft are directly tickled with the finger. The response takes longer if only kissing or caressing of the breasts is resorted to.

Changes in the breast: Masters and Johnson describe a series of changes in the female breasts. According to them, the first sign during sexual excitement is erection of the nipples. Erection usually does not occur simultaneously in both breasts—one nipple may become erect and tumescent, while the other may take a little longer. In right-handed male partners, the females (from a sample survey) reported that they usually responded with erection of their left nipple first. The nipples may increase in size from 0.5 to 1 centimetre. With increased blood supply, the veins on the surface of the breasts become dilated and the breasts become bigger. Erection of the nipples is a tell-tale, easily visible sign that the female is responding to sexual stimulation.

STAGE 2 is the Plateau Phase. The normal vagina is potential space but during Stage 2, the upper two-thirds balloons out and forms a cavity to accommodate the erect penis. The lower one-third is narrowed because of vasocongestion and grips the penis firmly. The uterus also enlarges during this stage, and a remarkable yet consistent change takes place in the clitoris. The whole clitoris retracts upwards in front of the symphysis pubic bone, while the glans is withdrawn beneath the foreskin. It is not easy to locate the body and the glans of the retracted clitoris with the finger and inexperienced males often fumble searching for it.

The clitoral body retraction is a sure sign that the female is about to reach her orgasm if stimulation is continued, otherwise the clitoral body and glans promptly return to their original overhanging position. In fair women, the inner lips (labia minora) become congested and appear bright red in colour. The colour change is not so prominent in dark-complexioned women.

The Plateau Phase may last from 30 seconds to a few minutes before culminating in an orgasm. If the orgasm does not take place, pelvic congestion may persist for a few hours and may lead to tension and frustration.

STAGE 3: The Plateau Phase culminates in the climax or orgasm which is characterised by sudden peaking followed by a release of sexual tension. The responding woman may feel the muscular contractions in her vagina, rectum and the pelvic muscles as well as in the arms, legs and back of the neck. A sense of fulfilment and contentment permeates her whole body as she floats into a different world. The orgasm lasts for 10 to 15 seconds. There are many aspects of female orgasm which are separately discussed in Chapter 11.

STAGE 4 is called the Resolution Phase, when the response cycle moves backward through the Plateau and Excitement Phases to the passive unstimulated state. After climbing the sexual peak, the female returns to the plains. The pulse and blood pressure return to normal. The muscle tension and the vasocongestion also disappear.

The two basic changes which all the organs undergo to return to normal are: (1) release of muscular tension in the body, and (2) return of the blood to the heart from the congested blood vessels. The heart rate, blood pressure and respiration return to normal within minutes. If a woman has had a sex flush of her skin during the Plateau Phase, it will rapidly disappear; she may also have a thin layer of perspiration on her body.

The congested areolas around the nipples return to normal as the venous constriction is relieved. This rapid relief of areolar congestion makes the nipples look more erect. The tell-tale secondary erection of the nipples is another sure, externally visible sign that orgasm has taken place.

Within five to ten seconds after orgasm, the clitoris returns to its normal position as during the pre-excitement phase. In cases where manual stimulation of the clitoris is resorted to produce an orgasm, its return to the normal overhanging position is another indication that an orgasm has taken place. The contracted outer-third of the vagina relaxes and the orgasmic platform is lost.

Where the female partner has not gone beyond the Plateau Phase, the resolution takes much longer. If an inadequate male partner leaves her high and dry at the Plateau Phase, chronic congestion of her pelvic parts occurs, resulting in backaches, a constant feeling of congestion in the pelvic area and, in some cases, local irritation causing vaginal discharge. Intercourse makes her more tense, irritable and frustrated.

The female is ever ready to scale the sexual summit once again if restimulated, unlike the male who cannot respond immediately. Hence the necessity of an ever-potent male to fulfil the evergreen female. However, in this Stress Century, the civilised man is a tired man and does not have the energy to carry repeated sexual burdens.

Chapter 8

THE ROLE OF THE SENSES IN
SEXUAL AROUSAL

No barrier of the senses shuts me
How good is man's life, the mere living!
How fit to employ
All the heart and the soul and the senses
forever in joy!

ROBERT BROWNING

THE SENSORY pathways of touch, sight, hearing, smell and taste, besides keeping us attuned to our surroundings, play an important role in turning us on and enhancing sexual pleasure (see Chapters 6 and 7). If these sensory pathways are blocked owing to inhibitions or mental preoccupations, not only do we fail to enjoy sex, but diminished sensory perception can lead to impotency in the male and frigidity in the female. Hence the importance of knowing the functions of these emotion-generators.

The touch of love

Of the five senses, the skin's sense of touch has a peculiarly vivid and explosive quality and differs from other sensations in arousing response. It is the most extensive sense, as the sensory organs of touch are distributed all over the body in the skin and the adjoining mucous membrane. The sensation of touch is of two types—active and passive. If you touch your partner the sensations you feel are active sensations. On the other hand, if your partner touches you, it is termed a passive sensation. Both types of touch sensation are necessary to enhance sexual excitement and pleasure and lift sex from the level of the humdrum to the sublime. However, to feel these sensations normally or to be sensuous, the sensory centre in the brain where these sensations are interpreted should be free and uninhibited. As I shall describe in the next section, it is very easy to inhibit or brake the sensations from childhood. If your sensory motor is braked from childhood, you can never respond freely and totally in sex: you are like a car trying to accelerate with the hand-brakes on. But you can learn to release the brakes, even if your parents have anaesthetised you sensually. Robert Browning wisely advises:

'You should not take a fellow eight years old
and make him swear to never kiss the girls'

Touching plays an important role in the normal, well-balanced emotional growth of babies. Infants thrive on cuddles and caresses. Without contact their personalities become deprived and warped. Harry Harlow in a series of experiments isolated the young ones of monkeys from their parents, thus depriving them of early childhood experiences like touching and fondling by their mothers or playing with other baby monkeys and watching adult monkeys having sex. When the secluded monkeys grew up and attempted sex they were very clumsy. In another experiment, Dr. James Prescott of the National Institute of Health, USA, demonstrated that young infants, when deprived of sensory experiences like touching and fondling, grew up mentally retarded. It is customary in our culture for mothers to hug and kiss their daughters, but not the sons for fear that they may grow up into 'sissies'.

'Namaste' culture
Unfortunately in our country, with its innumerable castes, customs and rituals, we have developed an allergy to touching and being touched. A male greeting a female or even a male does so with folded hands. In a *namaskar* even hand-contact is absent.

Caste distinction abounds, despite our Constitution forbidding it. We do not touch individuals of certain castes. This unwillingness to touch has led to sensory deprivation and affected our sexuality. The male, owing to ignorance and upbringing, does not touch or feel the need of touching the female partner, except during sex. This is unfortunate, as true touch is the most powerful means of sexually exciting and gratifying the female. Dr. Masters calls it 'sexual touching pleasuring'. It is the common grouse of many women that their partners do not touch them for touch's sake. Many males are surprised when I tell them about the importance of touching their partners.

'HE NEVER TOUCHES ME EXCEPT DURING SEX': 'Tony thinks I am untouchable except when he wants to go to bed with me,' moaned Celine. On my taking Tony to task, he said defensively, 'If I touch her, doctor, she might think I want sex.' It was impressed upon Tony and Celine that touching need not necessarily culminate in sex! It can be just touching your partner to reassure her that you love and care for her.

A woman's greatest torment is her man's indifference. 'Oh, doctor, if only my husband would give me a hug or a kiss occasionally, how different I would feel! Women are like little puppies. We long for the loving look or touch. A little male attention makes the world so wonderful,' Sakar said wistfully.

Do you know, Mr. Tarzan, that touching plays a very important part in women's sexuality? Physical affection for its own sake and not just sexual touching is important to women. They crave to be touched by their beloved. It costs you nothing to use your hand non-sexually, yet it will bring you lasting dividends—a contented and responding partner. Mere sexuality without adequate sensuality where body contact gives little or no pleasure to one or both partners, results in mechanical sex. When sensitivity to varying touches is heightened in both partners, either naturally or through exercises, a unique and totally sublimating experience is felt in sex.

Sensuality is the spark which ignites you sexually when you are not only giving but also receiving—in fact, total pleasuring. It is the hallmark of a great lover with a touch of class.

Erogenous zones
The whole body in both sexes, especially in women, is sensitive and

sensuous to touch. But certain touch spots stimulate greater desire than others and are termed EROGENIC or EROGENOUS ZONES. They are located mainly around the body openings—the lips, the mouth, the outer side of the eye sockets, the ears, the vulva in the female, the penis in the male and the area around the anus, are all highly sensitive as they are richly supplied with nerves.

'EACH KISS A HEART QUAKE': Kissing with lip-to-lip contact brings into play the senses of touch, smell and taste. Erotic kissing is basically a Western form of love-play. Orientals have the nasal kiss. There are different types of kisses—the kiss of love, kiss of affection, and parting kiss between friends. The first is mouth to mouth while the other two are usually on the cheek or forehead. Kissing is not a common form of foreplay in our culture. Shashi, hero of many conquests, once told me, 'It is much easier to get at the breasts than at the lips in our culture. If I tried anything like that in the West, I would instantly be slapped!'

SENSITIVE EARS: In most sensual women, the ear is a highly erotic zone which when sucked, tickled, kissed or gently bitten makes them breathless with desire. Men are not generally aware of the tremendous arousal potential of the ears. While examining the ears of Swapna, she screamed. I removed the ear speculum immediately and asked, 'Sorry, did I hurt you?' She blushed with embarrassment as she replied, 'No doctor, not one bit, but my ears are so ticklish. I wish my husband knew about my sensitive ears!' 'Why don't you tell him?' I said to her. She replied, 'How can I do that? It is for him to find out.' The path of love would be simpler and smoother if both female and male partners indicated to each other where and how they like to be fondled.

You can easily find out your own erogenous zones by your response to touch spots which when lightly touched or tickled by your partner give you maximum pleasure. Sensitivity varies from person to person and there are two ways in which your partner can discover zones which are sexually exciting and so give the utmost pleasure. Firstly, by trial and error, the male can discover the erogenous zones by employing different types of touch on his partner and observing her facial expressions. It is a time-consuming method and I have known males who have spent years trying to find out what their partners wanted. I must add here that most males and even their partners are under the impression that they do not like or want to be touched except during intercourse, which is far from the truth. The caressing of the genital organs and the stimulation of the breasts and the clitoris are discussed separately in Chapter 9 and so are omitted here. A man's sexual performance can also improve tremendously if he is tenderly touched and his sensuality developed by his partner.

Second, ask your partner about her erogenous zones. Most women are shy and reticent but you could communicate to her your likes and desires which would help overcome her shyness and allow her to tell you, if not in words, by pointing with her hands, or as Vatsyayana says, by looking at the erogenous zones she would like to be stimulated.

In conclusion, touch is the mainspring for sexual stimulation. It kindles the flame of arousal into a ravaging fire of desire in both sexes, particularly the female. Dear male reader, you can occasionally dispense with touching, stroking, petting and caressing and be like an animal penetrating her with your erect penis. She may suffer such an assault silently, but remember that for rewarding sex there are no short cuts. You have to go through the whole works. This is because in a male, the seat of desire is his erect penis, but in a female, it is her whole body that is sensual and not merely her genitals. A normal individual can increase his sensuality by doing the recommended exercises (see Appendix A) whilst for persons suffering from sexual inadequacies (premature ejaculation, impotency and frigidity), the exercises form the sheet-anchor for restoring normal sexual functioning.

Language of the eyes

Next to the sense of touch, visual sensations play an important role in turning us on. The sexual impact of first impressions is sometimes so powerful that it has won the name of love at first sight.

In the West, where love leads the way to the altar, poets, authors and media have romanticized the lover's gaze. But in India most marriages are arranged with the parents choosing the future partners of their sons and daughters. They are the first to see the prospective bride or groom. The boy and the girl see each other much later, and the eyes therefore play a limited role in mutually turning on the partners even after marriage. 'I was 14 years old and my wife only nine, when my parents got me married off,' said Ramkumar, aged 48. He was suffering from impotency, because from the beginning he was never sexually aroused by looking at her. However, even in the West, the arousal effect of the sense of sight wears off after some time, unlike the sense of touch which persists. As John Donne says: 'Love built on beauty, soon as beauty dies.'

Mention must be made of the sexy parts of the female body which arouse strong desire in men. The breasts invariably attract attention, especially in an alluring choli with a plunging neckline and exposed midriff. Shapely legs also turn on men, but in India most women wear saris, so they are hidden from view. A sari-clad female who walks gracefully with hips swaying invariably attracts male attention. And of course, the female face that launches a thousand ships holds the male spellbound.

Women on the other hand are attracted to tall, broad-shouldered, virile men. However, there is a basic difference between the sexes. For most women, beauty in a male is mere surface attraction; they are drawn like magnets to gentleness, politeness and character.

VISUAL APPRECIATION OF MOVEMENT: Bodily movement, especially rhythm, is also very appealing to the eyes. A person who walks, sits and dances gracefully stirs the senses. The rhythmic folk dances of India with their varying tempo and movement arouse the senses of sight as well as of hearing. The modern Western dances with the partners dancing separately opposite each other combine visual and audio effects. The slow and lilting older numbers—the waltz and the fox trot—with the partners holding each other close, gladden the senses of touch, sight and hearing.

In conclusion, if the eyes are used sensually, they provoke strong desire and improve the quality of sex. On the other hand, if one is preoccupied as most males usually are (including myself), you may be looking at an alluring, curvaceous female but the perception produces no visual impacts; you just cut her dead. But she makes an immediate visual impact on the sensual man. This is not to suggest that his sense of sight is uninhibited: he has just not braked his arousal system. For a normal man, 'A thing of beauty is a joy for ever: Its loveliness increases; it will never pass into nothingness.'

'Heard melodies are sweet'

The ear has a particular biological role in animal mating. Observations on crickets have shown that the male produces the chirping sound and the female seeks him out. In man, hearing attains its highest utility in the sound of music and of speech.

Music is 'the food of love' says Shakespeare. A song or a tune often arouses emotions and desires and creates the right mood for love. The whispered intimacies between two people in love are very potent arousers. However, the haste and bustle of modern life are the greatest enemies of carefree sex. The so-called 'quickie', a product of the Stress Century, has speeded up man's reactions. He is swiftly stimulated and quickly satisfied; but not so the female, except rarely. She likes her partner to talk to her, tell her how much he desires her, wants her and loves her. The sound of the three magic words 'I love you' genuinely said is sweet music to her ears and removes mountains of inhibition in her and gets her ready for sexual intimacy.

'THE MELTING VOICE': 'I fell for his sexy voice,' Malti, an advertising executive, said to me about her husband. 'You can never imagine what it does to me even if I hear it on the telephone. My bones turn to jelly. I pity the innumerable women who must be turned on just listening to him on the radio.'

Smell attracts or repels

Smell is a very potent sexual arouser in animals. Its role in humans is limited except in individuals of the olfactory type, in whom the sense of smell is (as in primitive man) more sexually pronounced. Nose-to-nose contact and inhalation or the nasal kiss is an important act of foreplay in Orientals.

Our body odours vary from individual to individual and differ also from race to race. The armpits and the genital organs in both sexes have their peculiar body odour, which is more pronounced in females, especially during a period. Modern man with his soaps and deodorants has lost the ability to be naturally turned on by smelling his partner. He relies mainly on colognes and after-shave lotions and the female partner on perfumes—artificial arousers of the sense of smell.

DISAGREEABLE BODY ODOURS: Rancid sweat and bad breath in either partner is off-putting to both sexes. Many men think it is masculine to jump into bed with their partner without a bath after a day's sweating at the office. Similarly, many females are blissfully unaware of the repelling odour from their armpits or during a period when they have not paid enough attention to personal hygiene like washing and changing pads frequently. Some women do not bathe during a period, thinking it might harm them. Nothing is further from the truth. A bath is more essential at this time and does no harm.

PHEROMONES are chemicals with scents that influence the sexual behaviour of animals. For example, the sex pheromone in female animals attracts the males from miles around. Men use different types of after-shave lotions to turn on females. A search is on to isolate the normal pheromones in males. A British research team at the University of Warwick is reported to have isolated from the sweat, a natural pheromone smelling like sandalwood oil which will 'create between people, even strangers, immediate empathy, if used like a cologne.'

Taste the beautiful
Like the sense of smell, very few individuals experience the taste of their beloved. The lip-to-lip and tongue kiss is a cocktail of three sensations—touch, smell and taste. Dr. Van de Velde in his pioneer book *Ideal Marriage* writes about 'the individual flavour of a beloved's kisses' of the ancient Romans. 'For instance, the kisses of Poppoea, Nero's second wife, are described as tasting of wild berries.' The clitoris when licked with the tongue is saltish in taste.

The sensual partner
The single characteristic which distinguishes a good lover from an ordinary one is sensuality. Such a man is emotionally mature, confident in his powers and believes in reciprocal pleasure in sex. The key to great sex does not just depend upon technique or how long you

can carry on, or how handsome you are. It depends upon how responsive and relaxed you are. To sum it in just one word, how **sensual** you are. The senses are within you, ready to be tapped. All of us can become more alive sensually and therefore more responsive in sex. Your arousal could be psychic or through any of the senses. When once aroused, the others senses increase it in geometrical proportion. This chapter and the sensuality exercises outlined in Appendix II are the twin keys to the exalted and glorious kingdom of sex.

Chapter 9

THE ANATOMY AND ART OF INTIMACY

*And the eyes of them both were opened, and
they were naked; and they sewed fig leaves
together, and made themselves aprons.*

GENESIS

LET US PAUSE for a while and briefly recapitulate our journey through the first eight chapters. Out of ignorance we believe anything and everything that we read or are told about sex. We believe as real all the stories of the sexual stereotypes who date and mate by the hour and think ourselves the unlucky ones not endowed with the super-sex model. As a result we develop an inferiority complex, producing anxiety and sexual inadequacies. The earlier chapters should help us shed these myths and stop us making comparisons with non-existent sexual monsters, as well as make both partners knowledgeable about the anatomy and physiology of the male and female sexual organs and evaluate one's own sexual potential.

In the male the erect penis is the yardstick of arousal. It takes place naturally when you are turned on and is not under the control of the will. For example, if you say to yourself, 'I will have an erection' or 'I must have an erection', you will never get one. In a normal man it takes place as spontaneously as breathing, when he is aroused. Arousal in the male is almost instantaneous in the younger age group but takes a little longer with advancing age. In older men it may take still longer, sometimes necessitating female fondling. Arousal in the female is much slower and is a complicated multi-channel process, unlike the single-channel arousal in the male. Her whole body is sensual or sensitive to stimulation, the sex and accessory organs being more responsive. The effect of arousal is concentrated in the penis in the male whilst in the female it is more diffused or generalised all over her body. The response to sexual stimulation varies from region to region. When aroused, both partners go through four stages: (1) Excitement, (2) Plateau, (3) Orgasm, and (4) Resolution.

New dimension

Up to now we have considered the male and female response separately. In this chapter on sexual intimacy, we shall tackle it from a new dimension—the male and the female interacting with each other and mutually responding. I have stated earlier that the female is slower in her responses than the male and therefore it is the duty of every male to arouse the female thoroughly, so she can also be an active participant, enjoying intimacy. It is imperative that the male should not consider his partner a mere robot but should arouse her artfully with the knowledge that he has gained in the previous pages and with the guidance he can glean from this chapter. The greatest sexologist of his times, Vatsyayana, recognised the importance of this as early as in the 4th century, and laid down a very elaborate and time-consuming procedure for winning the confidence and love of the female partner.

The previous chapter, one of the most important in the book, lays stress on the sensuous male who uses all his special senses in arousal without inhibitions. His sensory pathways are not blocked and he therefore knows the art of loving women and giving pleasure to his partner. Vatsyayana always preached that sex is not only for procreation but also for pleasure. He observed that animals do it mechanically without any feeling, thought and foreplay. Sex in them is a compulsive drive for procreation. But man is different. He has a mind, he can think, and therefore Vatsyayana advocated *kama*, the science of erotic passion where both partners, particularly the male, learns the art of giving pleasure to the other partner during sex.

Your requirements for satisfactory sex

It is important to realise that all or most of us have certain requirements before we are turned on and can engage in sex. If these prerequisites are not met in either partner, the male is unable to get an erection and the female does not enjoy sex or become orgasmic. You may ask in surprise if anything is at all necessary to get a good erection? The fantasyland culture has made you believe that erection is automatic and a sideways look at a female is enough for your penis to get erect. If this were so, there would be no sexual inadequacy and no necessity to study sex manuals. Unfortunately, it is not all that simple. The penis was never meant to perform without prerequisites, except for a few men who function mechanically when they are anxious or under stress or unduly worried.

I will clarify. Tarun, aged 40, could never get an erection unless his partner fondled his organ with her hand. Joe was fine on the hard bed in his bedroom but discovered to his horror that when he went with his partner to the beach-house and attempted sex on a soft Dunlopillo, he could not get an erection. When he returned to his bedroom, Joe was his normal self again. Cyrus told me, 'I have been impotent for the last seven years. Nothing worked till I met Mary, an expatriate who had come to India with her husband. One night after a dinner-dance when I dropped her home and kissed her good-night on the lips, Mary was so excited that she opened my flies and grasped my penis hard. I immediately had a very powerful erection after years. It is strange but unless my partner undresses me and catches hold of my organ, I don't get a hard-on.' Tarun, Joe and Cyrus did not get an erection till their requirements were met by their partners.

There is nothing wrong in having a requirement. Your car, your air-conditioner and your refrigerator need regular servicing if they are to function smoothly. You gracefully accept that they need looking after, but what about your penis? You are mistaken if you believe that it can function like an automaton. Try and find out what you need in sex. Don't be a needless martyr. Communicate your desires to your partner, always verbalising it tactfully.

The woman also has her own special requirements before she can be orgasmic. For example, just before orgasm she may require her nipple or her ear bitten hard by her partner. A husband told me that his wife could only enjoy sex if she held a hand-mirror and watched coitus. A liberated lady professed the woman-on-top position for satisfactory sex. Surprising as it may seem, there are women who only enjoy sex if their male partner beats them prior to coitus. A few long to be raped by the man they secretly admire!

SEXUAL INTIMACY

Intimacy can be divided into four stages: (1) Prelude, (2) Foreplay, (3) Sexual union, and (4) Afterplay.

Prelude

In India most marriages are arranged and a woman has little chance of meeting her prospective bridegroom. The prelude is, therefore, a very important factor in the approach to sexual intimacy. In fact, both partners do not know anything about each other and wonder what sort of sexual life lies ahead of them. The winds of change are slowly but surely affecting our conservative society. Many girls now attend college and their sexual horizons have broadened by mixing with the 'mod' crowd. They will no longer be satisfied with churning out babies when they get married but want sexual pleasure and fulfilment as well.

Males should anticipate this change and become proficient in the art of arousing and fulfilling their partners. Vatsyayana was keenly aware of this and in the *Kama Sutra* (translated by Dr. Umendra Verma), he strongly advocates that the husband should approach 'his bride with as much gentleness as she desires, and treat her with great kindness and consideration so that she is no longer afraid and thus lead her subtly to the perilous brink of desire.'

In those days, when everything moved at a leisurely pace, Vatsyayana suggested that for the first three days after marriage, the partners should abstain from any sexual pleasure and have food which is free of salt and chillies. For the next seven days they should take their 'bath, toilette and meals together amidst the sound of auspicious musical instruments.' On the tenth night, the male partner was supposed to allay his wife's fear and get her ready for the great event. Though today most bridegrooms would not have the patience to wait so long, without having sex with their brides on the wedding night, it is most essential that if he does not know her before marriage, he should wait for a day or two before attempting coitus. However, in mod society, where the boy and the girl have gone out together and know each other, such lengthy preludes are unnecessary, though a certain amount of conversation is absolutely essential. Sony complained, 'He never talks to me, Doctor. I tell him often, "Talk to me, darling", but he is so impatient that he just wants to get into me.'

In the Prelude, the sense of sight, hearing and smell come into play if the partners are close together. It is most essential to create the mood for romance by listening to music, or enjoying a movie or doing anything together like dancing. The sense of touch plays a very important role in arousing the woman. In modern dancing, however, the women is not held in the man's arms, but the rapid rhythm and beat of the drums act as a strong sexual arouser.

In conclusion, it is not possible to draw a hard-and-fast line between Prelude and Foreplay—one blends imperceptibly with the other.

Foreplay

I have stated that a woman is basically slow to arouse and her sexuality extends to all the pores of her body and not merely the genital region. Men should therefore realise that foreplay is extremely important to satisfy a woman. Touch plays a vital role in arousing a woman while sight more than touch arouses a male. Enjoy foreplay. Only the highly passionate female does not want lengthy foreplay; she is aroused very quickly and is ready for coitus as soon as intimacy starts.

FOREPLAY IN MALES: Surprising as it may seem, men also need foreplay. Most men in middle age need skilful handling of their male organ by their female partners. However, most women do not realise that a certain amount of firmness is necessary in fondling the organ though there may be times when a light touch may turn him on instantaneously. The partner has to discover the moods of the male and how he likes to be aroused by mutual discussion. Dr. James Woolsley, a psychiatrist, says, 'Both sexes need a bit of love-play and it is just as insensitive for a woman to automatically assume a man is ready for penis stimulation, as it is for a man to neglect his warm-up strategies.'

Dr. Woolsley asserts, 'Good foreplay goes a long way towards eliminating impotence. With most men who have trouble, the problem isn't that their mothers failed when they were three, but simply because they're tense or angry or threatened or feeling some such inhibiting emotion now. Definitely, a lot of affectionate love-play is needed to put an out-of-sorts male in the right mood for making love.

EROGENOUS ZONES: In a sample survey conducted at a clinic on 440 married males aged 25 to 35 in the junior and middle management group, when asked about women's erogenous zones, nearly 70 per cent replied, 'The breasts and the vagina.' Almost 75 per cent of them were surprised when asked whether they used their finger in clitoral stimulation. They honestly believed it an insult to their penises to call upon the finger for help! However, 75 per cent of the senior managers were aware of the various erotic zones in the females but only 50 per cent indulged in clitoral stimulation (see Chapter 5). I am laying particular emphasis on erotic zones because in the West, knowledge about them is kindergarten stuff; more recent books do not even mention them, except perhaps in passing. But there is a great deal of ignorance about them in the land of Vatsyayana and Kalyanamalla. Vatsyayana lays great emphasis on love-play to excite a female and describes in great detail the various methods by which she can be aroused.

According to these ancient authorities, there are eight different avenues of love-play and each is supposed to consist of eight varieties—in other words, there can be in all 64 different ways of love-play called *chatushshashti.* The eight basic types are: (1) Embrace, (2) Kissing, (3) Scratching with finger-nails, (4) Love bites, (5) Position during intercourse, (6) Stroking and producing sounds by both partners, (7) Woman-on-top position, and (8) Oral sex.

EMBRACE: How to embrace a woman is described in great detail and it is emphasised that embracing should always precede kissing. There are different ways of embracing women who have never been embraced and those who have had experience of love-play. For both types, there are four methods, from the extremely slight contact or touch in the first to the complete fusion clasp in the second, where the partners are locked passionately in embracing each other and coitus is about to begin. The sage also emphasises and explains how to embrace the partner during coitus.

KISSING: The same meticulous attention is paid to the art of kissing, which should always follow the embrace. The various parts of the body to be kissed are the forehead, the eyes, the cheeks, the side of the neck, the breasts and, lastly, the lips. According to Vatsyayana, in ancient Gujarat it was usual to kiss the woman in the armpits, the joints of the thighs and the vulva. I shall revert to the subject of kissing a little later.

After the embrace and the kiss, when the partner is sufficiently aroused, the sensitive regions of her body should be scratched gently with the finger-nails and occasionally bitten. Our ancient sexologists recommend this kind of love-play only occasionally, but in highly passionate women it can be resorted to more often. The erotic bite is also recommended for passionate lovers. The parts of the body to be scratched with the nails are the arms, the armpits, the side of the neck, the chest of the male partner and the breast of the female, the lower abdomen, and the upper part of the thighs. Male marks were supposed to be finger-prints on the sands of passionate love—thrilling reminders of ecstasy both partners had experienced.

Oral sex and intercourse with the woman on top, and the woman from different regions who enjoy this type of sex, are also mentioned. For instance, the women of Afghanistan and Baluchistan are said to enjoy sex in a different position but do not relish kissing, scratching or biting, while some others from old Sind (after partition Sind in Pakistan and Punjab in India) particularly enjoy oral sex. It is indeed sad that all the teachings of these grand masters have been gradually lost till we evolved into a completely conservative society where sex became taboo except for procreation.

I repeat that the whole body of the female is erogenous—in fact, every pore of her body can be stimulated by a maestro. The main erogenous zones in the female are the forehead, the eyes, the nose, the lips, the breasts, the armpits, the upper part of the thighs, the clitoris and the vagina.

The forehead, the eyes and the nose are moderately erotic, while the bony margin of the eye socket, the upper eyelid, the cheek and the tip of the nose are erotic zones, especially in women who initially resist being kissed on the lips. It must be mentioned that gentle stroking of the hair is very pleasing and a protective non-sexual means of gaining tne confidence of your partner in the early stages.

EARS: Males are generally unaware that the ears are highly erotic in most women. I told you the story of Swapna who was extremely sensitive to the ear speculum. The lobule of the ears are sensitive to kissing and nibbling with the lips and in highly passionate women the ears are so sensitive that merely touching their ears leaves them breathless with desire. Many males make the mistake of biting hard the lobule of the ear, which is painful and should be avoided.

LIPS: The lips are intensely sensitive and help to turn on the female partner. Vatsyayana has suggested an ingenious classification of lip-kisses. In the first type if the girl is shy or is just being initiated into the art of eroticism, the male partner merely brushes her lips gently with his own without pressure. During the second stage when she has over-come her inhibition to the initial lip-kissing, the partner gently grips her lower lip between his lips, and keeps it up for a little while. Finally, when the female has got over her initial shyness, she grasps the lower lip of the male between hers.

The male partner should observe these few important principles while kissing:

1. Never crush her lips hard.
2. Don't hold her so tight as to squeeze and make her breathless.
3. Don't attempt stimulation with the tongue initially.
4. Don't bite her hard; just nibble. Don't push your tongue right in her mouth at the beginning but wait for the right opportunity till she is more receptive.

BREASTS: Seven out of ten Indian men after a fleeting glance at the face, invariably gaze at a shapely bosom—whether they are seeing it in real life, a movie or a magazine. There is nothing wrong with that. Men have always worshipped the breasts which have sustained and nourished them from the day they were born!

Women are also very breast-conscious and know that a shapely bosom arouses envy in their friends. The graceful sari-wearing Indian woman can play a subtle game of 'hide and see' with male gazers by constantly covering and uncovering her breasts with the *pallav* of her sari which her dress-wearing counterpart cannot employ.

In the West, although the so-called topless and braless revolution has taken place, bra manufacturing remains a multi-billion dollar industry all over the world. Suitable advertisements like 'small is sexy', flatter women and boost their ego. Women in Indian cities invariably wear a brassiere but in the villages the breasts are bare and covered only by the sari. Unless he is sexually aroused, a clothed female body is more appealing to the male than a naked one and the same applies for the breasts—what is partially hidden arouses his curiosity.

Unlike the lips and the ears which are uniformly erogenous in practically all women, the sensations from the breasts vary widely. Some women are so sensitive to touch that they become orgasmic by the male fondling the breasts, while others are not so sensitive and breast stimulation does not arouse them. Most males spend a little time caressing the breasts. There are various ways in which this can be done: by moving the palm of the hand across the breasts and gently rotating them or titillating the nipple with the thumb and index finger. The hands do not stimulate the breasts much in moderately passionate women; the lips provide more excitement for both partners, especially when kissing or gently biting the nipple. Vatsyayana also recommends scratching of the nipple, but most women do not enjoy it as it leaves visible marks.

Here are two don'ts when stimulating the breasts:

(1) Never be rough with her breasts. Handle them gently.
(2) Don't be a grabber or imagine that you are squeezing a juicy mango.

No woman will like such roughness on your part, except perhaps very occasionally. Please remember that just before the monthly periods, the breasts become very tender in most women and you have to be more gentle than normally. As sexual tension builds up the same female partner who initially complained about your rough handling might want her breasts to be tightly grasped or her nipples bitten. This is more pronounced in the plateau stage just before orgasm. She will give you a subtle indication like pressing your hand on her breast or she may stroke the breast with her own hand. Watch out for it.

THE SIDE OF THE NECK is a very sensitive area in many women and kissing this excites them, while the armpits and the upper part of the thighs are moderately sensitive.

CLITORAL STIMULATION: According to Ruth Hercherberger, 'In the symphony of love, the lost chord is a small organ—the clitoris, named by the Germans as *wallustorgan,* the ecstasy organ'. The artistic lover knows how to extract ecstasy after ecstasy from the clitoris. Nature has bestowed the female with the clitoris exclusively for her pleasure. It is the only organ in the human body—male or female—without any other function. The penis, apart from giving pleasure, serves also as a channel for procreation and voiding urine. Yet as I have stated in Chapter 5, 'full many a clitoris is born in Bharat to blush unseen', without being titillated by the male.

I shall recapitulate a few salient points on how to caress the clitoris artistically and not with heavy hands.

(1) You should be thoroughly conversant with the location and anatomy of the clitoris. Look at it in the picture (Fig. 5-1 page 46). If your partner is not too shy and if you love her, she may permit you to have a look at it. You need to separate the inner lips slightly to see it

(2) The mons area should be well-lubricated preferably with a little lubricant from the vagina by inserting a finger inside it. Alternatively, a non-irritant jelly like K.Y. Jelly can be applied to the mons area. Vaseline or hair oil should not be used as it cannot be easily cleaned and irritates the delicate skin of the clitoral region.

(3) During the early stages of caressing the clitoris, it is advisable not to manipulate the clitoral body or the glans. Many women are hyper-sensitive and feel uncomfortable if the glans is touched.

(4) It is better to start stimulation of the mons area and gradually move on first to one side of the clitoral shaft and then the other side. Initially the manipulation should be very gentle, the pressure applied varying in intensity and location. Women are more sensitive on the left or the right side of the clitoris, depending on whether they are left-handed or right-handed.

(5) Encourage your partner to verbalise what she likes best during stimulation. Perhaps it would be a good idea if you first tell her your likes and dislikes and what you expect of her during foreplay. She may be reticent for a little while but with gentle persuasion she will ultimately express her desires verbally or indicate them.

(6) During the end of the excitement phase the clitoris retracts up-wards and an inexperienced lover loses contact with it. It is essential

that stimulation of the mons area should be continued rapidly with the finger, otherwise your partner who was about to reach an orgasm is left unfulfilled and marked sexual frustration occurs.

(7) Bear in mind that the female needs to be stimulated throughout her orgasm, unlike the male.

(8) If she wants to come once again, continue the manipulation. Some women prefer a brief pause before being restimulated, whilst others like continuous stimulation till they have had three, four or even six orgasms. She will herself indicate when to stop. Most women with their conservative background are content with one or two orgasms.

(9) Some women like deep vaginal stimulation with the finger. In such cases do a to-and-fro thrusting movement with the finger in the vagina.

AVOID EXCESSIVE STIMULATION: If you suddenly press the accelerator of a car, it jerks before picking up speed, similarly if too much pressure is applied to the clitoris, your partner jerks or twitches—a sure indication that you are pressing too hard on her accelerator of arousal. Should this happen, stop stimulating her clitorally for a few seconds till the jerking or twitching has ceased, then restart titillating her more gently till she reaches an orgasm. However, at the time of orgasm, she may thrust her pelvis forward wanting excessive pressure from your finger, but as too much pressure on the clitoris makes it numb and insensitive, just continue the firm pressure.

INDICATORS FOR COMMENCING INTERCOURSE: When your partner is thoroughly aroused after sufficient foreplay the areolas of her breasts are tumescent including the nipples, the vagina is moist and well-lubricated, and the clitoris cannot be felt vaginally. It is the right time for beginning genital union. The method of introducing the penis, the anatomy of genital union and various positions in which intercourse can be conducted are described in the next section.

Genital union
Genital union begins with the penetration of the penis into the vagina and culminates in male ejaculation of the semen into the female vagina. In ideal intercourse, orgasm or climax in both partners is

almost simultaneous. However, in many cases the female needs a much longer time, and the couple should not worry if their orgasms do not coincide (see 'Orgasm in the Male'). After the penile penetration comes the most active phase in intercourse—the copulatory movements where the penis is thrust to and fro and is rubbed and pressed against the velvety soft vaginal walls, resulting in heightened sexual tension and pleasure.

In the initial stages erection is psychogenic, but during copulation the friction of the penis against the vaginal passage produces and maintains local stimulation, leading to a stronger erection. As the movements proceed, sexual tension mounts till it reaches a climax just before ejaculation.

Often the male ejaculation takes place before the partner reaches her orgasm and in some cases, he ejaculates immediately after insertion or even before the penis penetrates the vagina. The subject of premature ejaculation is dealt with in Chapter 15.

Can a male partner prolong his ejaculation and if so how can it be done? It is possible to temporarily postpone ejaculation by diverting the mind during intercourse to some other topic like a card game or a game of golf! The intensity of the thrusting movements can be reduced in the early stages till the female partner is about to reach orgasm when vigorous movements may be resorted to by the male. In some cases, an early discharge is due to increased sensitivity of the glans penis. This can be diminished by the application of a local anaesthetic ointment about half an hour before intercourse or by using a condom. The latter is objectionable to many women and also to men as it diminishes pleasure though it prolongs intercourse. It is essential that the male should never be selfish in sex, seeking only his own gratification but should try actively in every possible way to bring his female partner to an orgasm. The effort is worthwhile, for increased sexual excitement and desire in her enhances his own pleasure. And gentlemen, you will earn her eternal gratitude for fulfilling her.

MEN USE YOUR HANDS: Women need a wide variety of stimuli to bring them to the point of orgasm and in some females coital movements alone cannot culminate in an orgasm. A frustrated lady patient of mine remarked, 'If only my husband knew how to use his hands, sex would be so much better.' What a profound statement! Men instinctively use their penis and think that it is all that is needed. The use of the hands is an art to be cultivated. The piano virtuoso can bring out the best tone from the piano by a skilful use of the hands. Similarly, the maestro in sex can get the best response from his female partner by knowing where, when and how to use his hands.

Some women require stimulation of the mons area during intercourse to reach an orgasm. This can best be done by the man lying on his back and the woman sitting astride on him. She is the active partner in coital movements in this position and it is easy for a male partner to stimulate the mons area and clitoris in this attitude. To have each other's understanding and co-operation, both partners should freely discuss sex and communicate their sexual needs and requirements.

LUBRICATION: The vaginal canal adapts itself remarkably to the penis but in some women if the pre-coital stimulation is insufficient and the vagina stays dry, coitus can be harmful and uncomfortable. In case of weak erection and a dry vagina, penetration is difficult for the male. A sensitive male who is unable to penetrate a few times may develop psychological inhibitions, resulting in loss of erection and even impotency.

In these cases the use of a lubricant, like KY Jelly, by the male facilitates easy entry of the penis into the vagina. Many such preparations are available in the market. It is better to use a preparation which is water-soluble and can be easily removed by soap and water. Vaseline or greasy ointments if left in the vagina turn rancid and are difficult to wash off. Similarly, antiseptic ointments containing dettol or antibiotic creams cause irritation in these sensitive areas or an allergy as they contain antibiotics like penicillin or terramycin. There is the added danger that an individual can get sensitized to these ointments and subsequent injections or oral administration of these drugs can produce a violent allergy.

Positions in intercourse

Variety is the spice of life and sex with the same partner in the same position can be as monotonous and boring as an insipid Goa curry. Frank Beach, a fellow of the American Psychological Association, did a series of interesting experiments on mating behaviour in animals. He found that 'if a male rat was placed with an estrual female and allowed to mate freely he eventually tired and the interval between ejaculations became progressively longer. But if the exhausted male was offered a new estrual female, he immediately for a while resumed copulation (though this did not last long).' Similar behaviour was noted in male rhesus monkeys. About human beings Frank Beach says, 'Men often report dramatic increases in sexual ability when they change partners.' In many Western societies, swapping of partners is done regularly to introduce an element of variety in sex. It is therefore vital that both husband and wife should introduce as many variations as possible in foreplay and intercourse techniques to avoid boredom, in our monogamous society.

Vatsyayana and other ancient scholars describe over 20 different positions and attitudes in which the partners can indulge in sex. They recommend different positions for close-fit communion, when the vagina is large and does not firmly grip the male penis, and when the vagina is small and the penis is large. Normal couples will find some positions described by Vatsyayana very difficult as they require extreme mobility of the body joints. Such sexual acrobatics are better left out! A couple should only indulge in positions they find easy and enjoyable. The two main positions are: (1) man-on-top, and (2) woman-on-top. Needless to say, there are different attitudes or variations in each of these positions to enhance erotic pleasure and increase the joy of union.

Man-On-Top

THE CONVENTIONAL OR USUAL POSITION has the man on top and is also called the Missionary Position. There is an interesting story behind its name. Some natives of the South Sea Islands secretly watched a missionary couple indulging in intercourse. The natives who only practised the rear entry coitus (the female squats on her elbows and knees and the male enters her vagina from the rear) as animals do, were surprised to discover the new position, which they called 'Missionary'.

The female partner lies on her back with her thighs separated and the knees slightly bent. The man lies on top of his partner, supporting

(Fig. 9-1)

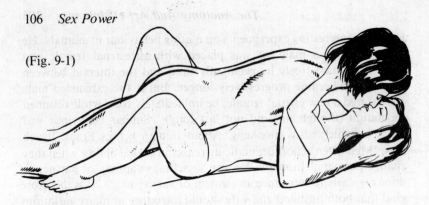

his weight partially on the bed. A hard bed is preferable to a soft or spring bed or one with a Dunlopillo mattress; however, each couple can choose what suits them.

The man-on-top is the most frequently practised and suitable position in coitus when the organs of both partners are proportionately well-matched. However, medically it is inadvisable in certain situations. During the latter part of pregnancy or if the male is heavy or has a protruding belly, sex causes a lot of discomfort to the female. During convalescence after a heart attack or after surgery when the man is less vigorous and violent coital movements may cause harm, the woman can help out by adopting the woman-on-top position. Also in sexual inadequacies (see Chapters 14 and 15), it is necessary in the initial stages for the female to sit astride over the male for the treatment of these disorders. Later, when normal sexual functioning is restored, the couple can adopt any position they like in sex. Finally, a major drawback with the male-on-top position is that there is no direct contact between the clitoris and the penis during intercourse. The former is stimulated indirectly by the movements of the glans of the clitoris. If the stimulation is inadequate and the female is unable to reach her orgasm in this position, the female-on-top position is recommended as it permits better clitoral contact with the male pubic bone.

Variations in attitude

EXTENDED POSITION: If the organs of the two partners are disproportionate and the erection is partial, intromission becomes difficult or,

even if introduced, the penis-vaginal clasp is loose. In a sexually inadequate partner, the erection may die down before the female reaches
her climax. In such cases, the male should keep his thighs on the outside and after intromission of the penis, the female should draw her
thighs close together to provide a firmer grip of the male organ during
sex. However, deep penetration of the vagina is not possible in this
position (Fig. 9-2).

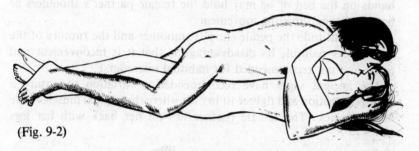

(Fig. 9-2)

In another variation of the extended position, the female straightens
her knees after intromission has taken place in the conventional
position. She then brings both legs together, thus pressing on the male
organ between her closed thighs (Fig. 9-2).

The penetration of the penis is not deep into the vagina but as the
thighs are brought together the vagina grips the male organ tightly,
thus producing a stronger erection as well as prolonging it; it also
provides increased indirect stimulation of the vagina, giving greater
sexual gratification to the female. However, for women who desire
profound penetration of the penis in the vagina, the couple should
adopt a position of flexion described later in this section.

A variation of the extended position is to keep a thick, hard pillow
or a bolster under the loins (the part of the body above the hips) of the
female partner who lies on the bed with both her legs straight. The
proper positioning of the pillow is important; it should not slip above
or below the loins. This inclined position produces a greater extension
of the lumbar region and better stimulation and accessibility of the
clitoris to penile thrusting.

Another variation of the extended position was specially recommended by many ancient cultures for deflorating the hymen. It is,

however, a somewhat inconvenient position and not easy to adopt in a modern bedroom with low beds. The male is required to stand upright on his feet between his partner's knees, while the female lies on her back on a high bed or table, bringing her pelvis near the edge of the bed. Her legs hang down, but her feet have to rest firmly on two stools. The male partner stands between the stools and introduces the organ. It is more convenient for a man to bend forward and rest his hands on the bed or he may hold the female partner's shoulders or breasts during thrusting movements.

In this attitude the penile entry is smoother and the rupture of the hymen less painful. Its disadvantage is that it is inconvenient and tiring and not recommended for habitual intercourse.

The ancient sages have recommended a variation to ensure a stronger erection and tighter fit in case where the vaginal muscles have become slack. The female partner lies on her back with her legs

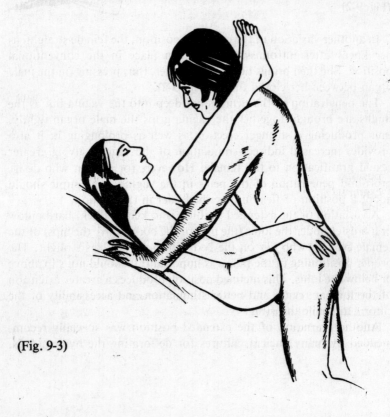

(Fig. 9-3)

straight initially. But after the penile penetration, she crosses one leg over the other, tightly gripping the male, as he does the thrusting movements. A difficult one for the male partner is where she crosses her thighs and the male attempts to penetrate her and finally with a strong erection succeeds.

FLEXED ATTITUDE: The attitude of flexion is extremely suitable when deep penetration of the male organ is desired. It has a two-fold advantage. It gives direct access to the male, and more pleasure to the remale who prefers the penis to nestle deeply into the folds of the vagina. This in turn stimulates the male partner resulting in a stronger erection. In this position, the female partner lies on her back with both legs lifted at right angles from the hips with the feet resting on her partner's shoulders. As the lower spine becomes bent forwards and upwards, the vulva slopes vertically, the vagina points downwards and the male organ enters the rear of the vagina (near the perineum) without contact with the clitoris. However, the male can digitally stimulate it manually during coitus. There is one risk in this position. If the vagina is comparatively small, an attempt at deep penetration with a well-endowed penis can easily lacerate the vaginal wall or in rare cases even rupture it.

In another variant of extreme flexion the male kneels, bringing his partner's thighs and legs almost parallel to the abdominal wall and continues the thrusting. However, such extreme attitudes of flexion require very supple joints, and everybody cannot do them.

A modification of the position of extreme flexion is the 'lithotomy' position which doctors find convenient for visual and internal examination of the female genitalia, for minor operations like dilation and curettage, and during confinement. The female partner lies on her back and bends her thighs, keeping both legs as apart as possible with the knees bent and the toes and heels touching the back of the thighs. Intercourse in this position is more convenient than in extreme flexion.

LATERAL ATTITUDE: This is much less demanding energywise and is therefore suitable during convalescence and in pregnancy, as there is little pressure on the abdomen. The male mounts as usual by resting his weight mainly on his hands and knees. After inserting his penis, he rolls over on his left side with the female partner on his left. The female draws up the leg on which she is lying and the male has his superior leg (away from the bed) stretched across hers. Alternatively, the male can roll over on his right side with the female partner on his left but generally right-handed males prefer to turn on the left side so that their superior right hand is free.

FEMALE ORGASM WITH MAN-ON-TOP POSITION: According to Dr. Masters, all orgasms in the female are caused by clitoral stimulation. During thrusting of the penis to and fro in intercourse, the prepuce of the clitoris is rhythmically pulled back and forth, which is responsible for producing the female orgasm. However, the noted author of the *Hite Report,* Shere Hite, and many other sexologists do not agree with Dr. Master's suggestion that all women during intercourse are orgastic by the prepuce-glandular mechanism. Dr. Master's very select subjects could easily reach orgasm this way but most women are unable to reach it in the man-on-top position. In women who were orgastic during intercourse there was intimate contact of their mons area with the men's pubis. This is possible with the woman on top and moving to and fro so that the clitoris rubs against the base of the penis while the penis remains stationary. It can also be done by the grinding movement of the pubis by both the partners where after a complete penile penetration, either the female or the male moves around and around, causing intimate rubbing of the two pubic areas. Alternatively, the two pubic areas can be stimulated rhythmically with the woman on top and the penis moving to and fro gently at first and finally rapidly when she is about to reach her orgasm. Lastly, manual stimulation of the clitoris by the male or by herself when she is sitting astride on him can also achieve an orgasm. In conclusion, as Shere Hite states, 'Intercourse was never meant to stimulate women to orgasm.'

Woman-On-Top

Many males as well as females are averse to having sex in this position because the man lies passive while the woman plays the dominant role. 'It is still a man's world,' Lawrence told me. 'Why should I permit my partner to be on top? It will put her in a very dominating position—the sign of a liberated female.' I had a hard time convincing

(Fig. 9-4)

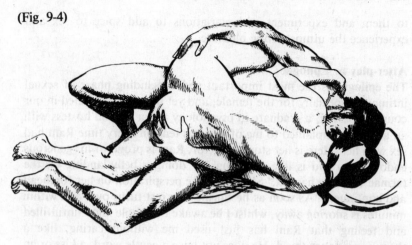

Lawrence that to relieve boredom and increase erotic pleasure for both partners there is nothing like trying different positions.

Successful sexual intercourse needs the active co-operation of both partners. 'My partner enjoys me on top,' said Roopa. 'He does not have a thing to do! As for myself, don't you think, Doctor, a female can only have full gratification if the male lies on top of the woman—in every sense of the word.'

For the woman-on-top position, the male lies on his back with his legs apart. The female sits astride the male with the legs bent at the knees near the male partner's nipples and then glides her vagina downwards over the erect penis. This position permits penetration of the penis up to the hilt as well as direct clitoral stimulation against the body of the penis, if the female partner bends forward during thrusting. A variation of this position is for the female partner to move backwards instead of forward. She can also squat on the male's erect penis. Kissing and embracing are not possible in this posture. As I have stated earlier, this position is particularly useful in certain situations as when the male is physically below par or suffers from sexual inadequacies.

In conclusion, various attitudes and positions during intercourse have been briefly explained and their advantages and disadvantages outlined. Couples are however free to choose the positions that appeal to them and experiment with variations to add spice to sex and experience the utmost erotic pleasure.

After-play or Epilogue

The epilogue is the most important and concluding phase of sexual intimacy, especially for the female, and yet the most neglected in our country. Savitri, a graduate in psychology and a ground hostess with an airline, complained to me of nervous tension every time Ram had sex with her. Here is her story. 'Doctor, Ram is proud of his generous endowments and is like a Boeing 747 doing a belly-landing on the tarmac when he has sex.' She wiped the perspiration on her forehead and continued, 'As soon as he finishes, he just turns over and within minutes is snoring away, whilst I lie awake the whole night unfulfilled and feeling that Ram has just used me without caring, like a throwaway paper towel. He does not have a gentle word, a kiss or an embrace after he has ejaculated. Do you think it is too much to expect of him at the end of sex? I have been asking my friends and they tell me the same story.'

Firoza, an artist, said her husband gave her a splitting headache every time he slept with her. 'He will be furious if he learns that I have been talking about him. I don't want to break up my marriage but I'd like to get it off my mind,' she said. 'As soon as he has come off he literally runs to the bathroom to wash himself. He puts on his pyjamas and plays loud rock music whilst I hold my throbbing head. He thinks a woman is unclean and it seems his mother has told her darling son to have a wash immediately afterwards. I get hopping mad with him. Why can't he spend a few minutes with me after sex? You should write in the *Times of India* about these things, Doctor.'

Savitri and Firoza are typical examples of their men's neglect of the very vital after-play for women. Mr. Casanova, please remember that after-play following coitus is the most important aspect of sexual union for your partner. She has readily surrendered her body to you for your gratification. Is it too much for her to expect you to spend a few more minutes with her? Give her a loving kiss or a tender embrace so that she feels protected and appreciated, otherwise she will think that you have merely used her to satisfy your selfish urge... and perhaps she's right!

Let me explain why it is wrong for men to turn over and go to sleep immediately after a sexual encounter. While for innumerable men intercourse and ejaculation are the be-all and end-all of their sexual profile, it is a different experience for women. Firstly, she takes a long time to get aroused as well as to return to normal. Secondly, while the male after ejaculation has a refractory period during which time he does not like sex or even being touched, for a woman the whole sexual experience is meaningful from the word go, and her sensations of pleasure do not come to an immediate end with an orgasm but continue much longer. After her orgasm she still loves to be fondled and caressed by her partner. The post-coital period is a time of heightened sensitivity and awareness when closeness and intimacy can be developed between the partners. It is the time for sharing intimate thoughts. Every woman desires this togetherness and no male should deny her these moments of rapture. According to psychologists Dr. Mark Shermen and Dr. James Halpern, authors of *After-play,* 'Women in fact, consider the first five minutes after sex as slightly more important than orgasm.'

Here are a few don'ts for men.

(1) Please do not go off to sleep immediately unless your partner also desires it. She can lie in your arms and both of you can sleep together.

(2) Don't get up and dress immediately after coitus and leave your partner with excuses that you have an urgent appointment.

(3) Don't get up and watch the TV or turn on the radio or go for a bath immediately; don't fail to communicate your love and appreciation for the joyous experience you have shared of being one.

Chapter 10

ORGASM IN THE MALE (EJACULATION)

Press not, although the tempest urge, thy pace!
Lest she thou lovest linger far behind.
Soar side by side! And mingle flesh and mind
In one joint moment of supreme embrace.

OVID

ORGASM AND EJACULATION in the male are separate events, though interlinked. The male reaches the orgasm first, and a second or two later ejaculation of semen takes place. During copulatory movements as the penis is moved to and fro, the sexual tension mounts in the male and soon reaches its peack when he can no longer control himself. This is the beginning of the orgasm in the male. At the point of orgasm, the male stops the coital movements and thrusts his penis into the female partner very deeply. For the purpose of description, the events during the male orgasm can be divided into physiological and psychological.

Physiological

Physiologically, orgasm in the male is a total body response with all the organs and systems participating. The main body reactions are vaso-congestion, and muscle contractions with spasm of most of the muscles of the body. The pulse rate quickens and is 100 to 170, the systolic (maximum) blood pressure rises by 40 to 80 millimetres of mercury (mm of Hg) while the diastolic (minimum) blood pressure goes up by 20 to 40 mm of Hg. The respiration rises to about 40 per minute and many males perspire profusely as well.

The male genital organs are the centre of attention. Orgasm in the male has two distinct phases—expulsion and emission or ejaculation. It may be compared to loading a pistol and later firing it. During the first phase the internal genital organs like the prostate, the seminal vesicles and the inner portion of the urethra pump the seminal fluid into the firing area, the prostatic urethra; simultaneously the urethral bulb increases two- to three-fold in size. Early in this stage, the urinary bladder is sealed off so urine is not voided during ejaculation. In the second phase, the urethral sphincter muscle contracts at intervals of 0.8 seconds, expelling the semen into the vagina in six to eight consecutive jets. It is interesting to observe that the vaginal muscles in the female contract with the same frequency.

Psychological

The psychic manifestations are a feeling of ecstasy, a moment of profound joy. The man loses conception of time and space during these few sublime moments. However, all good things come to an end, and the male soon returns from love to his normal work. Men often engage in sex when they are tense, tired, bored, preoccupied or in a hurry. They mechanically go through the motions of reaching orgasm and then complain that sex fails to stimulate them. But if a man wisely indulges in intercourse when he has active sexual desire, orgasm stimulates and exhilarates his whole being. Refreshed in mind and body, he is able to pursue his normal activities with more zest after a brief rest.

Psychologically there are two phases in the male orgasm. It would be interesting to correlate them with the two-stage physiology of male orgasm. During the first phase, the male feels ejaculation is 'inevitable now' and he can no longer control it. It takes place immediately prior to the first phase of emission and later accompanies it. However, there is a delay of one or two seconds between the feeling of inevitability of ejaculation and actual ejaculation taking place while the semen fills up the urethral bulb. During the second phase as ejaculation occurs, the male passes through two stages: the sensation resulting from contractions of the urethral bulb, and the pleasurable sensation created by the volume of the seminal fluid.

In other words, the greater the volume, the more pleasurable the feeling of release. This is most marked when one has sex after a period of abstinence. The greater volume of fluid at the first orgasm gives him more pleasure than the second orgasm after the refractory period. Thus the first orgasm is most satisfying to the male, unlike the female whose second or third orgasmic experience is reported as more pleasurable than the first. According to Masters and Johnson, the first two or three contractions of the penile urethra are more gratifying than the rest (often they are hardly perceptible), as after the first few forcible contractions males develop a sort of anaesthesia along the urethra and do not feel the later contractions.

There are exceptions, however. Bhagvatiprasad, a businessman, meticulously counted the number of his urethral bulb muscle contractions during an ejaculation and compared notes with his friends. He was shattered to learn that one of them beat him in the numbers game! In a very agitated and perturbed frame of mind, he telephoned me, 'Doctor, there is something wrong with my ejaculatory motor. Kuldip can score eleven whilst I have never gone beyond eight.' I advised him not to be performance-oriented and count his contractions or compare notes with others as it would only make him self-conscious and miserable.

Male and female orgasms compared
The most significant difference in the orgasm of the two sexes is ejaculation in the male while there is no emission in the female. The male is quicker in reaching an orgasm, its duration is shorter and he returns to normal more quickly than the female whose orgasm lasts much longer and is slower to come on and return to normal; some women enjoy the orgasmic thrill for hours afterwards. The other difference is that while the male almost always reaches an orgasm, only about 30 per cent of females have an orgasm every time (see Chapter 11). The male can reach an orgasm during intercourse only once while the female is capable of a single or multiple orgasms during the same intercourse, or often none at all.

The female experiences a greater variety of orgasms in intensity and duration as compared to the male. Dr. Masters has called the sexual experience in the male as 'a-rose-is-a-rose sort of thing', while in the female it 'goes all the way from poppies to orchids.' In other words, the female may have a very mild orgasm of short duration or an explosive one continuing for some length of time. Dr. Masters maintains that in terms of intensity and duration, all males experience the same kind of orgasm, though the pleasure they derive may differ from partner to partner. Many sexologists have challenged Dr. Masters' observations and Barnard Zilbergal in *Men and Sex* states that 'men are capable of variety in duration and intensity like the female. There are many males whose orgasmic experience varies from orgasm to orgasm.'

Coitus Interruptus

We have stated earlier that the male reaches the orgasm first and a second or two later ejaculation takes place. The male can thus utilise this time-lag between orgasm and ejaculation to withdraw his penis from the vagina and discharge outside.

If the penis is withdrawn from the vagina during the sex act before ejaculation takes place, it is called *coitus interruptus* or withdrawal. This was the commonest method of preventing conception before the advent of modern contraceptives like the condom, the loop and the pill. Many couples still indulge in *coitus interruptus* as it is the simplest and most inexpensive birth control method. But the method is harmful, especially for the female, as the sexual tension mounting in her is not relieved, and the sudden withdrawal of the male organ before ejaculation jars her nervous system, leaving her pelvic organs congested with blood for a long time, unless the male partner manually stimulates her clitoris and relieves her tension or she herself masturbates. The male also is tense and anxious to withdraw in time lest he discharges inside the vagina; this is not as pleasurable as discharging inside it. Finally, in spite of both partners sacrificing their pleasure, it is not a very safe method of birth control because unwanted pregnancies often occur. *Coitus interruptus* is the enemy of carefree sex and should be resorted to very rarely—only when it is not possible to use other birth control methods.

Simultaneous orgasm

Most manuals on sex recommend that the partners should ideally have a simultaneous orgasm. The male ejaculation strongly triggers off orgasm in the female partner. However, in practice it is difficult to achieve a dead-hit or a photo-finish coitus with both partners simultaneously orgasmic, because unlike the male who is almost always orgasmic, only 30 per cent of women always are, according to the *Hite Report*. Secondly, women usually take longer to come and many men just cannot prolong their ejaculation. In such cases, the male should stimulate his partner's clitoris while the penis is in the vagina. This is easier if the couple are using the woman-on-top position. Another alternative for the male who has a tendency to come too quickly, is to lessen the intensity of his pelvic thrusting and so reduce his sexual stimulation and prolong ejaculation.

In conclusion, as Dr. Masters has said, 'There is no quarrel at all with mutual orgasm if it happens naturally but to strive for it and to feel frustrated if you don't attain it—that's a bad hang-up.' Besides, at the height of orgasm both partners are so self-oriented that it is not possible for one to enjoy the orgasm of the other.

Pre-orgasmic emission

Two newly qualified and engaged-to-be-married doctors, Sapna and Rajesh, looked lovingly at each other while I waited for them to talk. 'You tell the doctor about my problem,' said Sapna, nudging Rajesh. Turning to me, Rajesh said, 'We are getting married within two months and because of the excitement Sapna has missed two periods.' After doing a general examination of Sapna, I told her to come back the next morning with her urine. When the couple returned two days later, I told Rajesh that Sapna's urine showed that she was pregnant. 'How could that be? We have never had intercourse. I think we should recheck the urine.' Rajesh said in a shrill voice.

While sympathising with their plight, I questioned them in depth. What Rajesh said was true—they had never had sex, but they had indulged in heavy petting with his organ just touching her vulva. In an aroused male, two or three drops of mucoid secretion escape from the opening of the urethral meatus (opening). Frequently this fluid contains a few motile sperms which travel through the external genitals, the hymen, the vagina, the cervix and the fallopian tubes to hunt for the female egg, fertilise it and cause a pregnancy. Rajesh and Sapna were unfortunately not aware of pre-orgasmic emission.

Marathon sex

Men erroneously believe that sex should be a marathon affair and last for an hour or longer. They wrongly assume that women admire the long-lasting stallion. I will illustrate what I mean with the story of Nuru and her two husbands. 'Sikander was a sex machine,' Nuru told me, her pretty face crinkling into a frown. 'Thank God, Doctor, I divorced him after seven years of torture. Like the Arab stallion, sex for him was a marathon race, where he prided himself on his staying power—the longer it lasted, the better,' Nuru paused, whilst she looked thoughtfully at Hussain's painting in my office, depicting the types of women in the *Ramayana,* then said, 'Like an animal, he pounced on me and battered me endlessly, sometimes for half an hour, occasionally for an hour. He never caressed or touched me except during sex and was shocked to learn that I had never had an orgasm with him who considered himself a Casanova! I remained dry and sex was so painful I got sore and had to consult my gynaecologist.'

There are many Sikanders in this world who believe that intercourse is the be-all and end-all of the sex game and wonder why in spite of their generous proportions and prolonged sex, their partners do not enjoy it—in fact, sex revolts them. Let me explain why: First the male partners must understand that the sex act by itself is low down on the priorities of what women want in bed. What women look for is warmth, gentleness and a partner who makes them feel wanted all the time. It is easy for such women to be orgasmic, irrespective of the size of the male organ or the duration of the act. Males do not realise that the concentration of nerve fibres in the female is in the vulva (external genitalia and the clitoris). The vagina is relatively insensitive, except the lower third, and if it is not properly lubricated by foreplay, intercourse becomes very painful as in Nuru's case. With her face radiant with joy Nuru said about her second husband, 'Anwar is so gentle and he appreciates me not only sexually but in all the things I do. I feel great comfort when he puts his hand on my shoulder and when he lies next to me. I feel so protected and loved. He was very understanding and patient with me and gradually I got over my abhorrence for sex. Within six months of our marriage, I became orgasmic and have an orgasm every time I have sex with Anwar. He is a man I worship, adore, respect and love even though he has no staying power and does not possess a huge battering ram.'

Priapism

The erection sometimes continues for five minutes after ejaculation before it finally disappears. Initially the individual is very happy with his new windfall. He enthusiastically indulges in sex again and his partner is delighted with his new 'Sex Power'. But his new-found happiness is short-lived as ejaculation is impossible, and the harder he tries the more mulish his penis becomes. Pain now replaces pleasure, he feels tired and fagged out and has no desire left, yet the endless erection continues.

This persistent abnormal erection is called *priapism* and is a rare condition. Priapism usually occurs in injuries or diseases of the spinal cord like spinal tumours, or a stone in the urinary bladder or if the veins of the penis (dorsal vein) are obstructed, thereby irritating the nerves of erection. Occasionally with rest and a strong sedative, the abnormal erection subsides but often surgery is necessary on the penis to remove the accumulated blood from the reservoir of the corpora with incisions along the side of the penis. Surgery on the penis is mainly palliative in priapism. The disease or injury which caused it has to be treated to prevent recurrence and restore sexual functioning.

Painful ejaculation

Males occasionally complain of severe pain during ejaculation and after. In some cases it is very acute and continues for days. It is sometimes due to an inflamed prostate gland. But if the examination proves negative, the syndrome is caused by powerful contractions of the ejaculatory muscles. Psychological causes like guilt about masturbation, religious beliefs or sexual conflicts may be the reasons.

Sexologists like Helen Singer Kaplan equate this syndrome with vaginismus in the female which causes the vaginal muscles to contract and produce severe pain, the moment the penis is about to penetrate the vagina. The therapy for the male consists in acquiring a detailed knowledge of the mechanism of ejaculation and the psychological factors responsible for healthy sexual conditioning (see Chapter 13). Most cases improve by reviewing by their attitude about sex, but professional guidance from a sex therapist may sometimes become necessary.

Chapter 11

ORGASM IN THE FEMALE

And they were both naked, the man and his wife,
and were not ashamed.

THE BIBLE

D EAR LADY READERS, I am deeply conscious that as a male, I am handicapped a great deal in writing about something which I do not experience myself. I have therefore shown this chapter to lady sex therapists, knowledgeable women and some of my female patients and have incorporated their valuable suggestions. I have made a sincere effort not only to make you more knowledgeable about yourselves and your own sexual responses but, more important, to create a consciousness and a healthy respect for your sexuality.

Vatsyayana in A.D. 400 and Kalyanamalla in A.D. 1600 gave a vivid account of orgasm in the female, centuries before Freud or other Western authorities were even aware of it. Vatsyayana states that 'sexual satisfaction in woman is as important as in men'. He even goes so far as to warn his readers that without sexual satisfaction, a woman's physical and mental constitution may become unbalanced. Vatsyayana notes that 'at the approach of the orgasm the following signs manifest themselves in a woman—lassitude of the body, closing of eyes, absence of bashfulness and greater pressure applied towards the man's pubis with that of her own, so as to effect closer contact. Just before she attains her final pleasure, she shakes her hands, perspires, bites her partner, prevents him from detaching the sexual connection or from rising and beats him (on the legs or buttocks) with her feet. If the man attains satisfaction (ejaculation) first, she would not let him rise, and would exceed the man in forwardness and want of restraint, contrary to her natural bashfulness.'

In *Ananga Ranga,* Kalyanamalla says, 'A man versed in the art of the sports of love can subjugate the gazelle-eyed one by pleasing her with his various accomplishments and making her finally attain her orgasm. Towards the end of the sexual act the woman, when she does secrete the coital fluid (attains her orgasm), dances with pleasure, speaks too much and cries; she becomes deranged, her beautiful eyes become half-shut and she cannot bear any great exertion!'

Unfortunately, the teachings of these great sexologists were lost in our country with the advent of Manu's 'moral code' which promoted the cult of male superiority. The woman was considered inferior and was to provide merely the soil for a man's seed. She was not supposed to enjoy sexual intercourse.

Western culture imposed similar constraints on the female, the Victorian Age exemplifying prudery at its worst. Women who were orgasmic were considered to be of 'loose' character. The naturally responding women in sex had therefore to suppress and inhibit their sexual responses for fear of being branded as 'cheap' women by society.

The clitoral vs. vaginal orgasm controversy

At the dawn of the present century, western women were grudgingly permitted by male medical pundits to be 'orgasmic' only during intercourse, and not by auto-manipulation (see Chapter 12, 'Masturbation'). However, there was heated argument among the high priests of sexuality whether the site of her orgasm was the clitoris or the vagina.

I shall mention a few prominent psychoanalysts of those days who debated and decided how a woman should have 'a normal orgasm'! Sigmund Freud in 1910 presented his three essays on the Theory of Sexuality. According to him, women can experience two kinds of orgasm—clitoral and vaginal. Little girls during masturbation achieved orgasm by stimulating the clitoris. When they married they were supposed to transfer their sexual response from the clitoris to the vagina. A number of women failed to undergo such a transfer. Freud called them 'vaginally frigid', even though they could be orgasmic during manual stimulation of the clitoris, because they were frigid as far as the vagina was concerned.

Innumerable analysts wholeheartedly agreed with Freud that clitoral orgasm in a female was a sign of immaturity. Even female analysts supported Freud, the most noteworthy being Marie Bonaparte who went a step further than the Maestro by claiming that a mature woman performs a unique biological feat in transferring an orgasm from the clitoris to the vagina. She later modified her views slightly and suggested that there were women who were capable of having both types of orgasm—the clitoral and the vaginal. Although the majority of psychoanalysts supported Freud's viewpoint, some expressed serious doubts and the controversy continued. Meanwhile millions of women suffered silently till the arrival on the scene of Dr. Masters and Mrs. Johnson in 1959, who after scientific research demolished the citadel of pure vaginal orgasms. Researchers proved that all orgasms in the female originate in the clitoris. Innumerable women who were erroneously labelled frigid or masculine heaved a sigh of relief. They at last felt that they were normal women responding to normal sexual stimulus.

The Masters and Johnson research findings showed that during vaginal intercourse, the thrusting in and out of the penis stretches the inner lips (labia minora) at the entrance of the vagina. These lips are joined above the vaginal opening to form the hood or the prepuce of the clitoral glans. The rhythmic thrusting of the penis in and out slides the hood back and forth against the sensitive glans of the clitoris, resulting in its stimulation and culminating in an orgasm. During normal intercourse with the man on top, the clitoris participates indirectly, as there is no direct friction. A large number of women find it difficult to reach orgasm in the so-called 'missionary' position; they need direct clitoral stimulation by the hand or by adopting the female-on-top or lateral position, where the clitoris is directly stimulated by maintaining contact between the male and the female pubic regions.

The researchers also stated in the *Western Journal of Surgery, Gynaecology and Obstetrics* (September-October 1962) that the response of the pelvic viscera (organs) to effective sexual stimulation occurs 'regardless of whether the clitoris is stimulated manually or during natural coitus or just by stimulating, the breasts. In other words, the response of the human female is identical irrespective of the source of stimulation, psychic or physical.' They concluded that there is neither a pure clitoral nor a pure vaginal orgasm. In fact, during orgasm both the clitoris and the vagina respond according to their physiological pattern in sexual intercourse.

This 'judgement' of the Supreme Court of Sexuality by a bench comprising the Hon'ble Dr. Masters and the Hon'ble Mrs. Johnson permitted all women to have sexual orgasm. In other words, their 'Lordships' meant that it is the fundamental right of a woman irrespective of her caste, colour or creed to have one or many orgasms, either during sex or during auto-manipulation. She is even at liberty not to have an orgasm, if she so desires!

Single vs multiple orgasms

Male sexologists have been claiming that a woman, like a man, is more than satisfied with a single orgasm during intercourse. But Masters and Johnson's finding that a normal woman can invariably have more than one orgasm during auto-manipulation upset the male apple-cart! The media gave wide publicity to the 'judgement' that the female partner during sex can have many orgasms. Women were delighted with their new sexual power. After age-long humiliation they were one up on men. But many unfortunate males found themselves inadequate to last the gruelling four- or six-set rubber! The result was a tremendous pressure on the male to perform, which in many cases even caused impotency.

This feeling of inadequacy if the penis cannot produce multiple female orgasms is uncalled for. The researchers' findings relate only to auto-manipulative technique in the laboratory where women were multi-orgasmic. The male can use his obliging hand equally or perhaps more effectively in the mons area to stimulate the female for as many orgasms as she wants.

Orgasm: fantasy and reality

In our permissive twentieth-century society, writers about sexual eroticism have had a field day describing with their fertile imagination mind-boggling and earth-shaking orgasms. If such writers are to be believed even the seismograph would record shocks of mild intensity when a woman becomes orgasmic! Many women read erotic literature with high hopes of achieving explosion during sex and are deeply disappointed when such mind-shattering volcanic explosions do not actually happen. Such erotic fantasies exist only in the imagination of the authors and the gullible readers. An orgasm—the real thing—is an extremely pleasurable event, though it has none of the components of fantasyland sex for the majority of women. A few passionate and excitable women do have violent orgasms where they wriggle, sigh, cry, scratch or bite the male partner. The poet Heine in *Hastings Battlefield,* vividly describes such a love-bite during orgasm:

And on his shoulder she beheld three scars,
And kissed them once again: wounds of no wars,
    No foeman's brand had smitten—
    Three little scars, her own white teeth had bitten.

ORGASM: THE HEIGHT OF PLEASURE

The credit for accurately describing the physiological and psychological changes during orgasm goes entirely to Dr. Masters and Mrs. Johnson. According to the researchers orgasm in the female is a total-body response with sudden release from extreme vasocongestion and myotonia or muscle tension. At orgasm time, her facial expression appears painful, there is contraction of all muscles with those of the arms, legs and hands in spasm. Some females tightly grasp their partner with their hands. The muscles of the abdomen, back and buttocks are tightly contracted to increase sexual tension and eventually obtain orgasmic release.

The onset of orgasm is heralded by involuntary contraction of the vaginal wall, five to eight times, at an interval of 0.8 second. The total number of contractions vary widely and so does the intensity. The longer the duration of the contractions the longer is the interval in-between. Along with the vaginal contractions some women also experience contractions of the external rectal sphincter (the muscle guarding the opening of the rectal canal which controls the passage of stools) and the external urethral sphincter (the muscle which enables us to hold the urine). The clitoris, which was withdrawn upwards, returns to its normal overhanging position. The vasocongestion in the breasts and particularly the areolae disappears rapidly after the orgasm, making the nipples erect and prominent (false-erection reaction). The prominent, erect nipples with wrinkled areolae provide a visual evidence of orgasm. Dr. Masters found that at orgasm, the heart rate went up between 110 to 180 beats a minute, the systolic blood pressure increased by 30 to 80, the diastolic pressure by 20 to 40 mm of Hg, and the breathing became more rapid with a respiratory rate of over 40 per minute. The skin over the whole body is flushed at the peak of orgasm. The sex flush is most noticeable in fair individuals and disappears immediately after orgasm.

These physiological changes occur irrespective of the method of stimulation—sex with a partner or auto-manipulation or mechanical manipulation with a vibrator or, rarely, just stimulation of the breasts.

Psychological response

Dr. Masters and Johnson compiled a detailed subjective response of women undergoing orgasm in their sex laboratory. There were three distinct stages. The first stage which lasts only a second is characterised by a sense of suspension or stoppage, followed by intense sensual awareness beginning in the clitoral region and radiating upwards into the pelvis. The intensity of this feeling varies widely from a mild to an extremely intense sensation, accompanied by a generalised loss of sensory feeling. During the second stage, a sense of warmth suffuses the pelvic region, spreading rapidly all over the body. During the third stage, the contractions of the orgasmic platform give rise to a throbbing sensation in the pelvic area, which a little later merges with the quickened heartbeats. Women can feel the rapid pulsations of the arteries in the pelvis and vagina.

Is every orgasm accompanied by contraction of the vaginal wall?

I have given you a detailed account of the orgasm in the sex laboratory of Masters and Johnson as they observed it, mainly during auto-manipulation but also in sex with a partner. Does it mean that what happens in the laboratory during orgasm also applies universally to every woman in the bedroom, where she is frequently beset with cares and worries? Innumerable women in the West and some in our country have started comparing their experiences with the laboratory model orgasm.

While orgasm in most women is accompanied by contractions of the vaginal wall which can be felt by the male penis or by a finger in the vagina, there are some who do not feel these contractions and therefore think that they are deficient and have not reached the climax. A number of sexologists and lady sex therapists maintain that orgasms without vaginal contractions can occur. Irving Singer in *Goals of Human Sexuality* argues that orgasms without contractions take place in many women and are normal for them. Hence the Masters and Johnson type which is always triggered off by the stimulation of the clitoris, is not the only type of orgasm.

Many women in spite of the vaginal contractions, do not even know that they have had an orgasm. Zarina told me, 'Poor Ahmed tries his level best but I never seem to come. Doctor, I have read from cover to cover Masters and Johnson's *Human Sexual Response,* the *Hite Report* and every conceivable book on sex. I know the theory but in bed nothing happens. Is there something wrong with my anatomy? I even saw my gynaecologist who assured me that everything is normal. Then why is it that nothing happens?' When questioned, Ahmed had a different story to tell. 'Zarina is a sexy dame. Doctor, she has at least three to four orgasms every time during intercourse.' Why was Zarina not aware of her orgasms though Ahmed invariably felt the contractions of her orgasmic platform (vaginal wall)? The reason is psychological. Zarina's upbringing had been orthodox and puritan. She was never permitted to mix with boys and her mother had indoctrinated in her that sex was dirty and that only cheap and wicked girls enjoy it. Was it any wonder that Zarina was mentally blocking off her own sexual responses? Similarly, Sarita, as reported by her husband, would always mutter during her orgasms, 'I don't want to feel it. I don't want it. It is dirty,' and as a result she blocked out the orgasms from her conscious mind. I explained to Zarina and Sarita that their stern upbringing blocked their reactions and reassured them that they were experiencing normal orgasms and that it was essential that they respond naturally at the climax and not try to block it. They were also told that the pattern of response varied from woman to woman.

What should a woman feel during orgasm?
It is extremely difficult for a sexually aroused woman to describe accurately her feelings, and especially during orgasm. Dr. Alfred Kinsey says, 'The participant in a sexual relationship becomes physiologically incapacitated as an observer. Sexual arousal reduces one's capacity to see, to hear, to smell, to taste, or to feel with anything like normal acuity, and at the moment of orgasm one's sensory capacities may completely fail.' This difficulty in objective reporting on the orgasm was overcome by direct observation of Dr. Masters and Mrs. Johnson in their sex laboratory. It was means of double-checking on the statements of the participants.

The response differs from female to female and even in the same individual at different times. Her sensations today may not be the same as those she would feel tomorrow. There are, however, certain common denominators.

(1) A gradual build-up of muscular tension and later a sudden release followed by complete relaxation.

(2) A feeling akin to climbing up a steep hill on roller-skates and suddenly feeling quite breathless for a second on reaching the top.

(3) Wave upon wave of intense contractions which come in rapid succession, then stop suddenly.

In other words, the three common denominators of a female orgasm are:

(1) Reaching a peak.

(2) Experiencing sudden relaxation as the muscular contractions subside and the blood is drained away from the genital organs.

(3) Finally, extreme sensitivity of the clitoris. A woman does not like her man to caress the clitoris at this point.

The female experiences two types of sensations during an orgasm. The orgasm may be centred in the genital area and is therefore not felt acutely in the rest of the body, or the orgasm may involve the whole body. The second type usually occurs during prolonged love-play when the female is greatly aroused. As the sensations are felt over the entire body, they are spread out and diffused, so that the female is often unaware that she has had an orgasm. On the other hand, as the local pelvic orgasms are concentrated in a small area, intense sensations can be easily observed by the responding female or during auto-manipulation. She can even count the vaginal muscular contractions.

Types of orgasm

The majority of moderately sensitive women have an individual orgasm where the sensation reaches a peak for a brief period (about 30 seconds to one minute) and then dies out. It is like a Diwali rocket soaring skywards and blowing up with everything over in a magic instant.

The other type of orgasm is usually present in more passionate women. It lasts much longer and when she reaches saturation point she does not want any more stimulation. In this group of women who have sustained orgasms are some women who cannot stand prolonged stimulation but want what is called the stop-start type of orgasm. After she reaches the peak, the male pauses and then restimulates her until she reaches the next peak. This goes on till she is satisfied. Some of these women may break out into tears or become violent and scratch the male partner all over during orgasm. The male should not be alarmed or worried at having to handle a sexually violent female who may swoon or even faint. She is like an explosive mass of dynamite reacting intensely.

Can a woman reach an orgasm the natural way?

Innumerable women still believe that they should have an orgasm as nature meant them to have—only by penile penetration. In other words, they feel that they should have what is called 'a no-hand orgasm'.

Women should give up this notion. The twentieth-century male needs the aid of his index finger to bring about his partner's orgasm and she should not mind. The idea is to enjoy sex and have more orgasms if possible, whichever way they come. There is no hard-and-fast rule that an orgasm should be achieved with the penis only. In fact, the flexible finger is often a better method of producing a more intense orgasm than the penis. However, for deep emotional satisfaction vaginal penetration by the penis is necessary for a woman.

She feels her partner deep inside her and it provides her additional stimulation.

If one looks at a picture of the female external genital organs, one will realise that the clitoris is situated some distance away from the vagina, and therefore the penis does not come in direct contact with the clitoris during sexual intercourse. Masters and Johnson have conclusively proved that an orgasm always originates in the clitoris, and therefore if the clitoris is not stimulated, how can it reach an orgasm? But the researchers observed that during the penile thrust, the clitoral hood gently rubs against the clitoris, paving the way for an orgasm.

The other way to reach an orgasm is by direct stimulation of the clitoris. For a natural climax, the clitoris must be sensitive and the position must be such as to provide direct contact with the male pubis. This can be achieved with the female-on-top or lateral position. In this position, there is intimate contact between the man's groin and the woman's clitoris.

I repeat that a woman may have a different orgasm from the ones described. Individual experiences are wide and varied.

Like premature ejaculation, is there a premature orgasm in the female?
A woman may reach a climax immediately after the male enters her, and occasionally go off to sleep, thus depriving the male of his pleasure! This is rare and women who climax easily still enjoy the sex act and may come again a few times before the male ejaculates. In such cases, the couple may try the stop-start technique; the male stimulates her clitoris, stops for a while and restarts stimulation. He employs the same technique during penetration. It is better to adopt the woman-on-top position, so that she can regulate the pace she desires and postpone the orgasm.

Is it essential for a woman to have an orgasm?
In the West, owing to the age-long taboo on sex, it was erroneously believed that the majority of women had neither the desire nor the capacity for sexual enjoyment and gratification. The few women who achieved orgasmic release were branded defective or wicked and

freaks of nature. Aristocratic parents in the Victorian era had clitoridectomy (surgical removal of the clitoris) performed as a preventive measure, if they suspected or found their daughters deriving pleasure from auto-manipulation of the clitoral region. Removal of the clitoris or suturing the vulva is prevalent even today in some societies in Africa.

India was way ahead in recognising sexuality in the female and both Vatsyayana and Kalyanamalla stated that it was a man's duty to gratify his partner. The teachings of these great sages were gradually lost and women were considered the weaker sex whose basic function was producing babies; if she derived enjoyment in sex, it was a bonus. With Sita as her model, she was expected to be at her husband's beck and call whenever he wanted to gratify himself and did not bother about her own sexual pleasure and orgasm.

The *Kinsey Report* on the possibility of multiple orgasms, followed by Masters and Johnson's findings that women could not only enjoy sex but were capable of multiple orgasms, caused a sexual explosion in the West. After centuries of suppression and male domination women have started demanding their rights! This obsession with orgasm has greatly troubled the twentieth-century Western woman. She feels that if she does not have an orgasm, there is some inherent defect in her or her male partner is inadequate. She thinks she is a failure and feels cheated of the supreme delight in the central game of life. This is an irrational and unwise outlook. There are innumerable women who have never had an orgasm yet are happily married. However, Western sexologists opine that an orgasm, though not necessary every time, is desirable for women to feel fulfilled in sex. Whether it occurs by a penile thrust or is brought about by hand is immaterial. In our conservative society, female orgasm consciousness is almost non-existent except in a handful of liberated urban females. Most Indian women not only put up with sexually inadequate men but are not particularly bothered about having an orgasm. It is however likely that, as women become more knowledgeable about their sexuality, they will want to experience orgasm during sex.

Frequency of orgasm in the female

Men almost invariably have an orgasm during intercourse. One can therefore say that men are almost 100 per cent orgasmic. However, there are a few who do not have an ejaculation and therefore do not reach an orgasm. Although such men do not derive any pleasure from sex, they can, because of the prolonged sex act, bring about innumerable orgasms in the female partner. There have been many documented cases of such personalities, including some of our old rajas and maharajas. In a biography on Prince Aly Khan by Leonard Slater, Juliette Greco says about him, 'It always made me feel sad. Here is a man who cannot bring things to an end for himself. I don't think it was a matter of choice; it was the way he was. I felt it because I am a giving woman as well as a receiving one. But another woman, perhaps, was attracted by a man who took so much time. It flattered her. He was thinking only of her. Too many men only think of themselves. Or maybe, she was helped in a way she had never been helped before. With another, it could be a challenge: "I'll be the one who makes him do it" '

The ultimate aim of many of our sophisticated males is to prolong the sex act by taking gold, silver and other medicines. However, this is not the case with the female. In a limited survey of 109 women interrogated by us, 51 per cent were not aware or had no orgasm during sex with any regular frequency, 20 per cent never having had an orgasm during sex. About 19 to 20 per cent reported a pleasant tingling feeling after sex either in the genital region or in the whole body, whilst the remaining 30 per cent had orgasm almost every time they indulged in sex. For a woman, having an orgasm is not as important as the whole feeling of being close, touched, caressed and kissed by her partner. I repeat that the female in this respect differs from the male, for whom the main pleasure is centred in the orgasmic phase. He derives comparatively little enjoyment from the sense of touching, as modern civilisation impresses on the males right from childhood 'that boys should not be cissies, and should avoid touching each other or girls.' Even a mother is self-conscious about cuddling her son as he grows older, although she will shower kisses on her daughter. When men meet they usually shake hands and that is the end, except after a few drinks when they loosen up a bit, and sometimes peck the cheek without deriving any sensory pleasure. But Arab males kiss and embrace each other from childhood, and even as adults it is the usual practice to hug and kiss each other in greeting.

Girls, on the other hand, right from childhood derive a lot of pleasure from touching other girls; they enjoy the sensation of touching their own bodies, combing the hair or washing the face.

Neither the female nor the male partner should worry unduly if she is not orgasmic during sex. The male should not divert his energies and concentrate entirely on producing an orgasm in her. If, however, the orgasm does not occur with repeated frequency or she has never had an orgasm and it bothers her, the pair should try and find out the causes. (1) Is the male adequate? (2) Does he provide her the right sexual stimulus? (3) Does she have any childhood hang-ups that sex is dirty? If the pair themselves cannot sort out their problem, it is advisable to take professional help from a qualified sexologist.

How does the male know his partner has had an orgasm?

Often an anxious male eagerly awaiting his partner's orgasm asks, 'Darling, have you come?' A woman is put off by this awkward cross-examination. She usually avoids a direct answer but sometimes just to please him she may nod.

Instead of asking her, Mr. Casanova, look for the tell-tale signs which are written in large capitals on her body. Firstly, the sudden increased prominence of the nipples is an infallible sign that she has had an orgasm. She may try to please you by feigning an orgasm but she cannot make her nipples prominent unless she has had one.

Secondly, you can feel the vaginal contractions during orgasm either with the penis or, if it is manually induced, with the finger. It is another tell-tale sign that she has had an orgasm. However, some women, as described earlier, do not have vaginal contractions during an orgasm. In such cases the male has to rely on the secondary erection of the nipples and immediate return of the clitoris to its normal overhanging position. The clitoris during the plateau phase of the sexual response cycle is retracted upwards and cannot be felt by the male partner. Finally, the woman who was clasping the partner, taut and tense, suddenly relaxes and becomes calm and still.

Chapter 12

MASTURBATION

*'There is nothing good or bad
but thinking makes it so.'*

MASTURBATION OR AUTO-MANIPULATION is one form of sexual outlet and may be defined as self-stimulation of the genital organs. Masturbation also occurs in domesticated animals when there is no opportunity for natural sexual outlet. It is universal in both sexes from childhood to old age. According to Dr. Alfred Kinsey, the pioneer researcher in human sexual behaviour, 92 per cent of the American population is involved in masturbation. While in a more recent study of male sexuality by the noted author of the *Hite Report,* Shere Hite, only one per cent of 7239 men who answered her questionnaire did not masturbate. Those who do not masturbate are from the beginning involved in heterosexual intercourse or their sex drive may be so low they do not feel the necessity for a sexual outlet through masturbation. In Europe and America, masturbation is a stepping stone to intercourse with a female. In the East, up to recent times, the joint family system prevailed and marriages took place early, so masturbation was unnecessary. But conditions have changed, the joint family system is disintegrating, the age of marriage in men has gone up, therefore masturbation is more prevalent. Masturbation is more common in boarding schools and college hostels. It is more frequently practised in cities than in villages as a large number of villagers who emigrate for work to the cities have to leave their wives behind. There is no normal sexual outlet for this large floating male population. Where there is opportunity for normal sexual union at puberty, as among the primitive tribes, masturbation is unknown.

AGE OF ONSET: The sex instinct is present from birth in both sexes, and infants derive a lot of pleasurable sensations playing with their genitals. Infantile masturbation is harmless and innocent. Parents should not be anxious about adolescent masturbation. The sex urge becomes very demanding at puberty and finds an outlet in masturbation. The average age at which boys begin auto-manipulation is 13 to 14, though it may be delayed up to 16.

FREQUENCY: This varies from individual to individual. In a sample survey at a boarding school, the frequency was once a week among boys aged 14 and three times in two weeks among the older boys of 15 to 18. Besides this, nocturnal emissions were the only source of sexual outlet.

Among collegians and young unmarried men the frequency was about twice a week, though there were wide variations. I had three cases who masturbated twice every night, and in addition once or twice in the afternoon on Sundays and holidays. Most young adults gave up masturbation after marriage. There were quite a few, however, who had the best of both worlds—normal sex as well as masturbation. 'I love my wife and love myself in solitude,' said a 37-year-old advertising executive, Ramesh. 'The former is emotionally satisfying while the latter is intensely stimulating, physically. I have masturbated all my life since I was 13.' 'Does your wife know about your other love?' I asked. 'No, not yet,' replied Ramesh.

The middle-aged and elderly usually practise normal coitus with a female partner in preference to masturbation. But I had the case of a 53-year-old foreigner, married for 26 years, who preferred masturbation exclusively to intercourse. Unmarried individuals or spinsters in both groups practised masturbation as well as heterogenous sex.

TECHNIQUE: This varies from individual to individual. The majority of males manipulate the body of the penis by holding it between the fingers and the thumb or the fingers and the palm. The rate of stroking also varies. Some prefer rapid excursions, while others like slow excursions. Some others stimulate the undersurface of the glans. I have known several collegians who held each other's penis and masturbated. A few males take great delight in getting their wives to hold their penises and masturbate them. The time taken to reach an orgasm varies considerably. If the stroke movements are rapid, orgasm is reached within half to one minute. If on the other hand, the stroking movements are slow, the time taken to reach an orgasm may be much longer—about 5 to 15 minutes or more. A few individuals though they masturbate do not want to reach an orgasm and ejaculate semen, which they believe is a very vital fluid. Many young men wrongly pre-suppose that to maintain sexual vigour, strength and concentration they should retain the vital body fluid. Masturbation for most males is a love session with wide and varied fantasies where they are alone and do not have to worry about a female partner.

FANTASTIC NONSENSE: Never in the history of medicine has so much been written by so many as on masturbation. For centuries the Jewish and Christian churches, educational institutions, and the medical profession have all denounced masturbation as perversion and given innumerable warnings about the dire consequences of indulgence in this evil practice. In no conditions have the so-called harmful effects been so exaggerated as in masturbation, and in no condition has education of the educators been so necessary as in their opinions and knowledge of masturbation.

RELIGION: In the West from very early times the Christian and Jewish clergy have strongly condemned masturbation as sinful. Fortunately in India our approach to sex was more enlightened, thanks to the science of sexology which existed and flourished as early as 2300 years ago. Secondly, the custom of early marriages provided ample opportunities for heterosexual contact, so masturbation was unknown in India during the Hindu and Muslim domination. But with the coming of the Portuguese, the French, the Dutch and the British, came the missionaries who dominated the Indian scene from then onwards and the supposed evils of masturbation were naturally preached to the people of the East.

EDUCATION: With the advent of Western influence on Indian culture, a large number of educational institutions were set up under European management for the benefit of the natives. Their culture and opinions on social and sexual matters influenced and moulded our thinking and attitudes. We aped the West and started denouncing masturbation as an undesirable and immoral practice.

MEDICAL OPINIONS: Western influence infiltrated the sphere of medicine and our Ayurvedic systems were gradually replaced by modern allopathy. A large number of allopathic doctors of those days condemned masturbation as an evil habit. The Ayurvedic practitioners borrowed these ideas from their Western counterparts and masturbation became the favourite whipping boy. Here is an extract from a book on the evils of masturbation, *Mysteries of Sex* by A.L. Saksena: 'A mental conflict or guilt is produced in the boy which results in anxiety symptoms like loss of sleep, palpitation, sweating, and worry about his potency.

'The victim awakens to the fact only when the intellect is weakened and he becomes a physical, mental and moral wreck. If a bright, cheerful, obedient, frank and energetic boy becomes seclusive, sullen, stupid and reticent the evidence is sufficiently strong that he is a victim of the evil practice. Sudden decline in health or senile looks, without any acute illness or apparent cause such as intestinal worms, dyspepsia, loss of sleep, overwork or overstudy may be traced to this vice. Unnatural languor, lassitude and dullness, especially in the morning, may give rise to suspicion.'

In more recent years the pioneer contributions of Kinsey and Masters and Johnson have helped considerably in demolishing beliefs about the so-called harmful effects of masturbation.

The effects of masturbation can be discussed under three heads: (1) Physical; (2) Mental and Emotional; and (3) Socio-sexual adjustment.

PHYSICAL EFFECTS: The physical effects of masturbation are not different from those of normal sexual intercourse.

MENTAL AND EMOTIONAL: Masturbation by itself is harmless and produces no emotional ill-effects, if the boy is properly educated on sexual matters. It is a sexual safety valve which reduces tension when a female partner is not available. On the other hand, if the boy is told not to masturbate or that masturbation is sinful or that a little self-abuse is good but more is harmful, it may result in emotional instability and impotence in later life.

SEXUAL ADJUSTMENT: Man is primarily meant to have a heterogenous sexual outlet. It is necessary for him to merge his ego with the ego of his loved one for proper establishment of a 'we relationship'. Because opportunities for sex between unmarried men and women are not readily available in modern civilization, masturbation is invariably practised. Compulsive masturbation is common in individuals suffering from an inferiority complex, and unable to face real-life situations. They seek solace by indulging in fantasies of sexual conquest during masturbation. Masturbation should be regarded as an infantile substitute for heterosexual sex. Where it is practised in preference to normal sex it indicates a deviation from the normal and the individual should consult his doctor.

Advice on masturbation

The word 'treatment' for masturbation found in many textbooks is purposely avoided here, implying that masturbation is one form of normal, natural sexual outlet, and all that is necessary is to give the proper advice. It would mean educating the parents, educationists, medical profession, clergy, and last but not the least, the individual himself.

PARENTS should be made to realise that infantile masturbation is harmless and that infants show an innocent, instructive interest in their genital organs. If the infant or the young child is unceremoniously snubbed, 'It is dirty, do not touch it,' 'Don't play with it. It is naughty for young boys to play with their organs,' he wonders why and does it on the sly. In addition if the scolding is peppered with a sense of guilt or shame the seeds are sown for a textbook case of neurosis about sex in later life. If the father or the mother frightens the boy about masturbation being an evil practice leading to complications, the boy will in time develop the very condition that his parents have mentioned. For example, if the boy is told that masturbation will lead to loss of manly vigour or intellect, he will in course of time develop these conditions. I appeal to parents to always satisfy the basic curiosity of the infant and young boy about his genital organs. The boy, whilst not encouraged to masturbate, should be informed that it is a passing phase of adolescence that he will outgrow after marriage. It should be explained to him that it is a natural sexual outlet that does not result in any physical or emotional damage.

We as doctors should never be shocked or horrified by anything a patient says and should always give him a sympathetic hearing and understand his viewpoint. Sex is a subject on which patients have distorted ideas, and the doctor may also have certain pre-conceived notions which he must give up to give the correct lead to his patients. Patients are shy to talk about this intimate subject and tremendous confidence in the doctor is therefore absolutely essential. Not only must there be sympathy for the patient but also empathy. Only then will the patient open up and talk about sexual matters. I have frequently had cases of young boys complaining of palpitation, sweating of the hands, loss of sleep, and inability to concentrate. These are all cases of distorted fear of masturbation and great tact and care is needed in handling them. I generally gain their confidence by assuring them that most young men masturbate, and there is nothing to worry about. It is then that they pour out their tales of woe. All they need is reassurance that masturbation has not damaged their delicate sexual organs permanently. In this connection it is interesting to observe that the modern Indian woman is less reticent to talk about sex than her male counterpart. Emancipation of women has indeed gone a long way in free India.

THE CLERGY: Religious upbringing in infancy and childhood has a lot to do with an individual's behaviour in adult life. While Judaism and Christianity in their original form considered sex sacred, they now denounce certain sexual outlets like masturbation as sinful and an individual has to make a 'confession' for them. Such a myopic outlook on sex makes a poor lonely boy who masturbates into a sinner and produces in him a tremendous guilt feeling. Ashamed and remorseful, he makes war on masturbation. He clenches his teeth, hammers his fist on the table and says to himself, 'I will never masturbate again.' His energies are dissipated in fruitlessly trying to quell the sexual urge. Every New Year he makes a new resolution, which he breaks within hours or days. Every time he breaks his vow he feels more discouraged and remorseful and loses his interest and zest in life. If only this poor boy had been brought up with common sense and told that masturbation is not a sin against any religion, but is only a natural sexual outlet, he would never become an overwrought emotional wreck.

In this respect the teaching of Hinduism is commendable. It does not consider masturbation a sin, but some *swamis* preach sexual abstinence as good for the soul and advocate not only abstinence in intercourse but also in masturbation. There is also a belief among many Hindus that semen is a vital body fluid and 40 drops of blood go to prepare one drop of semen and that loss of this vital body fluid causes general debility, and decreases sexual vigour. Therefore every time a boy masturbates he feels he has lowered his vitality and injured himself. Islam has no inhibitions about sexual intercourse or masturbation.

To conclude, religion and modern medicine in the 20th century should go hand in hand for the well-being of mankind. Not only the medical profession but also the clergy should give up their outdated ideas on masturbation and accept the modern view that it is a passing phase and a normal sexual outlet for young adolescents before marriage.

THE INDIVIDUAL: A boy who masturbates does so secretly and is ashamed to admit it to his doctor. He therefore consults his physician for some other complaint like forgetfulness, headache, dizziness, palpitation, sweating or sleeplessness. It is then up to the doctor to tactfully elicit the history of masturbation and assure the poor frightened boy that it is normal for most young men, and does no harm physically or emotionally. It should be explained to him that medical studies have conclusively proven that boys who masturbate have no difficulties in marriage, if they have been properly briefed, and are prefectly normal individuals. On the contrary, boys who have abstained from masturbation out of fear or on the advice of their parents or teachers have been found to be emotionally unstable. Apart from organic diseases, the individual most fears impotence as a result of masturbation. He should be reassured that masturbation does not lead to impotence—but that the guilt feelings which accompany it may do so.

FREQUENCY OF MASTURBATION: An individual wants to know how often he can masturbate without harming himself, just as a married man likes to know how often it is 'safe' to have sexual intercourse. A number of authorities have recommended that once a week is normal — which implies that if an individual goes beyond it he is likely to harm himself. I have stated earlier that sexual capacity varies considerably from person to person and there is no hard-and-fast rule governing the frequency of masturbation or intercourse. You can masturbate as often as you like.

SIGNIFICANCE OF MASTURBATION: In the pre-adolescent and adolescent years masturbation is a sexual outlet when heterosexual contact is not possible. After marriage, the individual automatically switches over to a normal sexual relationship. For most males, coitus is primary and masturbation secondary.

A large number of young men suffer from an inferiority complex and fear of impotence, and are afraid to risk a sexual situation with a woman. An innate shyness prevents their switching over from masturbation to normal intercourse. They try to escape from reality by fantasies during masturbation of themselves being Casanovas, sleeping with a different woman morning, noon and night. But they are unwilling to have normal intercourse and risk failure. Female partners can with tact and patience help to build confidence in these unfortunate men. Alternatively they should seek the help of a sexologist.

In certain men masturbation is an outward manifestation of deep sexual perversion. These men always practise masturbation in preference to normal intercourse because masturbation lets them enjoy the specific fantasy that turns them on.

A 24-year-old male, married for two years, consulted me for impotence. He could only have an erection during masturbation, when he fantasised that he slept with his male roommate in college. With his wife he was impotent. He had been masturbating three or four times a week since the age of 14 and blamed it for his impotence. It was only during the interview that I found out that he had homosexual inclinations which I pointed out to him. In this case, therefore, the homosexuality was the cause of impotence, of which masturbation was merely an outward symptom, like fever being the symptom of many organic diseases.

Similarly, deep religious bias also makes men impotent. They believe that masturbation has caused impotence, but a careful analysis shows that deep at heart they are religious in a very puritanical way and suffer from a guilt complex. They are extremely sensual men with all sorts of fantasies about women which they repress because they think they are immoral, and this culminates in impotence.

To conclude, masturbation is self-stimulation of the genital organs. It is a perfectly normal sexual outlet during adolescence before intercourse with a woman is possible and has no physical, mental or emotional ill-effects.

Young man, you can masturbate as much as you like. In the Stress Century, no one can deny or dispute your right to masturbate. With women evaluating your sexual performance, it is only when you masturbate in solitude that you are a sexual king.

Masturbation in females
Females also masturbate but not as frequently as males. This is because in the latter the sexual urge is overpowering and localised in the penis while in females it is less demanding and diffused over her whole body.

Unlike the Kinsey and Hite Reports in the USA, statistics about the frequency of masturbation among Indian women are not available. But its incidence is much lower than in the West, as most Indian girls are married off at a young age. Masturbation, however, especially in the cities has been showing an upward trend during the last four decades as a growing number of young women are embarking on higher education and a professional career before marriage. In these days of inflation, an earning bride commands a higher premium in the matrimonial market. Modern movies and magazines provide an erotic stimulus arousing her sexuality and sheltered 'Miss Touch-me-not' is suddenly exposed to the pawing animals in the executive jungles. She has been forewarned about them but that does not mean she is forearmed. Her puritan background prevents her from taking the ultimate plunge so she secretly resorts to masturbation to relieve her sexual tension.

Needless to say, she enjoys it physically. It gives her a feeling of intense ecstasy followed by release. But she is mentally and emotionally disturbed and unhappy, being plagued by innumerable doubts. Will masturbation damage her delicate organs? Can her future partner find out that she has been masturbating? Is playing with herself childish and inconsistent with being a grown-up young lady? Will she get hooked on stimulating herself and prefer it to normal sexual intercourse? Will she become sterile and not have babies? The answer to all these questions is a definite 'NO'. 'Masturbation is our primary sex life,' writes Betty Dodson in *Liberating Masturbation*. 'It is the sexual base. Everything we do beyond that is simply how we choose to socialize our sex life.' Apes and monkeys also masturbate from childhood.

A large number of married women and widows also resort to masturbation. Innumerable males still lack sexual skill and invariably leave their partners unfulfilled during penis-vagina intercourse as they are ignorant of the art of manually stimulating women to orgasm. Besides, the jobs of so many executives, salesmen, *jawans* and seamen involve long separation from their wives. In many cases, the acute housing shortage in cities forces wives to stay away from their husbands and live with their parents. Nor is it uncommon to find an eighteen-year-old girl married to a male of fifty-plus. Often the husband dies a few years after marriage, leaving a young widow. Our tradition-bound society still wrongly frowns on such unfortunate females if they want to remarry and permissive sex is prohibited. So for all such women masturbation is the only outlet from sexual tension.

How do women masturbate? Like the male the female learns instinctively to masturbate, by stimulating her clitoral-vulva area. According to Shere Hite, 73 per cent of women masturbate by lying on their backs and stimulating the clitoral-vulva area with their hand or a vibrator (see Chapter 11, 'Female Orgasm'.) Many orgasm-conscious, gadget-oriented and time-dominated Western women, especially in the USA, lean heavily on a vibrator to produce clitoral orgasm. 'Me and my vibrator,' quipped a single lady from the consulate. 'Back home, I rarely have the time to resort to the slow-moving yet tremendously satisfying manual orgasm. When I am racing against the clock and need a quick release from tension, a blitzkrieg with the vibrator does the job.'

The remaining 27 per cent of women, according to the *Hite Report*, either masturbate lying on their stomachs, or thrusting themselves back and forth against a pillow, while a few cross their legs and contract and relax the leg muscles. Women usually fantasise or listen to music or read erotic literature while they masturbate. A common fantasy is that they are forcibly possessed by their lover while they lie helpless and without a will to resist!

SO-CALLED EVILS OF MASTURBATION: Young women are brought up not to masturbate in our puritan society. If ever she is discovered by her parents 'touching herself there', she is severely admonished, and warned of dire consequences like insanity, blindness, sexual promiscuity and perversion. Millions of women in Africa and West Asia have their clitoris excised when young, so they can never masturbate, or later derive pleasure from sex.

To conclude, masturbation is a perfectly normal and harmless sexual outlet in the female until heterosexual intercourse is possible.

Part II

Prevention Of Impotence And Frigidity In Adult Life

Chapter 13

HOW TO PREVENT SEXUAL INADEQUACY AND PERVERSION

Use it or lose it.

JAMES FRIES

D EAR PARENTS, the seed of sexual inadequacy and perversion is
often sown in the cradle. You can teach your children healthy
sexuality in order to prevent sexual dysfunction when they grow up.

The dawn of the Stress Century and the conquest of infections with
antibiotics has brought about a change of diseases. For example,
billions of dollars are spent all over the world on the prevention of
heart disease and cancer. We are told what to eat to maintain good
health, how to cope with stress and prevent diseases. Yet little or
nothing is being done anywhere in the world to curb the curse of the
twentieth century—sexual inadequacy.

Why this neglect of sexual disorders at all levels? It is because sex is
still taboo. It was only after Masters and Johnson's unique experiments in the sexual laboratory that world attention was suddenly
focused on sex, and a veritable sexual revolution took place in the
West. The Masters-Johnson team advocated their intensive two to
three weeks' behaviour therapy for sexual inadequacies. Yet cases of
failure have been reported even with this treatment.

It is now recognised that the foundation of healthy sexuality must
be laid in the cradle and sex treated as part of general character-
building. Because once sexual inadequacy such as psychogenic
impotence sets in, although treatment can restore sexual functioning,

it is not quite normal. A broken vase can be mended by sticking together the pieces but the crack shows. A man can recover after a heart attack, but his chances of a relapse are four times higher than in a person with a normal heart. Similarly, behaviour therapy puts Humpty Dumpty together again but impotence can recur. Except in cases of congenital defects, sexual inadequacy is a hundred per cent preventable disorder. Knowledge of preventive measures is, therefore, vital. For purposes of convenience, advice is outlined separately according to the stages of physical development: (1) infancy and childhood; (2) puberty and adolescence; (3) adulthood; (4) middle age; and (5) old age.

Section 1 is essentially meant for parents, particularly for the mother who is the greatest influence in the child's life and is therefore responsible for his future development. Section 2 is meant to be read by parents as well as adolescents. Section 3, 4 and 5 are for individuals of different age groups who are interested in keeping themselves sexually fit.

1

PREVENTION IN INFANCY AND CHILDHOOD

The Child is Father of the man.

WILLIAM WORDSWORTH

The poet Wordsworth implied that what the child is, the man will become. Suppression of normal sexual urges in infancy and childhood by puritanical, over-zealous and strict parents is often the foundation for impotence in later life. Most sexual problems are the result of parental failure to treat sex as a natural learning process along with other aspects of education. Many parents erroneously believe that the sexual urge suddenly appears at puberty. The sexual instinct is present in all of us from the day we are born and it is therefore essential to understand its nature and development.

An INSTINCT is an inborn capacity for purposive action. Bees build a beehive through their inborn capacity. A bird instinctively knows how to build a nest with twigs at the first attempt, without previous training. The three basic instincts present in birds and animals are the self instinct, the herd instinct, and the sex instinct. Each has a definite purpose in the biology of living. The self instinct is for self-preservation and self-advancement and enables an animal to find food and prepare itself to meet any threat from man or other animals. The instinct of self-preservation makes the animal fight or flee when attacked—that is, fight and vanquish his opponent or run away to save his life. The herd instinct is for protection. Animals instinctively know that 'united we stand, divided we fall' when exposed to danger. They therefore move in herds. The sex instinct is for procreation and propagation of the species.

During evolution, Man also inherited from lower animals the basic instincts—self, herd and sex—which are essential for life and living. In man, the basic instincts have been modified to serve his diverse needs. The three major schools of psychoanalysis, Freud, Adler and Jung, postulated that Man has different basic needs. For example, Freud believed that man most of all wants to be loved, while in Adler's view, Man's basic need is that he wants to be significant. Jung, on the other hand, thought that man needs security most. The biological urges in modern man are the urge for food, which is the strongest, the urge for security and love, and the sexual urge. Every human being is born with a natural capacity for sexual enjoyment. The development of the sexual urge depends very largely on training and upbringing and the moral and cultural norms and environment in which the individual grows up.

The basic instincts are like a fountain—water from a reservoir forcing its way out through numerous jets, fanning out into a fountain. If some jets get blocked, the shape of the fountain is altered. Similarly, the life stream from within us, flows into consciousness as instincts which supply the energy for living. If some outlets are blocked, the personality becomes distorted. It is therefore important that the channels through which the instincts flow are kept open, otherwise they affect a man's personality. In a normal mature personality, the instincts freely enter consciousness through their natural outlets to reach the desired aim. For example, the sex instinct finds its normal goal, firstly through meeting girls socially at college or work, then physical intercourse and finally procreation.

Development of the sexual instinct

The sexual instinct is present from birth. It is not single or homogeneous but a group of impulses which are predominantly auto-erotic in the infant. The infant obtains gratification from his own body and, unlike adults, the sexual impulse is not directed towards others. The daily routine of the infant—sucking milk from the mother's breast or feeding bottle, voiding urine and stools, playing with his genitals or displaying them—gives him tremendous satisfaction and pleasure. The normal infant thus leads a rich sensual life and derives innocent gratification from different regions of his body. The sexual impulse is first diffused and the infant gets satisfaction from tickling the skin of his whole body (skin eroticism). The next zone which acquires importance is the mouth, the lips and the tongue. Sucking milk and dribbling saliva and playing with it are also sources of immense joy to the infant. The centre of interest next shifts down the alimentary canal to its termination—the anus. The period is called anal eroticism. The infant in its natural state is interested in his own stools and enjoys lying in the mess after passing a stool.

Finally, the erotic focus shifts to the most important zone—the urethra. The infant enjoys passing urine and later, as a child, gets a thrill playing urinary games like seeing who can project the stream higher or longer. The genital organs now take over as the centre of attraction. The infant loves playing with his genitals.

SUBJECTIVE AND OBJECTIVE EXPERIENCE: In the early stages the infant is incapable of distinguishing between subjective and objective experiences. His world is extremely subjective. For example, the baby believes that the feeding bottle is an extension of his own mouth. The child gradually learns to differentiate between two different experiences, what is 'me' and what is 'not me'. In the life of the child what is 'not me' is soon recognised as an ever-present element—his mother. She is the indispensable bond between him and the outside world. The child is now capable of objective love. The whole world including himself becomes objective. This has to be distinguished from auto-eroticism when the infant has an aim but no object.

PRIMARY NARCISSISM: In Greek mythology, Narcissus fell in love with his own reflection in the waters of a spring. Freudian psychologists used the term 'narcissism' for a condition in which the subject is interested in his own body. This is the first experience of the child in objective love—he is in love with himself and this is termed 'primary narcissism'.

OEDIPUS COMPLEX: One of the most famous Greek myths, the Oedipus legend talks of a prince who unwittingly killed his father and married his own mother. Freud used the legend to illustrate what he considered a universal truth that when the child outgrows narcissism, his love is directed at his mother who gives him comfort and sensual gratification. He regards the father as a rival claiming much of his mother's time and energy and resents him. But his feelings of rivalry, jealousy and hostility are forbidden in his mind and conflict with the love, respect and regard he has for his father. These conflicting feelings produce mental tension and his natural tendency is to repress them.

The Oedipus situation is always present when there is a father. In most cases the child does not suffer anxiety or tension because of his inherent ability to put up with stress. But an emotionally charged experience can intensify the Oedipus complex and cause neuroses in later life. For example, if a child sleeps in the same bedroom as his parents and sees his parents having sexual intercourse, it can produce tremendous anxiety as he has no knowledge about sex. In later life this could lead to disturbed sexuality.

A little boy wants to marry his mother and a little girl wants to marry her father. In a normal healthy child in course of time this attachment diminishes. In abnormal cases however, the child continues to be attached to the parent. The mother's image is also associated in the infant's mind with frustrations and reprimands. The mother might scold the infant or enforce discipline which he does not like. The infant thus has a love-hate attraction for the mother.

SECONDARY NARCISSISM: After the Oedipus complex, there is a latent period between 5 and 11 years when the child concentrates on himself or loves himself. The child is self-centred and emotionally there are no violent upheavals till puberty.

Preventing impotence

Infancy and childhood are very vital periods for development of adult sexual behaviour. The normal infant leads a rich sensual life by striving to derive bodily pleasure and avoid pain. Tickling the skin, sucking, passing stools and urine and playing with his genitals are a source of immense satisfaction and pleasure to the infant. Anything which interferes with this normal and innocent sensual pleasure represses the sexual instinct. The prevention of psychogenic sexual disorders therefore depends entirely upon the parents' understanding of the normal sexual instincts and the infant's need for love and affection. The structure of most of the organs like the heart, lungs, the alimentary canal and the kidneys is complete at birth. They merely grow in size for some years afterwards. But the newborn infant has only the rudiments of his personality structure. The brain is a clean slate which can be written upon by experience. The experience of the young infant is the experience he gets from his parents. Parents leave an indelible impression on the infant's personality.

The parents, and especially the mother, can do much to prepare the child for a healthy life of sex and sexuality. The way they train the infant depends in turn upon their own upbringing and training in childhood. They can, however, improve their knowledge by consulting doctors, friends and the right books. They should not impose a strict moral code on the baby; the relationship between them should be normal and natural.

Types of parents

NORMAL PARENTS: The husband-wife relationship is based on love, understanding and respect. There is no competitiveness between them and they do not lie to each other to win the infant's love. They do not subscribe to social or religious taboos on sex. They understand the normal sexual instinct in the infant and do not suppress it in any way. They are emotionally mature individuals, free from unnecessary anxieties and tensions.

FRUSTRATED PARENTS: If there is frustration in marriage due to sexual or emotional maladjustment, one of the parents may try to obtain emotional satisfaction by a very close bond with the child and prevent him from growing up emotionally and sexually. I am reminded of a patient whose sexually frustrated mother was so possessive she never let him out of her sight, never allowed him to date young ladies or move in society without her. She got him married to a girl of her choice—and was it any surprise that the young man consulted me for impotence? He could not love any other woman but his mother!

INDIFFERENT PARENTS: Most parents in this group are 'social climbers' who spend a lot of their time running after material success. By worldly standards they have everything in life. They are, however, lacking in emotions and feelings and believe that by buying the best toys and sending the infant to the best school they have done everything for him. They are unaware and insensitive to the infant's need for warmth, comfort and emotional security.

OVER-PROTECTIVE PARENTS:This group of parents over-protect the infant and child. All the important decisions are made for him. He is cocooned from all dangerous situations and disappointments. Such a child cannot become emotionally mature and is unable to face complicated situations in life. He may find difficulties in facing sexual situations.

Effect on the infant
The last three groups of parents are unknowingly guilty of causing personality defects and sexual inadequacy in their child in later life. 'Doctor, how can our son have a problem? We have given him everything in life,' moan the mother or father. I wish such parents realised that the child craves most for emotional security and not merely material things like a teddy bear, an electric train, a bus or a tricycle. A pat, a hug, a little time spent by the father with the toddler is more important to him than the costliest toy.

In the small world of the child, affection should always be expressed physically and not just verbally. A pat, a hug or an embrace by the father will make the child emotionally confident and secure and prevent sexual inadequacy in later life. What about the mother? The mother also plays a vital role as she looks after all the daily chores like breast-feeding, weaning, toilet training, dressing and playing with the infant. However, over-dependence on the mother can make him a mother's darling, quite unable to transfer his love from his mother to another woman when he marries. The result: impotence.

Civilization and childhood experiences

It is interesting to observe what modern civilization has done to the normal childhood experiences of feeding, weaning, toilet training and genital play. Among the primitive and poorer classes of society the infant is breast-fed for a longer period. He is fed when he is hungry rather than by the clock and he spends more time with his mother as they cannot afford a nanny. Toilet training is not strict and does not take place at a very early age. In civilised society, especially among the upper classes, there is so-called 'civilized control'. The infant is weaned earlier, he is fed more by the clock than by his hunger, to suit his mother's convenience and social engagements. He has to learn toilet training earlier and the mother is more strict. In other words, he has to give up present satisfaction for the promise of a brighter future. This cultural difference causes sensual discontent in the civilized child with the result that he masturbates more and his personality is inhibited. In later life, this is turn affects his sexual capacity.

Milestones in the infant's life

FEEDING: In the infant's small world feeding plays a very important role. The feed should be given at the right time by the right person who cares for him and loves him. This results not only in normal growth but also builds a feeling of security. He derives a lot of sensual pleasure from the feeding process and for the future development of a relaxed personality free from tension, it is essential that feeding should leave pleasant memories.

WEANING: This is the process by which the infant is gradually induced to give up feeding from the mother's breast (or, in case of bottle-fed infants, from the feeding bottle) and switch to solid food. The infant has a very limited capacity for adapting itself to a new experience. If, therefore, he is weaned suddenly or the mother or nurse shows impatience during weaning, he develops anxiety which persists in later life and may hamper his sexual functioning, as anxiety and sex do not go together.

THUMB SUCKING: This is done by most infants at some time and psychiatrists agree that it is harmless. Sucking gives pleasure to the infant and he resorts to it when he is hungry or tired or needs attention from the mother. If the infant is scolded or the thumb pulled out forcibly it can produce anxiety and tension.

TOILET TRAINING: The infant derives pleasure in passing urine or stool at his own sweet will and enjoys lying in the mess. There comes a time towards the end of the first year when he has to learn to deposit his stool or urine in a specified place at a particular time. The young one naturally resents being disciplined as it is a new experience for him. The mother or the nurse should educate the infant with the utmost tact and patience. In their anxiety for toilet training if the parents tell him that voiding urine or stool is a dirty habit, the young infant will grow up in the belief that anything to do with genital functioning is a dirty, messy affair. Is it any wonder that when these infants grow up they consider sex dirty and messy? This often produces inhibition or repression which prevents erection during intercourse, resulting in impotence.

SEXUAL CURIOSITY: The healthy infant at the age of three or four has solved his toilet problems, and becomes more interested and curious about the outside world and himself. He wants to know the why and wherefore of things. All his questions are generally answered by the parents—except those on sex. They feel, without any rational basis, that knowledge of sex should be kept away from the infant. In modern cities with residential flats becoming smaller due to spiralling costs of land and building materials, a child inadvertently seeing the sexual act, gets anxious and wonders what is going on. It is therefore necessary that children should be given information on sex in a matter-of-fact, cheerful manner, whenever they ask for it.

SEX AND SEXUALITY: There is a vital difference between sex and sexuality. Sex is physiology, or the changes that take place during intercourse. Sexuality in our sexual profile or personality develops from the sexual instinct. The infant learns sexuality from the parents. Mature sexuality is the capacity to be human in love, to be tender, warm and understanding.

GENITAL PLAY: It is normal for children to play with their genital organs and for older children to masturbate. As I have stated earlier, the genital organs are an erotic zone and masturbation gives pleasure to children. If this normal habit is harshly suppressed or the child told that it is dirty and wicked, it can ultimately lead to disordered sexual function in adulthood. Masturbation is a natural sexual outlet and does no harm physically, mentally or emotionally (see Chapter 12, 'Masturbation').

SEX AND MORALITY: It is wrong of parents to instil in their children's impressionable minds that sex is immoral or to give a religious twist to sexuality. The sensitive boy grows up thinking that all forms of sex are immoral, which can give him a guilt complex and seriously impair his sexual functioning. It is also wrong of parents to tell their son to 'treat all women as sisters'. The boy may grow up and treat his wife as his sister, with the sexual component non-existent! The guilt or shame that frequently darkens the first sex experience is the result of attitudes inculcated in childhood, and often prevent a husband and wife from behaving naturally towards each other.

GENITAL FUNCTIONS IN THE MALE: The male genital organs have the dual function of voiding urine and procreation. In the animal kingdom and among primitive men, normal sexual functioning is totally unconnected with any false feelings of guilt or disgust, anxiety or shame. It is most unfortunate that while civilized man will unhesitatingly explain the role of every organ of the body to his child, he should be so inhibited about explaining the nature of the sex organs. Parents and teachers should not desist from giving sexual information about the facts of life to young people, who need it desperately.

CASTRATION COMPLEX: This is the fear a young boy develops that his parents may cut off his penis if he is naughty. 'I'll cut it off if I ever see you playing with it,' threatens the father. The poor boy is petrified, because he cannot differentiate between fact and fantasy and believes that his father may really cut off his penis. Due to the Oedipus complex, the child already has hostile feelings towards his father and fears reprisal. There is in the mind of the child an association between physical pleasure from manipulating his own organ and the possibility of his penis being amputated, causing tremendous anxiety. The castration complex often becomes intolerable and is repressed, but can emerge later as an anxiety neurosis with impotence.

The foundation for male potency is laid in this period. Let us therefore build an everlasting edifice for the ever-potent male. Infancy and childhood is the time.

2

PREVENTION IN PUBERTY AND ADOLESCENCE

Boys will be boys, and so will a lot of middle-aged men.

F.M. Hubbard

Puberty according to Schonfeld is the age at which a boy or a girl is capable of procreation. The age at which this takes place is soon after the first menstruation in a girl or the first discharge in a boy. Many authorities dislike the term puberty and recommend the word adolescence, which better defines this very vital and highly explosive stage in development.

Puberty is a stage of development when important anatomical, physiological and emotional changes take place. The child now becomes an adolescent and is capable of reproduction. The age of onset of puberty varies from individual to individual and also depends upon the climate. Generally the onset is earlier in the tropics than in colder climates. The average age for males in the tropics is twelve to thirteen while in temperate zones it is thirteen to fifteen years. Adolescence is the difficult transitory stage between childhood and adulthood. It is a continuously evolving period when momentous somatic, sexual and psychological changes occur due to tremendous glandular activity. The so-called peculiar behaviour of the adolescent which bewilders adults is due to the tremendous internal and external changes taking place at this stage. Adolescence is also the period between sexual and emotional maturity. Unlike mammals who mate as soon as they are sexually mature, human beings, even though they are sexually mature and capable of reproduction, undergo a waiting period till they become emotionally mature to undertake marriage. They have to finish their studies and become economically independent so that they can support their wives and families. During this period the adolescent gradually breaks away from the dependence on his parents to lead a comfortably independent life.

CHANGES IN GENITAL ORGANS: At puberty, the testes rapidly increase in size. The testes consist of the seminiferous tubules which form the sperms and the interstitial cells which secrete the male hormone testosterone. The testes thus produce bodily changes by means of hormones secreted in the blood. The hormones produce growth of the accessory organs of reproduction: the epididymis, the seminal vesicles, the prostate and the penis. The secondary male sex characteristics also make their appearance—hair on the trunk, face, axillae (armpits) and the pubis. The voice breaks owing to growth of the larynx. The penis is now capable of erection and occasionally there may be a discharge of semen. The age of sexual maturity varies from boy to boy, so also the growth in size of the penis. These changes are due to the effect of the glands, pumping hormones into the blood stream.

The hormones which stimulate the development of the above male sexual characteristics are known as androgenic hormones. In mammals with periodicity in breeding, testosterone is secreted only during the breeding season, but in man and monkeys who have no periodicity, this hormone is secreted continuously. It is interesting to note that under-nutrition and lack of Vitamin B diminish the formation of this hormone. Correct nutrition and adequate intake of Vitamin B are therefore essential in the diet to maintain normal potency. Testosterone is responsible for retaining the secondary male characteristics in adulthood and for emotional well-being.

CONTROL OF TESTICULAR ACTIVITY: The growth and activity of the testes are controlled by the anterior pituitary gland, the leader of the endocrine orchestra. The anterior pituitary secretes a hormone which stimulates the interstitial cells of the testes which manufacture testosterone. The testes normally inhibit secretion of the pituitary hormone, gonadotrophin. The hormone from the thyroid gland situated at the root of the neck, is responsible for proper development of the secondary sex characteristics.

SOMATIC CHANGES: Children grow more rapidly during puberty and adolescence than at any other period except the first year. There is a sudden spurt in height, weight and muscular development though there are wide variations in the growth pattern. Some children mature early, others late, while some may follow a pattern which is midway between these two groups. Usually girls mature about two years earlier than boys do, and their growth pattern is also different. Pre-adolescent girls suddenly grow twice as fast during this period for about two years. They are taller, weigh more and are more mature than boys of the same age. This sudden difference in growth produces a tremendous sense of inferiority and resentment in boys towards girls. Boys at this stage therefore dislike girls and their company, and prefer to keep to themselves. The growth pattern in boys is also different. Some mature early, others late. For example, if the height of two boys, both 11 years old, is the same, the early maturer at 14 may be 10 centimetres taller than the late maturer, but the latter may then grow faster and both the boys may again be of equal height at the age of 17. These differences in the rate of growth can affect boys psychologically. The boy who matures late is teased in his school, feels inferior and worries whether he will ever develop normally. The same applies to the weight of the early and late maturing boy. He, therefore, faces problems because of these normal differences in attaining maturity.

PSYCHIC CHANGES: At puberty the child becomes an adolescent, capable of reproduction. The sex instinct which was up to now autoerotic or objectless becomes heterosexual (directed towards the opposite sex) and crystallizes into one unit with the sole aim of reproduction. In the male, the erect penis becomes capable of penetrating the vagina and discharging semen into it. The intensity of sexual desire depends upon the endocrine pattern, heredity and the type of environment in which the child has grown into adolescence. The oestrogens and the androgens circulating in the blood determine sexual arousal and desire, with heredity playing an important role. Fathers with low sexual capacity generally have children whose sexual performance is also below par. The type of environment also has a considerable bearing on sexual capacity. If the child has been brought up on correct lines he will have normal sexual desires. On the other hand, faulty sexual upbringing suppresses or inhibits the child's sexual urge, which may necessitate treatment before he can function normally.

The adolescent develops a more mature love-sex feeling than the young boy. He may develop a strong attraction for a member of the opposite sex like his teacher, a film star, or an athlete. Generally, the object of attraction is older than himself and may be single or married. He loves, respects and adores his loved one but does not expect a reciprocal response. Often he imagines her to be his wife and has imaginary intercourse. This thought can lead to masturbation. The fantasy figure during masturbation becomes his new object of love.

Puberty is a period of crisis for many youngsters. The adolescent is not only self-conscious but also sex-conscious. He passes through a period of turmoil and unrest which are often associated with anxiety symptoms brought about by a disorder of body image. There is heightened self-awareness in his mind due to the tremendous physical, sexual and emotional changes taking place in his body. He often worries about the slow development of his body. He is still thin and short with long lanky legs and narrow chest, while the neighbour's daughter has suddenly blossomed into a smart young lady. His best pal in school has shot up 5 centimetres while his height has remained the same. He is worried about his not yet broken voice and feels shy talking on the telephone. Another source of worry is the absence of axillary hair in the armpits and consciousness about gynaecomastia (prominent breasts). The universal fear among adolescents is about the size of the testes and the penis. His friends have told him that the larger the penis the better the sexual act, and the bigger the testes the more virile the man. Modern civilization has always laid false stress on bigness for male virility.

Fear about his potency is the commonest outcome of these factors. He compares himself with an imaginary virile Casanova and has doubts about himself. His views on normal anatomy and physiology as learnt from misinformed friends or parents are often distorted and wrong. He may also fail to accept his new self, because his mother subconsciously wants him to remain her darling little boy.

The other important change during this period is the tremendous sense of power that the youngster develops and which needs to be channelised. In modern society adults bring up their children in the belief that 'little children should be seen and not heard.' This attitude produces tremendous frustration. The young adolescent longs to behave like a grow-up and shake off the shackles of parental authority and control.

Failure to understand the adolescent's deep desire to act like an adult in society results in delinquency. Instead of normal healthy outlets through sports, games, education and work he rebels against society and normal social behaviour. The delinquency may take various forms. He may become a member of a gang aimlessly loitering about to pass time between adolescence and marriage. Some of these gangs may indulge in antisocial activities like eve-teasing, stealing, rowdiness, looting and arson.

Sexual promiscuity is also common among adolescents in search of kicks and thrills. The sex instinct becomes more demanding and sexual outlets can take different forms. Some resort to call girls and sex with them is initiated in a very crude way. It is often difficult for such an adolescent to establish sexual rapport with his wife in later years, who is quite often shocked by his unnatural behaviour on the first night. It is also easy for an adolescent moving in gangs to become a homosexual as a ready-made contact is at hand and the trials and tribulations of dating girls who may not play the game are dispensed with. The more violent types rape young girls and get into trouble with the law. In the countryside, bestiality is often practised.

The commonest cause for abnormal adolescent behaviour is lack of opportunity to utilise excess energy. The tremendous sense of power which accompanies puberty must have a healthy outlet and adults should provide opportunities in the form of sports, games, hobbies and group discussions to take care of this innate restlessness and aggression. One of the commonest causes of adolescent misbehaviour in modern society is that teenagers are not treated as grown-ups. In general, individuals tend to behave as we accept them. A dog usually bites a nervous man because he expects to be bitten. Similarly, because society brands an adolescent's high spirits as antisocial, he becomes a rebel. The treatment of antisocial behaviour lies in socio-therapy of the individual, the group, the local community and society.

PARENTAL CONTROL: During adolescence parents should give more freedom to their children, encourage them to think independently and make decisions. If the mother keeps the son tied to her apron strings and the father makes the daughter dependent on him, the man becomes impotent and the woman frigid and incapable of loving anyone else except the parents. It is suicidal for mothers to advise their sons to 'treat all women as your sisters.' It is the surest foundation for future impotency. Parents should also desist from telling their children that sex is immoral.

SEXUAL OUTLETS FOR THE ADOLESCENT: Free indulgence in sex is not permitted in our societies. In primitive and some Western societies, free sex is normal while in our culture, a school- or college-going boy or girl is not permitted sex till he or she marries. What can he do till then? What are the alternatives to free sexual expression? The easiest remedy is to masturbate. Other alternatives are: (1) Self-control; (2) Repression; and (3) Sublimation.

SELF-CONTROL: This is the ideal solution. The individual accepts that the sexual instinct is a normal biological urge in all humans but its expression is disallowed till marriage in our society. Every society has its own laws and code for the sex instinct. If a man attempts a solution outside legitimate bounds he comes into conflict with the normal code and is shunned by society. What can he do? He can convert the sexual energy into physical energy by playing outdoor games like football, hockey, badminton and tennis or take up an absorbing hobby or become involved in charitable and social uplift activities.

REPRESSION: As instinct unable to find natural expression results in mental tension or conflict which is a painful experience for the individual. He instinctively suppresses the urge, pushing it from the conscious into the unconscious. Such an individual may be abnormal in adult life.

Let me illustrate with a case report. Michael, a 29-year-old businessman, married for three years, consulted me about his inability to consummate his marriage. A clinical examination did not show any organic lesion and the laboratory tests were normal. The patient's mother, a very strict, religious-minded lady had impressed on him from childhood, 'My moppet, I want you to be a great man one day. If you love me, my son, promise me that you will never touch a girl or think about her. Sex is dirty. Almighty God is always watching us. If ever you break your promise you will commit a sin against Him.' The young man was so closely watched by his mother that apart from masturbating he had no other sexual outlet. When Michael married he found himself impotent. Every time he attempted intercourse he was seized by the fear that 'Almighty God is watching' and 'sex is dirty'. The inhibitions naturally produced complete loss of erection and impotence.

This is a typical example of how a mother can, through faulty sexual upbringing unwittingly make her child impotent when he grows up. I am confident that if the mother knew the harm she was doing to her child she would never have repressed the normal sexual instinct in Michael.

SUBLIMATION: This is an unconscious mental process by which the individual redirects the instinctive sexual energy into a different channel. He thus avoids a conflict between the demand of an instinct for expression and his ideals of life which prevent it. Sublimation of the sexual instinct is often resorted to by a person without realising it. For example, an inventor can convert his sexual energy into an invention, an artist into his paintings, and an author into his books.

To conclude, the driving force in an individual is provided by the instincts. The natural expression of an instinct is the ideal outlet but it is not always possible in life as we live it. Control and temporary sublimation are healthy alternatives when natural expression of the instinct is not possible. Repression of an instinct is harmful and might cause a personality defect.

Sexually transmitted diseases

Adolescents should be told about venereal diseases. But morbid stories should never be recounted to impressionable adolescents as fear of venereal disease also produces impotence. To help non-professional readers, here is an account of the four important venereal diseases; syphilis, gonorrhoea, soft sore, and herpes genitalis.

The mode of infection in almost all cases is through intercourse with an infected partner. The organisms causing these infections can also gain entry into the body through minor skin or mucosal abrasions. Such an infection is called extragenital infection and can occur on the finger, lip, tongue or breast.

SYPHILIS is a venereal infection by a spirochaetal organism which can infect any tissue or organ of the body. The initial lesion is the chancre, which appears on the penis, the labia, or the cervix about three or four weeks after contact with an infected individual. There is also enlargement of the surrounding lymph glands. Unfortunately, in some cases the chancre heals without treatment, lulling the patient into false security. The untreated disease progresses slowly but surely to the second and third stage, involving almost every tissue of the human body—the skin, mucous membranes of the lips and cheek, bone joints, heart, liver, brain and spinal cord. It is therefore most important to take proper treatment and check the disease's progress at the initial stage.

GONORRHOEA is a venereal infection caused by a bacillus called *Neisseria gonorrhoeae*. The diseased mucous membrane of the male genito-urinary tract causes a discharge from the penile urethra and a burning sensation at the tip of the penis. The severe burning while passing urine, the discharge and the painful inflammation at the tip of the penis bring the patient to the doctor, unlike syphilis where the patient does not bother about the painless sore on his penis.

INGUINAL GRANULOMA is the third venereal disease, and its incubation period is eight to twelve weeks. It produces lesions on the skin or mucous membrane of the genitalia or perineal area, and an enlargement of the surrounding lymph glands.

HERPES GENITALIS: The latest addition to the unholy family of venereal diseases is herpes. There are several types of herpes virus. Herpes Zoster, also known as shingles, causes inflammation in the nerve roots in the regions supplied by a nerve. At first, small blisters appear along with a rash which is painful or stinging. The rash usually occurs on the face or back and the infection clears up in two or three weeks in most instances. The other type, also called herpes type two, produces painful blisters on the genitalia, and can affect both sexes. The mouth and other mucous membranes may be infected. In the males the blisters appear on the glans penis. They dry up after a week or so but unlike type 1 the vesicles keep on recurring, every three or four weeks. The genital type of herpes is transmitted by sexual contact and in the West has become a common venereal disease. There is no specific treatment for this viral scourge apart from small-pox vaccination at intervals of a week or two, 8 to 10 times, and large doses of Vitamin B 12 injections.

PREVENTION: Avoidance of illicit sexual intercourse is the surest prevention, but this is easily preached but difficult to practise. Pre-marital intercourse is on the increase in most modern societies, resulting in a corresponding increase in venereal diseases all over the world. It is therefore imperative that every adolescent is told what precautions are necessary to prevent venereal infection. The standard rubber condom is the most effective but protects only the covered parts. The individual should immediately after intercourse pass some urine and wash the genital organs with soap and water and apply 33 per cent calomel ointment with lanolin on the genitals.

Modern sexual trends in adolescents

Civilised society has not provided any legal and moral sexual outlet for the adolescent when he needs it most. Sexual desire is strongest in boys from 14 to 18 years. All that society offers the sex-starved adolescent is continence and chastity till he gets married. 'Be a good boy and keep away from the forbidden fruit' is the parental advice from the days of the garden of Eden, which few modern adolescents follow.

In olden days, the basis for morality in the adolescent was fear of pre-marital sex being a sin, and fear of pregnancy in the female. These fears do not beset the present generation. Religious leaders are also moving with the times, and no longer preach that pre-marital sex is sin. The contraceptive revolution has made safe contraceptives easily available and eliminated the threat of unwanted pregnancies. Lastly, modern women, especially in the West, demand equality with men in all matters including sex. The previous double standards, where the man was permitted a certain sexual liberty but not the woman, are no longer operative.

All these factors have led to a tremendous increase in pre-marital sex among adolescents who no longer consider it immoral. Such experiments in free sex have been carried out in primitive tribes and the West.

The advocates of free sex aver that it removes the guilt feeling about sex and ultimately results in better adjuted sexual partners in marriage. We still do not have conclusive evidence that the Western experiment in free sex is an unqualified success. The divorce rate has remained the same. But there is an increase in extra-marital relationships and foster homes and orphanages have more children today than formerly because they have no parents to look after them. The West itself is having second thoughts about the wisdom of free sex.

3

PREVENTION OF IMPOTENCE IN ADULTS

A sexual pattern finally establishes itself in adults. Marriage usually takes place during this period and the majority of males switch over from masturbation or occasional intercourse to regular coitus. The prevention of impotence is therefore important in this age group.

The factors that are primarily responsible for producing sexual inadequacy are: (1) lack of knowledge about the anatomy and physiology of the sex organs; (2) fear that masturbation and nocturnal emissions have caused impotence; (3) fear of performance; (4) belief that erection never fails; (5) indulgence in competitive sex; (6) failure to communicate with your female partner; (7) avoiding sex; (8) fear of venereal disease; (9) inhibition during sex; and (10) sublimation.

KNOWLEDGE: To prevent impotence in adolescents and adults the first and foremost need is knowledge of the normal anatomy and physiology of the male genital organs, the female genital organs, and sexual intercourse. It is regrettable that even medical students are ignorant about the normal anatomy and physiology of the genital organs. In spite of a tremendous awakening on the subject, the basic knowledge of sex and sexual physiology is still an unexplained chapter. There are many doctors who are eager to learn and help their patients but have never been taught sex and sexuality, nor are good books on sex easily available. If one wants to play cricket or golf, one first learns the rudiments of the game from a book. The same is true of sex. It does not come naturally, but is a learning process (see Chapter 3).

To understand the anatomy and physiology of the male genital organs, re-read Chapter 4. I repeat that potency is a gift of God to all men. Erection is possible from the cradle to the grave and nothing can extinguish it if the correct sexual attitude and training have been imparted.

For knowledge of female anatomy and physiology, re-read Chapter 5. Most males know something about their penis or testes, but are not only ignorant but completely put off by the female genital organs. For successful coitus, knowledge of female anatomy is vital. The male should also remember that the female responds best to touch and is quickly aroused by the skilful use of his hands.

FEAR OF SO-CALLED HARMFUL EFFECTS OF MASTURBATION AND NOCTURNAL EMISSION: Masturbation is the commonest sexual outlet in the adolescent (see Chapter 12). Most young men have masturbated at some time or other. As I have told you before, 'Ninety-nine per cent of young men masturbate and the remaining one per cent are liars.' It has been conclusively proved that masturbation by itself produces no harmful effects. It is the guilt or fear about masturbation which damages the individual's sensitive nervous system. Masturbation never produces impotence if it is guilt-free and is used as an outlet when sex with a woman is not possible.

Nocturnal emission is another normal sexual outlet, common in single males between adolescence and marriage. Psychic stimulation can produce erection and orgasm. During sleep, the individual is not so inhibited and therefore can have an erection and orgasm. I have known few male patients who have never had a nocturnal emission in their life. Nocturnal emissions do not result in impotence. It is the false fear of frequent emissions damaging the sexual system that causes inadequacy.

FEAR OF PERFORMANCE: This is the commonest cause of sexual disability. The moment fear enters your mind, erection dies down. One is not afraid of other natural processes like breathing or the heartbeats stopping or the urinary bladder or the bowels not functioning. Why then have such an irrational and morbid fear of penis failure? It also comes naturally. So stop doubting your powers of erection.

INABILITY TO PENETRATE: During the first few attempts at intercourse it is common for a healthy man to have trouble in penetration because of inexperience and fear of injuring his partner during defloration. The woman should for some time guide the penis with her hands into the vagina.

KNOW THAT MOST MEN FAIL OCCASIONALLY: Your penis is a temperamental organ. It is not fail-safe. You may find that sometimes it remains limp and lifeless and there is nothing you can do to make it erect. Please don't pull the alarm chain of anxiety and think that the end has come! Accept your temporary impotence as normal. The failure of erection may be due to tiredness, stress, too much alcohol, mental preoccupation or an attempt at intercourse without a strong desire for it.

INDULGENCE IN COMPETITIVE SEX: Many performance-minded individuals are dead serious about sex and go through the motions as if it were a competition match that must be fought and won! Many young men's attitude is 'Grit your teeth and you can do it'. Sex is for enjoyment, so laugh and be carefree and relaxed. You can never enjoy sex if you are glum and serious.

LACK OF COMMUNICATION WITH YOUR PARTNER: It is important that you talk and communicate with your partner and find out her likes and dislikes, though initially, she may be shy and non-communicative. It is better if you verbalize your needs. She may later open up and tell you what she wants or, as women often use sign language, she may look at or touch the part she desires to be caressed. For example, during coitus, she may keep her hand on her breast to indicate that you should caress it.

AVOIDING SEX: All bodily organs function best if used regularly. The muscles of the leg and thigh atrophy if one does not use the legs for a fortnight. If the fingers are bandaged they become stiff. One can say the same about the penis. If not regularly used it becomes lazy, and stays limp when intercourse is attempted. If sex is not indulged in regularly, the male may find difficulty in erection and if he abstains for very long he may become impotent and the penis may even shrink in size.

It is a wrong belief that regular and frequent intercourse leads to loss of vitality and premature ageing. Indulgence in sexual intercourse when there is active desire is the best natural tonic. It refreshes mind and body and tones up the entire system. I have come across individuals who were wrongly forbidden sexual intercourse because of a minor organic disease. A patient aged 40 had suffered from typhoid, and general weakness followed the infection, which is usual. He was advised not to indulge in intercourse. The healthy, strapping, virile male became a complete physical and mental wreck! I had difficulty convincing him that sexual intercourse could never harm him. Longevity in males is often associated with intense sexual desire throughout their lives. To conclude, the preaching of moderation in sex is the greatest myth. Each individual should go entirely by his own desires.

Avoid preoccupation. A male in order to have successful intercourse has to perform and produce an erection, unlike the woman who is at the receiving end. 'Will I or won't I get an erection?,' the diffident male wonders. These negative thoughts are inimical to sex. Sex should always be carefree. Like any game you play, practice makes you perfect. If my golfing friends, whom I find enthusiastically swinging golf clubs in their bedrooms when I visit them, devoted one-tenth of the time, effort and energy they spend on golf to the perfection of their sexual relationships, it would pay them rich dividends.

FEAR OF VENEREAL DISEASES: This often haunts many males even after marriage. Every time they go to bed they think they might catch the dreaded infection and be impotent forever. Percy told me, 'Doctor, my college friend Ramesh has put the fear of God in me. He had the works—both syphilis and gonorrhoea—when he visited a call girl. "No woman is safe. She can infect you," Ramesh warned me. Ever since, I have been haunted by fear, and cannot go to bed even with my wife.'

Have yourself checked by a doctor before marriage. If Percy and his fiancee had had themselves medically examined before marriage and if Percy had seen a doctor about his fear of venereal disease, their marriage would have started on a happy, confident note.

You may have read reports about penicillin-resistant gonorrhoea in the Far East but you have nothing to worry about if you take basic precautions, if you must indulge in a fling or two outside marriage.

Get yourself treated at the first sign of a urethral discharge or a pimple. It is unpardonable if you do not take treatment and infect your wife.

INHIBITIONS DURING SEX: Be your normal, natural self, be a good citizen certainly, but do not inhibit your natural instincts all the time. Inhibition is the greatest enemy of sexuality. The mother's darling is a well-behaved, goody-goody boy but certainly not the ideal lover. Modern civilization, with its curbs on natural sexual desire, has led to inhibitions. For normal sexuality to develop, these inhibitions in the form of brakes on sexuality have got to be removed.

AVOID SUBLIMATION: In modern societies, sex is often sublimated in different ways. The millionaire who has set his heart on making a million has sublimated his sexuality for the sake of making money. A religious-minded individual who thinks sex is dirty or messy or is against the diverse laws of nature has also sublimated his sexuality and redirected it into channels like meditation or asceticism. The compulsive worker who works 14 to 16 hours a day and thinks he has got to be busy continually has also sublimated his sexuality.

PREVENTION OF DISEASES: To remain healthy and potent it is necessary that the important 'killers' like coronary heart disease, diabetes and peptic ulcer are prevented. Prevention of these diseases depends upon a thorough periodic medical examination which those over 40 should undergo at least once a year. This examination should include a routine physical check-up, evaluation of dietary, smoking and drinking habits, a complete pathological test of blood, urine and stool, and an electro-cardiogram and X-ray if necessary, as well as an assessment of the sexual pattern, so that the doctor can give advice on any change in sexual performance. Individuals who have a family history of diabetes should be particularly careful about having their blood and urine sugar checked every six months, so that it can be detected and controlled at the initial stage. Neglected diabetes is one of the commonest causes of organic impotence at this age.

REDUCE MENTAL STRAIN: Each of us is blessed by nature with a fixed amount of nervous energy which can be utilized for work, recreation or sex. This is determined partly by heredity and partly by upbringing and habits. All of us cannot be a Jawaharlal Nehru or a Winston Churchill, with boundless energy.

The competitive business economy of today and the tremendous time and effort that an individual has to put in to reach his goal produces excessive strain and tension. He spends a tiring and worrying day at the office, and returns home exhausted and ready to drop into bed after dinner. Sexual intercourse requires a lot of energy and vitality. In order to maintain sexual alertness one should not be fagged out at the end of the day.

CONVERSION OF SEXUAL ENERGY: In the good old days, one became a millionaire at 60. Then there were millionaires at 50. Now we have a race of super robots who are millionaires at 30 and 40. From sunrise to sunset, these individuals talk of nothing but how to double or treble their fortunes. They have converted their sexual drive into a lust for power and money, thus diminishing their potency. One cannot obviously burn the candle at both ends. Money can buy a woman's body physically but only male virility can earn her everlasting love.

Most important, cultivate a positive attitude and have faith in your potency. As I have emphasised time and again, erection in the male on which normal potency depends is present from the cradle to the grave. It is the conditioning by modern civilization which has produced doubts in the minds of older men. In the Victorian Age the age of 50 was the accepted limit for becoming impotent. Naturally, this fear played a big part in producing increased impotence. Apart from the physiological changes produced by age which have been described earlier, remember that potency does not diminish as you grow older.

4

PREVENTION OF IMPOTENCE IN MIDDLE AGE

Wives are young men's mistresses, companions
for middle age, and old men's nurses.

FRANCIS BACON

Bacon brilliantly portrays the conventional thinking of society about the sexless years which are in store for the middle-aged and the elderly. 'My husband is getting old,' said Roma at a cocktail party. 'He comes home, lazes around for a while, has dinner, watches TV and is off to bed.' She looked at me and asked, 'What else can a man of 50 do?' She was shocked when I told her, 'Everything he was doing at 40.' The media and folklore constantly sway the impressionable minds of middle-aged males that their manliness is gradually lost after 40. If they consult doctors, the standard reply is, 'What do you expect at your age?' The deflated individual just grins and miserably bears his loss of sexual power.

Sexual response in middle age

The anatomical and physiological response of the middle-aged to sexual stimulation are slightly different from those of adolescents and young adults. It is necessary that the middle-aged male knows about these changes so that he is not alarmed or frightened but accepts them as normal physiological changes prevalent in his age group. These changes will be described in detail in the next section.

The young adult has an immediate erection within seconds of effective sexual stimulation. In middle age, erection takes a little longer and I have known cases where it is necessary for the female partner to caress the penis with her hands before erection takes place. This normal delayed response worries many individuals and, if the male becomes self-conscious, it can lead to impotence. However, erection once achieved is maintained till ejaculation. Occasionally, if there is a distraction and the erection is lost, it is difficult to regain immediately. This is in sharp contrast to the younger age group where erection if lost is regained almost immediately. The middle-aged man has to wait for some time till the refractory period is over. He may even have to postpone intercourse at that given moment. If he is aware that this is a natural phenomenon in some individuals and that erection will return after some time, he will not worry. Some do not reach full erection except just before ejaculation, though this is more common in old age. If these males find difficulty in penetration because the penis is not fully erect, the use of a lubricant (K.Y. Jelly) on the penis just before intercourse enables the penis to glide easily into the vagina. Once in the vagina the erection naturally becomes stronger. Middle-aged males usually do not suffer from premature ejaculation as the sexual tension is not as high as in young adults and as they become experienced sexually they do not tend to come off quickly. The orgasm and ejaculation are less intense as compared to young adults.

Erection is usually lost more quickly after ejaculation in middle age. The refractory period (inability to perform again) gets more prolonged as age advances. The refractory period varies widely. Some middle-aged men, accustomed to a high sexual outlet since the days of their youth and free of inhibitions or debilitating disease, continue to enjoy a high sexual outlet. There is a sudden increase in frequency of impotence in the age group 40-45. In many studies there were at least six times more cases of sexual disability in this age group compared to adolescents and adults. It was interesting to observe that diminution of sexual power was more noticeable among top executives and senior management as compared to their staff members. What are the causes of this sudden increase in impotence in this age group?

Causes of impotence in middle age
(1) Fear of failure; (2) sexual boredom; (3) 'that tired feeling'; (4) overeating and obesity; (5) alcohol; (6) excessive strain; and (7) organic diseases.

FEAR OF FAILURE: Middle age is a period of uncertainty and self-doubt in many men. It is caused by a feeling of insecurity. An individual may worry about his health. The other cause of insecurity and worry is that he is getting old and has a feeling of failure. He had high hopes of success at the start of his career which have been dashed to the ground. He now feels frustrated and his personality disintegrates. In a number of individuals, apart from job frustration, lack of financial insecurity in old age also enters the picture. Will he be able to maintain the same standard of living when he retires? Last but not the least, he has always been conditioned to the thought that potency diminishes with age and therefore fears that the days of his potency are now numbered. 'Let me make the best use of these last few years,' he says to himself, and to prove his potency he attempts sex outside marriage, which quite often results in failure.

To conclude, therefore, one has doubts about one's health, financial and job insecurity, and is haunted by the accepted belief that erection disappears with age. These factors increase in geometrical progression to 'I am now impotent for the rest of my life.'

SEXUAL BOREDOM: This is the giant killer of sexual arousal in the male. After ten to fifteen years of married life the male is tired of the same old sexual routine with his female partner. Variety is the spice of life and I would advise wives to remember that variety maintains sexual excitement and promotes virility.

'THAT TIRED FEELING': 'I am dead tired, darling. I had a very exhausting day at the office,' he says and slumps into a reclining chair, smoking a cigarette as he sips his cup of tea. He has neither the time nor the inclination to inquire about his wife, who has eagerly waited for his homecoming all day. She is naturally disappointed and dejected. Fatigue in the male and frustration in the female are the greatest enemies of sex. It is really amazing how a modern healthy man sitting at a desk for seven or eight hours gets so physically and mentally drained of energy at the end of the day.

OVEREATING AND OBESITY: The metabolism slows down during middle age and the individual who was used to an active outdoor life in his younger days becomes a sedentary worker in an office. There is thus a reduction in the total calories required to maintain ideal weight. Yet many individuals tend to overeat during middle age. This may be due to social and business entertainment or a higher financial status which permits indulgence in calorie-rich delicacies like cakes, sweets and pastries. A number of people overeat to compensate for emotional stress. Overeating results in obesity and sexual disability. In such cases, by merely reducing the weight of an obese individual, the sexual power returns to normal. A 45-year-old 170-centimetre medium-frame executive weighing 83 kg. consulted me for diminishing sexual power. He had put on about ten kg. in two years. Apart from overweight due to excessive intake of carbohydrates in his diet, the clinical examination and blood chemistry were normal. He was not suffering from diabetes. I put him on a low-carbohydrate reducing diet and assured him that his potency would return. He lost 12 kilos in four months and his sexual performance improved tremendously. Obesity is an important contributing factor in reducing potency in the middle age group. I have observed that active, virile men are never obese. The carbohydrate metabolism is related to virility in man. In diabetics, with derangement of the carbohydrate metabolism, impotence is common.

OVER-INDULGENCE IN ALCOHOL: A small quantity of alcohol relaxes an individual and removes inhibitions but imbibing large quantities depresses the brain and reaction centres in the spinal cord, resulting in impotence (see Chapter 14).

EXCESSIVE STRESS: I have stated that modern man is a tired man in spite of his sitting in an office for seven to eight hours. Most modern executives are engaged in a perpetual rat-race with an anxious eye on the top of the ladder. The industrial revolution has produced tensions. There is keen competition for advancement. For example, there might be a conference of all the salesmen in an organisation with one salesman pitted against the rest as the sales in his area are not as good as those of the others. In trying to improve his sales against heavy odds, the poor man undergoes such intense tension that it could ultimately result not only in a heart attack or ulcer but also impotence. Stress is the deadly enemy of potency. Innumerable individuals who are continuously under stress in the twentieth century, stimulate the sympathetic nerve which inhibits erection. (see Chapter 4, 'Nerve supply of the Penis').

Many individuals spend their lives doing dull, monotonous jobs which also lead to stress, tension, frustration, boredom and sexual inadequacy.

ORGANIC DISEASES: Coronary thrombosis, peptic ulcer, chronic bronchitis, leukaemia and cancer often make their first appearance during this period in life. The near-perfect human machine starts creaking and protesting against the years of abuse and craves for attention. Many of us care ten times more for our car than our body. We take care there is not a single scratch, we get the oils changed, we get it serviced every month. Yet we seem to care very little for our most precious possession—our body.

Prevention of impotency
A little time and effort spent on prevention is more rewarding than

undergoing the humiliation of impotence and getting it treated. Nothing stimulates the human engine and charges it with vim and vitality as normal intercourse. It makes the man tick. It refreshes his mind and body and gives him a new lease of life. In fact, normal healthy intercourse is only possible for a man with a 'healthy mind in a healthy body'.

Having outlined the causes of impotence in the middle-aged and the normal physiological and anatomical changes that take place in the sexual cycle, the necessary precautions for prevention of impotence are: (1) faith in potency; (2) practising variations in sex; (3) keeping fit; (4) avoiding overeating and maintaining ideal weight; (5) avoiding excessive alcohol and smoking; and (6) coping with stress.

HAVE FAITH IN POTENCY: Nature has given the power of erection to every man from the cradle to the grave. The heart keeps on beating till we die. The lungs keep on functioning as long as there is life. Apart from disease or degeneration these organs are built to last a lifetime. Man accepts this as his birthright and is not normally conscious of the heart-beat or breathing. It is only when there is a disease or disorder that he becomes aware of his internal organs. On the other hand, most middle-aged men accept loss of sexuality as a natural phenomenon. 'Ramesh is getting old,' says the wife with a twinkle in her eye and a chuckle in her voice, to the merriment of her other girl-friends and the embarrassment of Ramesh. He accepts the situation. 'I cannot fight the inevitable,' he thinks and gives up his potency. It worries him a great deal, consciously or subconsciously. He seeks solace by saying to himself, 'What cannot be cured must be endured.'

I repeat that the middle-aged male must cultivate a confident, positive attitude and have faith in his potency. He must not give it up. Like the heart and the lungs, which function as long as he lives, he must remember that nature has given potency to every man from the cradle to the grave. He must use it, so as not to lose it.

PRACTISE VARIATIONS IN SEX: If we ate the same food every day, and followed the same routine, life would lose its charm and soon get monotonous. The same applies to sex. It soon loses its novelty and thrill. Here I would like to emphasise to women that they should be ready to explore new horizons and provide both themselves and their male partners with much-needed variety in sex. Every sex act can be a new and stimulating expression of love. All that is necessary is the knowledge and will to elevate it from a drab routine to an exhilarating experience. For details of the techniques of sexual intercourse the reader may refer to pages 104 to 111.

Man is polygamous by nature, and primitive societies are not bound by monogamy. It is modern society and the institution of marriage which have virtually bound a single male to a single female, 'for better for worse,... till death do us part'. This was forced in olden days by religion and control that the priestly class had over the masses. With the advent of the scientific revolution and the diminishing influence of religion there are marked changes in society. The contraceptive revolution separates sexual intercourse from reproduction and has had a tremendous social impact.

Dr. Helena Wright visualises a society where sexual relations before marriage would be socially approved, provided the couple is self-supporting or has the agreement of those who support them. After marriage 'we shall have to achieve a new kind of sexual relationship which is free from possessiveness and jealousy. Except when a child is to be conceived, fidelity to one partner will no longer be demanded.' Lest her ideas sound like an invitation to promiscuity, I should add that the first (and most difficult) item in Dr. Wright's new code is that 'no new sex relations should cause damage or distress to an existing one. Whether distress will in fact be caused must presumably be left to the two people concerned. Except for marriage and parenthood, all sexual relations in this new world are to be private.'

If man is to be bound down to the monogamous band-wagon it is necessary that his normal natural polygamous instincts, which he has inherited from his primate ancestors, are respected and the necessary variation provided. The problem of the male who is impotent with his wife but potent with other women stems from lack of interest in sex due to boredom.

BE FIT: One of the causes of impotence in middle age is 'that tired feeling' which a number of males complain about. They wake up tired, go through the day tired, come home in the evening more tired and go to bed still more tired. Working hours have become shorter, office and factories have become more comfortable, modern man has more leisure, yet he complains of more tiredness! What are the causes of this tiredness? Is it the race against time? Is it emotional stress? Is it the boredom produced in modern factories and offices? Some daily physical exercise is a must for desk-bound workers to keep physically fit and active and mentally alert.

PREVENTING DISEASES: To remain healthy and potent it is necessary that the major 'killers' like coronary heart disease, diabetes and peptic ulcer are prevented. Prevention of these diseases depends upon a thorough medical examination which the elderly should undergo at least once a year. This examination should include a routine physical check-up, evaluation of dietary, smoking and drinking habits, a complete pathological test of blood, urine and stool, an electrocardiogram and X-ray when necessary, and most important, a proper evaluation of the sexual pattern, so that the doctor can advise if there is any change in sexual performance.

The carbohydrate metabolism is intimately connected with potency. Often impotency is the first symptom of raised blood sugar levels (especially two hours after taking glucose or having breakfast) and diabetes mellitus. The correction of raised blood sugar by diet or anti-diabetics restores potency to normal. Impotency in these cases is due to thickening or spasm of the arteries which supply blood to the penis. Diabetic neuritis also impairs the nerves of erection. Why the impaired carbohydrate metabolism produces the earliest changes in the penis in these unfortunate individuals is not known. But there are many diabetics of long standing whose potency is not appreciably affected. Individuals with a hereditary tendency towards diabetes should have their blood and urine sugar checked every six months so that if signs of sugar appear, it can be detected and controlled at the initial stage. Neglected diabetes is one of the commonest causes of organic impotence in this age group.

COPING WITH STRESS: Stress is the essence of life, the master-key to the lock of living. Unlock the mysteries of stress and you have mastered the art of living happily, and enjoying carefree, spontaneous sex—the noblest of nature's gifts to man. For coping with stress you may read my book *Rock Around The Clock*.

5

PREVENTION OF IMPOTENCE IN THE ELDERLY

*In men, the capacity for erection begins on the day
of birth and extinguishes with death.*

WILHELM STEKEL

Can old men be potent? Definitely yes, if they do not give up their potency and stop thinking that indulging in frequent sex leads to dissipation of energy and an early grave. The reverse is true. As Lorand has said. 'Persons with a pronounced sexual desire often reach advanced age.' I have known patients who are capable of normal sexual intercourse at the age of 75 or 80.

A young wife brought her 75-year-old husband, an active and successful businessman, for a check-up. 'Doctor, he wants sex every single day and occasionally even twice. I am terrified he might damage his heart and drop dead. I married him for companionship and security, not sex.' She waited. Proud as a peacock, her husband winked as he projected his manliness to me. How could I tell the wife that as she refused him, he had found himself a girl-friend in the office! I therefore impressed on the young lady that sex was the best anti-age tonic for her husband. There are many old men who have not lost the zeal for a shapely thigh or a sexy bosom. Even at the age of 94, the U.S. Supreme Court judge, Justice Oliver Wendell Holmes, had an eye for a pretty maiden. 'Ah!' he once sighed, admiring a lovely leg, 'What would I give to be seventy again!' The sexual exploits of Charlie Chaplin, making love twice or thrice a day, often three or four times a week when in his eighties, have become a legend.

Wilhelm Stekel states that 'nature has placed no limitation on man. The so-called licentious men like Louis XV, Tiberius and Retif de la Brettone were by popular standards dissipating their vital sexual energy yet they were virile all their life.' Retif de la Brettone was proud of his unusual potency. 'Not a single day passed but that I at least once rendered homage to Venus,' records Wilhelm Stekel in *Impotence in the Male*. However, society looks upon the few males who continue to be potent as freaks and often condemns them as lecherous and anti-social. You will say the cases I have quoted are exceptions. What about the vast majority of old men who live sexless lives? Read on and join the ranks of the virile again!

Causes and prevention

In the old days when men were prey to numerous infections and died young, they had the consolation of spending only a few sexless years. But with the advent of antibiotics, infections were conquered. No longer do individuals die from pneumonia or septic meningitis. With advances in the science of nutrition and preventive medicine, men live much longer today than they did at the turn of the century. For instance, in 1930 the average longevity of an Indian male was 30 years; it is now over 50 while an American male lives to be 75. It would therefore be a great shame if these men lived lifeless years without sex in their old age. In his investigations of the American male, Kinsey has found out that males who were most active sexually during adulthood were also active during middle and old age. However, if their desire was low from the very beginning, potency flickered out in later years. It is essential not only to grow old gracefully but also to maintain a healthy sexual tempo. The popular saying 'You are as old as you think' applies to a lot of individuals who think themselves old and become old.

By knowing the common causes of impotence in the elderly, we can take adequate steps to prevent it. The causes of impotence are: (1) lack of knowledge of the physiological changes in sexual response; (2) refraining from sexual activity; (3) mental attitudes; (4) belief in sexual myths; (5) fear; (6) organic diseases; (7) lack of exercise; (8) faulty diet; (9) excess alcohol; (10) inadequate sleep and intake of drugs; (11) fear that masturbation may cause harm; (12) abstinence; (13) boredom; (14) inability to cope with stress.

LACK OF KNOWLEDGE OF SEXUAL RESPONSE: Erection is present from the cradle to the grave, but physiological changes in the sexual responses become evident as we grow older. It is lack of scientific knowledge of these changes in the elderly that results in sexual inadequacy after 40 or 50. Men are generally obsessed with chronological age. We take it for granted that potency declines after 40. We grow up believeing this myth, which Dr. Harry Benjamin aptly calls the tyrannical rule of the calendar'. Masters and Johnson did a scientific study of the changes that take place in the sexual response cycle and found out that while erection is immediate in youth, in the aged it takes much longer and often requires the help of the female partner. Many men erroneously believe that they must have an instantaneous erection throughout their lives and that delay is a sign of impending impotency.

Dr Combard Kelly in *So You Think You're Impotent* describes the two types of erection which occur in men. In the cerebral type, a quick erection response takes place, generally in boys and young men. For example, a boy sees a beautiful girl or a picture of her or thinks of her and he gets an instantaneous erection. The impulse passes from the brain to the spinal cord and stimulates the nerves of erection and the penis. The second type of erection, generally prevalent in the middle-aged and the elderly, is called the reflex or tactile erection. Here erection does not take place generally from mental stimulation but from physical tactile stimulation. The female partner has to fondle the male organ before erection occurs or alternatively the male masturbates to get a hard-on. It is therefore essential to know about the normal delayed erection response in the elderly.

A 76-year-old businessman told me, 'Now my female partner supplies the stimulus for an erection. In my youth I could get immediately erect by looking at a female a mile away! But once erection takes place, it continues longer than in youth.' He went on musingly, 'In my young days, I was quick on the trigger. Now if I pull the trigger nothing happens. Previously the ramming rod was a mere showpiece for the partner. Now it is really useful, goes on and on at low peak.' The elderly male should not mount early if the female takes longer to come. This permits more prolonged love-play. Finally, as he does not ejaculate quickly, the female has a greater chance of reaching an orgasm. You should therefore be happy that nature and ageing have equipped you better to match the slower responses of the female.

REFRAINING FROM SEXUAL ACTIVITY: Many individuals at 40, 50 or 60 give up sex, believing that it is time for them to retire not only from the office but also sexually. All the organs in our body especially the penis work best if they are constantly used. 'Use it or lose it,' James

Fries of the Arthritis Clinic, Stanford University Medical Centre, advises his patients. Like all other organs, the penis also needs exercise to keep it in trim. So indulge in sex regularly and never surrender your potency.

ACT OLD AND YOU BECOME OLD: Many men in their fifties slow down physically, mentally and emotionally. They slow down their walking pace, do not climb stairs lest their hearts get damaged. This negative thinking produces unhealthy emotions like depression. They stop living and merely exist. The 'lazy' penis is the first to take advantage of this mental and physical lethargy and becomes limp and lifeless.

BELIEF IN SEXUAL MYTHS: Many men in our country are convinced that loss of vital bodily fluids like semen weakens them, and the seminal discharge during sex drains their vital fluids. 'My husband has given up sex,' Clara, wife of 60-year-old Vernon told me complacently, 'I entirely agree with his philosophy that just as we save money for a rainy day, he should save the vital fluids to live longer.'

Clara has strong supporters in our country as well as abroad. Dr.R.W. Bernard claims that semen contains a high concentration of spare vital constituents of our blood like lecithin, phosphorus, nucleoproteins, iron and calciums. With every seminal discharge during sexual intercourse, masturbation or nocturnal emission, these vital constituents are lost. The individual is depleted by such repetitive losses and feels run down, weak and exhausted. On the other hand he saves all these sparse constituents through abstinence. The logic behind this thinking: like a savings bank account, if you do not withdraw, balances accrue.

Nothing is further from the truth. The semen is like any other body fluid, say, the gastric or pancreatic juices. There is nothing special about it, except that it contains sperms, the creators of a new life. The chemical constituents of semen are constantly replenished from food. The semen that is discharged is stored in the accessory sex organs like the epididymis, the seminal vesicles and the prostate and does not come directly from the blood during intercourse.

Physiologists have proved that the body is self-regulating and the loss of semen is quickly restored in individuals eating a normal diet. The so-called weakness, loss of vitality and draining of energy is entirely due to psychological conditioning by popular myths. The earlier you give up the belief that semen is a vital fluid to be conserved, the better you will feel after sex.

FEAR: This is the greatest enemy of erection. 'Men are supposed to perform', is drilled by cultures of all ages and races. The elderly individual develops a deep concern about his virility and, beset by fear, is unable to have an erection and thinks he has become impotent. Besides, fear of old age grips most men. 'Old age is catching up with me,' said 55-year-old Sushil. 'Formerly I could stay awake till two or three at night and start work at eight in the morning. Now I am dead beat all day even if I come home shortly after midnight.' This fear stems from ignorance about the ageing process and male menopause, fear of incapacitating illnesses and organic diseases like heart attacks, strokes and impotence.

ORGANIC DISEASES: With ageing the body's resistance decreases, making men more vulnerable to diseases like high blood pressure, heart attacks, diabetes and arthritis. The evil day can be postponed by keeping yourself cheerful and happy and having regular check-ups.

THE HEART AND SEX: Faint heart never won fair lady, says an ancient proverb. The heart has since times immemorial been the symbol of life and love. Heart attack has become the No.1 20th century killer in the West. In India, it presently ranks third among the killers but with the conquest of infections and urbanisation and industrialisation, it is rapidly ascending the list. Is it any wonder that the elderly male worries whether sex will precipitate a heart attack or a stroke? The answer is definitely 'No', if the heart and blood pressure are normal and the individual indulges in sex with a partner of his age group. However, some males in their second childhood chase young birds to prove their manliness (during their first childhood they were content running after the winged ones!). High-pressure sexual activity in males who have suffered a heart attack or have high blood pressure is definitely detrimental to health.

HEART ATTACKS AND RESUMPTION OF SEX: 'My sex life has ended with my heart attack,' 55-year-old Joseph told me mournfully and asked what he should do to relieve his sexual tensions. 'Where is your wife?

Doesn't live in Bombay?' I asked. 'She is here,' replied Joseph, 'but my G.P. has advised me to refrain from sex after my attack.' There are many unfortunate Josephs for whom sex has been prohibited or who have themselves practised abstinence after the heart attack thinking that it is the right thing to do and who needlessly suffer sexual tensions. According to Dr. Heiman Helterstein of Cleveland Work Classification Centre, 'The vast majority are able to resume after a couple of months.' However, each person should be assessed individually depending on his heart condition, blood pressure, the type of sex he wants and his emotional make-up. In the early stage after a heart attack, the woman-on-top position is the least strenuous and mutually satisfying.

Here is the story of Mr. M who had a heart attack when the money-spinning medical toy—Intensive Care Unit—had not invaded Bombay hospitals. I treated him at his residence with day and night nurses in attendance. On the eleventh day, I paid a surprise visit in the afternoon. The sister on duty said, 'Please wait. Mr. M has a lady visitor and he has asked me not to disturb him.' I told the nurse that I was in a hurry so she knocked on the door. No answer for ten minutes whilst I waited impatiently with a frown. At last the door opened and a 35-year-old lady came out and said demurely, 'You can see him, Doctor.' I could tell by the glint in her eyes and her disordered face that my patient had made love to her. I was frightened out of my wits and expected to find him dead as I entered the bedroom. Mr. M was laying sheepishly on the hurriedly made-up bed. His ruddy face still had an after-glow, yet it was relaxed and the depression following the attack had momentarily disappeared. 'Forgive me, Rusi, I have been a bad boy. I promise you I will never do it again,' he said, wiping the perspiration on his face and body with a towel. 'I thought you would prohibit sex for the rest of my life. I had to do it, just once before I die.' I felt his pounding pulse, greatly disturbed by what my patient had done. 'Don't look so sad and worried,' he chided me. 'I am going to make it. Nothing is going to happen,' he said, giving me his right arm to take his blood pressure. M was right. His heart grumbled for a day or two but eventually he made an uneventful recovery.

Not long ago, a patient recovering from a heart attack believed that it was the end of his sex life. If he dared to ask his doctor, the standard reply was, 'Better forget it. It might precipitate another heart attack.' 'Today, the physician far from prohibiting it, will actually prescribe sex for him,' says Dr. E.B. Mozes in *Living Beyond Your Attack*. He states, 'Normal sex life undoubtedly represents the most satisfactory means for release of inner tension.'

Diabetes is frequently seen in this age group and an unusually high rate of impotence is observed in diabetic men. Dr. Klebanow and Dr. Macleod, reporting in *Fertility and Sterility*, state that diabetic impotence in their patients took different forms. About one-third of patients complained not of weakness of erection but difficulty in ejaculation, which became progressive until complete loss of function resulted. Another one-third of the diabetic patients had retrograde ejaculation and discharged into the bladder because the nerves closing the bladder neck during ejaculation were affected. The remaining one-third became progressively impotent (see 'Diabetes in the Middle-Aged').

LACK OF EXERCISE: According to Dr. Ernest Jolk, 'Regular exercise is an anti-age antibiotic,' and keeps a man young. An individual must do regular hard physical exercise like jogging, running, walking or playing games, depending upon his liking. Walking is the simplest and safest exercise throughout life. The longest-living pockets of people are usually in mountainous regions where constant walking up and down hills in fresh air exerts a powerful anti-age effect.

FAULTY NUTRITION: As we grow old, and particularly if we live on our own, we tend to consume more carbohydrates and neglect the intake of proteins, which contain the essential amino acids—the building blocks of life. More carbohydrates are consumed as they are easily and cheaply available, and because they need little mastication and so can be taken even if one has a number of teeth missing. For example, rice, porridge, fruit juice and soft sweets like *barfis* and *pedas* need little chewing. A moderate intake of proteins, about 50 gm. daily, is advisable. Excess intake of proteins, however, can strain the kidneys and raise the urea and uric acid.

The principles of good nutrition are:

—Eat well-balanced meals by including one item every day from the four main food groups—proteins, carbohydrates, fats and vitamins and minerals—as well as adequate roughage.

—Your diet should contain adequate quantities of vitamins and minerals. Due to inactivity, the bones of the elderly become decalcified, resulting in osteoporosis causing severe aches and pains in the back and lower limbs. Your diet should therefore include adequate amounts of calcium and vitamin D. Take minimum salt as there is a tendency of the arteries to harden with age, resulting in raised blood pressure.

—Eat at regular intervals. Do not keep your stomach empty for more than four to six hours and do not skip meals.

Eat to live and do not live to eat—even if you are alone and bored.

MEALS AND SEX: It is important not to attempt intercourse after a heavy meal as more blood is diverted to the stomach and small intestines for digestion. The man feels sluggish and potency is diminished. If the coronary arteries have become atherosclerotic, sudden exertion like intercourse after a meal can produce angina or pain in the chest.

In a nutshell, eat the right amount of calories, proteins, fats and carbohydrates. If you are overweight, bring your weight down to normal. Scientific studies have not shown that any particular food is an aphrodisiac.

ALCOHOL: Experiments have shown that a small quantity of alcohol relaxes the individual and removes inhibitions. Imbibing a little alcohol acts as an aphrodisiac by removing inhibitions and stimulating the sexual centres. But excessive intake of alcohol depresses the brain and erection centres, producing impotence (see the section on 'Alcohol' in Chapter 14).

SLEEP: This is essential for recuperation. The amount of sleep an individual requires varies from person to person. Younger people need more sleep than older persons. As a rule, about seven or eight hours of sleep are necessary, but some people can do with just four or five hours of sleep while others need eight or nine hours. Each person is his own best judge.

SLEEP AND DRUGS: It has become fashionable to take a pill for sleeping, another for waking and a tranquillizer to reduce tension during the day. The sleeping tablets and tranquillizers generally depress sexual activity and therefore should not be taken routinely every day. I may mention here that the *Rauwolfia serpentina* group of drugs used for lowering high blood pressure also diminish potency (see the section on 'Drugs' in Chapter 14).

FEAR THAT MASTURBATION MAY CAUSE HARM: As I have previously emphasised, masturbation is normal, particularly if there is no opportunity for heterosexual outlet. It relieves the elderly of sexual tensions if done without guilt or fear.

ABSTINENCE: It is an erroneous belief that sex saps vitality, especially in the elderly. The belief is so deep-rooted that even males in their forties complain to me, 'I feel completely drained after sex for days, sometimes weeks. I feel the vitality oozing out from every pore of my body.' Satish said while flipping the pages of his diary, 'The last time was twenty-one days ago, and I am still drained out. My wife sulks and goes into temper tantrums if I deny her sex for long periods. What do I do, Doctor? Surely I don't have to cripple myself for her sake?' It was a herculean job convincing him that carefree sex does not tire but infuses vim and vitality. The so-called tiredness is neither in your body nor in your sexual apparatus but in your mind. Remember that if you think tired, you become tired.

BOREDOM: The elderly have little to do after retirement. Unless they are active and gainfully occupied they suffer from boredom. Boredom in turn breeds tiredness. Sex in such cases is a great rejuvenator. It drives away tiredness. In fact, any activity like walking is also helpful.

COPING WITH STRESS: In the Stress Century, the elderly have to face many kinds of stress. There is the fear of ageing and suffering from a protracted illness. With increasing longevity, the fear of impotence and facing sexless years without relief from sexual tension also produces stress. Retirement with diminished income and increased expenditure, coupled with nothing to do, produces boredom. The children lead their own lives, and the elderly are 'alone and palely loitering'. Finally, while the pace of living is accelerating, the mobility of the elderly is diminishing. All these factors combine to produce stress disorders like high blood pressure, heart attack, asthma and duodenal ulcers. It is therefore essential that the elderly should learn how to cope with stress.

TOTAL FITNESS: Sex needs a lot of energy but it does not deplete the body of vitality. Carefree sex produces a healthy fatigue; within a few minutes you recharge your batteries and feel full of vim and vitality. On the other hand, performance-oriented sex can leave you tired. You can enjoy sex only if you are totally fit—that ·is, physically, emotionally and mentally. A tired man has no erection as nature wants to conserve his energy. Total fitness depends on heredity, healthy nutrition, ability to cope with stress and knowledge of how to combat middle-age maladies and killers like high blood pressure, heart attacks, strokes and ulcers. (For further·details please refer to my books *Are You Killing Yourself, Mr. Executive?* and *Rock Around the Clock.*)

REMARRIAGE: If a spouse is lost should an elderly individual remarry? Children talk disparagingly about elderly parents who have sex. They have difficulty in recognising their parents as sexual human beings. The myth of no sex after 40 prevails amongst them, even though they want free sex for themselves. In other words, the young are conditioned to believe that sex is the prerogative of the young.

With this cultural background, if the father or, more important, the mother remarries, they raise a hue and cry. With the knowledge that sexuality is present even at an advanced age and that therefore sex is necessary for the elderly, the taboo against remarriage, and especially against the mother remarrying, should gradually disappear. If a spouse is divorced or dead, there is nothing wrong in the living spouse remarrying.

Sexual expression in the elderly
It is not the purpose of this section to convert you into a Casanova—far from it. It is to help you to rediscover your own sexual potential which has been inhibited over the years due to cultural conditioning and ignornace of the sexual response, and help you to unlock your true sexual power. It is written for elderly individuals who are still interested in sexual activity and are doubtful about what is expected at their age and where to turn for help. Just as water finds its

own level naturally and effortlessly, similarly you should rediscover your true sexuality, free from inhibitions and sexual myths. Elderly individuals who feel they should retire gracefully after a hectic sexual innings or suffer severe incapacity due to organic diseases like multiple osteo-arthritis or stroke are, of course, free to do so. But for the vast majority the show goes on. Having outlined the cause, how can the elderly prevent sexual inadequacies?

KNOW YOUR SEXUAL RESPONSES: You are like a slumbering volcano, slow to arouse but once activated you can smoulder for much longer than you did in youth. Please remember that you may not get a hard-on by merely looking at your partner's nude body. Do not jump to the conclusion that you have become impotent. Your penis now responds better when it is touched and fondled. It is a matter of normal natural physiology, so accept it gracefully. You don't shout from the house tops, when you wear eyeglasses for reading. You say it is natural in middle age. Similarly, it is natural for the penis to require manual stimulation to produce an erection. As a general rule, a woman does not appreciate a Divali rocket that zooms into the sky and flickers away in an instant. She much prefers a sparkler which goes on sparkling till she is orgasmic.

DO NOT ACT OLD AND REFRAIN FROM SEXUAL ACTIVITY: Your chronological clock rings the alarm of old age. Your culture indoctrinates you to slow down mentally, physically and put a brake on sex. 'Fancy, sex at your age!' jeer the other sexless cronies continuously in your ears. The result: you give up your potency.

Do not believe a word of all this cultural nonsense. You cannot help believing it as you have been brainwashed all your life and so have your parents and grandparents before you. You cannot overnight change your belief system. Initially, you must have faith in your sexual power. Convince yourself that erection is possible, except in a few cases of organic diseases. You cannot snap out of the years of faulty conditioning overnight; it may take some time to work it out of your system. Please read this section again and again.

LOSS OF SEMEN IS PHYSIOLOGICAL: Semen is no different from the gastric or the salivary or the pancreatic juices. During digestion all these juices are required and used and our vital organs like the stomach or the liver are in no way the worse for it. In the same way, discharge of semen during sex, masturbation or night emissions is not harmful. Your body soon replaces the so-called vital fluid if you take proper nutrition.

FEAR OF OLD AGE AND ORGANIC DISEASES: You can overcome them by growing old gracefully. Maintain physical fitness, have yourself checked regularly by your doctor once every six months, after the age of 60. If a parent or an uncle suffers from diabetes, take prompt preventive measures like reducing weight if you are overweight, cutting down on sugar and sweets, exercising regularly and learning to be one up on stress.

If you have a tendency to raised blood pressure, control it by reducing weight (if you are overweight), decreasing salt intake, and taking regular exercise and relaxation. If in spite of all these measures the pressure remains high, you have to consult your doctor, who will probably prescribe drugs for lowering the pressure. Please take them regularly. However, many of the drugs given for high blood pressure depress sexual functioning and produce impotency. If this happens to you, tell your doctor, who will change the antihypertensive for you. Sleeping tablets and tranquillizers also affect potency and should be taken sparingly. The same applies to alcohol. (For details on drugs and alcohol, see Chapter 14).

EXERCISE: Walking is the best anti-age and potency vitamin and the best exercise for the elderly. But do not tire yourself unduly by over-exercising. Stop the exercise and rest at the first sign of fatigue.

TIREDNESS AND SEX: You must be at your peak performance during sex, as tiredness and erection do not go together. It is better to indulge in sexual activity when you are full of vitality rather than late at night when you may feel too tired and lazy for sex.

THE FEMALE PARTNER: You must provide the spark to keep the male engine going. Please remember that in youth when his sexual batteries were fully charged, the sexual engine throbbed instantly by just pressing the self-starter. With age, the sexual self-starter does not function at the flick of the button. It needs to be manually cranked or pushed, just as one pushes a car with run-down batteries. But once it is cranked, there is no looking back. Maxine Devis in *Sexual Responsibility of Woman* states, 'The responsibility for longevity of love rests with the wife. From middle age onwards a wife had better take steps to jolt her husband out of his rut and open new doors to adventure and romance.'

'In all domains of life,' says Dr. G. Lawton in *Ageing Successfully,* 'we must try to obtain through strategy and skill what we formerly did by means of physical force and speed.'

EXPRESSION OF SEXUALITY IN THE ELDERLY: Sexuality is an expression of an individual's total personality. Sexuality is always present in the elderly—the sexual urge once kindled is only extinguished at death. However, owing to culture conditioning and the taboo on sex for the aged, sexuality does not in most elderly individuals find expression in sexual intercourse. The aim of this section is not to preach the need for sex in old age. It is an attempt to enable you to rediscover your true sexuality and express yourself without inhibitions. Whether you want or do not want sex, the choice is yours. But the decision must be made by you, not because society says so or expects it, but as a result of healthy sexuality—totally free of guilt and unconscious sexual anxiety.

In conclusion, as H. Benjamin has said, 'Even if the actor on the stage of life has become more and more a spectator, life can still be interesting and enjoyable provided we learn to evaluate those late years in their own terms and not in the terms of youth.'

Part III

Impotence,
Premature Ejaculation And
Frigidity

Chapter 14

IMPOTENCE, ITS CAUSES
AND TREATMENT

If there's no light anywhere
And you've got no one to turn to
I'll lead you out of the darkness and then
I'll put you together again.

HOT CHOCOLATE

THE MAN suffering from impotence is frustrated, anxious and
depressed, as he has tried every remedy under the sun—pills and
potions, hormone injections, extracts of pearls and diamonds, the
famous *palangtod paan*. He has visited quacks and as a last resort
even changed his partner. He is excited and aroused, and wants a
sexual encounter, but his penis remains limp and lifeless. He feels
wretched and humiliated by his repeated failure in front of his aroused
partner. His confidence in his manliness and faith in his penis are
rudely shattered. He had grown up believing that nothing could go
wrong with his missile. Other men could have erection problems, but
he, never! The car could stall or the TV black-out, but his gadget had
always been fail-proof. The space shuttle could run into problems, but
he could shuttle in and out of bed at will. Like most men living in the
Fantasyland of Sex (see Chapter 2), he believed that penises are made
to last forever. He is surprised when I tell him that over half the male
population at one time or other has a temporary problem of
impotence.

The word impotence implies 'powerless' or 'wanting in natural strength' and is a misnomer which should not be used. Sex therapists have coined a new term, erectile dysfunction or erection problems. However, I have continued to use the word impotence because readers have got used to it and understand it more easily.

1

CAUSES OF IMPOTENCE

What is impotence?

Dr. Masters and Mrs. Johnson have defined an impotent male as one who cannot achieve or maintain an erection sufficient for intercourse. He is therefore unable to obtain or give gratification during the sexual act. According to them, there are two different types of impotence: (1) *primary impotence* where the male has failed every time he has attempted sex because of his inability to achieve an erection or maintain it; and (2) *secondary impotence* which is a highly frequent complaint in males who have functioned adequately for some time but develop erection problems later. It usually begins with an initial erective failure, resulting in anxiety and fear of failure in subsequent attempts at sex.

Impotence has to be differentiated from *premature ejaculation*. Premature ejaculation is a condition where the male ejaculates immediately after interomission, leaving his partner unsatisfied. In premature ejaculation, the erection is present but the ejaculation is early. It is therefore different from impotence, though premature ejaculation after some time may lead to impotence.

Sterility is inability to procreate or to have a child. Sterility and impotence are often confused by laymen, and even by doctors. A sterile man can be potent; that is, he can have normal intercourse, but he will not have children. An impotent man, on the other hand, may not necessarily be sterile; he can have children, as pregnancy can result by merely depositing the semen on the external genital organs of the female. One of my female patients had two children, though the husband was impotent. In a divorce suit filed by her, the wife had difficulty in convincing the lawyers that an impotent man can have children.

Primary impotence

Primary impotence is an almost cent per cent preventable disorder, but its prevention begins in the cradle (see Chapter 13, 'Prevention of Impotence') as soon as the young infant discovers his genitals and derives innocent pleasure by touching them. All are born with a clean sexual slate on which the infant, and later the child and the adolescent, inscribes his sexual alphabet. All of us agree that there is only one way to write a letter of the alphabet correctly. The same applies to the sexual alphabet. There is only one way of learning sexuality—the right way.

ROLE OF THE MOTHER IN PRIMARY IMPOTENCE OF HER SON: The unfortunate male with primary impotence will be relieved to learn that he is not responsible (barring a few cases) for his present plight. Who is then responsible? His mother, of course, though unknowingly and unintentionally. Let me illustrate primary impotence with a case history. Dr. M once told me at a medical get-together, 'What I am today, is entirely because of my mother. She has been both a mother and a father to me ever since my father died when I was seven.' Turning towards his mother who had joined us, he said, 'Meet my mother, who means more to me in life than anybody else.' The stately, stern lady interrupted and continued talking for the next half-hour. 'My son right from birth slept with me,' she said, as she opened her handbag and fanned herself and her son. 'I sent my husband to the guest-room. I enjoyed spending the whole day and night with my priceless possession. I bathed him, dressed him, took him to school and fetched him back. When he was eighteen, I took him to London for his medical education.' Dr. M interrupted sheepishly, 'Mummy, tell Dr. Dastur about the naughty English boys.' She sternly replied, 'They teased my poor poppet and called him "Mummy's Darling"! I shouted back at them whenever they teased my little one. He passed all his exams with flying colours. After a brief holiday we returned to Bombay and he set up his practice.' The mother often dropped him at the consulting-room and invariably picked him up. The son soon made a name for himself and the mother went bride-hunting for him. Countless eligible young ladies were considered till she cast her eyes on the twenty-five-year-old, soft-spoken, gazelle-eyed pianist Sheela. The marriage was celebrated with the usual affluence common in India. The three even went on a honeymoon together!

Ten years later, I accidentally ran into Sheela at Santacruz airport as she was flying to Delhi to be with her father who had a sudden paralytic stroke. 'May I sit next to you?' she asked. 'I am alone and need someone to talk to.' Fortunately, the seat next to her was vacant. She was sweating, and her eyes were moist. 'I have been wanting for a long time to talk to you about my unhappy marriage,' she said. 'I will begin at the beginning. As soon as we entered the house after the wedding reception, the possessive old lady said to her son, "Darling, you must sleep with me tonight." I slept alone in the next room and cried all night. On the second night my husband came to me and, though a doctor, was completely ignorant and clumsy and did not know how to handle a virgin bride. During the night he tried twice, but could not do a thing. He dressed and walked away to his mother's room and slept there. After three months, he came back to me again. By this time he had read some books on sex and knew a few preliminaries of love-play. "Do something, darling, please," I inadvertently blurted, finding him limp. I tried to fondle him, but he pushed my hand away saying, "No woman will ever touch you there, my mother always told me." 'I was about to launch divorce proceedings when my father fell ill in Delhi. Nobody believes me when I tell them that I am still a virgin.'

At Delhi airport she thanked me for listening to her and as she was leaving said, 'Please keep our talk to yourself. I know it is not his fault. He is one of the finest human beings, minus his mother.'

It is unfortunate but true that the cause of Dr. M's impotence was his mother's possessiveness and the kill-joy sexual training she gave her son, without consciously realising the lifelong damage she was doing to his sexuality.

RELIGIOUS ORTHODOXY: Where the family background is highly religious and parents, particularly the mother, din into the ears of the impressionable young boy, 'It is a sin to have sexual relations before wedlock,' 'God is watching you all the time, my boy,' 'You will suffer mental and physical anguish if you sin against God,' the resultant guilt complex is enough to extinguish the delicate erection response.

IMPOTENCE FROM SEXUAL ENCOUNTER WITH A PROSTITUTE: Primary impotence often results from an unpleasant encounter with a prostitute. Let me narrate the experience of Nari, an engineering undergraduate, in his own words. 'In the college hostel Sunder and Balwant were always recounting glowing accounts of their bi-monthly visits to whores. "You will rust away in Bombay's salty air," the bearded Balwant told me. *"Arre bhai, aap ek baar try karo!"* Reluctantly I agreed to go on Saturday night though I felt very frightened. It was nauseating to see the disease-ridden women parading their bodies on hire. Balwant fixed up his old flame for me, and went in search of younger chickens. The place was stinking, the sheet dirty. I stood self-conscious in a corner as she threw her clothes on the floor and waited for me. I felt momentarily dazed and stood like a frozen statue. She got up from the bed in a huff, pulled down my trousers and ripped open my shirt. Next she caught hold of my organ and said, "Don't waste my time," as she took me to bed. I lay on her mechanically, motionless and tongue-tied. I was terrified and could not do a thing with my limp organ. She pushed me aside after a few minutes, saying I was no good. I put on my clothes, convinced I would never have an erection. On the advice of my office friends but against my better judgement, I got married. They told me that sex with a whore was different from intercourse with a wife. As soon as I go near Sunita, the face of the whore mocking my impotence, comes back to my mind and I am limp. At Sunita's insistence I have come to see you. Please help me.'

HOMOSEXUAL RESPONSE: According to Dr. Masters, individuals who prefer a homosexual response in adolescence are impotent during heterosexual sex. In most such cases, the dominant mother wears the pants in the house. The father of these unfortunate individuals is a mere figurehead, just the breadwinner and provider.

Secondary impotence

Secondary impotence results from diverse causes ranging from organic diseases to psychogenic reasons. It can be classifed as owing to: (1) medical causes and hormonal imbalances; (2) alcohol and drugs; (3) psychogenic reasons.

Until recently, it was believed that 90 per cent of cases of impotence were psychogenic and the remaining 10 per cent due to physical causes. The current thinking is that 75 to 80 per cent of cases are psychogenic and 20 to 25 per cent due to physical disorders and organic diseases. Most constitutional diseases depress sexuality, fortunately only temporarily. Alcohol and nicotine—mankind's artificial props for centuries—are sexual depressants. So also the newcomers: marijuana or pot, cocaine, Dexedrine and LSD. Finally, a large number of antihypertensives, tranquillisers, narcotics and anticholinergics (drugs to relieve pain in the abdomen caused by duodenal ulcer, intestinal or biliary colic) depress sexual functioning.

Although the most prevalent causes of sexual dysfunction are psychological, *physical factors must always be ruled out before commencing sex therapy or psychotherapy in deep-seated disorders.*

Medical causes

SEXUAL DYSFUNCTION: Normal erection and hence intercourse depends upon physically sound genital organs and their vascular, neurological and hormonal components. Any disorder—functional, organic or local—which directly or indirectly affects the parts responsible for normal erection impairs sexual function.

FUNCTIONAL MEDICAL DISORDERS are due to altered physiological or psychological states like tiredness, stress, anxiety and depression.

TIREDNESS: Like any other activity of our body sex is an energy-consuming exercise. The sum total of energy—physical, mental and emotional—which each of us has depends upon the energy generated and spent. In a bank account, if you deposit five hundred rupees and withdraw seven hundred rupees, the account is in the red. The same thing happens in our body. Very little energy is left for sex if you overspend it in work, sports, hobbies, reading or watching TV, or in indulging in negative thinking and unhealthy stressful emotions like jealousy, envy, aggression, fear, anxiety and anger. For example, the five-star expense-account executives after a hard day's work attend cocktail parties three or four times a week where they consume large pegs of Scotch on an empty stomach and return home not only inebriated but tired and bored; no wonder they flop in bed!

Sex is a low-priority item for most individuals. They think of sex after doing everything else. You cannot function adequately this way as very little energy is left. It must be a high-priority item in your activities. In short, the choice is yours. Either you consciously set aside time and energy to make love to your partner or you spend all your energy on 'work' and say to your partner if she makes a subtle advance at night, 'Darling, not today, I am dead tired. I have had a very busy day at the office.' She is not going to forgive you easily for neglecting her at a time of her cycle (just before or during a period) when she is most responsive. Mr. Tired, you may not have the surge of energy for coitus but you can make her happy by telling her you love her, holding her in your arms, stroking her and kissing her gently. As I have mentioned earlier, intercourse is low on the sexual shopping list of most women.

Besides work, you may be spending a lot of energy exercising or playing competitive sports, in which case you are left without reserves. Professionals like lawyers, doctors, architects, executives and champion sportsmen are generally lousy lovers. These are high-energy-consuming vocations involving thinking, planning and organising. On the other hand, artists, musicians and actors are better lovers as they are engaged in creative activities.

Remember, tiredness and sex never go together. Total physical fitness, vibrant energy and giving sex a high priority in your list of daily activities are necessary ingredients for supreme and fulfilling sex.

STRESS: 'I function best sexually when I am under severe pressure of work and tension,' Arif Khan, president of an advertising agency, told me. 'My brother is the exact opposite. He only enjoys sex when he is completely relaxed.' Khan is either an exception or resorts to sex merely to relieve tension. If his partner were asked, she might have a different story to tell. One can never indulge in relaxed satisfying sex under severe stress.

Stress is mediated by the sympathetic branch of the autonomic nervous system and the stress hormones from the hypothalamus-pituitary-adrenal axis. It has recently been demonstrated that serum testosterone levels in the blood are not constant but fluctuate widely. It has also been observed that blood testosterone levels fall considerably when a man is under constant stress but that the levels return to normal when the individual has learnt to cope with stress. The hypothalamus-pituitary axis is believed to be responsible for the fluctuations in serum testosterone levels. During stress, the production of FSH (Follicle-Stimulating Hormone) and LH (Lutinizing Hormone)—the two hormones which stimulate the testes to produce testosterone—also decreases, resulting in diminished sexual desire and erectile dysfunction.

Chronic stress also results in increased secretion of plasma cortisone from the adrenal glands which produces anti-testosterone (androgen) effects.

'Honeymoon impotence', according to Dr. Masahumi Shirai of Toho University, Tokyo, accounted for nearly 30 per cent of the impotence seen in a three-year study of 470 patients in Japan's 'do or die' high-pressure society. 'Most of these were young men in their twenties or thirties and were extremely tense and anxious. The system of match-making in Japan makes new couples very tense,' said Dr. Masahumi. Thus stress and sex are deadly enemies. Sex should be carefree, without anxiety.

ANXIETY AND FEAR: Fear of failure, and anxiety or worry about what will happen, are the commonest causes of erectile problems in the psychogenic group. Hippocrates, the father of medicine, recognized that 'the fears and terrors that assail us, some by night and some by day' are produced in the brain.

THE PHYSICAL ILLNESSES RESULTING IN SEXUAL DYSFUNCTION can be divided into the following groups: (1) Metabolic and hormonal, (2) Neurological, (3) Vascular, (4) Liver diseases, (5) General ill-health, (6) Local genital disorders, and (7) Surgical conditions.

Metabolic and hormonal imbalances

DIABETES MELLITUS: Impotence is frequently the presenting symptom in a patient suffering from Diabetes Mellitus. Disturbance of the carbohydrate metabolism leads to diminished potency. As soon as diabetes is controlled potency occasionally returns.

A group of New York clinicians recently reported in the *Journal of the American Medical Association* that they found a high frequency of diabetes in subjects suffering from premature ejaculation or impotence. The study was carried out on three groups of men without known diabetes. Known diabetics, alcoholics and drug addicts were excluded from the study. The first group suffered from impotence, the second from premature ejaculation while the third group (the control group) had normal sexual function. Laboratory investigations included 100 mg. 3-hour glucose tolerance test, sedimentation rate, and measurement of thyroxine, follicle-stimulating hormone (FSH), lutinizing hormone (LH) testosterone levels, lipid profile and liver function tests.

The results showed that the group suffering from impotence had higher levels of glucose at one-hour and two-hour tests. There was no significant difference in fasting serum glucose level. Seven from the group with impotence were diabetic. On the whole, 19 per cent of the impotency group, 7.3 per cent of those with premature ejaculation and 3.2 per cent of the control group had diabetes or impaired glucose tolerance test. Diabetes causes thickening of the arteries all over the body. It affects the arteries of the penis as well, resulting in less blood flow to it, preventing an erection. Diabetes also damages the nerves of the penis.

HORMONAL IMBALANCE: 'It is all in your mind,' doctors used to tell patients suffering from impotence. Until recently, 90 per cent of impotence was estimated to be psychogenic but modern methods of radio immunoassay enable us to determine accurately infinitesimal levels of various hormones circulating in the body. Dr. Richard Spark of Beth Israel Hospital, Boston, writing in the *Journal of the Americam Medical Association,* states that 'the problem in many cases is medical and not mental'.

DEFICIENCY OF TESTOSTERONE: Dr. Spark found that at least 35 per cent of the 105 impotent males studied had endocrine problems—too little testosterone or overactive thyroids—which had been overlooked. Medical treatment restored normal sexual functioning in all.

EXCESS PROLACTIN: The *British Medical Journal* reported on 29 males having increased prolactin (the hormone secreted by the anterior pituitary which stimulates lactation after confinement) levels in the blood as tested by a radio immunoassay. Twenty-three of them suffered from impaired sexual functioning. When prolactin levels were brought to normal with treatment, circulating levels of testosterone also returned to normal and so did sexual functioning.

ADMINISTRATIONS OF OESTROGENS: Excising one or both testes (orchidectomy) and administering 1 mg. of oestrogen daily is the usual treatment in cancer of the prostate. A depressing side-effect of oestrogen therapy is loss of secondary sexual characteristics like the growth of the beard, and moustache, impotence, and water retention in the tissues.

HYPOTHYROIDISM: In this condition, the thyroid gland becomes inactive and fails to produce the adequate quantity of the thyroid hormone. This hormone stimulates metabolism in the tissues by increasing oxygen consumption and generating heat in the body. In other words, the thyroid gland is the pace-setter of our activity, drive and energy, stoking the fire in our body cells. When there is deficiency of the thyroid hormone, the fire of metabolism becomes a flickering flame, slowing down all bodily activities including sex. The individual becomes impotent.

Oral administration of thyroid acts like a charm, not only making the individual alert and active but also potent. Let me tell you about 50-year-old Virchand, a highly successful man in business and sex. For five months he had been gradually developing impotence, which worried him no end. Incidentally, according to my dear friend Abdulla Shirawi, a business magnate from Dubai, 'a man has to be first successful in sex to be successful in business.' There is a lot of truth in what Abdulla says, and one finds innumerable examples among our captains of industry!

Like Abdulla, Virchand was always confident of his masculinity and business capability. Is it any wonder that his impotence shattered him completely! He slowed down visibly in everything and could no longer take bold decisions. He thought it was due to approaching male menopause and deficiency of male androgens. A detailed clinical examination and a battery of tests (see the next section for details of tests) including thyroid function revealed that he was suffering from hypothyroidism. His potency returned soon after the deficiency of thyroid had been corrected with Eltroxin (Thyroxine sodium) tablets. But Virchand has to take these tablets for the rest of his life.

CASTRATION is removal or destruction of the testes by disease, injury or radiation. Unlike the female ovaries which are situated deep in the pelvic cavity and well protected by the back and the abdominal wall, the male testes suspended in the scrotum between the upper thighs are very vulnerable to injuries. As the testes secrete the male hormone, testosterone, impotence results if both testes have to be removed because of, for exmple, gun-shot injuries or malignant tumours. Severe radiation also destroys the hormone cells producing testosterone.

HYPOPITUITARISM AND HYPOADRENOCORTICISM: Diminished secretion of gonadotrophin by the pituitary gland causes male hypogonadism, a condition characterised by diminished function of the sperm-manufacturing cells of the testes. This results in azoospermia (absence of sperms in the semen) and sterility. The secondary sex characteristics regress and impotence gradually sets in. Reduced secretions by the adrenal glands can also lead to sexual malfunctioning.

CRYPTORCHIDISM is a defect where one or both testes fail to descend into the scrotum but remain either in the abdomen or the inguinal canal. When both testes fail to descend the condition is due to a hypothalamic or pituitary disorder and is often linked with other congenital abnormalities. Due to hormonal interference with the production of testosterone, impotence is usually present. As the sperms cannot mature at body temperature there is often azoospermia and sterility. Favourable results are reported in abdominal cryptorchidism with the administration of 500 I.U. chorionic gonadotrophic hormone thrice a week for six weeks, when the child is between five and seven years old.

If the testes fail to descend, surgery is necessary to bring down the testes into the scrotum. However, many cases continue to remain sterile, though presently testicular hormone deficiency can be corrected and potency restored by administering testosterone.

NEUROLOGICAL LESIONS: Impotence results from injury or diseases of the second and third sacral segments of the spinal cord, where the erection centre is located. Such injuries or diseases may be caused by car accidents, falls, spinal cord tumours, tuberculosis of the spine and myelitis or inflammation of the spinal cord.

If the injury or disease is at a higher level of the spinal cord there is temporary impotence during the stage of shock of the spinal cord. After recovery, erection is not spontaneous unless it is manually produced or the bladder is full. In case of paraplegia or quadriplegia, we instruct the wife to help.

Mawdeloy and Fergusson (1963) reported impotence in boxers following injury to the brain. Impotence has been observed in certain frontal lobe diseases, especially tumours. Impotence has also been reported with temporal (side) lobe disorders by Hierons and Saunders. According to them, 'Impotence occurs in association with organic disturbances of the temporal lobe and clinical and experimental evidence supports the involvement of the anterior temporal region as the higher centre of the sexual function.'

VASCULAR CAUSES: The two basic responses to adequate sexual stimulation are vasocongestion and muscle tension (contraction). The penis becomes erect when the cavernous tissues are engorged with blood; erection is lost when the blood returns from the penis to the general systemic pool. The response is controlled by the autonomic nervous system. Any disorder that interferes with prompt vasocongestion of the penile arteries leads to erection problems. It is well-known that arteriosclerosis or thickening of the arteries of the heart and brain reduces blood supply to these vital organs, making the individual prone to heart attacks and strokes. Dr. L.H. Hiranandani, Bombay's well-known E.N.T. specialist, says that arteriosclerosis of the vertebral arteries causes postural vertigo and deafness. More recently it has been found that arteriosclerosis of the penile arteries in diabetics reduces blood supply to the penis during erection, resulting in sexual dysfunction. An additional factor in diabetes is also damage to the delicate nerves of the sex organs.

LIVER DISEASES: Liver disorders like hepatitis (viral or amoebic) and early cirrhosis of the liver depress sexuality. A damaged liver is unable to neutralise the circulating oestrogen in males. The three cardinal symptoms of liver disorders are loss of appetite, nausea and loss of libido.

GENERAL ILL-HEALTH: Constitutional disorders like acute or chronic infection, severe anaemia, cancer and degenerative diseases may result in penile dysfunction. However, the disability is temporary and erection returns as soon as the disease is eradicated. Many workers claim that infections like pulmonary tuberculosis and leprosy are exceptions as sexuality is not depressed until the disease has reached an advanced stage.

LOCAL GENITAL DISORDERS: Phimosis or tight foreskin of the penis, and a thick, fleshy hymen which does not perforate during penetration by the male, interfere with normal erection and proper sexual functioning. Both can be corrected by minor surgery. Other disorders causing sexual dysfunction are urethritis and prostatitis (inflamed urethra or prostate), a large hydrocele, inguinal hernia, orchiditis (inflamed testes) and injury to the testes.

SURGICAL CONDITIONS: Dangerous surgical procedures in grave conditions may damage the nerves to the sexual organs resulting in sexual disorders. For example, sympathectomy done for TAO (thrombo-angina obliterans) or a perineal prostatectomy often results in sexual dysfunction. Castration of both testes for a severe injury also causes an erection problem.

ALCOHOL AND IMPOTENCE: Shakespeare recognised the powerful effect of alcohol in precipitating impotence nearly 400 years ago. In *Macbeth* the drunken porter says, drink 'provokes the desire, but it takes away the performance; therefore much drink may be said to be an equivocator with lechery: it makes and it mars him; it sets him on, and it takes him off, it persuades him and disheartens him.'

Quite often, secondary impotence occurs the first time after a few drinks. Shankar, an advertising executive, narrated to me his tale of woe. 'Last Christmas Eve I lost my manhood for the first time. Sushma was furious as I kept on consuming large Patiala pegs of Chivas Regal, my favourite brand of Scotch. I paid a lot of attention without intention to a number of women at the cocktail party while my wife was turning green with jealousy. The more I drank, the more I kissed and hugged the other men's wives, while their husbands contentedly smoked, drank and chatted idly.' Putting his hand on his forehead, Shankar continued, 'I decided to crash the sex barrier between me and my wife, quite forgetting that while alcohol increases the desire, it diminishes the performance. After a lot of coaxing she agreed. I thought it would be my best performance but I could not do a thing. I was furious with my organ and my wife. "How dare you misbehave!" I said to the former and to the latter, "You don't know how to arouse me." I tried again the next morning and night but my penis remained limp and lifeless.'

Alcohol when drunk is diluted in the stomach by the digestive juices. If the stomach is empty about 30 per cent of the alcohol immediately enters the blood through the tiny capillaries in the wall of the stomach and small intestine. If, however, there is food in the stomach absorption is delayed. Alcohol is the only substance absorbed directly from the stomach without digestion. From the stomach and small intestine alcohol is carried to the liver where it is oxidised, that is, oxygen transforms the chemical energy of alcohol. If, however, more alcohol is consumed than the liver can oxidise, it reaches the heart via the veins in the liver. From the heart it is pumped with the blood to all parts of the body including the brain. Thus in a few minutes the individual begins to feel the effects of the drink.

Experiments have shown that a small quantity of alcohol relaxes the individual and removes inhibitions. Thus a little alcohol acts as an aphrodisiac by removing the inhibitions and stimulating the sexual centres. On the other hand, alcohol in excess depresses the brain and erection centres, producing impotence. As the sense of judgement is also depressed, the individual thinks that he is a Casanova but is unable to consummate the sex act. The question you will naturally ask is how much alcohol should one take? The capacity for intake of alcohol which might affect potency differs with each individual. Beer has a reputation among laymen of prolonging coitus and preventing premature ejaculation. In conclusion, alcohol in small quantities stimulates potency by relaxing a tense individual and making him feel happy and carefree, which is necessary for normal sex. Large quantities of alcohol, on the other hand, always depress sexual power and may cause temporary impotence.

DRUGS AND SEXUALITY: It is not generally realised that a large number of drugs commonly prescribed today have sexual side-effects and depress sexuality. Innumerable individuals in the Stress Century swallow some forms of medication like tranquillisers, narcotics, anti-hypertensives or anti-cholinergics. The depressing effect of these drugs on sexuality is better documented in the male than the female, as erection and ejaculation are more easily visible and' registered than vaginal lubrication and orgasm.

In any male who complains of erectile or ejaculatory dysfunction it is therefore necessary to rule out physical causes (like diabetes mellitus, hypothyroidism, etc.) and use of drugs before diagnosing the case of psychogenic impotence.

Drugs which stimulate or depress sexuality can act on any one or more of the three components, neurological, vascular and hormonal, responsible for normal sexual functioning. Erection in the male and vaginal lubrication in the female is brought about by local vaso-congestion which in turn depends on the reflex dilatation of penile and circum-vaginal blood vessels during arousal. Erection is controlled by the parasympathetic division of the autonomic nervous system whilst ejaculation is mediated by its sympathetic division. Th arousal centre is located in the hypothalamus and preoptic area of the brain.

Drugs which depress sexuality
Sexual depressants act either on the central or the autonomic nervous system.

DRUGS ACTING ON THE BRAIN: Sedatives and narcotics like barbiturates and heroin in general decrease the libido and sexual responses.

Opium was well known to ancient Egyptian priests and was used as early as 1550 B.C., as a sedative, soporific and pain-killer. Tincture of opium, also called Tincture Laudanum because of its many laudable qualities, was popularised by the Swiss physician, Paracelsus, in the fifteenth century. Before the advent of modern tranquillisers, 30 minims of Tincture Laudanum were extensively perscribed to relieve the anxiety of a sexually inadequate male and improve his performance. It is, however, habit-forming.

Anti-anxiety drugs like Librium, Valium and Meprobromates taken for a prolonged period depress sexuality and, as they are muscle-relaxants, can occasionally cause disturbances of orgasm. They are frequently used to relieve anxiety, which is a predominant cause of impaired sexual functioning, and thereby improve the sexual responses. Prolonged administration and in large doses however depresses sexuality.

The phenothiazine antipsychotic drugs like chlorpramazine (Largactil), thoriadazine (Melleril), or trifluoperazine (Eskazine) are commonly prescribed is schizophrenia and frequently cause 'dry ejaculation' due to non-closure (paralysis) of the internal vesical sphincter just prior to ejaculation, resulting in discharge of semen into the urinary bladder.

The tricylic antidepressants like Depsonil, Depsodiaz, Impranil, Tryptanol or Sarotena usually have no direct effect on sexual responses. In general, the libido and performance improves as the depression reduces. In rare cases these drugs cause ejaculatory and potency disorders as they have a slight effect on the autonomic nerves.

Monoamineoxidase (MAO) inhibitors like Marplan, Nardil or Parnate, when used in the treatment of endogenous depression, tend to cause premature ejaculation.

Anticholinergics like atropine, belladonna, banthine, probanthine and other similar drugs used in the treatment of hyperacidity and peptic ulcer inhibit the action of acetylcholine on organs which are innervated by the parasympathetic nerves. As erection in the male is also mediated by the same nerves, these group of drugs can cause impotence though sexual arousal is not effected.

Anti-adrenergics are commonly used in the treatment of hypertension and can be divided, according to their sexual side-effects, into two groups, as suggested by John Buffam, a pharmacist at the V.A. Medical Centre in San Francisco. The first group consists of those which are reported to cause a 50 per cent or greater incidence of sexual dysfunction like me methyldopa (Aldomet) clonidin (Arkamine or Catapress), and guanithedine (Ismelin). The second group causing lower than 50 per cent sexual dysfunction are propranolol (Inderal, Ciplar); hydralazine (Apresoline); reserpine (Serpasil), and spironolactone (Aldactone). Those with no reported sexual side-effects are thiazide diuretics, minoxidil (Loniten). These drugs act on sympathetic autonomics producing ejaculatory problems. The reserpine group also has a central action on the brain and may cause impotence.

Hormones

ANTI-ANDROGENS: Oestrogens employed in cancer of the prostate, cortisone, ACTH and Aldactone oppose the action of androgen on the brain and the sexual organs, producing impotence and lack of desire.

In conclusion, while a number of prescription drugs depress sexuality, yet the search for a true aphrodisiac continues. In fact, as Alfred Kinsey rightly concluded, 'Good health, sufficient exercise and plenty of sleep still remain the most effective of aphrodisiacs known to man.'

2

PSYCHOGENIC IMPOTENCE (CAUSES)

Psychogenic impotence is the commonest form of impotence in the Stress Century. Its peculiar characteristic is that the male does not have an erection during intercourse with his female partner but has very strong 'morning erections' or has erection during masturbation or a sexual dream. Many authorities attribute morning erections to the reflex action of a full bladder (the accumulated urine in the bladder causes an erection). Steke I described the above explanation as a 'psychological absurdity'; if the individual did not have unconscious sex anxiety and inhibitions, he would function normally. If a person has morning erections but does not have erections during intercourse, he can be sure that his impotence is psychogenic and can be cured in most cases with sex therapy, while in a few cases psychotherapy may be necessary.

Doctors have agreed to disagree on the various psychological causes of impotence. But they generally agree that male sexual dysfunction is produced by experiential factors. The real disagreement arises about what exactly causes psychogenic impotence. The psychoanalytic theory advocated by the founder of psychoanalysis, Sigmund Freud, holds specific childhood conflicts responsible for sexual dysfunction. Psychoanalysis is a lengthy treatment and continues for many years. While the male is analysed the unfortunate female partner feels frustrated and left out. Another drawback is that while the patient gets a better insight into how his childhood experiences cause dysfunction, the impotence continues as immediate causes like coital anxiety and fear of failure are not removed. Impotence naturally persists till he overcomes these fears.

The psychopathology theory postulates that sexual dysfunction arises from a sexually destructive environment created by the partners. For example, a female partner may pass derisive remarks about the male's sexual performance, laying the foundation for psychological impotence. Finally, behaviour or learning therapy believes that sexual dysfunction is a learned process, arising from sexual ignornace which can be unlearnt by sex therapy.

The various concepts in the evolving pattern of sex therapy are highlighted mainly for the professional reader. The average reader is primarily concerned with knowing the causes of his sexual dysfunction and how to overcome them in the shortest possible time.

Psychoanalysis and psychotherapy were the main tools in the treatment of impotence till the arrival of Dr. Masters and Mrs. Johnson on the sexual stage. They suggested for the first time that sexual anxiety, fear of failure and spectatoring (the patient watching all the time to see if he is getting an erection) were the immediate factors responsible for sexual dysfunction. If these factors are removed by sex therapy, sexual functioning soon becomes normal. The Masters-Johnson fourteen days away from home, intensive team treatment (both partners are simultaneously treated) of sexual dysfunction was a great milestone which revolutionised sex therapy. The noted psychiatrist and sex therapist Helen Singer Kaplan states, 'In many cases, the sexual dysfunctions have their roots in the more immediate and simpler problems, which were ignored until recently, such as the anticipation of failure of rejection and humiliation by the partner.' However, in some cases merely removing the immediate causes is not enough and psychotherapy is necessary to tackle the remote causes.

The causes of psychogenic impotence can therefore be conveniently divided into two groups: (1) immediate causes, and (2) remote causes. Such a classification is helpful in the treatment of impotence. If the impotence is due to immediate causes, a reversal of these factors results in adequate sexual functioning. In impotence due to remote causes, psychotherapy may be necessary for a more lasting cure.

Common immediate causes

The common immediate causes contributing to male sexual dysfunction are:

(1) Lack of adequate sexual skills;
(2) Fear of failure during the sex act;
(3) Spectatoring and spying on oneself resulting in lack of sexual abandonment and eroticism; and
(4) Failure of communication.

LACK OF SEXUAL SKILL or know-how is a frequent cause of impotence. I shall illustrate with a case history. Twenty-eight-year-old Popatlal, a bank clerk from Porbandar, had been married to a commerce graduate for six months, yet the marriage had not been consummated. Popatlal tried several times to penetrate his wife without success. Repeated failure produced loss of erectile ability. Both of them were ignorant about the anatomy of the sex organs. Popatlal had never seen a picture of the female genitals. When I showed one to him he asked in amazement, 'Which is the cavity for the penis?'

Popatlal's futile attempts at penetration were prohibited and the couple were asked to indulge in mere pleasuring (stroking) each other's body without touching the breasts or genital organs (see Section 3, 'Treatment of Impotence'). After five days, genital stimulation was encouraged without any attempt at intercourse. The wife was asked to hold the penis in her hand and guide it into the vagina in the woman-on-top position. Initially she was averse, but later agreed. Popatlal's potency soon returned to normal and the treatment was discontinued after three briefing sessions at weekly intervals.

Another case is that of 30-year-old Surinder who brought his 26-year-old wife Leela for treatment of her so-called 'frigidty'. 'I am highly potent and virile,' said Surinder, 'I can continue for over half an hour but she does not come naturally.' I asked Surinder what he meant by coming 'naturally'. 'With the penis alone without touching her genitals,' was his immediate reply.

The couple were shown the position of the clitoris and the vaginal entrance. The role of the clitoris in producing orgasm and how it is situated far away from the vaginal opening were also explained to them. There is no direct contact between the penis and the clitoris in the normal man-on-top position. I told them that the overrated king, the male penis, was merely a figurehead in the kingdom of sex. Just as a king needs a prime minister to rule his kingdom, the penis is powerless in most cases to produce an orgasm in the female without his prime minister, the index finger.

While Surinder readily agreed to try his hand at it, Leela firmly said that it was unnatural. It took a lot of explaining before she was convinced that a woman initially needs to be stimulted with the finger in most cases.

Sexual functioning soon returned to normal in both the cases described above as there were no infantile hang-ups. However, all cases do not respond to therapy so promptly.

FEAR OF FAILURE: A male has to produce an erection in order to penetrate the vagina. As long as the sexual mechanism works normally he is not conscious of it, as erection, like the beating of the heart, is not under conscious control. But if the erection fails to takes place, consciousness is immediately alerted and panic sets in. The individual is full of self-doubt the next time. 'Will I or won't I?' is the incessant and persistent long-playing record in his mind. A state of fear is generated which makes him focus all his attention on his erection. The inevitable result of this self-fulfilling prophecy is, of course, impotence.

SPECTATORING OR SPYING ON SELF: Once the failure of erection occurs the unfortunate individual usually grinds his teeth and says, 'I must succeed. I must not fail.' Instead of letting himself go during the preliminaries of love play, he constantly watches or spies on his penis. Erection never occurs when the will power is altered; the organ remains limp and lifeless which in turn starts a vicious cycle of anxiety, fear of failure and spectatoring. Dr. Kaplan believes that generally 'insecure men and men whose behaviour is excessively governed by a need to excel and to compete are particularly vulnerable to the fear of sexual failure.' Sex therapy is directed towards combating this performance-orientation in sex by methods like forbidding intercourse for a few days and merely resorting to mutual pleasuring—touching or stroking each other and learning complete sexual abandon and eroticism. The most effective distraction from spectatoring is fantasy. Different fantasies of a successful sexual encounter are very useful in intensifying sexual experiences.

FAILURE TO COMMUNICATE: Very few couples freely communicate their sexual feeling and what they want in sex. If they could or would, a great obstacle to sexual dysfunction would be removed. 'The most important cause of my impotence with my first wife was my complete lack of communication,' Rajan told me. 'We were completely nude yet total strangers to one another while attempting sex. With Sushma it is entirely different. Knowing my sexual insecurities and impotence, she took the initiative and asked me how I would best like to be stimulated. Her free and frank attitude soon restored my confidence and erectile power.'

It is most essential that partners communicate freely their sexual wants to each other. It not only makes sex carefree but also more enjoyable.

Remote psychological causes

All of us are conditioned about sex during infancy and childhood. If the mother considers sex dirty, the boy grows up believing that it is dirty. At the critical moment when he initiates intercourse, a voice whispers in his ear, 'Sex is dirty. Remember what your mother taught you.' He does not get a hard-on or the erection is lost as there is a conflict between the conscious desire to enjoy sex and the subconscious fear or guilt of doing so. Thus an emotional conflict is responsible for the impotence. The resolution of the conflict is the basis of psychotherapy in these cases. For example, the inherent fear the little boy has of being punished for peeping into his parent's bedroom while they are in action, or his belief that his naughty father is 'harming' or 'injuring' his darling mother during the sex act, or a persistence of the Oedipus conflict which is universally present in childhood, are often responsible for sexual dysfunction in adult life (see Chapter 13, 'Prevention in Infancy and Childhood').

Freud was the first to point out that sexual conflict in childhood was the most important cause of adult sexual dysfunction. He also suggested the existence of unconscious psychic processes. Prior to Freud, it was believed that man was in constant touch with his basic needs, desires and conflicts and that he was, as the poet Oliver Wendell Holmes, says 'built in such a logical way'. The dark unfathomed caves of the unconscious were unknown. Freud exploded the myth that man's behaviour was entirely governed by reason and will. He formulated a three-dimensional model of personality. Firstly, there is the ego—the rational and reasoning component. Secondly, the id or unconscious, consisting of primitive sexual wishes and desires, all neatly packed in the id of which the ego is unaware except during psychoanalysis. Finally, there is the superego or conscience which makes cowards of us. It produces guilts about enjoying sex which in turn causes sexual dysfunction. The unconscious is also the storehouse or godown of old junk—discarded, unpleasant sexual memories which are not cast off but preserved and waiting to pop out into the conscious.

Freud termed this conflict about sex, its denial and subsequent diversion into the unconscious, repression. Anxiety is the sentry which guards these hidden sexual wishes and prevents them from coming into the open—consciousness. In other words, as soon as the conscious is alerted, the individual puts up a stiff symbolic resistance and pushes back the thought into the unconscious. This explains why individuals during psychotherapy resist the emergence of unacceptable sexual material from the unconscious into the conscious. Some of these individuals do not want to get well.

WHY DOES THE CONFLICT ARISE? Freud was the first to suggest that childhood experiences shaped the destiny of adults. Even little children, according to him, are dominated by sexual desire and fantasies. However, they suppress them for fear of incurring the wrath of their parents. The little chap likes to play with his penis but mainly the mother and also the father prevent him from doing so. 'Don't touch there,' scolds his mama. The little boy is now torn between the desire to enjoy the erotic feeling of touching himself and fear of his mother's anger and loss of love. 'Mummy must be right,' he thinks. 'It is bad to enjoy myself by playing with myself.' So he suppresses his erotic desires and shuts them off in the unconscious where they lie buried but surface into consciousness when he attempts sex as an adult: 'Mama said sex is dirty. Don't do it.' The inevitable result of the conflict is impotence.

Sexual conflict can also result from fear of retaliation by God or society. 'I am a sinner. God will punish me.' 'What will my community think if I go out with a Muslim girl? I am a Hindu.' 'Love is blind' he says to himself, 'I just cannot take my thoughts off her. I know that I am doing a wrong thing. My parents and society will never approve of my marriage. The only way to marry her is to run away from home and have a civil marriage.'

OEDIPUS COMPLEX: Freud postulated that the infant passes through three stages of psychosexual development. He called them oral (from birth to about 18 months), anal (18 months to 4 years) and genital (4 to 6 years). During these stages the child's life is dominated by varying erotic pleasures arising from the different zones of his body. During the oral stage the infant derives pleasure from sucking the mother's milk. During the anal stage, the little toddler loves to pass his stool and derives intense pleasure lying in the mess. However, he is subjected to parental control at this stage which produces a conflict. The parents want him to pass the stool in a potty at a particular time, which he resents. Finally, during the genital stage the infant's main source of pleasure is touching his genital organs. He now passes through the Oedipus stage made famous by Freud, who thought it to be the only cause of adult sexual dysfunction (see Chapter 13).

In Greek mythology, the prince Oedipus was raised by his foster parents. One day he quarrelled with his real father, killed him and later married his mother. When he discovered the mistake he blinded himself. A little boy is always attached to his mother and thinks the father is his rival, monopolising his mother. Similarly, a little girl is attached to her father and imagines that the mother is her rival. In other words, the child always chooses the parent of the opposite sex as the object of his or her eroticism.

The boy at this stage feels an intense urge and longing for his mother and loves her while he hates his father. The impossible romance with his own mother leads to a conflict with the father, a guilt about his secret love for his mother to which is added an element of anxiety. Freud terms it 'castration anxiety': the fear that his jealous father will castrate him (cut off his penis) if he finds out about his love. As he cannot fulfil his wish and is scared of his father, he represses his love for his mother. If, however, there is fulfilment of his erotic dreams or he can identify himself with his father, the conflict is resolved.

Usually, the Oedipus reaction is temporary and the boy soon outgrows it. If, on the other hand, the conflict is unresolved sexual dysfunction occurs in later life. Freud rates unresolved Oedipal conflict as the sole cause of adult sexual dysfunction, though he was unable to identify how it produces loss of erection at the critical moment. He merely suggested that when a man suffering from this complex attempts intercourse, his hidden fear of castration prevents him from getting an erection.

Helen Kaplan believes the Oedipal conflict produces sexual dysfunction only if it causes acute anxiety at the time of love-play or the individual unconsciously does not want to get aroused. She reports cases where the sexual functioning remained excellent despite the Oedipal situation in adult life. The Freudian concept is no longer accepted as the only cause of impotence in the adult. Psychoanalysts have suggested that many other factors are responsible for sexual dysfunction in the adult.

SEXUAL CONFLICT IN CHILDHOOD: Sexuality is an extremely pleasurable and powerful drive in a growing child, but its expression is denied in our sexually-constraining society. Sexuality is taboo. Sex is dirty. Sex is sinful.

The incessant desire to express his sexuality and its constant denial produces a conflict in the child. He grows up with a feeling of guilt and fear which can damage his sexual functioning. For example, every time the youngster wants to touch his genitals or wants to make love to his mother while the father is away, he is extremely worried about the small size of his penis. His father and school friends have much bigger organs than his. Why has nature been unkind to him? Can he ever satisfy a girl with such a small penis? How can he make it bigger? Is there a tablet he can take? Will some electric treatment help him? His life is made miserable by such thoughts. He does not know where to turn for help. The same negative thinking plagues him, when he attempts intercourse. The result: loss of erection and inability to penetrate.

FEAR OF HARMFUL EFFECTS OF MASTURBATION: Most boys and adolescents have practised masturbation as a natural sexual outlet, where coitus with a female partner is not possible before marriage. All authorities on sex are now agreed that masturbation is not harmful, but it invariably produces a sense of guilt. In many schools, the young and impressionable minds of boys are frightened by threats about the so-called harmful effects, with the result that every time the boy masturbates he suggests to himself that he will be impotent in heterosexual contact.

These powerful suggestions actively result in impotency. Were it not for the pernicious literature that is published about the harmful and sinful effects of masturbation, this state of affairs would not have existed. The impotency in these cases is entirely psychological and has nothing to do with masturbation. A twenty-three-year-old adult consulted us for his inability to perform the sex act after marriage. He was most worried that he was impotent and life for him was not worth living. He used to masturbate once or twice a week since the age of fourteen and was firmly convinced that his present plight was entirely due to this harmful practice. He had become such a slave that he could not give it up in spite of every effort. Time and again he willed and willed himself never to masturbate again, only to find that the very next hour he had masturbated, thus producing tremendous depression. We reassured him that most young men masturbate and that there was nothing to worry about. It is fear about the harmful effects of masturbation that produces impotency. He wanted a magic pill which would produce an erection, and was most disappointed when we pointed out to him that once he is convinced that masturbation leads to no harmful effects, his normal potency would soon return. He left most disappointed but telephoned four days later to say that he had been successful in consummating the marriage.

FEAR OF HARMFUL EFFECTS OF SPERMATORRHOEA: Spermatorrhoea is loss of semen in the urine. Spermatozoa appear quite often in the urine and mucous discharge of a healthy man. This is a frequent cause of anxiety and alarm, and is very common in cities, as a result of enforced abstinence from lack of a heterogeneous sexual outlet. Spermatorrhoea can be detected by the presence of spermatozoa in a slide, when a centrifuged specimen of urine is examined under a microscope. Spermatorrhoea is a harmless physiological loss. It does not have any connection with potency nor does it create other harmful effects like weakness or loss of vitality. It is the anxiety and the worry about losing semen' which is responsible for the so-called bad effects. Men should be warned not to be 'semen-conscious' and not watch for the presence of semen every time they urinate.

PHOSPHATURIA: This is a condition where cloudy urine is passed and where patients observe white agglutinated masses at the end of urination, due to the presence of phosphates. Phosphaturia is very common in the tropics, where the vast majority of the population live on a vegetarian diet. Phosphaturia is often mistaken by laymen and even medical students for spermatorrhoea, because of the white, cloudy appearance of the urine in both conditions. If the cloudiness of the urine is due to phosphaturia, a few drops of hydrochloric acid clarifies the urine immediately, thus distinguishing it from spermatorrhoea. A vegetarian medical student, nineteen years old, consulted us for loss of semen, lack of energy and very poor erections. He had been passing white cloudy urine for the last year. Every time he urinated he collected the urine in a glass and was alarmed by the amount of semen he had lost. 'It must weaken me, Doctor,' he said. A few drops of hydrochloric acid were put in the cloudy specimen and it cleared up immediately.

FEAR OF HARMFUL EFFECTS OF NIGHT EMISSIONS: It is popularly believed that forty drops of blood go to make a drop of semen. Like gold, silver and diamonds, semen is considered to be the body's most precious fluid and frequent loss of it is—quite wrongly—thought to lead to dissipated nerves, mental and physical exhaustion, and marked impairment of intellect and thinking—if there is a combination of masturbation and frequent 'wet dreams'.

The widely published theory, that athletes, weight-lifters, boxers and wrestlers would have diminished vitality if they had frequent night discharges, is entirely without foundation.

Like the fear of the harmful effects of masturbation, nocturnal emissions have no bearing on potency. This is one of the normal sex outlets when there are no chances of heterosexual contact during adolescence.

THE SIZE OF THE PENIS AND TESTES: Boys and young men are often worried about the size of their penis and testicles. It is a common practice in school dormitories and bathrooms to compare the size of one's penis, and if it appears to be on the smaller side it is a source of great worry to the individual concerned, producing a sense of inferiority and shame. This is based on the fallacy that the larger the penis the more effective is the male during intercourse. Masters and Johnson have shown that the length of the penis has nothing to do with sexual adequacy. Even a small penis is very effective, because of the involuntary accommodative power of the vagina during intercourse.

FEAR OF VENEREAL DISEASE: Indoctrination of the adolescent and susceptible mind by preachers and teachers instills a tremendous fear of venereal disease. They are told that if they attempt intercourse with women, they are likely to get venereal disease, which will ruin their life for ever. As the saying goes, ' A few seconds with Venus and the rest of your life with Mercury', which in the good old days was the anti-venereal drug. This subconscious fear of venereal disease is known to affect potency, even though the man knows that his wife is a *virgo intacta* and free from any blemish.

FIRST NIGHT IMPOTENCY: Young men who have not had premarital sex find it difficult to penetrate the vagina unless the woman actively cooperates and helps at the beginning of intercourse. Many men suffer from the primitive fear of the woman's body and her vagina. Young boys are often told by their elder brothers, 'If you ever enter a vagina, go there with a lantern, lest you be lost.' These fantasies persist in later life and produce tremendous fear of the woman's body, which may finally lead to impotency.

There is also the fear of hurting the loved one, which results in diminished potency. If the female partner is not psychologically and sexually prepared for what is in store for her, she grows very tense and rigid, thus making penetration by the male difficult or well nigh impossible. The male partner mistakenly believes this inability to penetrate to be failure on his part, which in turn might result in impotency.

Last but not the least, if a couple wants to practise *coitus inter-ruptus* or premature withdrawal before discharge of the semen, the preoccupation can often result in impotency in the male, more so in premarital or extra-marital sexual intercourse.

DOMINATING DAMES: Many women do not realise that they completely dominate their husbands. The modern emanicipated dame (who wears the trousers in more senses than one!) has economic, social and sexual freedom, thinks that she can compete with her male partner in everything—as in the flim *Annie Get Your Gun,* where Annie sings: 'Anything you can do, I can do better.' Is it any wonder then that an American psychiatrist reported to the American Medical Association that out of every 100 persons who applied for a sex change operation, 66 per cent were males. The equality of sexes and sexual freedom is leading to increased female domination and assertiveness. Society is becoming increasingly matriarchal. Is it surprising then to find that the poor paper tiger finds difficulty in tackling the tigress? The noted anthropologist Margaret Mead has called this 'emasculation of the modern male'. Of course, women do not do it consciously, and express great surprise in the consulting rooms when their dominating characteristics are pointed out to them. A charming, smartly turned out lady once complained about her husband's impotence. She was very thorough and meticulous and dominated all his activities. The husband was a nice, reticent man, who casually mentioned that his wife ran his life to the minutest detail. He was also worried about his business which had run into difficulties. I explained the husband's difficulties to the wife and, in a very roundabout way, told her that she was 'wearing the pants' in the house. She was most understanding and co-operative. She felt sorry that she had been so dominating. She immediately changed her tune and the couple went off for a short holiday. On her return she told me: 'I cannot stop my husband; he has gone the other way now!' If both men and women decide to give some thought to what constitutes masculine and feminine roles, potency in men will invariably assert itself. We must here point out that most women are not conscious of their dominating traits, but, once things have been explained to them, they are convinced and invariably try their best to change. A lady patient of mine once very rightly said, 'The female can have full gratifiction only if the male is on top of the woman—in every sense of the word.'

GUILT FEELINGS: Over-religious parents impress on the child that sex is something immoral. This leaves indelible marks on the young mind. When such an individual gets married, he runs into sexual difficulties, because deep down inside him he thinks sex is immoral and dirty.

HOSTILITY AND RESENTMENT: Though this cause operates a few years after marriage, in some cases the subconscious hostility and resentment towards the wife can lead to impotency. Unless the pair, through their own efforts or through their marriage counsellor, resolve their differences, potency is not likely to return.

FAILURE FROM WEAKNESS OF DESIRE: In the normal male, sexual excitement is aroused by the presence of the beloved—through sight, sound, touch and smell—which results in erection. Even though the woman may not be present, the mere thought of or psychic image of the woman can result in normal erection. If the sexual urge is repressed in childhood, the child grows up showing lack of interest in women. In later life, this lack of interest makes him avoid women. Women are not his preserve; they are meant for other lucky males. He represses his urge, until ultimately sexual desire and night emissions stop and impotence sets in. When to such individuals an explanation is given that the repression of the sexual urge has led to their present difficulties, they soon return to normal.

PROLONGED ABSTINENCE: Prolonged abstinence is a common cause of impotence, if the male has remained abstinent because of the death of his wife or has married late in life. During the two World Wars, when men had to remain abstinent for a long time, many on their return from active service were shocked to learn that they had become impotent because of prolonged abstinence. If fear and anxiety had not set in, their potency would soon have returned to normal. In the human body, all important organs remain in shipshape condition if they are constantly used. The same is true of the sexual organs, which, if not constantly used, can cause problems and difficulties.

SUBLIMATION: Many moralists and religious leaders have advocated self-control, abstinence and suppression of sex, so that the Soul may reach a higher level and ultimately become one with the Creator. Sublimation, that is, conversion of sexual energy into other energy, not only results in impotency but also leads to nervous disturbances.

RELATIVE IMPOTENCY: Relative impotency is a condition, where the male is potent with one female but with another his potency diminishes at times.

FAILURE WITH ONE WOMAN BUT NOT WITH ANOTHER: The wife of one of my patients sued him for divorce on the grounds of impotency. The young man had failed to consummate the marriage with her, in spite of every effort. It so happened that on the wedding night, when the tense, sensitive boy could not perform because he was self-conscious about getting a proper erection, his wife ridiculed him about his inability. This set up a tremendous inferiority complex in him, with the result that he was never successful with her. Two years later, after his divorce, he remarried a childhood friend of his. This girl had tremendous understanding of her man, with the result that he was able to function normally with her and in a short time she became pregnant. There are also cases where the husband is impotent with the mistress and yet has a normal sexual relationship with his wife. In the latter case, where the man is impotent with his mistress, the cause may be guilt or fright that they may be found out. Conversely, the impotence with the wife can be due to getting tired of the same woman. Man is basically a polygamous animal and quite often likes to pay attention to other women without any dishonourable intentions.

IMPOTENCY WITH LOVED FEMALE: Freud described the type of characteristic impotency where a man loves his wife and yet is unable to have intercourse with her, yet is perfectly normal with other females. Freud said: 'When such men love, they have no desire, and when they desire, they cannot love.' According to him, during the emotional development of a boy, the affection and love that he has for his mother is much older than the sensual sex feelings which arise at puberty. In an emotionally mature male, the older feelings of affection and love are detached from the mother and fused with the newer, sensual feelings of affection, and both of them in turn get attached to the loved one—the girlfriend or wife. The same transference has to take place between a girl and her father. According to Freud, the extent of fusion determines the degree of potency. If, on the other hand, the newer sensual feeling in a boy got attached to the old affection for the mother, impotency results. We had a patient, aged 27, married for four months, whose wife stated that their marriage was not consummated and that the husband complained of severe headache and always postponed intercourse. Before marriage the husband was a Casanova and was proud of his sexual conquests. Before marriage our sensual athlete was very attached to his mother, but when he moved out of the house to live with his wife, she became a mother substitute. He had strong guilt feelings whenever he attempted to make love to her, which ultimately made him impotent.

OCCASIONAL FAILURE: No man can ever be hundred per cent sure of himself. It is quite possible that even a normal man occasionally has premature ejaculation or complete failure. It is said that even Casanova occasionally failed with women!

We are reminded of a Captain for whom a very urgent appointment was asked by a shipping company. As I opened the door, I noticed a tall, strapping, rugged individual, pacing the floor of my waiting-room and wiping with his handkerchief the beads of perspiration from his face. His hands were trembling like an aspen leaf. 'Come in, Captain,' I said, putting my hand on his shoulder. As he sat on the chair, he burst out crying: 'Doctor, I want to die, I want to die, I want to commit suicide! Life is not worth living.' Depression was written on his face, and as I consoled him, he poured his heart out: 'I was a miserable failure with a woman last night. I have travelled the Seven Seas, and women had admired and loved me for my maleness. This is the first time I have failed. Is life worth living without women?' He went on sobbing for 15 minutes, at the end of which I reassured him that the most potent men have occasional failures, when they are mentally worried or physically tired or have indulged in excessive womanisation or had too much to drink. The Captain then admitted that the ship had a slight mishap and he was worried about it. We reassured him that, with a little rest, his potency was bound to return. Three days later, the overjoyed Captain gleefully reported, 'Life, Doctor, now is worth living!'

Impotence following vasectomy

Vasectomy is surgical removal of a part of the Ductus deferens (see Chapter 4) from both inguinal regions. It is one of the strongly recommended methods of male sterilisation since it can be performed easily as an outpatient procedure under local anaesthesia without the need of elaborate personnel or operating theatres. The operation has no sexual side-effects. However, an increasing number of males have reported erectile problems following sterilisation. 'Doctor, I was functioning fine until I was sterilised. I noticed that within two months after the operation, I lost my manliness,' said Vijaykumar, lamenting, 'I wish I had not succumbed to the surgery.' It is therefore imperative that the person having vasectomy understands its implications. He should be told that sterility and virility are two different things. A man can be sterilised so that the ejaculate does not contain sperms and yet be virile and perfectly capable of normal intercourse. Secondly, the operation does not affect his sexual pattern in any way. However, some patients feel that the surgery has castrated them and their own anxiety leads to a waning erection. It is their self-fulfilling prophecy that is responsible. Vasectomy has no sexual side-effects. Erection is dependent upon the male hormone testosterone which is released directly into the blood stream. Secondly, the testes contribute a very small portion of the liquid ejaculated, so the quantity of the ejaculate will not decrease appreciably. Finally, neurotic, psychotic (schizophrenic, depressive and manic) or impotent males should not undergo sterilisation.

Impotence in the middle-aged and elderly

In the middle-aged, sexual boredom (sex with the same partner in the same position), fear of ageing and loss of erectile powers are the main causes of impotence. Most males are unaware that erection in this group is not instantaneous as it is in the younger age group. After 40 it is necessary for the female partner to fondle the penis before it becomes erect. This is not a sign of oncoming impotence, as most males believe, but a normal physiological change due to ageing (see Chapter 13, 'Prevention of Impotence in Middle Age').

In the elderly, the most frequent cause of impotence is the self-fulfilling prophecy ingrained in our society that erectile power is lost in old age. Nature has given man the power of erection from the cradle to the grave. It is only modern man in the Stress Century living in a sexually restraining society that extinguishes it earlier (see Chapter 13, 'Prevention of Impotence in Old Age').

Why the penis lets us down at odd times
In order to understand the erective failure better let us compare the penis with our index finger, which is always obedient, under our command and ever ready to do what it is told. The poet Ralph Waldo Emerson vividly describes a quarrel between a mountain and a squirrel. Let us imagine a verbal duel between the penis and the index finger.

THE INDEX FINGER AND THE PENIS HAD A QUARREL
Index Finger

(I.F.):   You are the laziest and craziest of human organs. You don't do a stroke of work. Look at the lungs, the heart and the liver—they are on the job day and night.

Penis (P): I give pleasure which no other organ can. Without me, the human species would be extinct. And I do work by acting as a channel for voiding urine and discharging semen.

I.F.:   I can't understand why you suddenly sulk and go limp without rhyme or reason.

P.:   I am more sinned against than sinning. If my master does not know how to use me, is it my fault?

I.F.:   The heart and stomach stand a lot of nonsense before they pack up. Why must you go on strike like the Labour in our country, on the flimsiest excuses!

P.:   I am a no-nonsense organ. My erection response is very delicate and complicated. Like a burning matchstick it is easily extinguished.

I.F.:   I grant you erection is a complicated process but why should you, like a stubborn mule, remain limp and embarrass your master when he desperately wants you to be erect?

P.:   There is method in my madness. My master believes I should get erect at his command and sweet will. He sees a sizzling lady and 'thinks' he is aroused and curses me if I do not become erect when he wants to sleep with her.

I.F.:   Isn't he justified if you don't perform when he wants you to?

P.:   I am not an electrically operated robot that responds to commands with push-button frequency. He thinks he has only to press a button and I will become erect. Nature never intended that I should function this way.

I.F.: Why don't you tell him about the right way you can function and get erect?

P.: I have special requirements to get erect.

I.F.: I thought penises were fail-proof, beat-the-clock battering-rams, ever ready to get erect at a moment's notice.

P.: My dear chap, such penises only exist in the Fantasyland of sex portrayed by the media. In reality, things are entirely different.

I.F.: I get you, Sir. Incidentally, why don't you tell your master that the sexual machinery may occasionally fail like any other machine?

P.: Tell him? Never! Do you remember the other day when he had too much to drink and attempted sex—and it was a dismal failure?

I.F.: My dear friend, I immediately came to your rescue and produced a manual orgasm by clitoral stimulation.

P.: My master brought the roof down. He cursed and abused me. He believed that it was the end of the world. There is no tomorrow in his life.

I.F.: Why did you refuse to get erect the next day?

P.: He was gripped by fear and panic. The whole day at the office he kept saying to himself, 'I must get an erection tonight.' But I never respond to orders like 'I must' and 'I will'.

I.F.: Then how do you become erect at odd times during the day or during sleep at night, when no sex is required?

P.: Oh, you mean morning erections or piss-hards? They were formerly believed to be due to a full bladder. But I think my erection is due to his last dream.

I.F.: I can't understand your logic. You get erect during sleep but not when your master is awake and burning with desire. Surely you were never meant to be merely a showpiece but also a performer?

P.: I function naturally and normally all my life, if left to myself and if my master does not short-circuit his wiring or orders me about.

I.F.: I am so used to being ordered about by my master that I do instantaneously what I am told.

P.: That is because you and I are governed by different systems. Yours is the central nervous system, mine is the autonomic.

I.F.: Why are there different controls for you and me when we belong to the same person?

P.: We have different commanders-in-chief. Your boss is the cerebral cortex while mine is the hypothalamus. Your brain is the 'thinking' brain, mine is the 'feeling' brain, the seat of emotions.

I.F.: I get you! I only function when the man 'thinks' and asks me to do something. You never function if your owner thinks and consciously wills an erection. He has to 'feel' the desire.

P.: Right! My master may 'think' he is aroused and yet no messages reach me to get hard.

I.F.: You mean the messages are short-circuited?

P.: Yes. Often my master attempts sex when he is bored, or tired and tense. He does not really feel aroused and I do not react to half-hearted messages. I am a no-nonsense organ.

I.F.: You are a spoilt brat—just because you are a symbol of his manliness. Why during penis-vagina intercourse a number of women do not reach orgasm!

P.: True. But I am the glamour boy of my owner. Poets and novelists sing my praise. Only dull anatomists write about you and medical students curse you, as they dissect your intricate muscles and nerves.

I.F. Certainly not! Every sexologist writes about my tremendous powers and flexibility in producing multiple orgasms in the female. I am never temperamental like you. I am obedient, dependable and at his beck and call. My master cannot do without me.

P.: Utter nonsense! One finger is as good as the other—it can

	be chopped off! But I am the creator. Tell me, how do you produce an orgasm?
I.F.:	The clitoris is the most sensitive organ in the female. I first massage the mons area, then the side of the clitoris and finally the body and the glans. I continue doing it even while she is having an orgasm.
P.:	Women like to be orgasmic the natural penis-vagina way.
I.F.:	You're kidding! *The Hite Report on Female Sexuality* says less than one-third of women were orgasmic during penis-vagina intercourse without finger stimulation of the clitoris. Seventy per cent of them need my help to reach an orgasm.
P.:	You are my Man Friday! You help me out when I am in difficulties.
I.F.:	Shall we call a truce? We both need each other to satisfy the female of the species.

3
TREATMENT OF IMPOTENCE

This section is written not only for the lay reader but also for medical students and doctors. There is an acute shortage of sex therapists in India; only a few are found in the cities. Unlike the West, there is an innate shyness and reluctance among sexually inadequate males to seek professional advice though they are quite willing to consult their family physicians who are their friend, philosopher and guide. Ninety per cent of sexual inadequacies in the male are due to inadequate knowledge and needless anxieties about sexual functioning. The family physician is ideally suited to sort out such simple sexual problems and earn his eternal gratitude. The problems of the remaining ten per cent are too deep-rooted and need to be treated by a qualified sex therapist or a psychologist.

Sexology has made tremendous advances in the West in the last two decades. But in most of our medical colleges, sexology is not even included in the curriculum. All these institutions teach is the anatomy and physiology of the sexual organs and reproduction. This is the reason why general practitioners are ill-equipped to tackle emotionally charged sexual problems. What usually happens in a case of impotence is that the physician without the necessary background does a routine physical examination and informs the patient that 'there is nothing wrong'; his impotence is 'psychological'; it is 'all in his head'. This statement further disturbs and upsets the patient, as he is normal in every other way; in fact, many such men have attained eminence in their professions. He immediately asks, 'Why do I have the trouble if there is nothing wrong with me?'. The doctor routinely prescribes a few hormone injections and tells the patient not to worry. 'Everything will be all right. The injections take a little time to act.' As a parting short, he adds, 'Keep on trying. You will succeed.' The patient unfortunately is not cured by such treatment or advice and flits from doctor to doctor hoping for some magic pill or potion which would cure him. After years of gloom and despair he is referred for psychotherapy. Patients always prefer to consult their own doctors for impotence rather than go for prolonged psychoanalysis or psychotherapy which puts a great strain on both partners and on the marriage itself.

A few enthusiastic venereologists and urologists used to believe that impotence was due to congestion of the prostate and the urethra. They massaged the prostate to tone it up and instilled solutions of silver nitrate in the posterior urethra which caused a stricture of the urethra in later life.

Was it any wonder that patients thronged to quacks who had glowing certificates of making impotent maharajahs potent and converting weakly potent ones into Casanovas? The pills, potions and the *palangtod paans,* like any placebo, had a temporary effect. As John Money, the well-known psychologist at John Hopkins University School of Medicine, says: 'Patients expect to get better, so they do for a while. Any form of treatment is likely to work some of the time, at least to bring about a temporary reversal of symptoms because of a placebo effect.' After some time the unfortunate individual goes back to square one.

The past two decades of treatment
Great strides have been taken in the treatment of impotence in the last two decades due to the pioneering efforts of Masters and Johnson.

Before that, psychoanalysis, which went on for years, was the only treatment for sexual dysfunction arising from sexual conflicts in childhood. Even though the patient gained deep insight into his so-called conflicts, the impotence continued in many cases. Masters and Johnson demonstrated that if the immediate obstacles to sexual functioning were removed the patient made a remarkable recovery in a short time even though the remote causes like childhood conflicts were left untouched. The million-dollar question arises: Should we discard all the conventional beliefs of psychoanalysis and concentrate only on the immediate factors that cause sexual dysfunction? Helen Singer Kaplan says, 'Perhaps a more satisfying alternative is a synthesis which conceptualises the etiology of sexual dysfunction as being due to both remote and immediate causes. These two sets of causes operate at different levels but they are not incompatible.

Modern sex therapists concentrate on the immediate causes of sexual dysfunction while psychoanalysts dwell on anxiety resolution of the remote causes, ignoring the immediate causes. Kaplan advocates a happy marriage of both groups of causes, immediate and remote, for a wider therapeutic spectrum instead of exclusively concentrating on one or the other. I shall briefly outline the various therapies in vogue today.

PHYCHOTHERAPY: The main aim is to resolve the childhood sexual conflicts responsible for impotence. These have already been outlined in Section 2 of this chapter.

BEHAVIOUR THERAPY: Dr. Masters and Mrs. Johnson (now Mrs. Masters) formulated the unique concept that the marital unit must be treated as one, with both partners being treated simultaneously and not just the partner with a sexual problem. They along with the marital partners, form what is called the 'therapeutic foursome'. In India, there are a number of family physicians whose wives are also qualified doctors and can easily form the therapeutic foursome for the treatment of sexual dysfunction. The Masters-Johnson treatment is expensive and even in the USA a large number of solo therapists treat the marital unit.

SINGLE THERAPIST AND SINGLE PARTNER: This is used where the female partner is not available for treatment.

THERAPY WITH SURROGATE PARTNERS: In the early stages, Dr. Masters used surrogate partners. The word 'surrogate' means substitute. The sex foundation supplies a properly trained partner for the sexually inadequate male. Dr. Masters has given up this practice and so have many other American clinics.

NEW SEX THERAPY: Dr. Helen Singer Kaplan of Cornell University Medical College in New York has wedded the insight and techniques of psychotherapy to behaviour methods. Her method combines the best of behaviour therapy and psychotherapy at the surface, going deeper only if necessary. According to her, lack of knowledge of sex is the commonest cause which can be easily reversed by learning. If the sexual inadequacy stems from recent anxiety, Kaplan recommends a series of guided sexual exercises.

RATIONAL EMOTIVE THERAPY: This is an outpatient procedure for only one person. According to Dr. Ellis, the therapist instructs and educates an impotent male that it is not what happens that upsets him but his belief that he must have an erection when he is with a woman.

GROUP THERAPY: A sexually inadequate male feels that he is 'alone and palely loitering' in a world of sexual Casanovas. Besides, the cost of sex therapy in the West is prohibitive and many cannot afford it. To make the inadequate male feel one among many others in his neighbourhood who are sexually inadequate and also to reduce the financial burden, group sex therapy has been evolved in the West. Charles Lobitz and Joseph LoPiccollo were the first to demonstrate that women who have never reached an orgasm could be treated in groups where they were taught masturbation. However, group therapy is more popular among anorgasmic females learning to be orgasmic. Bernard Zilbergeld, Co-director of Clinical Training of the Human Sexuality Programme in the University of California, has developed a successful group therapy programme for males.

Treatment

The common causes of erection problems have already been outlined in Section 1 of this chapter. The reader will find a ready reckoner in tabulated form given in table 14:1 more helpful when taking the

TABLE 14-1
Causes of Impotence

PSYCHOLOGICAL CAUSES		ORGANIC DISEASES	DRUGS
	FUNCTIONAL DISORDER		
I. *Remote Causes*	(a) Tiredness	I. *Metabolic*	I. *Anticholinergics*
(a) Oedipus problems	(b) Stress	(a) Diabetes	(a) Banthine
(b) Denial of sexuality in childhood	(c) Anxiety	(a) Hypogonadism	(b) Probanthine
(c) Guilt	(d) Depression	(c) Hypothyroidism	II. *Sedatives*
(d) Fear of harmful effects of masturbation and nocturnal emissions	(e) Boredom		(a) Alcohol
	(f) Lack of desire	II. *Vascular*	(b) Heroin
		(a) Arteriosclerosis of penile arteries	(c) Morphine
			(d) Codeine
		(b) Liver diseases such as cirrhosis	(e) Antianxiety drugs
			(f) Antidepressants
II. *Immediate Causes*		III. *Nervous disorders*	III. *Antiadrenergic*
(a) Lack of knowledge		(a) Injury to lumbar or sacral segment of spine	(a) Beta blockers
(b) Fear of failure			IV. *Antiandrogens*
(c) Spectatoring		(b) Disseminated sclerosis	(a) Oestrogens
(d) Lack of communication			

history of the patient, ascertaining the true causes of the difficulty and planning therapy.

Both the family physician and the individual with an erection problem will want to know how to restore normal sexual functioning. The former will need a simple format which he can easily adopt in a busy practice. The latter should ideally seek the help of his family physician in erectile difficulties. For those individuals who are unable to obtain professional help, a 'do-it-yourself programme' is also outlined. If the female partner is not available, therapy for the single male partner is also given. However, the best results are obtained when both partners are seen together and undertake therapy together.

Case history

This section is written for the family physician interested in treating sexual dysfunction as well as the non-professional reader for whom sex therapy is not available or who is too shy and reticent to see a doctor. The doctor as well as the individual concerned will find the format useful in making out a detailed sexual history. An accurate history is of paramount importance in the treatment of sexual dysfunction. It forms the basis for ascertaining the cause of impotence and planning appropriate therapy. However, only simple problems like anxieties about the size of the penis or testes, masturbation and myths about exaggerated sexual function can be handled by the person himself. For more complex causes you have to consult a doctor.

If the patient is being seen for the first time it is better to complete the general medical history and clinical examination before going into the sexual history. This will help the partner to gain confidence and build a close rapport with the physician. On the other hand, if you know the patient intimately,you can start straightaway with the sexual history.

Sexual history

At the first interview, both partners are seen briefly when their history is taken in general and the main sexual complaints noted. After a while, one partner waits outside, while the history of the other partner is recorded. Later, the other partner is called in and the salient features of the history taken and cross-checked. Both the partners are asked not to discuss what was asked to them in the interest of better therapy and to preserve initially a cordial atmosphere.

Needless to say, sparks fly when both partners are seen together later! It is better to bring into the open the resentment or the hostility built over the years.

Getting a true history in sexual disorders is always difficult as most individuals are reticent in talking about sex. The physician should avoid asking direct questions like, 'How often do you masturbate?' Instead he can say tactfully 'Most young men masturbate. It is a perfectly normal practice when intercourse with a female partner is not possible.' This approach will put the patient at ease, remove his inhibitions and encourage him to talk freely about his sexual problems. The patient should always be given time to talk and unburden himself. He should never be hurried, but should have undivided attention and should be made to feel that the doctor is always interested in him, understands his problem and will do everything to help him get over his disorders. The physician should never show any personal embarrassment during the interveiw.

The sexual history is taken in great detail to study the sexual make-up of the individual and find out the exact cause of his impotence. Psychological impotence occurs only under a certain set of conditions. The highly selective nature of psychological impotence distinguishes it from organic impotence and impotence due to drugs, where the impotence is present at all times and is not selective. For example, in psychogenic impotence an individual may be potent with his mistress but not his wife or vice versa, or may have erection and ejaculation during masturbation but not during attempted intercourse with a female.

He may have morning erections but not at any other time. Morning erections occur three or four times at night during a sexual or an asexual dream. Their exact cause is not known but according to Bernard Zilbergild in *Men and Sex,* 'Morning erections are erections which accompany the last dream of the night.' It was formerly believed that morning erections were due to the reflex action of a full bladder. If this was true the problem of psychological impotence would be immediately solved. All the impotent male would have to do was to attempt intercourse with a full bladder. Morning erections in a man who cannot achieve erection during intercourse are, according to Stekel, the most reliable symptom of psychic impotence. To prove that the impotence is psychic the following questions are asked:

(1) Do you have an erection in the early morning?
(2) Do you have erections during masturbation?
(3) Do you have erections during dreams?
(4) Do you have erections during sexual fantasy or daydreams?
(5) Is intercourse possible with a female partner other than your wife?
(6) Do you have erections under other conditions like riding or in a train?

In psychic impotence the answer to any of these questions is 'Yes'. If the answer is 'No' to all the questions, the individual is asked to observe for a week or two whether he has any erections in the morning. Many males have morning erections about which they are not conscious unless they are told to observe them. He is also asked to masturbate by recalling the same fantasy and see if he gets an erection. If the patient still reports no erection, the impotence is psychological, if other causes (organic or drugs) are excluded.

DURATION OF SEXUAL DIFFICULTY: When did he first notice it? Is there a complete loss of erection? General questions like 'How is your sex life?' should not be asked. Instead specific questions framed in a particular way should be asked. For example, 'Is there a desire for sex?' Detailed questions about the nature of erection, penetration, maintenance of erection, orgasm and ejaculation, and, similarly in women, about desire, lubrication, accommodation and orgasm, should be framed on the following lines.

SEXUAL EXPERIENCE IN BOYHOOD AND PUBERTY
(1) When did you first have an erection?
(2) What was the frequency of night discharge?
(3) Have you had intercourse?
(4) What was the result?

MASTURBATION
(1) What is your attitude towards masturbation?
(2) What is the frequency?
(3) Do you have remorse or guilt after masturbation?
(4) What were the nature of fantasies before or during masturbation?

INTERCOURSE

(1) Do you know the mechanics of intercourse? (Many men have difficulties because they are unaware of the anatomy and physiology of the male and female reproductive organs.)

FEAR

(1) Does any type of fear dominate your attitude towards sex? (The commonest fear is that of impotence. There may also be a fear about an unwanted pregnancy or venereal disease.)

PREREQUISITES

(1) Are there any prerequisites for your potency?

(2) Are you potent with a certain type of woman, like call girls or prostitutes?

(3) Do you need to take alcohol before you can have sex?

(4) Are there any other prerequisites, such as the female fondling your penis or wearing a particular sari or blouse or pantie?

HOMOSEXUALITY

(1) Have there been any homosexual tendencies? If so, at what age?

(2) Do you prefer the company of men to women?

(3) Do you enjoy the active or passive role in homosexuality more than normal intercourse?

(4) Was your potency normal during a homosexual experience?

THE SPOUSE

(1) Do you really love your wife or was it a marriage of convenience?

(2) Is there a secret hostility towards the wife?

(3) Are you sexually attracted to your wife?

(4) What do you think of your wife during intercourse?

(5) Is she highly passionate or cold and frigid?

(6) Do you think that she suffers from some obstruction or spasm of the vaginal muscles which prevents intercourse?

(7) What is her attitude towards your disability?

(8) Is she sympathetic and understanding or has she ridiculed you?

(9) Can she do without sex?

(10) Is she content to reach an orgasm through manual manipulation?

(11) Is she prepared to go on with the marriage for security or companionship?

THE FEMALE PARTNER should always be interviewed for a better understanding of the cause of impotence. There is no difficulty today in seeing her. The doctor should impress on her that what she communicates to him will remain entirely private, and the idea of seeing her is to find out more about the difficulty facing the husband.

It should be pointed out to her at the onset that inability to have an erection is the most humiliating experience for the male. Explain to her that the male has no conscious control over erection. Erection happens when he is in a particular frame of mind. It is but natural that her pride is hurt that in spite of her attractiveness she is unable to produce an erection in her husband. She should also be told that there is a wide gap betwen desire in the male and its fulfillment.

The doctor should impress on the wife that a little encouragement from her will work wonders for the partner. Many timid men need sexual arousal and that is why a mistress who knows the art is more successful than an inexperienced wife in stimulating his passions. She is also advised not to pass disparaging remarks about his disability. She should be very discreetly told that many males have certain prerequisites for potency. Has she observed any in her male partner? The female hand stimulating the male organ in the right way at the right time during foreplay is the best aphrodisiac in the world.

At this interview the doctor can also assess whether the female is suffering from inhibition or spasm of the vaginal muscles which may prevent them from having successful sexual intercourse. Discreet inquiries should be made about the character of the male. Is he fond of her? Is he kind and considerate towards her? The doctor can assess whether the female partner is very dominating. The male who cannot be aggressive in sex might suffer from impotence.

HISTORY OF ALCOHOL AND DRUGS

Alcohol, opium (a common ingredient of *paan), bhang, charas* and a number of medicines today can cause erectile depression and premature ejaculation (see the section on Alcohol and Drugs). A careful enquiry should therefore be made about the intake of drugs and alcohol, on the following lines:

(1) Do you take sleeping tablets or tranquillizers? If so, which, when and how many?

(2) Do you take any drugs for high blood pressure or for gastro-intestinal problems?

(3) What is the intake of alcohol?

(4) What is its effect on sex?

(5) Is there any history of chronic drug addiction like morphia, cocaine or pethidine?

(6) Why do you take drugs or alcohol?

(7) Is it to relieve anxiety and tension?

(8) What is the apparent cause for this anxiety and tension?

LABORATORY INVESTIGATIONS

It is necessary that all cases should have a complete physical examination, blood chemistry and hormone profile where available to exclude physical causes like diabetes, hypothyroidism and use of tranquillisers, sedatives, antihypertensives and anticholinergics. Tests should include: (1) Routine blood test; (2) Fasting blood sugar 2 to 3 hours after glucose; (3) Lipid profile; (4) Tests for bilirubin; (5) SGPT and electrophoresis of proteins to exclude liver disorders; (6) Thyroxine evels (T3 and T4); (7) Follicle stimulating hormone (FSH) and Lutenizing hormone (LH) levels; and (8) Serum Testosterone levels.

Although the most prevalent causes of sexual dysfunction are psychological, physical factors must first be ruled out before commencing sex therapy or psychotherapy for deep-seated sexual disorders.

ASCERTAINING CAUSES

With a thorough work-up in each case, it is easy to find out the cause of impotence:

(1) Is it organic? If so, what disease is responsible?

(2) Have any drugs individually or in combination with other causes, resulted in impotence?

(3) Is excessive alcohol intake responsible or playing a part in the production of impotence?

(4) Is it psychogenic? If so, what is the exact cause?

The treatment should be tailored to the cause. If the erection problem is due to a physical disease or disorder, the treatment should be directed towards treating the primary cause. However, sex therapy may also be required in these cases to combat the sexual anxiety and fear of failure which is invariably present. If drugs are responsible the physician should substitute another which has no sexual side-effects. For instance, in the treatment of hypertension, drugs like guanethidine (Ismelin) or methyldopa (Aldomet) cause sexual dysfunction in more than 50 per cent of cases. One can substitute them with thiazide diuretics or minoxidil derivatives (Loniten) which have no sexual side-effects. Similarly, in the case of alcohol, the remedy to restore sexual functioning is to give it up completely.

The only cause left is psychogenic impotence whose therapy is outlined in detail in this section. Psychogenic impotence may be primary or secondary. Secondary impotence most frequently occurs in a male who after years of successful sexual innings, develops erectile difficulties. More than 50 per cent of the male population have transient erectile failure but potency soon returns. Such cases should not be labelled impotent. However, the disability continues in a number of insecure males because of extreme anxiety generated by the initial erective failure—and they need sex therapy.

Primary impotence is much less frequent than secondary and is due to the Oedipus complex, sexual conflicts in childhood and cultural or religious orthodoxy. Such cases need professional psychotherapy and are best not handled by the family physician. The male with primary impotence, according to its definition, has never once been able to have intercourse successfully. However, one sees a number of impotent young men who have never had successful intercourse, the few times they have tried. Such individuals should not be branded as primarily impotent and subjected to psychotherapy. Most of them (like Popatlal) suffer from lack of sexual know-how about female anatomy, fears of the so-called harmful effects of masturbation, or fear about night discharges and phosphaturia which is fairly prevalent because of the predominantly vegetarian diet of our country causing alkaline urine (see Chapter 2). These cases respond as soon as they become knowledgeable about the normal anatomy and physiology of sexual response.

Pre-therapeutic concepts
For sex therapy to be effective certain pre-therapy concepts have to be observed in every case of sexual dysfunction.

GUIDELINES FOR MEDICAL PRACTITIONERS

(1) All cases of impotence due to physical disorders should be excluded from sex therapy until the patient has recovered. The primary disease or disorder resulting in impotence should first be treated before tackling erectile dysfunction.

(2) All cases of psychoses such as schizophrenia, paranoia, mania and endogenous depression should be temporarily excluded from sex therapy till recovery.

GUIDELINES FOR INDIVIDUALS

(1) The individual must understand how the penis works and show it some degree of tolerance. Learn to take an occasional failure in your stride (see Chapter 4 and section 2 of this chapter).

(2) Sex needs a lot of energy. You must maintain radiant health for adequate sexual functioning. Sex and tiredness do not go together.

(3) For adequate sexual functioning sex should be a high priority item. Most individuals attempt sex after doing everything else, have no reserve energy left for sex and flop disastrously.

(4) Avoid sex after overindulgence in alcohol, which provokes the desire but takes away the performacne.

(5) Attempt sex only when you *feel* aroused and go all out at it. There is no half-way house in sex.

(6) Most men have certain prerequisites for normal sexual functioning, such as the female caressing the penis. On the other hand, there are men who immediately lose their erection if their partner touches it. Similarly, in middle age, the penis usually takes a little time for erection and may need caressing by the female partner. Find out what makes you tick.

(7) Never attempt sex when you are anxious, upset, in a bad mood or under stress. However, the tolerance to stressful situations varies from individual to individual, depending on how they cope with stress.

(8) Variety is the spice of sex. Both partners should avoid boredom and routine sex. Experiment with different sexual poses to make it more enjoyable.

(9) Communicate all your requirements within reason and see that they are met. Also find out from your partner how and where she wants to be stimulated.

(10) Sex should always be carefree, without predetermined goals. It is

always better to float along with the experience.

(11) Be assertive without being rude or aggressive. Never indulge in sex as a matter of manly duty to please your partner. Have the courage to say you are not in the mood or how you like to be pleasured. Men have to learn how to abandon themselves to uninhibited eroticism. 'I like a man to be a tiger not a lamb, I mean assertive and dominating in sex,' Sophie told me—and most women think the same.

Basic principles of sex therapy

To recapitulate, the primary objective of any sex therapy is to relieve sexual dysfunction, which can be achieved by various therapy formats such as prolonged psychotherapy, Masters and Johnson's therapeutic foursome (two therapists and two partners), intensive 2-week behaviour therapy, marital therapy which resolves pathological inter-action between two partners, and Helen Kaplan's New Sex Therapy which is a happy marriage of behaviour and psychogenic therapy; single therapist and both partners, or single therapist and in excep-tional cases the single partner, have also been treated.

While psychotherapy and marital therapy aim at removing the patient's main conflict which has resulted in sexual dysfunction, all other therapies rightly concentrate on what Kaplan calls the immediate 'here and now' problems.

The other basic difference between the old treatments and modern sex therapy is that in the former the therapeutic interactions take place in the physician's office, while in the latter the erotic experiences are conducted in the privacy of the marital partners' home. Women in general desire love rather than mechanical sex and therefore are reluc-tant to go through what are commonly called 'exercises' in the therapy of sexual dysfunction. It is better therefore if the therapist uses the term 'erotic experiences' instead to prevent resentment and hostility in the female partner.

The basis of any short-term therapy of sexual dysfunction depends on two therapy formats. Firstly, remove the performance pressure on the male by imposing total abstinence for a week or ten days, permit-ting only initial non-genital tactile stimulation of each other's body, to be followed later by genital stimulation. Finally, when the male's confidence about his erection is established in a non-demand, nonperformance milieu, intercourse is permitted, first with the female on top. The male is told not to worry if he loses the erection. There is always another time. Finally, the male-on-top position is attempted.

The rationale of this therapy is to divert the attention of both partners from performance or, as Dr. Masters calls it, 'spectatoring' or watching with a pinched anxious face whether an erection is taking place.

The series of 'erotic experiences' help the couple to learn the art of giving and receiving sexual pleasure. 'What I am doing.' Dr. Harold Lear of Manhattan's Mount Sinai Hospital tells his patients, 'is giving you a licence to think and feel and be erotic.' The therapist should give instructions in a firm yet polite way. 'Patients are usually reluctant to come to grips with their bodies and emotions,' says Kinsey associate Wardell Pomeroy. 'I get very explicit. I say, "Take your clothes off, take a shower together. Make notes and tell me what happens. Think that I am giving you a prescription at the drugstore that you have to go out and fill."

It is very necessary to give definite and detailed instructions for success in sex therapy. Three decades ago when a patient with a fever asked me what he should eat, my stereotyped reply was, 'Eat bland food.' Naturally, such advice never worked. I have now learnt the hard way to give precise and clear instructions to a patient. Finally, the therapist should be comfortable with his own sexuality and not have any cultural hang-ups about sex.

A good plan would be to see both partners together at first, then individually, when the detailed history is taken of each partner and the nature of the sexual dysfunction is ascertained. A laboratory work-up as outlined in the previous section is ordered for the male. After a few days when all the tests are ready the nature of the sexual dysfunction, whether it is organic, or due to alcohol and drugs, or psychogenic, is confirmed.

At this interview the normal anatomy and physiology of sexual functioning with slides or pictures and the art of mutual pleasuring with 'structured erotic experiences' is explained to the couple. The partners begin mutual pleasuring (see Appendix II) and visit the therapist once or twice a week when further 'structured erotic experiences' are suggested and if any psychological conflict is observed, it is resolved. The therapy continues till normal sexual functioning is restored.

Within four to six weeks or earlier, the majority of cases of sexual dysfunction respond to the simple sex therapy outlined above. However, quite a few cases need the help of a sex therapist or psychotherapy. While the format outlined above is based on the model used by the pioneers of sex therapy, Masters and Johnson, every case cannot fit into a cast-iron mould. The partners may not like to do the sensate focus exercises (erotic sensual experiences), in which case instead of banging the rock of resistance which prevents further therapeutic progress, it is better to go around it and modify the procedure.

A six-week therapy format is outlined below, where the marital partners are seen twice a week. However, it can be condensed into an intensive two-week programme, depending upon the family physician's convenience.

Therapy programme

1ST DAY: Both partners are seen together briefly and the nature of the sexual dysfunction noted. It is necessary to reduce the anxiety of both partners by making the atmosphere cheerful and allaying their anxiety as far as possible.

The female partner is requested to wait outside while a general examination and sexual history of the male is taken.

The female partner is interviewed while the male waits outside. Relevant points of history are counter-checked and if a problem like vaginismus or fleshy hymen is suspected, a physical examination is done on her as well.

All pathological tests are ordered.

Both partners are told not to communicate with each other about what was asked in their sexual history. Intercourse is prohibited for a few days.

5TH DAY: Both partners return with the laboratory investigation reports of the male. If necessary, the sexual history is rechecked. The cause of the impotence is diagnosed and therapy planned.

The normal anatomy and physiology of sexual response in both sexes, with slides or pictures, are explained to the couple. Any doubts or difficulties are sorted out.

The importance of communication between the partners is emphasised.

The couple is now told to commence 'structured erotic experiences' without pleasuring the breasts or the genitals. The female usually begins first, followed by the male. Both are told to let themselves go.

The male is told not to look for an erection and even if he gets one, which frequently happens, not to indulge in intercourse.

The male or the female partner may wonder why such a childish exercise is prescribed, in which case the importance of touch is explained to the partners in depth (if time is short, call them again). It is impressed on them that in order to be sexual they must be sensual.

9TH DAY: The partners report on how they feel about mutual pleasuring. Ask discreetly whether they like it. Do they have any reservations? Are they more relaxed and communicative? Did they notice any erection while pleasuring each other?

It is again emphasised that erection can occur but if it is absent the male should not become a spectator and look out for one, as erection can never be commanded.

The partners are told to initiate genital pleasuring. The wife should pleasure the penis lovingly, in ways which give her partner pleasure. It should not be oriented to produce an erection. If erection occurs she adopts the teasing technique—stopping stimulation when erection has taken place, restarting when it is lost.

Intercourse is still prohibited.

12TH OR 14TH DAY: The progress of pleasuring is evaluated and the physician discreetly inquires whether erection has taken place. If the pair report good erection and the male by now has developed erectile confidence, the partners are complimented for mutually helping each other to resolve their dysfunction.

It is again emphasised that there is no way the therapist can teach a penis to get erect on demand. It must come naturally when he feels aroused.

When erection occurs spontaneously, the wife is encouraged to put herself in the female superior position.

Before stimulating the penis she starts caressing it from this position. If a full erection occurs, Dr. Masters and Johnson give very specific directions on how the wife should attempt intromission in a casual non-demanding way: 'No hurry to mount, no rush to obtain sexual tension release should be permitted. When she is attempting penile insertion, the penis should be angled at approximately 45 degrees from the perpendicular and directed towards the head. When mounting, the wife is encouraged to move back on the shaft of the penis rather than to sit on it (see Fig. 14-1).

The greatest threat to a male with erective dysfunction is penetrating the vagina. Initially, he may have a strong erection during 'erotic experiences', but at the critical countdown—intromission—he becomes anxious and starts doubting his powers. The result: the organ suddenly becomes limp as the erection disappears. It is therefore most essential that performance pressure on him during intromission is completely eliminated by making the female partner solely responsible

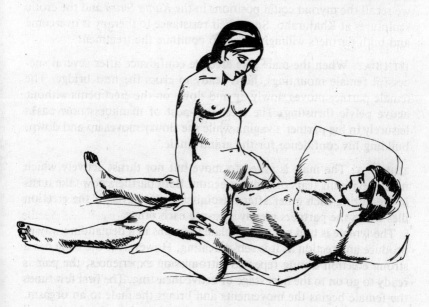

(Fig. 14-1, Non-demanding penile stimulation.)

for intromission. The above technique bypasses the most important obstacle every impotent male faces. He is now on the royal road to recovering his lost manhood and has only to contend with a few minor hurdles like losing the erection occasionally. The female partner is instructed to manually manipulate the penis while inserting it so that erection is maintained during her mounting. She is asked to lie still and not indulge initially in to-and-fro thrusting movements. The couple is asked to repeat the experience several times so that the male develops confidence in his erective ability.

There may be resistance from both partners to the female superior position. 'She will boss over me always, if you permit her to be on top of me,' objects the surprised male. 'How can I love him in that awkward pose? It is a man's duty to initiate sex,' protests the embarrassed female. We remind the former that his concern is to function normally, and normal intercourse is neither a power game between the sexes nor a battlefield. To the ever-sacrificing sexually inhibited wife, we recall the myriad coital positions in the *Kama Sutra* and the erotic sculptures at Khajuraho. Soon their resistance to therapy is overcome and both partners willingly agree to continue the treatment.

18TH DAY: When the male gets erective confidence after several successful female mountings, he is ready to cross the next bridge. The female partner moves slowly up and down on the erect penis without active pelvic thrusting. The erect flag-post of manliness now basks leisurely in his partner's vagina while she slowly moves up and down, building his confidence for the grand finale.

22ND DAY: The male is asked to move but not thrust actively which might revive his fears of losing erection. Both partners now take turns in pleasuring each other after intromission. However, if the erection dies down the partners merely pleasure each other.

The female is told not to stimulate the penis in a demanding way to produce an erection as it is self-defeating. However, if the male has a strong erection during repeated intromission experiences, the pair is ready to go on to the next stage of active thrusting. The first few times the female begins the movements and brings the male to an orgasm. Later, both partners participate in active thrusting, the female still helping out her partner.

30TH DAY: The male having gained further erectile confidence tries the male superior mounting. The female partner helps him with intromission, and later by holding the penis. The male graduates in this technique by passing through the same stages, that is lying steady at first, then gently moving up and down and, finally, active thrusting.

The therapy is discontinued when the male gains sufficient confidence for his erective endeavours. But he is reminded that there can be an occasional erective failure, in which case he should not panic and start imagining that he has become impotent. It is likely to be only a temporary phase and erection would soon return to normal.

'Do-it-yourself' technique

The 'do-it yourself' technique is useful only for simple cases of sexual dysfunction like fears of the harmful effects of masturbation and night pollutions, anxieties about the size of the penis, and erection failures due to lack of sexual skill, stress and fear of failure. Fortunately, a majority of erectile problems come under this category. However, in chronic sexual dysfunction it is necessary to take professional help. There is no magic potency pill up to now which can restore normal sexual functioning.

Nor is coitus a command performance; no penis ever gets erect on demand. In other words, there is no other way to produce an erection except the normal physiological way when you are aroused. An infant starts breathing as soon as he is born. Nobody teaches him how to breathe. Similarly, erection is present from birth. It happens naturally when you are aroused. You cannot grind your teeth, bang your fists and use your will power to bring about an erection. The moment you consciously say to yourself, 'I must have a rock-like erection,' even if you have one, it will disappear almost immediately. The next time you attempt intercourse you spy on yourself from the sidelines to see if you are getting a hard-on. Fear of failure grips you. Instead of enjoying carefree sex, you are spectatoring. You have therefore to overcome two great obstacles to restore normal sexual functioning—fear of failure and speactatoring. Your behaviour pattern must change. When a normal male is aroused, he approaches his partner sexually and starts stimulating her. Seeing her excited sexually stimulates him, resulting in an erection. This two-way sensory stimulation is called by

Dr. Masters and Mrs. Johnson 'give-to-get', and can be short-circuited in two ways. Firstly, if you become a spectator of your own sexual encounter, or secondly, if the partner fails to provide the necessary stimuli and remains passive, erection can be lost and result in erection dysfunction.

In order to function normally, follow these four rules.

(1) Cremate the sexual myths on which you have been fed all these years. Among the myths which should have no place in your belief system are: the bigger the better; forty drops of blood make a drop of semen; the penis becomes erect instantaneously; erection should be as hard as steel; sex is loss of vitality; masturbation and nocturnal emissions are harmful.

(2) Let yourself go while pleasuring your partner.

(3) Divert your attention from the penis with 'erotic experiences' (see Appendix II).

(4) Be free of performance pressure by not indulging in coitus.

The reader is requested to go through the section on pre-therapy concepts thoroughly once again as they form the groundwork on which a successful sexual outcome depends. Almost all men sometimes have erection failure when they eagerly want to be a success in bed. If such an experience worries or bothers you, it becomes a problem. You should take an occasional failure in your stride, as part of the sex game. Even batsmen Don Bradman or Sunil Gavaskar have been clean-bowled occasionally and failed to score runs. Why not you?

It would be a good idea at this stage to write down in detail your sexual history with particular reference to the following:

(1) When did you last have a successful sexual encounter?

(2) What do you think were the reasons?

(3) Do you think any of the myths mentioned in Chapter 2 are responsible for your dysfunction?

(4) What are your expectations for better sex?

(5) Are they in conflict with reality as outlined in Chapter 3?

(6) How have you handled your sexual dysfunction so far?

(7) Are you avoiding sex?

(8) Do you find excuses like tiredness, too much stress, bringing

work home from the office, returning home late at night to avoid a sexual encounter?

(9) Have you been able to communicate your requirements for good sex to your partner?

(10) Have you been potent with one partner and not another? If so, what is the reason according to you?

(11) What is your life style? Are you always in a hurry, chasing milliseconds?

(12) Do you cramp your working hours with endless appointments and non-productive activities?

(13) What about alcohol and smoking?

(14) Do you know that alcohol stimulates desire but diminishes performance? The onset of secondary impotence in innumerable men has been heralded by one drink too many. Similarly, nicotine also causes erective problems. Both alcohol and cigarettes in excess are arch enemies of sex. You can have one or the other in moderation—never both and never in excess.

(15) What about physical fitness?

(16) Do you do any exercises, yoga or meditation?

(17) Are you overweight? If yes, reduce your weight for better sexual functioning.

(18) Have you had a complete physical check-up to exclude organic causes like diabetes and hypothyroid?

(19) Are you taking tranquillisers, antihypertensives, sedatives and anticholinergic drugs? Most of them depress sexuality. Find out from your doctor if any of these drugs are responsible for your erectile dysfunction. If they do, ask him to substitute it with a drug with less or no sexual side-effects.

You now have your complete sexual profile. For the first seven days, go through it carefully every day and try to find out the deficit areas where you need knowledge and self-help. Gradually learn to change your erroneous beliefs built on faulty sexual conditioning. Learn to be able to produce an erection naturally; you never can by will power. You will need a sexually exciting exercise regimen to behave normally. You will naturally ask why you cannot take a potency pill instead. If such a potency potion existed, there would not be the slightest necessity for this book. Innumerable aphrodisiacs have been tried without any permanent therapeutic effect; their temporary effects, if any, are mainly mediated through the power of suggestion. The only alternative, therefore, to remedy a sexual disorder is to change your belief systems and give up spectatoring. A series of structured erotic exercises are outlined below which can be done solo or with a partner. In both cases you should attempt the exercises when you are relaxed and have sufficient time to do them without being disturbed.

Solo erotic experiences (single partner)

(1) Lie on a bed completely nude.

(2) Relax for 5 minutes (see Appendix I).

(3) Start sensory erotic experiences without touching the genital organs (as outlined in Appendix II) for four days. Enjoy the pleasurable sensations as you touch, stroke, tickle or gently pinch your body. Without concentrating on your penis or spectatoring whether you are getting erect, note sensitive areas and how you like to be pleasured. During the exercise, your mind will naturally wander to different subjects or focus on your limp organ. Do not worry but divert your attention to the pleasurable sensations you are receiving. How can merely touching or being touched by a partner restore normal sexual functioning, you wonder! The reasons are, one, your mind is diverted from spectatoring; two, the pleasurable sensation you feel during touching is the spark which ignites arousal and ultimately an erection. If you are inhibited, your sensations are shortcircuited, the penis will not get a proper message and stay limp.

(4) You are convinced by now that not only is masturbation harmless but that it is pleasurable and therapeutic in the treatment of sexual dysfunction. The pleasurable sensation you start experiencing from touching your body will gradually make you feel sexy or turned on. In case you feel like reinforcing arousal you can try and think of something that turned you on in a big way, like a memorable sexual encounter, an exciting picture or a fantasy. You can start masturbating the way you like best and enjoy the sensations. Do not bother whether you are getting an erection or not.

Do not snoop on your penis. Just let yourself go completely and revel in the thrills of stroking. You will soon start getting feelings you have never experienced before, with or without an erection or ejaculation. You may use a lubricant like vaseline or KY Jelly.

You should do this exercise in two or three stages by employing the 'teasing technique'. In case you have an erection (never force one), stop masturbating and think of a non-sexy scene, like what you have to do at the office. After the erection has died down, start masturbating once again. The penis is likely to become erect; if it does not, do not worry or start spectatoring. If it does become erect repeat the teasing technique once or twice. The exercise is designed to emphasise that erection is often lost and that you are not to worry if it does not come on again.

The invariable reaction of a male who fails sexually is to immediately withdraw from the anxiety-provoking situation. The exercise is structured to desensitize you. It will also enable you to prove to yourself tnat the world does not come to an end when an erection is lost. You can still do many other things which are outlined below in the exercises.

(5) Lubricate yourself and start masturbating while fantasising in great detail an imaginary attempt at intercourse with your partner. Imagine an initial tete-a-tete on the sofa, all the attention you paid her, your hand caressing her lovely locks, the kiss on her forehead and cheeks, the tight embrace as you kissed her bewitching sexy lips, panting with lust and carnal desire, your hands stroking the fire of love as she gasped with ever-accelerating desire, the undressing and pressing of bodies close to one another and feeling each other. But, alas! at the critical count-down you just grow dead. You withdraw in utter despair. Is it the end of manliness forever? Is life worth living? Stop masturbating at the point where you feel anxious and the erection if present is lost. You still have many options in your so-called predicament.

For instance, you can bring her to orgasm with manual stimulation. You can be close to her instead of withdrawing. When you feel relaxed start masturbating once again. While you fantasise that even if your partner fondles you nothing happens, you can explain to her that tonight is not the night for you. She will understand.

You must do this exercise several times after which the realisation will ultimately dawn on you that fulfilment in sex does not merely depend on an erect penis, and that ultimately 'all roads lead to Rome'. Normally, the exercise should take about half an hour but you can with practice reduce it to about 20 minutes. If you are interrupted, you can restart at the point where you lose the erection. You will need six to ten sessions to gain erectile confidence. Some may need more.

Handling a female partner

It is one thing to do these exercises in solitary splendour and an entirely different experience interacting with a partner. The insight, experience and confidence you have gained so far will give you the sexual skill to make love to her.

There are a few ground rules to be observed to cross the next bridge smoothly. First and foremost, the be-all and end-all of an individual with an erection problem is: 'If not quick in, quicker lost' There is always the fear that if an erection is not utilised as soon as it develops it will be lost—use it or lose it. With such an attitude, you cannot enjoy anything except the actual act of intercourse, and your attention is concentrated only on the end-point—intromission and ejaculation. Decide not to have intercourse the first few times you are with your partner. You are naturally afraid that she may be upset if you do not have sex. On the contrary, women are not interested in men with a one-point sexual programme—intercourse. If you therefore refrain from intercourse for a while she will continue to respect and love you. Your second worry is: what will she think if you don't get an erection or lose it quickly? In such a situation, a woman does wonder whether you find her unattractive or whether something is wrong with her. Since you have also learnt that communication with your partner is essential for good sex, talk your problem over with her. She will cooperate with you. Why not enjoy sensory erotic experiences (Appendix II)? A woman loves to be touched. Later, graduate to caressing the genitals and after a while stop her caressing yours. The erection will die down.

Do not think that she will be disheartened, if you have already communicated your problem to her. She will be happy to help you out as long as she is reassured that you love her and find her attractive. Perhaps it does not occur to you that she also enjoys caressing you. While a majority of women fall into the above pattern there is a small insecure minority whose only yardstick is the erection you produce. It is obvious that you cannot continue doing exercises with a woman of this type because with these exercises you will get an erection most of the time, though not always.

The real hurdle comes during intromission. Under such circumstances it is better for your partner to sit astride you, holding your penis with her hand while you caress her genital region and then she gradually introduces the penis into her vagina. You graduate in this technique by passing through the same stages (see 30th day, Therapy Programme): lying steady at first, gentle movements later, and finally active thrusting—never forgetting that there is many a slip between the cup and the lip.

Exercises with a partner
Both of you should be conversant with the procedures outlined in the previous section of the therapy programme. It is easy to modify these procedures to suit your individual requirements. The basic principles are:

(1) You should not indulge in sex for some time even if an erection takes place during these exercises.

(2) Both of you should be completely relaxed before starting them.

(3) Practise the sensory erotic experiences as outlined in Appendix II with your partner pleasuring you first.

(4) Initially avoid caressing the breasts and the genital regions for about a week.

(5) Let the female partner now fondle your flaccid penis, while you concentrate on not having an erection by fantasising a sexual experience where you fail to get erect. In case you get an erection ask your partner to stop for a while till the erection dies down. Repeat these exercises till you no longer feel awkward in making your partner caress a limp organ. For the success of these exercises it is necessary not to concentrate on whether you are getting an erection or not.

(6) On the ninth day adopt the teasing technique as outlined here. Both partners, after the preliminaries of relaxation and mutual pleasuring, initiate genital stimulation. You can visualize an encounter while focusing on the penis and enjoying the sensations you receive. Request your partner to caress you the way you like best as long as it is

not performance oriented to produce an erection. If your partner finds that you have become erect, she should stop caressing you till the erection dies down, then resume pleasuring. Repeat this exercise till you have gained confidence that erection once lost can be regained provided you are not spectatoring.

(7) Once erectile confidence is established, your partner stimulates you while sitting astride (see Figure 14-1). If erection is present she caresses her genitals while holding the erect organ. If the erection persists she gently introduces it into her vagina, but both partners should not indulge in any movement. The instructions given for the twelfth day (page 248) should be observed, namely, intromission in a casual, non-demanding way: 'no hurry to mount, no rush to obtain sexual tension release.' As stated earlier the greatest threat to a male with an erective dysfunction is penetration of the vagina at the critical countdown—intromission.

(8) Once you get erective confidence during female mounting several times, your partner moves gently without active thrusting.

(9) After acquiring more confidence you are ready to move but not actively. Both partners take pleasure in alternate movements. Finally, you are ready for superior mounting, gently at first, and then active thrusting. A single success with intercourse builds up supreme confidence, for, as you know, nothing succeeds like success. The flag of your manliness is now flying at full mast. You have been commissioned to the rank of potent men.

4

OTHER MODES OF TREATMENT

Aphrodisiacs

Apart from sex therapy, aphrodisiacs, mechanical aids and surgery, including silicon grafts and by-pass surgery, are also employed to treat impotence.

The term aphrodisiac—the word is derived from Aphrodite, the Greek Goddess of Love—is applied to a drug which arouses sexual desire and produces an erection of the penis hard enough to penetrate the vagina and prolonged enough for successful intercourse. Man's search for the potency potion is as old as history and as futile as his search for the philosopher's stone. But nothing is impossible in science today, and perhaps in the near future a potency chemical may be discovered. There are over 50,000 genes in our body and at the speed at which genetic science is advancing, the gene for erection may soon be located in the DNA double helix and surgically manipulated to produce an erection!

The search for the magic potion arises from man's cultural indoctrination that the penis should be as hard as steel, that intercourse is the only method for complete sex, and that coitus is a must every time he is with his partner. Man has also the deep-rooted desire to swallow pills and potions. 'The desire,' observes William Osler, 'to take medicines is perhaps the greatest feature which distinguishes man from animals.' An impotent man believes that if only he could find the right love potion he would again be a virile Casanova. He continues the futile search while each passing day prolongs the pangs of his impotence.

From the beginning of creation sex has been the dominating urge of life. The *Kama Sutra* was born in India long before Western civilisation was even aware of the science of sex. Intercourse was a sublime act and a supreme ritual sacrifice. 'Her lap,' says a line from *Brihadaranyaka Upanishad,* 'is a sacrificial altar; her hair the sacrificial grass. The two labia are the fire in the middle.' The naturally well-endowed Arabs gave prime importance to length and strength. Bernard Stern says the penises of Arab boys are pulled and massaged to make them long and strong. The Chinese craved for penises as hard as iron and as hot as fire. The French call the orgasm 'a little death'.

Vatsyayana was aware of impotence in some men and prescribed various concoctions and ointments like drinking milk mixed with sugar and a host of powdered roots and seeds to put life in a lifeless penis. A so-called fail-proof remedy which Vatsyayana recommended was a concoction of goat's testes boiled in milk and artistically administered to the chanting of certain *slokas*. As potency is in the mind, the herbs were temporarily effective.

The classical love potions (philtre, philtron) were well known to the ancient Greeks, Egyptians, Persians and Chinese. 'The women of

Thessaly,' says Dr. Van de Velde, 'were supposed to be the greatest adepts in philtres. The recorded ingredients were incredibly disgusting: the caul of a foal, other portions of the equine placenta, the vaginal discharge of mares in heat, the tongues of certain birds, pigeons' blood, fishes' roes and fins, insects, lizards, and other equally loathsome substances.' The various organs of animals were supposed to restore sexual vigour in sexually inadequate males and also enhance the powers of normal males who wanted an extra 'kick'.

In addition, to satisfy male lust, the testes from animals were given orally or its extract injected. Later, organ transplant was attempted. Brown-Sequard attempted to graft unsuccessfully the tails of rats and cats into a cock's comb and concluded that 'every tissue possesses its vital properties in consequence of its peculiar organisation'. Later he grafted the testes from young guinea pigs into old dogs to rejuvenate them. From old dogs to old men was but a hop, skip and jump for the crafty Russian surgeon in Paris, Voronoff. In the early part of this century he implanted the testes of apes in men to rejuvenate them. The transplanted testes from the monkey disintegrated in a few days; but its male recipient lived to tell tales of his new, though short-lived, virility—an entirely psychological delusion! Needless to add, gullible, affluent Indians also thronged to Voronoff.

Drugs

During the Middle Ages and succeeding centuries the accent was on drugs. Most were dangerous and produced harmful side-effects and even death. I shall describe a few—yohimbine, Spanish fly, nux vomica and its active compound strychnine, opium, marijuana and LSD.

SPANISH FLY AND ITS ACTIVE PRINCIPLE CANTHARIDIN: Man's eternal quest and ingenuity in treating sexual inadequacy at last found a useful but potentially dangerous ally—a small beetle called Spanish fly or blister bug, found mainly in the south coast of France and Portugal. An enterprising Spaniard probably crushed and sampled a few and got a prompt response—a painful rock-like erection and severe burning in the urine. He must have been jubilant initially—if pain gives pleasure. He must have attempted coitus a number of times and discovered to his discomfiture that his penis was standing at attention all day and all night. Defiant women who dared to humble 'him' in three straight sets of sex were left exhausted, humiliated, yet completely fulfilled. He must have drunk himself silly and swallowed pellets of opium to appease 'him'. Tired, restless and with urination very painful and scanty, death was deliverance from a terrible nightmare.

The story goes that if Spanish fly is dropped in the drink of a woman she gets aroused instantly and has insatiable sexual fires which no male can extinguish. It is, however, more probable that the woman may die and the one who gave the so-called potency potion faced a trial for manslaughter. The reason for this is that though cantharidin is a very potent aphrodisiac, the dose which produces tantalising sexual desire can also kill a human being. There is no margin of safety. A small dose is sometimes used in animals to arouse sexual desire and make them mate but because they are heavier there is a lot of safety between the oral and the lethal dose. In medicine, a tincture of cantharidin is occasionally used to produce surface irritation of the skin but it is a highly dangerous drug when taken internally.

YOHIMBINE: The generous sexual endowment of the African male and his powerful physique were the envy of European males and the secret longing of their better halves was to bed them. Naturally, male curiosity was aroused and was eager to discover the secret of their virility.

The whites discovered that the blacks were using the powdered inner bark of the African yohimbe tree. The highly suggestible European male mind believed that the bark if taken orally would restore lost manliness. Thousands of tons of yohimbine bark have been faithfully swallowed by millions of males all over the world. As usual, the power of suggestion worked, though yohimbine seldom did—in fact it is a must in every potency pill manufactured by drug companies all over the world.

NUX VOMICA AND STRYCHNINE: In the early part of the 19th century, the dried ripe seed of the plant *Strychnos nux vomica* claimed the limelight as a stimulator of the nervous system. The active principle strychnine in very small doses increases the response to sexual stimulation but larger doses cause severe convulsions and death.

OPIUM is a reddish-brown bitter drug obtained by over-drying the milky exudate from unripe capsules of a kind of poppy, *Papaver Somniferrum*. Opium was well known to ancient Egyptian priests and is mentioned among the 700 drugs in the Ebers Papyrus, as early as 1550 B.C. It was used as a sedative, a soporific (to produce sleep) and a painkiller. Tincture of opium is also called Tincture Laudanum because of its many laudable qualities and uses which were popularised by the Swiss physician Paracelsus in the fifteenth century. Before the advent of modern tranquillisers, Tincture Laudanum was extensively prescribed to relieve the anxiety of a sexually inadequate male and improve his performance. It is, however, habit-forming. The growth of the opium plant is now banned in most countries of the world.

MARIJUANA AND LSD are drugs whose use is banned by law. Marijuana is a potent sexual stimulant. Individuals who have taken it report heightened sensual awareness and are supposed to scale giddy sexual heights. 'Occasional use of marijuana can enhance sexual desire,' claim researchers at the University of Texas. 'However, chronic smokers may find impairment of sexual function.' The active principle of marijuana is tetrahydrocannabinal or THC. Low doses of THC, claims Dr. Susan Dalterio of the University of Texas, cause rapid increase in the levels of testosterone. However, if high doses are given there is a rapid drop in the testosterone level in the blood. The tests were done initially on mice, but the researchers claim that the same result may be expected in man.

Similarly, LSD, apart from being a powerful and even dangerous psychedelic drug which produces altered states of consciousness, is claimed to produce a sexual 'high'. Both marijuana and LSD are banned drugs and not available for field trials. It is safer to be on the right side of the law and not use these potent drugs until their side-effects are known and the law permits their use. Both may be habit-forming.

EXCITIN: Dr. Baize Turner, a Swiss physician, toured Africa and attended a fertility rite session of the Congolese Baluba tribe. He had earlier read a report of the Belgian Government which described the habits of the Balubas and the fertility sessions where there is a display of limitless sexual abilities by their males. The report also mentioned that the tribes used a secret drug. Dr. Turner found that the magic drug was from a jungle plant called *'kaji-kaji'*.

A Swiss pharmaceutical firm in Zurich has isolated the active principle from the root of the kaji-kaji and has been exploring its so-called aphrodisiac possibilities of producing a long-lasting erection. However, although erection is remarkably effective, even a small extra dose, as in the case of cantharidin, can cause organic frenzies and irritability, restlessness and insomnia.

PALANGTODS ('BED-BREAKERS'): No account of potency potions in our country is complete without the famous *palangtod paan*. Hats off to the ingenious *paanwala* who hit upon the brilliant idea of caging two birds with one *paan*—supplying two basic needs of the Indian male, a good digestion and a fail-proof erection!

What are the ingredients of the *paan*? An ordinary *paan* or leaf contains *supari* (betel nut), lime or *choona, katha* and in some cases *kimam* and *jarda* (tobacco). The potent *palangtod* contains *shelajit,* amber, *afim* (opium) and *kesar* (saffron).

Different types of *Palangtods* are available with a so-called built-in timer to produce erection for a specific period of time. Naturally, the price depends on the time-bound performance. For instance, the *palangtod* of 15 minutes duration is the cheapest, while the long-acting timer which lasts an hour or a whole night is the most expensive.

One would pity the female partner with such a marathon performing male but, according to the experience of a majority of males, nothing dramatic happens. The *palangtod* merely provides, in a few cases, a psychological prop to the highly suggestible lecherous male. In cases of impotency, the aphrodisiac *paan* has usually no impact on the limp and lifeless organ. A few ingredients of the *paan,* like cardamom and *choona,* have digestive and carminative effects.

ALCOHOL: Alcohol is the most ancient and widely used aphrodisiac known to man. However, it is not generally known that it is a highly frequent cause of secondary impotence in the male. As the drunken porter in Shakespeare says, drink provokes the desire but takes away the performance. This is because arousal and copulation are two different mechanisms and while alcohol stimulates the arousal mechanism, it depresses the copulation mechanism. But a little alcohol acts as a soothing tranquilliser and improves the sexual performance of a tense and overanxious male. Unfortunately, the line of demarcation is very thin between the quantity that acts as a stimulant and the amount that depresses sexual functioning—and most individuals do not know how much is good for them.

'Which is the best aphrodisiac?' I am frequently asked. No aphrodisiac up to now has any permanent effect in producing a powerful sustained erection. Think it over carefully. The all-potent, fail-proof aphrodisiac is the alluring, enchanting, bewitching female form. Accept it gracefully and you need not vainly search for a potency potion in the flora and fauna around you.

Sex hormone therapy

'Doctor, why can't I have a few hormone shots to fix me up?' Vinod asked me. Ever since Eugene Steinach in 1900 discovered that hormones were the mainspring of life, world interest in hormones, particularly the male hormone from the testes, was aroused. 'Sex hormones,' observed Steinach, 'are the motive power for the natural attribute of youth.'

The frantic search to isolate the male hormone followed. In 1935, two Dutch chemists were able to recover 0.28 grammes (1/100 ounce) from 1000 kilos of bull's testes—a prohibitively costly procedure. Next, the focus shifted to determining the chemical formula of the male hormone. A German scientist, Adolf Butenandt, isolated a few crystals from 25,000 litres of male urine showing male hormone activity, and painstakingly determined its chemical formula. Later Leopold Ruzicka, a Yugoslav chemist working in Zurich, was able to obtain from cholesterol, a substance present in all living cells, a synthetic male hormone. Dr. Russel Marker, an American chemist, developed the know-how of synthesising male hormones (as well as other hormones) from a natural plant called *labeza de negro* (head of a negro) growing wild on the west coast of Mexico.

Synthetic production of the male hormone laid the foundation of a new dynasty of sex hormones which have reigned supreme from 1940. In a book called *The Male Hormone,* the science writer Paul de Kurif says, 'The male hormone discloses magic far beyond the merely sexual. It boosts muscle power. It banishes mental fatigue. It eases heart pain. It even restores the sanity of men in midlife who suffer male hormone hunger.' From restoring sanity to curing impotency was but one flight of stairs of enthusiasm run amock. Injections, implants and sub-lingual pellets of the male hormone were indiscriminately administered in cases of sexual inadequacy. But the dead stick—the penis—would not come to life even after a lot of men had a lot of injections.

It is not well-known that the male hormone acts adversely in certain cases. If impotence is psychogenic and not glandular, administration of the male hormone stops the testes from producing testosterone naturally. The cells manufacturing testosterone stop functioning and atrophy and the testes shrink in size. Men with cancer of the prostate, penis or testicles should not be given male hormone injections and the male hormone may precipitate cancer of the prostate in susceptible individuals.

What are the uses of the male hormone in impotence? There are two groups of cases in which the male hormone works magic. In castration of the testes, the male hormone restores potency as well as the feeling of manliness and the secondary sex characteristics like the beard and moustache. It is also helpful in a small group of patients suffering from male menopause where deficiency of the male hormone is present as demonstrated by hormone assays. These cases improve remarkably after a few shots of testosterone.

In conclusion, just as water finds its own level, so is male hormone shorn of its glamorous trappings. Nevertheless, it remains a most useful weapon in the medical armament against some sexual disorders.

Sex aids

Artificial devices to produce an erection and keep it going are becoming increasingly popular in the USA and Europe among sufferers of prolonged impotency due to trauma, diabetes mellitus or non-response to sex therapy.

The simplest aid is the ordinary rubber band. When worn snugly at the base of the partially erect penis it permits the arterial blood to enter and prevents the venous blood from leaving the penis, thus maintaining erection. A modification of this simple rubber band is the hard rubber doughnut which the individual fits snugly at the base of the penis.

Splints have been devised to uplift the morale of the sagging organ. They are fitted at the side of the penile body, keeping the glans free for contact with the vagina. There are also artificial penises which fit over the natural one to permit intercourse. All these devices are, however, mechanical and many females object to having sex with an artificial aid.

The vibrator is an electronic gadget mainly used by females to masturbate and produce an orgasm. It is now being used frequently by males to produce an erection. The vibrator consists of a small electric motor, held to the back of the hand with an elastic strap. As the motor vibrates, strong vibrations are produced in the hand which are transmitted to the muscles, the penis or the clitoris. Applying the vibrator to a limp organ quickly brings on an erection because of the rapid, repeated stimulation of the nerve endings on the penis. A more sophisticated device is the electronic erection and ejaculation device working on the same principle.

Internal devices

Our friends, the surgeons, are ever ready to rescue surgically their medical brothers in distress. Name the disorder and the scalpel-wielding surgeon is waiting in the wings to cut it out! For instance, a neurosurgeon can remove a clot in an artery of the brain, restoring circulation and replacing the neurophysician. The heart surgeon bypasses not only the cardiologist but also the diseased plumbing in the coronary arteries of the heart; and the urologist, not to be outdone, swiftly substitutes the sex therapist by implanting silicone rods to produce a fail-proof erection when wanted. The inert material silicone is a great friend of plastic surgeons and has been extensively used in cosmetic surgery of the breast to increase its size, change its contour or make it firm. It was but natural that the urologist should think of a silicone rod in mechanically propping up a limp, lifeless penis.

The implant does not impair sensations or the ability to reach an orgasm and ejaculation. Two types of silicone penile implants have been developed in recent years. The first consists of one or two silicone rods which are surgically inserted in the corpora cavernosa of the penis. After the initial silicone implant the penis remains stiff and semi-erect. A patient asked Dr. Masters' advice about penile implants. 'Can you imagine,' quipped Dr. Masters, 'trying to get your pants on with such a device?' However, this was during the initial silicone treatment when the penis remained stiff and on perpetual duty. The hinge action in the modern implant allows the penis to hang down comfortably.

Finney Flexi Rod penile prosthesis is the most commonly used device. Some surgeons use a single implant instead of two. 'The quality of erection,' claims Dr. Gaur, a urologist at Bombay Hospital, 'is in no way inferior to that in double implant patients.'

The newer, more sophisticated implant is a hydraulic model consisting of inflatable cylinders in the penis, a fluid reservoir under the lower abdominal muscles and a pumping mechanism implanted in the scrotum. Whenever the man wants sex he pumps the bulb in the scrotum, thereby pumping in fluid in the reservoirs to inflate the cylinders. He has now produced a sophisticated erection! After intercourse, the scrotal bulb is activated again to deflate the cylinders.

The implant is a last resort in cases of severe organic impairment after all other avenues of therapy have been exhausted. It is merely a robot that functions mechanically, neither improving desire nor sexual skills. If your aim is just a mechanical erection, then an implant is the answer. But it is a surgical procedure and though fairly safe, surgery always carries a small risk.

BY-PASS SURGERY: By-pass surgery is the latest treatment for impotence due to physical causes like arteriosclerosis. In arteriosclerosis the arteries supplying the penis become think and lose their elasticity. 'In the past,' says American surgeon Dr. Milorad Jevtich, 'we did not pay enough attention to the one basic factor of a good erection—blood circulation.'

It is now possible to measure the blood circulation in the genitals and have the deficiency corrected by by-pass surgery. At the moment, the success rate of such surgery is about 50 per cent but as techniques improve so will the results. Just as in coronary by-pass surgery diseased coronary arteries are replaced with veins from the leg, in by-pass surgery for impotence, a healthy artery from the abdomen is transplanted into the penis, by-passing the diseased penile artery. Like its counterpart, coronary by-pass, this operation improves the circulation in the penis, resulting in a good erection.

5

HOW TO GET WHAT YOU WANT IN SEX WITHOUT AN ERECTION

The goddess of erection has forsaken you, you know not why! You think you were born destined to have a hard, rock-like erection. But performance-anxiety or an organic disease like diabetes has made you impotent. Initially you willed yourself to get an erection and failed. You panicked, yet had hopes that some magic pill would metamorphose your limp, lifeless organ into an erect, pulsating performer. You have tried them all—the pills, the sex hormone shots and all the therapies under the sun. You are depressed—but do not despair. All is not lost. Your cultural belief about the impregnable penis has given you your present blues.

Actually, when it comes to gratifying a woman the mouth and the hand play a more vital role than your prestigious penis whom you adore and have put on a pedestal. Bring him down from the clouds to earth, as my friend Dev did, down where it really belongs. 'You can call me impotent for the last twenty years,' confided 60-year-old Dev, 'but believe me, I can still make my innumerable mistresses quiver with joy and fulfilment.' 'How do you manage?' I asked, amazed. 'I learnt long ago,' he replied. 'To hell with the penis! I use my mouth and finger instead....though I may have lost one or two girls who were only interested in being loved with a stocking ram-rod.'

Dev is right. The vast majority of women do not rate penis-vagina coitus as a No. 1 priority in sex. In a study on the sexual preferences of women conducted by the prestigious magazine *Cosmopolitan*, penis-vagina intercourse was ranked low down on the list. It is not, as most men think, the be-all and end-all of sex. Let us look dispassionately at the possibilities. Love and romance, even reproduction, are possible without erection. So teach that obstinate mule, your tool, that the show can go on without him.

Vatsyayana was aware of the likes and dislikes of women. He advised males during the first two weeks after marriage to confine themselves merely to talking, admiring and appreciating their partners and be very tender and gentle. This was followed by gradual non-sexual touching; then sexual touching of the breasts, the vulva and, ultimately, intercourse. In those days, however, life was leisurely, and the male had all the time in the world for wooing. In the Stress Century everything moves at Concorde speed, including living and loving. The male's aim is to get it over with as fast as possible, with little or no consideration for the requirements of his female partner. Is it any wonder that in various studies, including the *Hite Report,* penis-vagina intercourse was low down on the list of priorities of most women? What they mostly craved for was gentleness, tenderness and non-sexual touching. Some women complained that they are immediately put off if their male partners have a one-point programme—of penetrating the vagina with their erect flag-pole.

A lady patient told Dr. Prakash Kothari, the well-known physician in Sexual Medicine, 'My husband uses me as a sleeping tablet.' On the other hand, cultural conditioning has made all males believe that women are always interested in coitus, and that the rougher and deeper they penetrate the greater is her pleasure. Nothing is further from such fantasies. As I have emphasised earlier, rough handling of the breasts or vigorous thrusting during intercourse is painful for the majority of women. Women want artistic lovers, not sexual drilling machines. 'Doctor, I want my penis so hard that I can penetrate this,' said Salim, a generously endowed engineer, pointing to the brick-wall of my office! I gently reminded him that the penis was not for drilling holes in a wall but penetrating the soft, sensitive vagina. On the other hand, Violet told me, 'Doctor, my husband became impotent after having an accident, but sex has never been better for me. He does a lot of non-sexual touching for prolonged periods, and stimulates me to an orgasm when I want it. I do the same to him. In fact, our closeness, togetherness, and gentle touching for hours have improved not only the quality of marriage, but brought us sexual fulfilment.' All women may not agree with Violet as some are culturally conditioned to want only penis-vagina intercourse. If your partner belongs to this category it is indeed hardship for her and heartbreaking for you.

By now you should be convinced that you can still live—not just exist—without a hard-on. You will next ask. 'What do I do with a limp, lifeless organ?' You can do everything you had been doing with an erect penis, even insert a limp one in the vagina! I will explain the technique later. An erect penis wants to get in and the semen to get out fast. You therefore find it difficult to resist the overpowering desire. A limp organ, on the other hand, can wait patiently any length of time.

Let us lay down a few ground rules on how to handle an occasional and a permanent loss of erection and also how you can save a situation when an erection suddenly disappears.

Temporary loss of erection
Do not imagine it is the end of the world and withdraw from sex with a sour face, leaving your partner high and dry and miserable. The show goes on. You need not apologise. Tell her frankly, 'Darling, today is not my day.' There are several interesting alternatives with your mouth, tongue, lips and index finger. You can lie next to her with your body in an intimate embrace. A woman's whole body is sensual and she will enjoy the intimate contact. If you have already aroused her, bring her to an orgasm manually or with your lips or your tongue by titillating her clitoral region. Do not touch the clitoris directly in the early stages. After you have brought her to an orgasm, don't leave immediately to wash yourself. Spend a few minutes lying next to her in a warm body-to-body embrace. If you ignore the occasional mishap, things will automatically right themselves and erection will soon return. But if you become anxious and angry and order an erection, your penis will go on strike and impotence may set in.

Permanent loss of erection
This occurs in severe untreated diabetes mellitus or injury to the spinal cord or spinal stenosis (narrowing of the bony spinal column housing the cord) or severe psychogenic impotence which does not respond to treatment. Such persons can still enjoy sex. You can use sex aids; a rubber band may be slipped over the partially erect penis to maintain an erection during intercourse. However, if worn for long it may

damage the delicate blood vessels of the penis. You will ask whether a silicone rod can be implanted. It sounds simple and logical, like wearing glasses or a hearing aid. But there are many difficulties. Spectacles and hearing aids are worn outside the body whilst silicone grafting is an operation. Any surgery, however trivial, carries with it a small risk of complications. Besides, silicone rod surgery is still in the experimental stage, is prohibitively expensive and is only performed in a few centres in India. Considering all the pros and cons, it is not feasible for a majority of individuals with erection failure.

How to make a limp penis enter a vagina
Upto now you believed that no erection, no entry. But a limp penis can enter a vagina—though the ritual differs from the standard code of sexuality. Here is Dev's technique, 'My partner lies on her back on a fairly high bed or table, in what you doctors call a lithotomy position—thighs flexed at the hip and legs bent at the knees. (See Positions in Intercourse, page 104). I stand in front of her, hold the organ in my hands and introduce it in the vagina of my aroused partner. It is nowhere near intercourse with an erect penis,' Dev concedes, 'but both of us enjoy it.'

In conclusion, penis-vagina intercourse is not the only way to sexual fulfilment. Even though your organ does not get erect, there are other possibilities. Both of you can lie side by side and indulge in non-sexual touching. The whole body is erogenous and you will discover that the heightened sensuality in both is a very rewarding experience. Next, you can do some sexual touching—fondle the breasts, titillate the vulva and bring her to a manual orgasm. She in turn can stimulate you to a climax and ejaculation with her hands. Lastly, if your partner enjoys oral stimulation (and most women do), stimulate the mons area with your lips or tongue. She would like to do the same to you.

Chapter 15

PREMATURE EJACULATION

> *There is no tepidity, no half-and-half in love. He who*
> *cannot embrace a woman with dominant virility will be*
> *neither respected by her nor loved. He bores her—and*
> *with her, boredom and hatred are near neighbours.*
>
> MICHELET

PREMATURE EJACULATION OR *ejaculation praecox* is the most frequent dysfunction in the male and is characterised by sudden ejaculation of the semen, just prior to or immediately after vaginal penetration during coitus. The word *praecox* means premature or 'before time'. In other words, it is a condition where the man has no voluntary control over his ejaculation. He is quick on the trigger once he starts intercourse.

Premature ejaculation was not rated a major sexual problem till recently. In a man's world sexual enjoyment was a male privilege—the feelings of the female did not count. Even Alfred Kinsey labelled a man who could discharge in 30 seconds a superior individual, although it is 'inconvenient and unfortunate from the standpoint of the wife in the relationship'. In the last two decades, the pendulum has swung to the opposite extreme. Lasting longer has now become a male obsession, in fact a disease, since Masters and Johnson demonstrated that the female can reach more than one enjoyable orgasm during intercourse. The all-consuming desire of males today is to make their partners multi-orgasmic. M, the author of *The Sensuous Male*, labels premature ejaculation a 'major disaster'.

After centuries of suppression, women have become orgasm-conscious and deem it a male's duty to make them orgasmic and fulfilled. This performance pressure has over-burdened the male, resulting in premature ejaculation becoming a major cause of sexual dysfunction in the West. The Westerly winds of change are sweeping over Bharat, and it is not unusual for the degreed, pedigreed modern female to drag her male partner to the doctor for treatment of premature ejaculation.

What is premature ejaculation?
Different authorities have given varying definitions of the disorder. Alfred Kinsey in a study of the sexual behaviour of about 1200 American males observed, 'For three-quarters of all males, orgasm is reached within two minutes of the initiation of the sex act and for not an inconsiderable number the climax may be reached within less than a minute or even within 10 or 20 seconds after coital entrance. Far from being abnormal, the human male who is quick in his sexual response is quite normal among the mammals'. Most animals discharge immediately after penetration. For instance, chimpanzees ejaculate within 30 seconds after intromission.

Masters and Johnson consider a male a premature ejaculator 'if he cannot control his ejaculatory process for a sufficient length of time, during intravaginal containment, to satisfy his partner in at least 50 per cent of their coital connections'. A medical centre in the USA has defined a premature ejaculator as an individual who cannot control his ejaculation for at least 30 seconds after vaginal penetration.

Helen Singer Kaplan disagrees with definitions of premature, ejaculation which 'are related to the time it takes a man to reach the plateau stage in the sexual response cycle'. The essence of prematurity, she says, is the 'absence of voluntary control over the ejaculatory reflex, once a high level of sexual excitement is reached'. A premature ejaculator cannot control his orgasm and, secondly, he does not feel the intense erotic or pleasurable sensations when he is aroused. Dr. Kaplan calls this phenomenon 'genital anaesthesia'

According to Bombay's well-known sex therapist Dr. Prakash Kothari, ejaculation and orgasm are two separate entities and the individual who is termed a premature ejaculator is actually suffering from premature or early orgasm. 'This disorder should therefore be called "early orgasmic response",' he says.

Reactions of both partners to premature ejaculation

Pranab, an officer in the armed forces, was 'quick on the trigger' ever since his marriage to Deepali three years ago. He had had no sexual exposure during his school or college days as his parents were strict and puritanical. His erection response was normal but he discharged within seconds after penetration. If he delayed the penetration he ejaculated outside the vagina. Pranab was away from his wife for long periods since he was stationed in the forward areas in Ladakh. He felt very worried that despite total physical fitness he should suffer from premature ejaculation. Deepali was warm and sensitive. Her parents were demonstrative and loving and she found Pranab cool, distant and anxious. 'My patience is exhausted as for three years he has left me unfulfilled,' she told me. 'I don't mind his "disease" but at least he can talk to me, kiss me, take me to the movies instead of finding excuses for running away from me to the club, morning and evening,' she said as tears welled in her eyes. 'Do you think he has V.D. from sleeping with prostitutes?'

After a thorough physical examination, I impressed on Deepali that Pranab was suffering neither from V.D. nor any dreadful disease, but a disorder caused by anxiety and lack of sexual voluntary control. Pranab was feeling equally anxious and frustrated. The moment he got excited he tried to suppress his arousal, lest he discharge outside—and so he appeared cold and distant to Deepali. Besides, there was no communication between them. Deepali never realised how ashamed and miserable Pranab felt.

Causes of premature ejaculation

A number of theories have been propounded about the causes of premature ejaculation. They could be physical or psychological (see 'Impotence', Chapter 13). It is therefore necessary to rule out the former before commencing treatment. The common physical causes are prostatitis and nervous disorders like multiple sclerosis. A detailed history and a thorough physical check-up, including blood chemistry (see Chapter 13, section 2), should be done to rule out physical causes or use of drugs, before starting treatment.

PSYCHOGENIC CAUSES: Freud suggested that childhood conflict related to the Oedipus complex is responsible for premature ejaculation. The psychoanalysts postulate that, firstly, a premature ejaculator is prone to sadistic feelings towards women. Secondly, he is emotionally immature in his feelings and finds in premature ejaculation a symbolic expression of causing suffering and disappointment to women (who are for him symbolic of his mother). As these feelings are in the unconscious mind, the patient is unaware of them. The therapy consists in discovering and resolving these childhood Oedipus conflicts by psychotherapy three or four times a week over several years. However, in spite of a better insight into their problems, very few premature ejaculators improve with psychotherapy.

PATHOGENIC TRANSACTIONS: Marital and family therapists believe that premature ejaculation may be due to hostile interactions in the marital relationship between the couple, also termed Dyadic problems.

Leon Salzman describes interesting sexual cases of premature ejaculation due to hostile relationships between the partners, in *Medical Aspects of Human Sexuality* (June '72). He quotes a case in which the husband became a premature ejaculator when the wife took the lead in love-play. Unconsciously, the male partner wanted to dominate in the power struggle and his prematurity was unconsciously directed against her. A similar case was that of Surjit, a chartered accountant who married a wealthy, haughty socialite, Swaroop, and went to live at her parents' home. Everything was excellent sexually for a year until Surjit began suffering from premature ejaculation. Whenever Swaroop wore the pants and attempted to dominate him in their day-to-day life, Surjit seethed with resentment and hostility towards her and had to keep quiet. Without her father's help he would not only be without a job but without a roof over his head! By ejaculating prematurely, Surjit was unconsciously showing his hostility and slighting Swaroop. In turn, she believed that he was no longer interested in her, did not bother to arouse her but purposely discharged quickly to get over with it as quickly as possible. She firmly believed that Surjit was having an affair with another woman. However, it has been observed that though marriage therapy improves the marital relationship, premature ejaculation persists.

EXCESSIVE SENSITIVITY TO EROTIC SENSATIONS: It stands to reason that excessive stimulation can result in early ejaculation. If, therefore, ways and means can be found to reduce this excessive sexual stimulation during foreplay or intercourse, the disability could be cured. Various therapies have been tried, such as applying an anaesthetic ointment on the glans penis (Procaine), Kegal exercises (see pages 55-56) involving contracting and relaxing the pubococcygens, mental diversion by thinking of something non-sexual and drugs like Melleril which produce a 'dry ejaculation' (see 'Drugs', Chapter 14) by paralysing the internal sphincter of the bladder. Unfortunately, all these treatments have merely diminished sexual pleasure without prolonging the time of ejaculation.

STRESSFUL SITUATIONS: Dr. Wordell Pomeroy suggests that anxiety producing stress is the root cause of premature ejaculation and 'possible repetition often becomes another self-fulfilling prophecy'. The therapy recommended is de-sensitization to reduce anxiety.

RAPID REFLEX MECHANISM: Urologist Dr. James Semans felt that the basic cause of premature ejaculation was an unduly rapid ejaculatory reflex which could be prolonged indefinitely by a simple treatment which he called the 'rapid reflex mechanism'. Dr. Semans and Dr. Donald Hastings were the pioneers in this brief treatment of premature ejaculation, which with a few modifications has been followed in sex therapy clinics all over the world.

His 'stop-start technique' consists in the female partner stimulating the erect penis without indulging in intercourse. As soon as the male feels the sensation to ejaculate he tells her and she stops the stimulation until the ejaculatory feeling has disappeared. She then starts restimulating him and continues till the male can hold himself indefinitely. Dr. Semans reported a hundred per cent disappearance of the symptom within a month, with this technique.

According to Masters and Johnson 'any learning opportunity that produces performance pressure can lead to premature ejaculation' Formerly most young men learnt sex in the cat-house, where it was 'hurry up, hurry up'. The men hardly had a chance to get their pants off. 'If a young man learned that way, it carried over to his marriage.' Masters and Johnson point out that today sex often begins in the back seat of a car where once again the same performance pressure is present.

Masters and Johnson have reported 98 per cent success with their intensive two-week therapy for premature ejaculation. Their technique is a modification of Dr. Semans' therapy or what he called 'rapid reflex mechanism'.

Dr. Helen Singer Kaplan believes that it is not rapid ejaculatory response but lack of voluntary control that is responsible for prematurity. Why are some males incontinent while others can control their ejaculation, she asks. She feels that the former 'fails to acquire ejaculatory control because he has not received or, rather, allowed himself to receive the sensory feedback which is necessary to bring any reflex function under control'.

All the reflex functions of our body, such as voiding urine or stool at specific intervals, are dependant on sensory feedback. An infant empties the bladder automatically, as soon as a certain amount of urine has collected. The reflex is mediated by the spinal cord; the infant has no voluntary control over it. Later, the child easily learns to establish voluntary control over urination and defaecation (passing stools) as the control for evacuation is transferred from the spinal cord to the higher nervous centres in the brain. This is brought about by sensory feedback—the child's ability to recognise the sensations of a full bladder. In other words, it is a learning process. If the child did not know what a full bladder feels like, he would have no control over it. In injuries of the spine, the higher cortical control is lost and the bladder reverts to autonomic functioning. The same analogy is applied to premature ejaculation. The brain gets the signal but for various emotional reasons the inhibiting mechanism fails. The individual cannot control the ejaculation as he has no, or very little, sensory feedback. But just as the child learns to control the urinary bladder, the man who is quick on the trigger can easily learn to control his ejaculation by specific sexual procedures outlined in the following section.

The professional as well as the unfortunate lay reader will naturally want a simple, easy-to-follow therapy format. With this in mind I have outlined two treatment schedules: (1) For the single individual without a female partner, and (2) Where both partners are available.

The general principles applicable to both groups are first outlined and, later, the method for each group.

Basic principles in therapy

(1) In every case of premature ejaculation a complete physical examination and blood chemistry is necessary to rule out organic causes in the nervous and genito-urinary system, such as disseminated sclerosis and prostatitis (see Chapter 13)

(2) Cases of schizophrenia, mania and paranoia should be excluded from the therapy.

(3) Men with a certain type of personality must accept the need for change in their patterns of behaviour. This refers specifically to the typical Type 'A' personality—the 'tiger' in the modern executive jungle, always in a hurry and counting milliseconds, must change his spots and learn to cope with stress for a sexual encounter. Performance-oriented sex is often the cause of erectile problems. In most cases, premature ejaculation can be eliminated merely by doing the sexual exercises outlined below. But for more scintillating sexual encounters, you have to learn how to cope with stress in all areas of your life—work, sex, home, your sexual partner, children and relatives, society and friends, leisure and sports. In general, exercise or take a brisk walk for an hour three or four times a week, and practise muscular relaxation, yoga and meditation; in extreme cases restructuring your stress profile will automatically improve your sex profile. (For details see my book *Rock Around the Clock*.)

(4) Be sensual to be sexual. You must be 'in touch' with your body and especially with the sex organs. Men are generally averse to touching themselves or being touched. 'I like only my penis to be fondled,' said Sudhir, 'but the moment she does it I trigger off. I do not like to be touched anywhere else.' The same story has been repeated for innumerable men. It is better if these exercises are done with a partner rather than singly (for details see Appendix II). However, some individuals are so hypersensitive that merely touching the body makes them come, especially if they fantasise about a female. Such persons should go directly to stop-start masturbation as advocated by Semans and subsequently modified by Masters-Johnson and Helen Kaplan.

(5) Most men feel embarrassed and bashful about telling their partners how and where they like to be stimulated. Women usually keep mum and never communicate their desires. They think men are omniscient! It is therefore necessary that both partners shed such mythical notions about each other and communicate their requirements.

(6) During penile stimulation, the male should not consciously try to control and prolong his ejaculation, but let himself go and enjoy the build-up of pleasurable sensations. Similarly, he should not introduce performance pressure by timing himself daily with a stop-watch—telling himself, for instance, that he took 10 seconds longer to feel the ejaculatory inevitability today than yesterday. Such exercises are self-defeating.

Exercises for males without a partner

LEARNING EJACULATORY CONTROL: While these exercises are primarily for the male without a female partner, even the male with a partner should do the sensate focus touching exercises (i.e. non-genital stimulation as outlined in Appendix II) by himself for three or four days.

MECHANICS OF THE EXERCISE

(1) Choose a time when you will not be interrupted for 15 to 20 minutes. Do not do these exercises when you are hard-pressed for time and under pressure to catch the ever-punctual, over-full local train or public transport.

(2) Remove all your clothes and lie on the bed.

(3) Relax for a minute or two. Recall a funny incident or an anecdote. Do not think you are appearing for a Master's Degree in Sexology.

(4) Learn to relax your body (see Appendix I).

(5) After relaxing for a minute or two, lie on your back and stroke your penis, while concentrating on the sensations in the organ. Hold the organ in the way you like best and stimulate it slowly. As you feel the tension building up, concentrate on the erotic sensations in the penis until you feel ejaculation is inevitable. Stop masturbating and squeeze the glans penis between the thumb, the index and middle fingers. Do not worry if you trigger off at first while attempting this

exercise. You will soon learn when to stop and start squeezing.

(6) When the feeling of ejaculatory inevitability has gone, restart stimulating and enjoy the pleasurable sensations within. Stop once again when you get the signal that you are going to come. Repeat the procedure a third and a fourth time. At the fourth attempt, masturbate till you ejaculate, and enjoy the feeling.

Initially do not use any lubricant or fantasy when you masturbate. You will soon find that you are gaining control over ejaculation. Enjoy the erotic sensations but do not attempt conscious control over your orgasm. After four or five days of dry stimulation introduce two changes: lubricate the penis with vaseline or preferably K.Y. Jelly, and repeat the procedure while fantasising about an exotic movie star or a seductive model. You will find this more exciting than the dry stimulation as it stimulates the type of sensations you feel in the vagina. Repeat the same stop-squeeze procedure as before and discharge at the fourth attempt. Your ejaculatory control will improve gradually. You are now ready to start exercises after a week or ten days with a partner if you have one but if you find you have not made much progress in controlling your ejaculation, it means that you have not relaxed enough and are tense. Practise relaxation for a few days before starting stimulation.

Exercises with a partner

It is much easier to learn ejaculatory control with a partner. Both of you should be nude and feel comfortable with and enjoy each other's bodies. If your partner agrees (many don't), both of you should look at yourselves in the mirror and get to know each other's anatomy. The female partner should accept that the treatment is directed at the male and that she has to be a little patient. If high levels of sexual tension are built up in her, the male partner after the exercise should stimulate her manually to orgasm. Many women initially object to pleasuring the penis but ultimately agree when it is pointed out to them that the longer the partner lasts the better it is for them in the long run. Perhaps the most powerful reason for undertaking the exercises jointly is that they will succeed in reducing the anxiety and tension felt by the male about his premature ejaculation and so build a closer, more fulfilling relationship. The female partner should also accept that even if the male's disorder is cured, the chances of her getting orgasmic are high but not assured.

MECHANICS OF THE EXERCISE

(1) Intercourse is banned for a week or ten days until better ejaculatory control is established and also to remove the performance pressure on the male.

(2) Lie side by side, completely nude, stroking each other in turn, but avoiding the breast and genitals. If by merely stroking the body, the male partner discharges, omit this exercise and go on to the next one.

(3) Lie on your back, legs separated.

(4) The female partner sits beside you (see Fig. 15.1) with one leg between your thighs and the other bent at the knee and lying almost parallel to your chest and abdomen.

(5) She holds the shaft of the erect penis and starts stimulating it gently. It is better if you tell her where and how you like to be stimulated.

(6) Focus your attention exclusively on the pleasurable sensations you

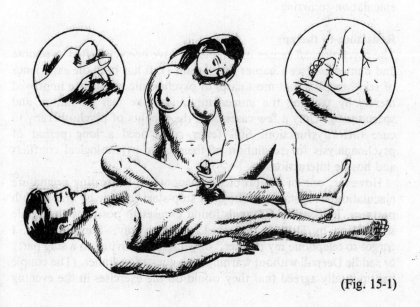

(Fig. 15-1)

are feeling. Do not worry about your partner or stimulate her initially.
(7) After you have developed some control with the stop-squeeze
technique outlined on page 279, the female partner is usually
permitted to start intercourse in the woman-on-top position. At first
she just holds the penis and lowers herself on you while sliding it into
the vagina.

(8) There should be no movement by either partner; you should just
lie motionless under the female for a few minutes. After the initial
desire to ejaculate has passed, she can gently start the up and down
movements. If you get an ejaculation, you should not worry unduly.
You will soon gain better control. After some ejaculatory control is
established, you may attempt the man-on-top positon, inserting the
penis gently into the vagina. If you feel like discharging, stop the
movements till the feeling has disappeared. You should practise the
stop-start technique at least three times before ejaculating. Then try to
bring your partner to an orgasm manually to release her tension.

(9) Once ejaculatory control is mastered by experiencing and feeling
intensely the erotic sensations, it lasts forever. But if the male abstains
from sex for a long period of time, there are chances of premature
ejaculation recurring.

Resistance to therapy

The psychological causes of impotence have been classified as remote
and immediate (see Chapter 14, Section 1). It has been the experience
of sex therapists that most cases of psychogenic impotence improved
merely by tackling the immediate causes like fear of failure and
spectatoring. Only a few cases need the insights of psychotherapy to
cure their dysfunction. Still fewer cases need a long period of
psychoanalysis for resolution of their basic psychological conflicts
and hostile interactions.

However, one of the problems encountered in treating premature
ejaculation is resistance to the brief stop-start therapy by one or both
partners. For example Pranab found excuses to postpone the penile
stimulation by Deepali. He would suddenly say, 'Sorry darling, I
forgot to telephone my mother,' or get himself invited to a stag party
or saddle Deepali without warning with guests for dinner. (The couple
had mutually agreed that they would do the exercises in the evening

after an early dinner and so would not accept any invitations to go out during this period.) Deepali was naturally furious at Pranab's excuses—while his reluctance to start therapy stemmed from his fear that she would dominate him completely. The passive role he was to play did not suit an officer of the armed forces used to ordering his men about! Pranab was told firmly but politely that he had two alternatives. Either he remain a premature ejaculator all his life or cheerfully go through the therapy. Initially Pranab rebelled as all men do, asking for a magic drug that could cure him without 'the male-ego shattering exercises' as he called them. He was even ready to go abroad if he could find a cure. It was impressed on him that at best, in some foreign sex therapy clinic he might find a surrogate partner to stimulate him. (Dr. Martin Cole at the Institute of Sex Education and Research in Birmingham, England, uses his wife as a willing surrogate partner.) After some persuasion and explanation Pranab was convinced that merely stimulating him did not mean that Deepali would dominate him.

Women often protest that mechanically stimulating their partners gives them no pleasure. 'It is so tiring and boring.' 'It is so disgusting.' 'Isn't there a better way of doing it?' 'No woman ever gets fun masturbating a motionless male.' If a woman shows resistance to therapy she is confronted with two alternatives: continuation of the sexual disorder or a better male performance with a good chance of gratifying her. These objections are usually the outer manifestations of the woman's basic insecurity about losing her partner if his sexual performance improves. More reassurance by the male that he loves her and is not going to desert her often works wonders.

To conclude, premature ejaculation, the most common and worrying sexual dysfunction, can easily be permanently cured in most cases with a short course of sex therapy. The cure lies within you.

Retarded ejaculation

Retarded ejaculation is a disorder where the male wants to ejaculate but is unable to do so. It was believed to be a rare condition but well known sex therapists Dr. Mahinder Watsa and Dr. Prakash Kothari report that they frequently come across patients suffering from this disorder. Sex therapists in the USA and Europe have also noted an increase in its incidence. Individuals complaining of retarded ejaculation get aroused, have a normal erection which persists, but cannot ejaculate in the vagina, though eagerly desiring orgasmic release. But they can easily ejaculate during masturbation or oral coitus with a partner.

In order to understand the paradox of a man being able to have a good erection without ejaculation, it is necessary to remember that the sexual response is biphasic. Erection is mediated by the parasympathetic division of the autonomic nervous system while ejaculation is dependent on the central nervous system (see Chapter 14).

The impotent male is unable to achieve an erection while the male with retarded ejaculation cannot come, although his erection is normal. In severe cases of retarded ejaculation, the extreme frustration of being unable to experience orgasm makes such men dislike intercourse and resort to masturbation alone for orgasmic release. One would think that the female partner would welcome the delayed orgasmic response of the male, but it is not so; she considers it a rejection of herself.

Causes of retarded ejaculation

ORGANIC DISEASES: The most common cause is undetected diabetes, which causes not only impotence but also retarded ejaculation. Nervous disorders affecting the sensory or motor pathway of the ejaculatory reflex can cause orgasmic disturbances, such as impaired sensation to the prepuce due to injury of the spinal cord.

DRUGS: Phenothiazine, psychotics like Melleril and antiadrenergics like methyldopa (Aldomet), clonidin (Arkamine or Catapress), guaninthedine (Ismelin), propranolol (Inderal, Ciplar), hydralazine (Apresoline), reserpine (Serpasil), which are commonly used in treating hypertension can cause retarded ejaculation.

PSYCHOLOGICAL CAUSES: Psychoanalysts postulate that retarded ejaculation, like impotence, (see 'Psychogenic Causes,' Chapter 14) is due to the unconscious fear of castration for ejaculating into the vagina. The man enjoys the preliminaries of love-play but develops coital anxiety while depositing his sperms inside his 'mother'. This anxiety makes him hold back and so he cannot ejaculate. Dr. Kaplan states that in some men the problem arises from hostility and aggression towards their wives.

DYADIC CONTEXT: Transactional analysts believe that retarded ejaculation is due to a strained and destructive relationship between the partners. For example, a meek, timid husband may give in to all the demands of his dominating wife, but when it comes to ejaculation he subconsciously holds back. A husband who feels insecure about his wife reacts similarly.

LEARNING THERAPY: According to this theory, an acute traumatic event, like the man finding that the wife is in love with another man or his fear of punishment if his clandestine love affair has been discovered by his boss, can inhibit ejaculation.

In every case, a complete physical examination, including a check on the intake of drugs, is necessary to exclude organic causes before commencing therapy.

Treatment

Retarded ejaculation is due to intra-psychic traumatic factors like guilt, puritanical parents and religious orthodoxy. Attempts have been made to relieve this condition through pyschotherapy but the results have been discouraging. The therapy format currently used is a combination of psychotherapy and specific sexual tasks to modify the inhibitory ejaculation response. The therapy format has to be adapted to the specific cause which has resulted in retarded ejaculation in each case.

(1) The couple is asked for the first five to seven days to indulge in sexual activities that they mutually enjoy, but penis-vagina intercourse is prohibited,

(2) These non-demand erotic experiences usually result in increased sexual arousal and erection. If the male partner now desires to ejaculate he should leave his female partner and reach his orgasm alone by auto-manipulation.

(3) After mastering this technique, the female partner manually or orally stimulates him to orgasm. If he encounters any difficulty he can fantasize in any way he likes.

(4) Having perfected the technique described above, the male now

moves on to the next step, where the female partner stimulates him to an orgasm near the vagina. The idea of these sexual tasks is to gradually desensitise his inhibitions and let him progress naturally to enjoyment and ejaculation during penis-vagina intercourse. If it is difficult to ejaculate near the vagina the couple can resort to oral stimulation.

(5) The male now introduces the penis into the vagina while letting himself go to ejaculate. However, he may encounter many mental blocks during this stage and wonder whether he will be able to come; in other words, he spectators himself. Erotic fantasy at this stage helps to overcome such mental blocks.

(6) Finally, the sex therapist attempts during therapeutic sessions to resolve any existing marital conflicts.

Chapter 16

FRIGIDITY (ORGASMIC DYSFUNCTION)

*A woman's lack of orgasm is always an alarm signal
which means: There is something wrong with my love.*

STEKEL

FRIGIDITY IS feminine sexual anaesthesia or sexual non-responsiveness, a condition equivalent to impotency in the male. Until recently the term 'frigidity' included a wide range of sexual problems—the total inability of a woman to get excited, the lack of vaginal lubrication during foreplay, and incapacity to reach an orgasm, although wanting and enjoying sex. According to Dr. Masters there is no such thing as a sexually cold and totally non-responsive woman. All women are potentially capable of responding to sexual stimuli, as all men are born potent. But just as some men develop impotency in later life, so some women because of emotional or physical trauma reject sexual responsiveness. For example, a woman who has been sexually molested or raped may be unable to respond when stimulated.

The term 'frigid' means cold, apathetic or without ardour, and was probably coined by a male. Ever since then, millions of women have suffered untold misery by being derogatorily dubbed 'frigid' by their male partners. A man has only to call a normally responding woman 'frigid' and her sexual machinery gets out of order instantly. There is an immediate short-circuit in the sexual wiring between her brain and the vagina, and she will fail to respond to him forever. Modern sex-ologists do not brand a woman 'frigid'. They have coined a new word—*anorgasmic,* meaning having difficulty in reaching an orgasm (*an* means 'without'). Some prefer to call it *orgasmic dysfunction* or *preorgasmic,* implying that the women can become orgasmic—as hope springs eternal in the human breast! The word *frigidity* is used in this section as readers have got used to it and understand it more easily.

Gopal brought Shakuntala to me because he thought she was frigid and was not having an earth-shaking orgasm. With total lack of tact, he blurted·out, 'Doctor, please do something for Shakuntala, she has become completely frigid.' Shakuntala flew into a rage and started sobbing. 'He always calls me frigid. I do not know what is wrong with me but he has made me believe that I am cold and unresponsive.' On close questioning I found out that Shakuntala was a healthy, sexually responding female who could be orgasmic if she was stimulated adequately, but that Gopal had premature ejaculation and that intercourse finished fast. It is common to find men dubbing women frigid when really the fault lies with them. Shakuntala told me wryly, 'It is still a man's world. How can I tell him that I am a healthy female but fail to respond because of his sexual disability?'

Another instance was that of the college girl, Charmaine. 'We were thinking of getting married after Asif got his law degree. But like most men, he could not wait for the happy event,' she said and started crying. Covering her face she burst out, 'He called me a frigidaire as I did not respond in bed. He wants to marry a hot sex bomb and not a cold cucumber like me! Can anything be done for my frigidity, Doctor?' I assured Charmaine that just because she did not respond once did not mean that she was frigid or under-sexed. On further questioning I found out that the young man, without having taken the least trouble to arouse her, had wanted to enter her forcibly. Was it any wonder that poor Charmaine was cold and unresponsive? Such a traumatic incident may well have made her incurably frigid but, fortunately for her, her parents were sympathetic and a year later arranged for her to be married to a very understanding boy, who with great patience overcame her resistance to sex. She now responds normally.

Impotency and frigidity compared

An impotent man does not have an erection; without erection, penetration of the female vagina is difficult, if not impossible. On the other hand, the so-called frigid woman can indulge in intercourse without enjoying it or reaching an orgasm. However, a man possibly suffers more mental agony because impotency is considered a loss of manhood and is excruciatingly hurtful to the male ego.

SEXUAL DYSFUNCTION

Sexual dysfunction can be divided into two main areas: (1) general sexual dysfunction or total lack of response to sexual stimulation; and (2) orgasmic disorder, where the woman is unable to reach an orgasm.

General sexual dysfunction

This is the most severe form of sexual disorder in the female. She becomes devoid of total sexual feeling owing to extreme repression and inhibition. Primary sexual disorder is a condition in which a woman has never experienced sexual arousal or erotic pleasure; whereas secondary sexual disorder is a condition in which she may have responded to kissing and petting earlier in life but after marriage develops an aversion for intercourse and becomes totally nonresponsive.

Orgasmic disorders

These are the most prevalent complaints in women of our country. Primary orgasmic disorder is a condition in which a woman has never experienced an orgasm. On the other hand, if the disorder develops after a period of ability to reach orgasm, it is called secondary orgasmic disorder. Women who have only orgasmic problems are usually normal in every other respect. They have a strong sex drive, delight in sex-play, lubricate vaginally and enjoy penile penetration. However, they just cannot go beyond the plateau phase and make the last lap to orgasm. Many women can achieve orgasm when they are masturbating or when their male partner stimulates them manually. In a few obstinate cases of orgasmic difficulties, a vibrator may be used by the woman or even by the male partner to help her achieve an orgasm (see 'Treatment of Frigidity').

Incidence of sexual dysfunction

Frigidity is the most widespread and most talked about functional sexual disturbance in the female. A few decades ago, women were not supposed to be orgasmic and nobody bothered about it. Worldwide consciousness of frigidity has arisen because of over-emphasis in the media of the widely reported finding of Dr. Masters that women can have not only a single orgasm but even multiple orgasms. Western women immediately started feeling that they must reach an orgasm, or something was wrong with them.

The incidence of sexual disorders in women varies from country to country. A report from the USA shows a rate of 45 to 90 per cent. In France, a recent survey quotes the figure at 30 per cent, while in Sweden the incidence is 50 per cent. No reliable data of the prevalence of frigidity is yet available for Indian women but in a few sample surveys the incidence varied from 76 to 96 per cent.

CAUSES AND PREVENTION OF FEMALE SEXUAL DYSFUNCTION

It would be useful to recapitulate briefly the normal sexual development and mechanism of female sexual arousal and find out how it can become deranged (see Chapter 5). First and foremost, it is well to repeat and remember that no female is born frigid; frigidity develops later. At birth the complicated sexual machinery is in perfect trim (barring rare genital defects like the absence of a vagina). But it can function properly only if its owner learns the necessary skills of how to use it.

Restrictive upbringing

You therefore need a teacher who can tell you objectively how to keep the naturally responding machinery in good shape. If, however, the teacher herself doesn't know how to drive the sexual motor, obviously she cannot correctly instruct her daughter. The learning process begins in the cradle. For example, if the mother admonishes her infant daughter, 'Don't touch yourself there, it is dirty,' her sexual development is naturally warped. Insult is further added to injury by the parents' partiality and preference for the son. The little girl senses and notices this difference in affection and attention. Her sexuality is stamped by her experience. 'It is better to be born a boy; after all, boys have a penis,' she thinks. She grows up feeling inferior, a second-class citizen of our sovereign secular republic.

At school her innate curiosity and sexuality is suffocated by the teachers. Dr. Prema Bali of the All India Institute of Medical Science, New Delhi, in a study of 400 females from the family planning clinic found that 75 per cent of them started gathering knowledge about sex from friends when they were between 8 to 10 years. According to an Inter-country Seminar on Human Sexuality and Sex Education held by the World Health Organisation in New Delhi in September 1977: 'The problems faced by school girls at puberty were: (1) No preparation for her period; (2) Fear and unpleasant reactions at the onset of the menarche and no knowledge of the purpose of menstruation.' During adolescence parents segregate the daughter and prevent any normal meetings with boys, repeatedly dinning in her ears, 'You must be a good girl,' 'Keep away from boys,' 'Sex is dirty,' 'It is only for getting a baby,' 'All men are the same. They want only one thing—sex.'

Such a girl may be studying in a co-educational institute. She has to spend a lot of energy attempting to ward off male advances and keeping boys at arm's length; and as her sexuality is suppressed from infancy, she can easily develop frigidity and fail to respond sexually. When she marries she cannot give up her old self-protective devices easily, while her equally ignorant and inexperienced husband expects her to respond sexually on the wedding night. The result: she suffers from anorgasmia and develops sexual anaesthesia.

Since attitudes are implanted during the first twelve years of growth and development it is most essential that the growing girl is told in a phased way about development of her sexuality. For instance at the age of three or four, her curiosity about where babies come from should be satisfied. Later on, at the age of ten or eleven, she should be told about the monthly period, and how menstruation is a normal physiological process in the life of a girl during the reproductive years. She should have no hang-ups about the menstrual period. As she grows older, at about 16 or 17, the mother should explain to her daughter her sexual anatomy and erogenous zones like the lips, the ears, the side of the neck, the breasts, and the genital region, especially the clitoris. A number of schools these days teach basic sexual anatomy and the mother should tactfully find out whether her daughter's school does so: if not, she should impart it herself. For if neither the school nor the parents impart this vital knowledge to the growing adolescent, she is bound to derive wrong ideas on sex from her friends' jokes or from reading lurid novels. She could also be made aware about what normal intercourse is and how she is expected to respond in it. Most women in our country never initiate sex. They are completely male-dominated and feel that they will be considered cheap or aggressive.

Religious taboos

Religious beliefs play an all-important role in sexual conditioning. If the idea is instilled into a girl that sex is sinful, she develops feelings of guilt and becomes non-responsive. Sexual guilt is very common even in the West. Carole Wade, editor of *Psychology Today,* states, 'Many people need written permission to enjoy themselves sexually.' Many couples are ashamed to stand in front of each other naked or even look at themselves in a mirror. Sex is a learning process and among the primitive tribes in our country begins early in life. There is no false modesty and nothing about sex is hidden from these children. We can take a leaf from their book.

Conflict with the husband

Conflict with the husband is perhaps the most important cause of frigidity in women. If they tend to argue or if her husband is only interested in sex without showing his affection at other times in a non-sexual way, like stroking her hair or patting her shoulder, she may gradually develop orgasmic difficulties.

A woman needs to respect and have a strong bond of attachment. admiration and love for her male partner. Unlike a man who can, relatively speaking, go to bed with any woman he feels sexually attracted to, women usually respond freely only to their loved one.

Inability to let go

Some women who can easily become orgasmic are unable to let go at the critical moment because of fear of losing self-control and appearing unladylike to their partners. Some are also afraid that they might scream during their orgasm. In such cases sex therapists simulate an orgasm and teach their patients how to go through all the gyrations.

Fear

Danger and fear are the greatest enemies of erection in the male and orgasm in the female. Fear of how she measures up sexually, what her partner thinks of her, fear of an unwanted pregnancy or of children suddenly intruding, may prevent a woman from reaching orgasm.

FEAR OF THE MALE: In our country, Manu's Code is still the guide for conduct and innumerable women fear their husbands. The woman is brought up from childhood to be an ideal Hindu wife and look upon her husband as a god. Indira Mahindra states in her book *The Rebellious Home-Makers,* 'It is this submission, this meekness, this unquestioning obedience, that is infused into every Hindu girl from childhood—be an ideal woman, like Devi Sita.' Her puritan upbringing is mainly responsible for her lying like a sacrificial lamb during sex, and if she fails to respond, her life partner could always manage a 'kick' elsewhere.

But the winds of change have affected our women in a big way. Society is changing rapidly and all classes of women, especially in the cities, are more conscious of their own sexuality through the media. They are getting more and more interested in the mechanics of sexual response and how they can increase their eroticism. Some of them even bring their husbands along for treatment of inadequacy.

Lack of sexual know-how

The modern Indian male who invariably sits, so to speak, in the driver's seat in sex, displays an amazing lack of knowledge of sexual skills and of how to arouse a woman. He is often unfamiliar with her erotic zones, especially the clitoris. An inept male is mainly responsible for orgasmic disorders in the female. Dr. Masters has rightly said, 'There is no such thing as a sexually unresponsive woman.'

The Pill

A minority of women who take the birth-control pill for 18 to 36 months at a stretch, gradually lose interest in sex. Such women often tell their husbands, 'Darling, I must be getting old. I am not interested in sex these days.' It is advisable in such cases to stop taking the Pill.

TREATMENT OF SEXUAL DYSFUNCTION

Until a few decades ago, women with sexual dysfunction could not get professional help from their gynaecologists or family physicians except through prolonged psychoanalysis. Here is Myrtle, now in her early forties, narrating her story. 'I fell in love with my husband at first sight and married at 19 in 1959. At 23 I was the mother of two children. I love my husband, I enjoy sex, but somehow I just could not make it to orgasm, however hard I tried. I felt cheated and left out. I went from physician to gynaecologist here as well as abroad. Some doctors told me to go in for psychoanalysis to resolve my so-called sexual conflicts, and I even tried that for six months but gave it up in disgust. In short, what the doctors said amounted to, 'Grin and bear it. As long as your husband does not mind, why worry about it? Women are naturally asexual.' One of them even quoted a rhyme which I still remember:

> *For all the ailments under the sun*
> *Either there is a remedy or there is none;*
> *If there is one try to find it,*
> *If there is none, never mind it.*

'Then a strange thing happened. While travelling in an aircraft in 1971, I picked up a magazine for women in which there was an article describing the technique of becoming orgasmic again. I got the magazine and faithfully practised the exercises and my joy knew no bounds when for the first time I reached an orgasm during masturbation. After two months I became orgasmic with my husband for the first time and reach it frequently when I sleep with him. It has opened up a new dimension in my life. I now feel a complete woman.'

A new horizon opened up for non-responsive Western women in the 1960s when Dr. William Masters and Mrs. Virginia Johnson reported that they had successfully treated sexual problems in both sexes without extensive and prolonged psychotherapy. The characteristics of the Masters-Johnson behavioural therapy is the involvement of four individuals: the male and the female partners plus a male-female team of sex therapists, aptly called the 'therapeutic foursome'. The sexually inadequate wife is not treated by them without the husband.

In the 1970s Joseph LoPiccolo and W. Charles Lobitz improved on the Masters-Johnson therapy by introducing masturbation to attain orgasm. These sex therapies have brought new hope to non-responsive women. Almost 100 per cent of the patients can become responsive again.

A number of women object to behavioural and auto-manipulative techniques to restore their orgasmic capability. They feel that it is artificial and prefer becoming orgasmic naturally. It is important that such women realise the basic difference between love and sex. Love is a natural phenomenon, an attraction between the sexes, while sex is a learning process. If women bear this in mind they would not have such strong objections against auto-manipulative therapy. Men as well as women have a sense of guilt whenever they masturbate, and until recently even medical authorities claimed that masturbation was harmful in both sexes. It is now conclusively proved that auto-manipulation is not harmful and can improve the female sexual response in orgasmic difficulties. It provides natural relief in normal women, who cannot reach an orgasm during coitus.

Choice of therapy

Fortunately there is a wide choice of methods for treating sexually inadequate women: (1) psychotherapy; (2) therapeutic foursome; (3) single therapist for both partners or for one partner; (4) family physician; and (5) do-it-yourself techniques.

Psychotherapy

Until 1960, when the new behaviour sex therapy startled the Western medical world, the only hope for a sexually inadequate woman lay in psychotherapy—which lasted for one or two years, or even longer in some cases. It is pertinent to make a few observations on psychotherapy here. Firstly, it was observed that sexual problems were not confined to individuals suffering from mental disorders, psychoses or neuroses. Secondly, though there were no doubt many psychological reasons for sexual disorders in a female, they had no immediate relevance to the relief of her sexual inadequacy. Thirdly, long-maintained psychotherapy for the inadequate partner put a tremendous strain on the marriage itself. While one partner underwent treatment, the other was left completely frustrated.

Moreover, the results with this therapy were not very encouraging and over the last twenty years psychotherapy has been replaced in almost all clinics by the Masters-Johnson behaviour therapy. Masters and Johnson proved that behaviour therapy along with a knowledge of sexual anatomy and psychology and a very limited amount of psychotherapy are sufficient to treat most patients with simple disorders like anorgasmia, premature ejaculation and impotency. They felt there was no need to delve in depth into childhood experiences and untoward incidents like attempts at molestation and rape. Only a very few cases of sexual disorders with deep psychological problems require treatment in depth.

Therapeutic foursome

The pioneers of the new, simple, short therapy were Masters and Johnson. They postulated that in sexual disorders the marriage is at fault and not the individual partner. They work with both members of the family unit. As a result, not only is the sexually inadequate partner treated but they also enlist the complete co-operation and willing participation of the adequate partner. Masters and Johnson maintain that sexual problems in the female are due to psychological hang-ups, but they do not recommend prolonged psychotherapy extending for a year or more. They employ intensive specific training procedures for two weeks for the marital partners. The basis of their therapy depends upon exercises to become sensual, as one cannot be sexual without being sensual. Intercourse is forbidden during the early stages of therapy. The wife is thus freed from pressure to produce an orgasm. Secondly, the female is asked to caress her partner's body first to counteract her guilt at being at the receiving end of the union.

This form of therapy is used in many countries in the West. Its disadvantages are that it is prohibitively expensive and is unsuited in our country, for two reasons. Firstly, a therapeutic pair of sexologists like Masters and Johnson for the treatment of sexual inadequacy is unusual in our country. There are only a few sex therapists, but no pair. Secondly, both partners are not simultaneously available for treatment as outlined by Masters and Johnson; only the inadequate female seeks therapy. The typical male reaction is, 'There is nothing wrong with me. Why should I go for treatment?' He may be an inept lover, neglecting foreplay, but as long as he produces an erection and is capable of penetrating his partner, he honestly believes that something is wrong with her if she does not respond. May I appeal to all males to do a self-appraisal of their sexual techniques before labelling their partners under-sexed and sexually inadequate?

Single therapist

The principles of therapy remain the same, except that one individual sees both partners either together or separately, according to the needs of the treatment. It is ideally suited for our country where both partners are not available for simultaneous treatment. However, there are very few professionally qualified therapists in our country who can advise women on sexual dysfunction, and women are generally shy to consult doctors about their sexual problems. I have therefore outlined a do-it-yourself programme to help women who enjoy foreplay and intercourse but are unable to reach an orgasm and cannot find a professional therapist or are reticent about consulting a doctor.

Family physician

The family physician is the ideal person to handle most sexual disorders as his patients have implicit faith in him. However, as Dr. Masters states, there are three major stumbling blocks which hamper treatment. Firstly, the erroneous belief that patients do not reveal correctly their sexual history to plan adequate treatment. Secondly, the family doctor does not know enough formal sexual physiology and how to treat a patient with a sexual disorder. Thirdly, the prevalent myth widely ingrained in the fraternity here that sexual disorders are psychogenic in origin, and the only treatment is psychotherapy. In our country however, as there is a dearth of sex therapists, the female physician with a knowledge of human sexual responses is often the ideal person to treat sexual inadequacy.

Do-it-yourself techniques

This book attempts to combine our traditional age-old beliefs about sexuality with the most modern sex knowledge and therapies, and is a handy manual for acquiring the know-how of sexual anatomy and techniques. (The reader may consult more advanced books and monograms to further her knowledge.)

The treatment of sexual dysfunction is divided into two sections: (1) Women who are sexually responsive but have difficulty in reaching an orgasm (anorgasmia), and (2) Women who suffer from general sexual dysfunction and total lack of response (sexual anaesthesia).

Anorgasmia

I shall outline the do-it-yourself programme by which any woman can become orgasmic after practising the technique at home. However, I repeat that there is no substitute for a sex therapist in cases of severe sexual inadequacy. The exercises mentioned below are helpful if you have no aversion to sex, enjoy the preliminaries and love-play but cannot reach orgasm.

HOW MUCH TIME IT TAKES: You will initially need about 45 minutes to one hour, or even a little longer. You have to be persistent and persevering with these exercises and do them regularly. Some women respond in a few days, others take a few weeks while the majority need a few months. *Do not give up.* With practice, as you become sensual and orgasmic, you will respond in a much shorter time.

(1) BE ALONE: You must be alone in a room and choose a time when you are not likely to be disturbed. Housewives can easily do the exercises when their husbands are at work and their children have gone to school. Working women may have difficulty in finding the time. It would be advisable to take a short holiday or adjust your daily routine in such a way that you can be alone. The lights should be dim and erotic music can be an additional help.

(2) TAKE A HOT BATH: Feel the different sensations which are most acute in parts richly supplied with sensory nerves like the hands, the forearms and the face. After the bath, rub yourself vigorously with a Turkish towel, systematically going over the whole body, and enjoy the different sensations as the towel rubs against your body.

(3) KNOW YOUR BODY: Stand in front of a mirror and look at your

nude body. Learn to like it and be comfortable with it. If you are worried about your height, the size of your breasts or your crooked nose, look for your plus points; do not give undue importance to the negative ones. There is always something bad in the best of us and something good in the worst of us.

(4) PRACTISE RELAXATION: Lie in bed completely nude and practise relaxation for about 15 minutes. The easiest way to relax is to first contract your muscles one by one and then relax them. The details of how to relax are given in Appendix I.

(5) BECOME SENSUAL: Women right from childhood are not in touch with their bodies. They have systematically suppressed physical sensations, turned off the sensory switch and so find it very difficult to switch on sensuality during sex. This is due to the differences in the upbringing of girls and boys. Girls are expected to suppress their sexual urge and curiosity while boys proudly display their lust. Society expects girls to be models of modesty and virtue and say 'No' to male advances and also to their own sexuality. This continuous repression of sensations prevents a girl from being aroused.

Be in communion with your body by lying in bed nude and, with your fingers, leisurely touch, caress and fondle your body, including the legs, thighs, hips and breasts. For the first few days exclude the genitals. Gradually, you'll get used to your loving caressing of your body and be able to distinguish the different sensations. You have to learn to be a narcissist—self-love, up to a point. Practise these exercises for at least four days for 15 to 20 minutes every day. You will gradually find a very pleasant tingling feeling developing when your body is stroked. India's veteran sexologist Vatsyayana was aware of the erotic value of touching and strongly recommended it 1500 years ago before Masters and Johnson rekindled it again.

(6) SELF-STIMULATION OF THE GENITALS: The word 'masturbation' is strongly resented by women in our country. They will admit to pre-marital sex or an extra-marital affair after some persuasion, but if questioned about masturbation one draws a blank. The majority of women masturbate in different ways yet they will not admit it or often are unaware of it. While boys masturbate by directly holding the organ in their hands and rubbing it, initially girls do not resort to

clitoral stimulation with their hands. They do it indirectly by rubbing their genitals against objects—like climbing a tree or a pole, or sitting cross-legged and shaking the legs. I repeat that masturbation is not harmful and does not lead to any untoward effects or dreadful diseases as was believed more than three decades ago. Secondly, you should have no feeling of guilt or remorse while you are masturbating. I shall refrain from using the word masturbation in this section and instead call it *self-stimulation* which does not arouse feelings of resentment and guilt.

Virgins wonder whether self-stimulation harms their virginity and would be found out by their partners when they marry. It is very important to realise that only the mons area and the clitoris are titillated and it is not at all necessary to introduce the finger into the vaginal cavity, so no harm whatsoever can result to the intact hymen. Self-stimulation makes a woman more sensuous, which her male partner will appreciate.

After being comfortable with stroking and pleasuring your own body for a few days, learn to derive pleasure from your genitals and ultimately become orgasmic.

HOW TO STIMULATE YOURSELF: First become thoroughly conversant with your anatomy, particularly the clitoris and the mons region. You are now ready to enjoy the thrills of self-stimulation and your rising tension will ultimately culminate in an orgasm.

Genital titillation will show you the places where you are most responsive, the type of manipulation you like best and determine your orgasmic pattern, that is, whether you are single or multi orgasmic. It is normal not to have an intense orgasm initially during sex. Many women are disappointed with the mild orgasm, but with more sexual experience the intensity improves and so does the quality. However, the most intense orgasms are during auto-manipulation and not during coitus. The latter orgasms are more gratifying as the female partner feels the male organ nestling in her vagina during sex, and later the male ejaculation in her gives supreme joy.

The technique of becoming sensual and of self-stimulation are outlined below. However, different women prefer varying techniques. Each is free to do so, for all roads ultimately lead to the same destination—orgasm.

(a) *Your Anatomy:* You must know the exact location of the clitoris and the vagina.

(b) *Lubrication:* Apply some jelly (preferably K.Y.) in the clitoral and the vaginal region. Do not use vaseline or coconut oil as it turns rancid and irritates the vagina and is also difficult to clean.

(c) *Fantasising:* Start fantasising about your favourite sex symbol. He may be a movie idol, the man you think is most handsome, the dashing executive you met at the party or the outstandingly attractive male you were with in the train. Fantasy will help you to become orgasmic early. You can imagine that your symbol desires you, wants to make love to you. Some women even like to be raped not by one but by many men! You can choose the fantasy that stimulates your imagination.

(d) *Titillation:* If you are right-handed, stimulate the right side of the body of the clitoris with the right index finger. Left-handers should stimulate the left side of the clitoral body. Most women do not like to stimulate the clitoral body or glans as it is extremely sensitive. Some women prefer titillating the mons area but the sensations here are not as intense as in the clitoris. Please remember that during the plateau phase, the body of the clitoris is pulled upwards and cannot be felt by your finger but the stimulation should be continued.

(e) *The build-up and orgasm:* As more and more sensations are built up, you reach a point where they burst into an orgasm. Continue stimulation whilst you are undergoing the orgasm. In case you feel like another orgasm or many more, you can achieve them by continuing the stimulation. Discover for yourself whether your body needs some pause after the first climax. If, however, the sensation does not build up in the clitoral region in spite of stimulation for some length of time, say, 30 to 45 minutes, you may have to use a vibrator to bring about an orgasm easily. The use of the vibrator is considered separately in the next section.

(f) *Time taken to reach orgasm:* If you have become orgasmic by constant practice, you will find that the time you need to climax gradually diminishes. When you have trained your body to respond almost invariably with an orgasm during auto-manipulation in about

15 to 20 minutes, you are ready to attempt orgasm with a partner during sex.

(g) *Auto-eroticism compared with love-making:* Some women find it difficult to switch over from self-stimulation to love-play with a partner and are unable to reach an orgasm with him during penis-vaginal coitus. Others respond during auto-manipulation or with a vibrator or if their partner stimulates them with his hand or orally, yet fail to reach an orgasm during coitus. This may be a normal variation of female sexuality or due to sexual inhibition. In such cases, it is better to consult a therapist immediately, who will be able to decide on the true cause of anorgasmia.

7. COMMUNICATE YOUR WANTS TO YOUR PARTNER: The most difficult part of your training is to tell your partner precisely how you need to be stimulated. You will say, 'It is expected of him. He should know. I feel too shy and reticent to tell him what I want.' May I point out to you that upto now you yourself were not aware of your sensuality. How, then, can you expect your partner to know what turns you on? You are afraid that he might think you bold and demanding and unladylike if you communicate your requirements. Let Freny narrate her experience to you. 'After regularly practising the exercises for two months, I at last became orgasmic during auto-stimulation but never with my partner. Robin just does not have a clue about what I want!' she told me exasperatedly. I told Freny, 'Why don't you tell him clearly what you want in sex? "Darling, please do this or that, in precise terms".' She left unconvinced but returned after a month, her face all smiles. 'I have at last made it,' she said triumphantly. 'Doctor, I could never follow your advice wholly, but instead during love-play I took Robin's hand and placed it on the region I wanted to be stimulated. If he removed his hand, I put it there again gently, caressingly, whilst kissing him and made him do it. Slowly but surely I took his fingers to my clitoris and made him stimulate me. If he did it too gently I pressed on the finger; if he was too firm, I released the pressure. Robin's performance has improved tremendously and now he instinctively takes my hand and asks me to fondle the part he likes to be caressed, including his male organ, and in the way he likes best.

The quality of our sex life has improved and boredom has gone out of it. We are lovey-dovey once again!'

AUTO-STIMULATION TO ORGASM IN FRONT OF YOUR MALE PARTNER: Western sexologists have used the technique of auto-stimulation in front of the male partner to achieve orgasm in the female. However revolting the procedure may seem at first sight, many anorgasmic women have reached a climax with it. Women complain that the step-by-step-to-orgasm techniques deprive them of spontaneity and makes sex mechanical. In fact, some even prefer spontaneity to responsiveness and pleasure. It is up to each woman to select the sexual lifestyle which suits her best. If she is to achieve the glory of being orgasmic she has to go through the mechanical motions of sexual stimulation and with the right fantasy of a male model always in her mind she can get a tremendous amount of involvement and the exercises won't seem mechanical.

GENERAL SEXUAL DYSFUNCTION

The most severe form of disability in the female is general sexual dysfunction, popularly known as frigidity or sexual anaesthesia, a condition in which she is totally devoid of sexual feeling. Unlike anorgasmia, it is therefore not easily amenable to therapy, and should be treated by a professional sex therapist. In many cases it is an unrewarding task as the wife cannot be removed from the conflict-burdened environment in which she lives with her husband or in-laws. Besides, it is not possible to change her basic nature and her inherent need for security, tenderness, affection, and her overt concern to meekly and obediently please her husband. I will illustrate what I mean with a case history.

'I am completely devoid of all feelings. I never get aroused and never feel anything in sex,' Shanta, a devoted social worker and mother of two children told me. She fumbled with her handbag as her eyes filled with tears and blurted out, 'Sex is the biggest ordeal I have to face twice a week but as a devoted Indian wife I grin and bear it. I have silently suffered the ordeal for twenty years and have resigned myself to my dominating and demanding husband.' 'Why don't you seek professional help for your sexual disorder?' I asked. 'No, doctor,

I will never go to a head shrinker,' she promptly replied. 'Gone are the days when women went through psychoanalysis for their sexual problems,' I told her. 'Certainly not that Masters-Johnson stuff where you artificially tickle and tingle yourself,' she said in a sharp voice. 'It must come naturally, not through my finger stimulating my insides. My mummy told me, "Shanta, never touch yourself there, never masturbate, or you will become mad".'

'It is not surprising that you have a sexual problem,' I told her. 'It is your stern puritanical upbringing. You were born with a clean slate of sexuality. But your parents repressed all your natural sexual urges and later you followed their advice and said an emphatic "No" to every feeling of arousal. Sacrificing yourself sexually to your husband without deriving any pleasure yourself is not the purpose of creation. You should be a little selfish now after twenty years and enjoy sex yourself.'

'What will my husband think if I suddenly start rolling and wriggling under him? He will think I am a cheap woman and not the prim and proper Shanta—the ideal Indian wife,' she told me anxiously. 'Perhaps your husband will derive much greater pleasure if you become sexually responsive,' I told her. 'I will do anything for my husband. May I, doctor, take his permission as he will have to foot the bill? I will call you again,' she promised.

The successful outcome of treatment for this severe sexual disorder in the female depends on many factors. First and foremost is the therapist himself, his experience, patience, sympathy, empathy with the patient and above all his professional skill. By this I mean, understanding the basic drives of the inadequate female and how to channelise the various streams flowing in different directions into a harmonious river of sensuality and sexuality which ultimately results in a torrential orgasm. I have known of some cases where an understanding family physician having access to the wife as well as the husband has been more successful than prolonged psychotherapy which the disabled female partner undergoes. According to Masters and Johnson nearly 75 per cent of frigid and under-sexed women can become sensually responding and orgasmic.

Helen Singer Kaplan, head of the Sex Therapy and Education Programme of the Cornell Medical Centre in the USA, maintains that the great majority of women who suffer from primary orgasmic inhibition can achieve an orgasm after a brief therapy. On the other hand, Professor H. Stamm, Chief Physician of the Department of Obstetrics and Gynaecology, Canton Hospital, Baden, Switzerland, reports that the treatment of this female sexual disorder is an unrewarding task and the majority of women remain uninfluenced and uncured by attempts at therapy. According to him, failure is due to the impossibility of removing these women from their conflict-burdened environment.

Conflict with the husband

If the wife is in constant conflict with the husband and has lost all respect for him, it is difficult to change the personalities of both to be at peace with their environment. In India, the joint family system still prevails and though it has many advantages, the young educated modern bride is in constant conflict with the conservative, dictatorial, doting-on-her-son mother-in-law. The tussle between the two women to possess the same man becomes a tense and charged situation in the house, which often converts a responsive young lady into a non-arousable, non-responsive and non-orgasmic woman.

Husband's lack of sexual skill

Dr. Masters asserts that there is no such thing as a sexually irresponsive woman. According to him, a frigid woman is one who does not achieve orgasm from any form of sexual stimulation. There are many women who are initially responsive to kissing and petting but after marriage develop an aversion for intercourse and cannot be aroused (secondary sexual dysfunction). These cases are almost invariably due to lack of understanding and skill on the part of the male partner. A woman is like a delicate musical instrument which must be tuned properly for the ideal response. Unfortunately, many males do not know much about female anatomy and or about the art of arousing a woman artistically. Dr. Helen Singer Kaplan rightly says, 'Too often men fail to realise that they can become good lovers if they simply supply their partners with gentle sensitive stimulation instead of perpetual erection.'

Principles of therapy

(1) The inadequate female should not feel rejected by her husband. He should be sympathetic, sensitive and understanding of her inadequacy.

(2) She should not be suffering from psychopathology like schizophrenia, paranoia or depression.

(3) Both partners should be available for therapy, the inadequate female first, the so-called adequate male next, and finally both of them together.

(4) The total involvement and desire to improve responses should be present in both.

(5) Exercises are prescribed for both to become sensual in a quiet, relaxed atmosphere conducive for love-making (see Appendix II).

(6) It is essential to open the avenues of communication between both partners, with each expressing wants and desires during the preliminary exercises which Masters and Johnson call *sensate focus*.

(7) Touching, stroking, caressing and fantasising:

(a) The female partner begins by stroking with her hands the body of the male, avoiding the genital region. She finds out from him whether he likes gentle or firm pressure, and the regions he prefers for stroking. The female first and the male next according to Dr. Helen Singer Kaplan, has a two-fold advantage. It counteracts the woman's fear that her husband may reject her touching, and her innate guilt about getting something done for herself.

(b) The couple is advised not to indulge in sexual intercourse, thus freeing the female partner from the performance fear of producing an orgasm. It makes her carefree, relaxed and she soon experiences erotic feelings in a day or two (in some cases longer), when the male pleasures her. In other words she is slowly but surely turned-on.

(8) When she reports a heightened feeling of sexual responsiveness she is advised to caress the penis while the male gently fondles her breasts and nipples, the clitoris and mons area and the vaginal entrance. If the male is too excited, Dr. Kaplan tells the patient to bring him to an orgasm manually or orally. During these exercises when she is aroused, and ready for intercourse, Dr. Kaplan advises the woman to be on top and start coitus with very slow thrusts whilst savouring the sensations which arise from her vagina. If the male partner feels that

he is going to ejaculate, he asks the female to demount and manually stimulates her, till his urge to ejaculate has passed off. The female mounts once again and starts thrusting movements. If she feels like having an orgasm she should proceed till she is orgasmic; otherwise she can enjoy the male partner discharging in her. However, these erotic exercises can in some patients evoke charged emotional responses which can be identified and therapeutically dealt with. In conclusion, as Frankle has stated, 'The more attention is shifted from the partner to the sex act itself, the more coitus becomes handicapped.'

(9) It is essential to emphasise, as stated by Shere Hite, that only 30 per cent of women become orgasmic during penis-vagina intercourse. The vast majority of women need clitoral stimulation to reach an orgasm.

Vibrator

In obstinate cases of orgasmic dysfunction in the female, the use of a vibrator is very helpful, particularly if she is unable to reach an orgasm during masturbation. There are many females who climax up to a point during auto-manipulation but fail to scale the peak.

Electric massagers have been in use since 1900 to relieve muscular aches and pains in stiff necks and cramps in the legs. In the swinging sixties this little gadget came into prominence as an excellent erotic stimulator.

Millions of women in the USA and Europe are using the little massager over their mons and clitoral regions to produce orgasms. They claim that the vibrator is a perfect lover available at a moment's notice, and can stimulate the erotic zone as long as one wants. But they are unanimous that a machine is no substitute for a man. It is merely a handy back-up system when the male partner is away.

Vibrators are also used in unlocking inhibitions and guilt attitudes which prevent a female from reaching an orgasm. 'In our desire to be good little girls,' says Betty Dodson, in *Liberating Masturbation*, 'many of us learned to cut off genital sensation. This negative conditioning can be reversed. The vibrator's strong, consistent stimulation allows a woman to achieve satisfaction very quickly, without the risk of becoming discouraged.'

Many women are concerned about reaching an artificial orgasm, as they call it, with a vibrator or even manually. They believe that the only right way to achieve an orgasm is *via* penis-vagina intercourse. But if women can use artificial aids like facial make-up to look more attractive, and domestic gadgets to make housework easier, why not a vibrator which is the most time-saving and least frustrating way to become orgasmic? It is not habit-forming, the user can easily switch over to respond manually after achieving orgasm. However, do not depend on the vibrator as the only means of scaling the sexual summit. As Dr. Shirely Zussman, President of the American Association of Sex Educators, Counsellors and Therapists says, 'Sometimes it is a good idea to begin with a vibrator, then once aroused, to proceed to orgasm manually. That gives you more of a chance to savour the sensations that build up to climax.'

HOW TO USE A VIBRATOR: Any ordinary electric massager is a multi-purpose gadget and an excellent erotic stimulator. However, never use it around water, on a wet body or while having a bath, as you will get an electric shock. Below is outlined how to self-stimulate yourself to orgasm with a vibrator.

(1) Have at least 30 to 40 minutes of uninterrupted time before you begin self-pleasuring with a vibrator.

(2) Practise relaxation for 5 minutes (see Appendix I).

(3) Get yourself in a sexual mood while relaxing by fantasizing. For instance, you can close your eyes and imagine that your partner is touching and pleasuring you the way you enjoy. Let yourself go with this fantasy and imagine the artistic way you want to be stimulated or you might like it rough or you might want to be forced or even raped!

(4) Apply a lotion or oil on your body, if you like. Begin exploring your body with the gadget, at first omitting the breasts and genital regions. Enjoy the erotic sensations as the vibrator slides over the different regions of your body while continuing the fantasizing. After a while move the vibrator to your breasts and genitals. If you initially find the nipples and clitoris very sensitive, change the pattern of stroking to barely brushing the nipples or the mons region or cover the genitals with a small towel to lessen the intensity of the sensations. After a few sessions you will be able to tolerate direct genital stimulation. You can also use a lubricant like KY Jelly over the mons and clitoral region.

(5) Julia Heiman and Leslie LoPicollo, who have considerable experience of treating anorgasmic women, recommend in the book *Becoming Orgasmic*, 'a reasonable amount of time, 15 minutes the first three times, then try for 15-30 minutes, and then 30-45 minutes, if that's what your body needs.' It takes about 30-40 minutes in the initial stages to become orgasmic with a vibrator. The amount of time you take is unimportant as long as you can reach an orgasm.

(6) After you have reached orgasm about 8 to 10 times with a vibrator and gained confidence, you are ready for the next erotic experience. Arouse yourself initially with a vibrator till you reach a high level of excitement and are close to an orgasm. Now remove the vibrator and switch over to manual stimulation to become orgasmic.

(7) Stimulate yourself manually to orgasm 10 to 15 times or more till you enjoy it without any feeling of guilt or shame. Get to know the regions which give you the most intense sensations.

(8) You are now ready to switch over to an understanding male partner who can stimulate you manually to orgasm. A convenient position for the male to pleasure you is to sit with his back propped up against the bed or to lean against the wall, while you recline between his legs, with your back against his chest. In this position, the male can stimulate the breasts and genitals and also kiss your head and neck. When you pleasure your partner, sit between his outstretched legs with both legs beside his chest. Tell your partner how you want to be stimulated. If you feel shy to tell him in so many words what you want, hold his hand and show him the way you like it.

(9) Abstain from normal coitus the first few times to avoid performance pressure of becoming orgasmic. You can manually or orally bring your aroused male partner to a climax, if he wants.

(10) You are now ready to move on to a few pleasuring sessions with your male partner. Initially after the male has stimulated you to orgasm or you have reached a high sexual peak, you should at first attempt the woman-on-top position, then thrust the way you like to reach an orgasm. Later, you can let the male have the posture of manliness—the man-on-top.

(11) What about women who are unable to achieve an orgasm with a vibrator after two or three weeks? Ask your partner to stimulate you manually when you have reached a high level of sexual excitement.

Many women reach an orgasm more easily with an understanding male partner than a machine. Finally, if nothing works, you should see a sex therapist as you need skilled professional attention.

VAGINISMUS

Vaginismus is an involuntary contraction of the muscles surrounding the vaginal inlet, when the male attempts to penetrate. The involuntary message is loud and clear: 'No Entry'. However, it is important to realise that the female does not consciously shut her vaginal inlet tight. The spasm is not under her will power. Just as the male cannot will an erection, so the female cannot prevent vaginal spasm by her will power.

Every attempt at penetration by a virile-man adds to her physical, emotional and psychological trauma. Frequently, the repeated failures act adversely on male confidence and the male begins to suffer from psychic impotence. Let me tell you about Prithi who had barricaded the gates of her vagina to sensuality and sex with a huge mental signboard: 'No entry for men'. The twenty-two-year-old girl had been married off two years earlier by her stern and puritanical parents to a most eligible bachelor. Prithi had not yet produced the much-wanted male heir and her mother-in-law, becoming anxious, took her to a female gynaecologist for her supposed sterility. It was then that the bubble burst! Prithi would not allow the doctor to examine or even touch her. It was therefore decided to do an internal examination under light anaesthesia. The doctor was amazed to find strong spasms of the vaginal muscles even though Prithi was anaesthetised. The vaginal inlet was so tightly contracted that the doctor could not insert a finger! It was only under deep anaesthesia that there was sufficient muscular relaxation for an internal examination which revealed that Prithi had an intact hymen. She was still a virgin! When asked to explain, Prithi said, 'Doctor, I permitted my husband to defile my whole body except my purity and virginity. I want to preserve it all my life. Sex is dirty. My mother always told me so.' Obviously Prithi needed psychotherapy for her ignorance and sexual inadequacy.

Causes

PHYSICAL: In every case, physical causes like rigid hymen, tumours of the pelvis, inflammation of ovaries and uterine tubes and narrowing of the vagina must first be ruled out, before concluding that vaginismus is psychogenic in origin.

PSYCHOLOGICAL: Psychoanalysts believe that vaginismus is due to childhood Oedipus conflicts (see Chapter 13), or penis envy or hatred of men. According to them penis envy is usually present during the phallic stage of development of the little girl, especially if parents show partiality and preference for the boy. If this conflict is not resolved when she grows up, she is likely to suffer from vaginismus—an expression of unconscious revenge by denying the man sexual pleasure. Her vagina is a 'no man's land'. Nature has 'castrated' her and made her into a woman. She therefore castrates the man, giving an eye for an eye and a tooth for a tooth. The psychoanalytical approach aims at resolving her so-called conflict by making her consciously aware of her subconscious hostility to men. However, sex therapists have found that the psychoanalytical approach does not work in most cases.

ENVIRONMENTAL FACTORS AND PSYCHO-TRAUMA: It is now believed that vaginismus is a conditioned response associated with factors like rape or sexual brutality, fear of men or fear of pain during initial intercourse and unconscious childhood conflicts associated with fear of vaginal penetration.

Principles of therapy
Vaginismus can be cured by simple treatment. An easy-to-follow therapy format is outlined below:
(1) It should be explained to the wife that vaginismus occurs owing to an imagined or real fear of being hurt during penetration, and may follow an unpleasant sexual experience. The doctor should explain that intra-psychic conflicts produce the spasm of her vaginal muscles. She should be told in simple language that 'a tight mind and a tight vagina go together'.
(2) Both partners are asked to examine their genitals in a mirror. It is often found that, apart from the male not knowing the female anatomy, the female herself is ignorant about it.
(3) 'Stay with your unpleasant feelings,' advises Dr. Helen Kaplan.

According to her, avoidance of the unpleasant incident which produced vaginal spasm perpetuates it. For example, all women who suffer from sexual trauma during childhood or initial coitus do not develop vaginismus as they do not mind facing a sexual encounter again. On the other hand, women who are the 'once bitten twice shy' type shy away from a repetition of the anxiety-provoking penetration and dilation of their vagina. The patient is reassured that she can overcome her problem by tolerating a transient psychic pain. The pain is not physical and she can divert her mind by fantasizing.

(5) She should, on her own, try to contract and relax the vaginal muscles for 3 or 4 minutes twice a day every day till she gains good control (see Chapter 5).

(6) Next she should lubricate her little or index finger with K.Y. Jelly and insert it into her vagina. At the moment of entry it is likely that she will suffer transient mental anguish but not physical pain. She must tolerate it and keep the finger still. After she has gained confidence and her fears have disappeared, she can move the finger to and fro and practise gently stretching the vagina muscles with her fingers. Later she can do the to and fro movements by inserting more fingers. She must practise till she can easily insert three fingers, but it is better if the female initially does it herself as she can withdraw her fingers whenever she wants.

(7) After two weeks of finger dilatation, the couple is ready to move on to the next stage: coitus. The male partner initially introduces a well-lubricated phallus and remains still. Later he gently introduces the to-and-fro thrusting movements while reassuring his partner with tender words and caresses.

(8) The outcome in most cases of vaginismus is excellent with the above therapy (Masters and Johnson have reported a cure rate of 100 per cent with patients treated according to their methods). However, a few cases of deep intrapsychic conflicts may need psychotherapy. Similarly, in several cases of marital discord, the strained relationship between the partners has to be resolved before behaviour therapy is begun.

Part IV

Putting Yourself
Together Again

Chapter 17

DO YOU MANHANDLE YOUR PARTNER?

Let me kiss you slowly
There upon your mouth,
Let me get to know you
North, east, west and south.

PAUL ANKA

THE OXFORD DICTIONARY defines the meaning of the word 'manhandle' as 'to handle roughly'. Adam has been rightly accused of manhandling and dominating Eve since her creation. If you want your partner to love you and respond wholeheartedly in sex, you should treat her as your equal and know her intimately—her likes and dislikes and what makes her tick. However, our heritage and culture wrongly presuppose that the male is a superior human being and the monarch of all he surveys—including women.

Is the male really a superior human being? How did he manage to dominate women?

Prehistoric man and woman, until about 300,000 years ago, were equal partners. Both hunted independently for food and fought side by side against threats from other cavemen, wild beasts and inclement weather. As soon as man harnessed fire to keep him warm in the Ice Age, the division of labour between the sexes began. The woman stayed indoors and kept the fire going while man became the hunter, protector and provider. As the woman stayed at home, she gradually became weaker and smaller, while the male with his outdoor life became stronger and bigger. Such a division of labour exists only among *Homo sapiens*. In all other species, the female hunts along with the male.

Moving to historic times, in the early Vedic period, the Aryan settlers respected their women, and sons and daughters were given opportunities for study and sexual freedom. But even in this progressive society, the status of the Aryan man was higher, since the woman's fate and freedom were decided by him. A few centuries later came Manu, the law-giver, who enacted a strict code of morality for Hindu women. Girls were denied education, had to remain at home and were considered inferior to boys. Manu's Code reigned supreme for centuries and even now largely governs the code of conduct for Hindu women in India.

In her book *The Rebellious Home-Makers* Mrs. Indira Mahindra vividly describes this male domination: 'Protection can presume upon possession of the protected. A woman who accepts protection of a male concurrently gives her protector a right over her. This is the historic reason for her subjugation to man. In acquiring a male to protect her she also reduced her level below his. She became his woman, his possession, his property, his slave—at his choice.'

An important corollary of the inferior status of woman was the change in the sexual behavior of the male. Man could now rape her—possess her forcibly. Rape is unknown in the animal kingdom. The male never copulates with the female by coercion. He never attempts to enter her except during the sexual cycle (oestrus) and, even then, not until he gets the go-ahead signal from her. He never trespasses into her territory without permission. The animals have therefore a strict sexual code, unlike man. We are indeed insulting animals when we say 'He raped her like an animal.' The human male is, however, ever ready for sex and can have it with any woman, at any time. In the old days, a husband could sell or trade his wife like any other commodity. Our ancient epics, the *Mahabharata* and the *Ramayana,* are full of such tales.

To give you a well-known example from the *Mahabharata,* Yuddhishthira wagered his wife Draupadi in a game of dice and lost her to Duryodhana. Modern man does not sell his wife, but he certainly uses her in more subtle ways for his advancement!

Male poets, writers and philosophers in all countries have not only condemned woman as evil but found her inscrutable and beyond their comprehension. I shall quote a few of them. In the *Mahabharata,* it is decreed, 'There is nothing more sinful than a woman. Verily women are the roots of all evil.' Even the wise Socrates did not have a kind word for them. He believed that 'woman is the source of all evil.' Aristotle pronouncing his profound judgement on women said, 'We should regard the female nature as afflicted with a natural defectiveness.' St. Thomas called woman, 'An imperfect man,' while Shakespeare moaned dramatically, 'Frailty, thy name is woman!' Later the great pyschoanalyst Freud, who spent a lifetime analysing the mental make-up of woman, finally, like a defeated soldier, 'put up his hands'. He was powerless to analyse this strange 'creature on our planet'.

Not content with mere condemnation, male arrogance regards it as its prerogative and privilege to determine and decide what is good for women—even in sex. The early sexologists were all males and the rare female who dared to raise her voice was outcast and ostracised. Fortunately, conditions have changed and many female sexologists have recently come forward and accurately described their feelings and responses during sex. I too am acutely aware of my limitations as a male attempting to write about female sexuality.

A lot of sexual inadequacy in both partners springs from man's conceited belief that a woman is meant for his pleasure. He wonders why she is as unresponsive as a log of wood to his love-making. The woman, on the other hand, resents being used at his will and command.

Vatsyayana in A.D. 400—sixteen centuries before the Kinsey Report and the Masters-Johnson sexual revolution—outlined in great detail how a woman is to be wooed, loved and treated with the greatest tenderness and respect. Unfortunately, the teachings of Vatsyayana were gradually lost and a woman became a mere receptacle for a man's sperm.

The status of women did not change much till the outbreak of World War II in 1939 and, in our country, the Independence movement. During the War, Western women worked shoulder to shoulder with men and a new awakening made them resent their inferior status. Similarly Indian women participated as equals with men in the freedom struggle. With this glimpse of equality, the seeds of female revolt against male domination were sown. Two major discoveries in the 1950s hastened the sexual emancipation of women and the birth of women's lib. One was the discovery of the contraceptive pill. With its advent, orthodox and restrictive sexual norms collapsed like a pack of cards. Henceforth, a woman could indulge in sex without the fear of unwanted pregnancy. Secondly, the laboratory research of Masters and Johnson in 1959 proclaimed to a startled world that a woman can reach one or several clitoral orgasms during auto-manipulation. Prior to their findings, investigators had been vainly trying to produce vaginal orgasms (see Chapter 11), and if the woman could not respond, she was labelled frigid. The pendulum now swung to the other extreme! The Western liberated female became acutely orgasm-conscious but the poor vulnerable male was incapable in most cases of climaxing her in the conventional man-on-top position. He needs his finger for the job and hence the validity of the French saying, 'As long as I have my little finger left, I will never be impotent.'

Let us examine both problems; that of male belief in his superiority and his inability to understand Eve, by a case history. Premkumar told me with an injured look, 'Doctor, I am utterly fed up of Sudha! I never know what she wants. Last night I made an advance but she rejected me immediately. "You men are interested in one thing only," she said. I was angry and lay sleepless for hours. After all, I am the master of the house. When I got up in the morning Sudha picked a quarrel and screamed, "You must be going to bed with someone else, that is why you did not love me last night!" Between you and me, Doctor, my telephone operator never refuses me whenever I want her. What a difference between my shouting, screaming wife and her!' he concluded.

Undoubtedly women come in different sizes, shapes, colours, temperaments and moods. Like chameleons, they can change their colours—the most ordinary woman becomes a smashing beauty queen with a little make-up, a little mascara, a new hair-do and a lot of 'performing'. The versatile Shobha Kilachand vividly describes her different *avatars* or forms in an article in the *Sunday Review*.

'I perform, oh yes, I do—anywhere, anytime. It has become a practised reflex which I can switch on at will. I have several roles in my repertoire. The dazzling Shobha K. The bright and witty party person.

The wry, wise-cracker. The 'together' woman. The doting and devoted mother. The sociable and glamorous wife. Even (believe-it-or-not) the vulnerable, little-girl-lost. I know I am in there somewhere. But where? That's the big question—to which I suspect there isn't really any answer.'

If a woman has so many *avatars,* how is a poor man to make out which role she is 'performing' and what her mental and sexual make-up are? It is extremely difficult but there are certain basic traits which, by and large, are common to almost all women.

In our clinic, we conducted a small survey on 386 women to find out what they expected from their male partners to make them tick and respond wholeheartedly in sex. The answers are very revealing and suggest a lot of male ignorance about women in general and female sexuality in particular.

COMMUNICATION GAP: The majority of women complained that there was either very little or no communication with their partners. Modern executives have learnt the importance of communication in business and industry and make every possible effort to keep the channels of communication open with their colleagues. But at home, it's a different story.

Here is a sample. 'Doctor, he never talks to me except when he wants sex. He then becomes a completely changed person. Otherwise in the evening he reads a novel or a newspaper, watches the TV or listens to music. I look forward to his return the whole day but all he says is "hello" and cuts me dead for the rest of the evening.'

I asked some men about their strange silence with their partners and am reproducing a typical male response. 'Doctor, I come home dead tired after a full day's work and as soon as I enter the house my wife starts playing the same old long-playing record of all her woes—the price of sugar has gone up, we are without cooking gas and there is no meat available in the bazaar. What can I do about all these things? I don't sell them! So I just pretend not to notice her at all.'

What does the referee advise in this undeclared war between the sexes? I would urge the wife to allow some time to the husband to unwind—with a welcoming smile and a piping hot cup of tea. After he is relaxed and refreshed he should devote some time to talking to his wife before burying his head in the newspaper or sitting glued to the TV.

HE NEVER TOUCHES ME EXCEPT DURING SEX: To be sexual one must be sensual. In other words, touching is the raw material for the development of good sex. Touching or mutual pleasuring also forms the basis of treatment of sexual dysfunction—impotence, premature ejaculation and fridigity. The relevant section on touching from Chapter 8 is therefore outlined once again, to emphasise its importance.

Touching plays a very important role in the normal well-balanced emotional growth of babies. Without it their personalities become warped. Infants feel good if they are caressed and cuddled. As they grow up, it is customary for only girls to be touched by their mothers (see Chapter 8). 'A man has got to be a man and must behave like one,' says the mother. She thinks that if she touches the boys they will grow up to be cissies, and therefore refrains from doing so.

'John thinks I am untouchable except when he goes to bed with me,' moaned Celine. Here is John's version: 'If I touch her, Doctor, she might think I am interested in sex.' We impressed upon John and Celine that touching need not necessarily culminate in sex! It can be just touching your partner and nothing more.

'Oh, Doctor! If he just put his hands on my shoulders or even kissed me, how different I would feel,' said Sakar. 'Women long for the loving look, the glance, the touch and a little attention. It makes our world completely different. He never treats me as his equal. He believes that women are inferior and never recognises my needs or ever has a word of appreciation for me.' Did you know, Mr. Tarzan, that touching plays a very important part in a woman's sexuality? Physical affection for its own sake, and not just sexual touching, is very important to women. They crave to be touched by their beloved. It costs you nothing to use your hand non-sexually, yet it will result in ever-lasting dividends—a contented and responding partner.

THE LOVING LOOK: By this I do not mean the lovey-dovey look of the Lailas and Majnus one sees on the silver screen. I mean the quick yet affectionate glance that shows that you have noticed the new hair-do or the lovely sari she has worn on her birthday. Your approval and admiration mean more to her than the HMT wrist watch you have presented her. If you fail to notice her, she is not going to ask you, 'Darling, do you like my new sari?' You will wake up with a rude shock at the cocktail party, when you find all the roving Casanovas praising her sleek outfit and paying her a lot of attention with only one intention! It need not be clothes alone; compliment all her efforts. Do not criticize the Russian Chicken she has attempted, even if she has forgotten the salt and instead added a generous helping of chilli sauce! After all, she will notice it herself when she tastes the first morsel. You can then console her that it will be perfect the next time and win her undying love. When you suddenly find a paper missing from your table, do not bark or shout. Count ten instead and simmer down! She cannot help having been bitten by the bug of tidiness ever since childhood. If you are too busy to have the time to show such affection, be prepared to foot the doctor's bill for her psychosomatic illness. In any case, how can a doctor cure her when you are the real cause of her heartaches, backaches and headaches?

THE MAGIC METAMORPHOSIS THAT THE FOUR-LETTER WORD 'LOVE' CAN CREATE: Here is Suma complaining about Paul: 'He has not once told me in the last ten years that he loves me. I think the word does not exist in his dictionary!' She said with a sigh, 'If men only knew the magic effect of the word "love" on our psychology, personality and well-being, they would use it more often.' Poor Paul was shocked to learn that it is necessary to tell your partner 'I love you'. But a word of warning. Never tell a woman you love her unless you mean it—for she may fall in love with you!

'IF YOU DON'T WANT TO TALK, YOU DON'T HAVE TO TALK' says a hoarding, advertising an internal telephone. It may be true for Super-phones but not for super-women. Birds and bees have their mating sounds and so do animals. But man, the only animal with the power to express his feelings, is tongue-tied before, during and after sex. Rajendra told me, 'How can I talk when, all the time, I am wondering if I will get a hard-on? When I concentrate I cannot talk. If my erection is not good, I give up sex and pretend to go off to sleep. How can I do *bakwas* with her when I am full of shame?' I told Rajendra,

'You are guilty of three cognizable offences under the Sexual Code of Vatsyayana.

'First and foremost, how can you get an erection if you intentionally concentrate on your penis? I have repeatedly emphasised that erection happens naturally when you are sexually aroused. You cannot order your penis, "Hey! I want to make love to Seema. Get erect." "Go to hell" will be the reply and it will keep obstinately limp! Secondly, if you had diverted your mind and had had a pleasant conversation and love-play with Seema, you would have been turned on naturally and would have had satisfactory intercourse with her. Finally and most important, if for some reason you do not have a good erection, please do not come to an abrupt grinding halt like a screeching car when the brakes are jammed. Continue to love her and bring her to a climax with your eternally obedient index finger. She will love you all the more for the consideration you have shown her. If you just turn over and go off to sleep she will think that something is wrong with her, and she has failed to turn you on.'

'SEX FOR HIM IS "BANG, BANG, FINITO AND SNORTO",' replied Dinah when I asked her why she was so tense and spent sleepless nights. I was taken aback but quickly regaining my composure asked, 'Dinah, what do you mean exactly by your crisp nine-word pronouncement?' Dinah's eyes flashed fire as she unburdened herself: 'Sex for men in the Space Age is just "bang, bang"—like firing shots from a .32 Colt revolver. For my husband sex means a kiss here, a finger there and within seconds he is on me. "Bang, bang", and he is finished! He then immediately goes off to sleep, leaving me high and dry and listening to his snoring. Every day he wants to bed me and says that I am frigid and should see a doctor. Do you think I am frigid?' she asked, expecting me to say, 'Certainly not'. Instead of a direct answer, I hedged and told Dinah that I would like to see her husband as well. I saw Denis first and confronted him with the cause of Dinah's insomnia. He looked shattered. He had thought himself an extraordinary lover and sincerely believed that sex in the Space Age should be 'quick in, quicker out'. I reminded him that supersonic speeds were for planes and not for women. He has now changed his technique and spends more time on the preliminaries and after-play. Dinah sleeps soundly and enjoys a better sex life.

'HE IS SO ROUGH WITH ME, HE MANHANDLES ME ALL THE TIME. Why can't men be more gentle and tender?' complained Kalpana. In spite of what is written in the popular literature on sex, most women want their partners to be gentle and tender. Unfortunately, the books have taught us that women have to be handled roughly and some women, having read these books, believe that it is part of their life to be manhandled by men. But you can never go wrong if, in the early stages, you try the twin approaches of gentleness and tenderness. It is only during the later stages of intercourse that some women prefer rough handling.

'Oh, Doctor, Bobby is so sweet. I can bully him wholesale,' Samira told me at a party. I reminded her gently that no woman really admires the man she can boss. I told Samira the story of one of my patients, a very attracive Australian blonde. Punctuality is a bee in my bonnet and the blonde was always half-an-hour late for her appointments. Her excuses were, 'held up at the hair dresser,' 'was playing cards,' 'got late at a lunch party'. I once told her firmly, 'If you are late next time I will not see you. You will have to see my colleagues at the clinic.' She repeated the performance and when I refused to see her, she created a scene and used the 'most effective water in the world'—tears. But to no avail. She left in a huff, swearing that she would never see me again.

Three weeks later she telephoned me personally and asked for an appointment. I told her I would certainly see her, provided she was on time. She arrived half-an-hour before her appointment and waited till I finished seeing the previous patient. It was a slightly tense meeting for both of us. As she was leaving, she asked, 'Doctor, do you have a minute to spare?' Then she went on, 'I have got my way with my looks all over the world, wherever my husband was posted. You are the first doctor who refused to see me if I was not on time. I will always respect you for it. I love to tease men, and try the power I have over them. But at last I met my Waterloo in you!' She pleaded, 'Just one more personal question. Did you not find me attractive?' Knowing that it is not a man's tyranny but his indifference that peeves a woman, I quickly reassured her and restored her ego, 'You are indeed attractive but attractiveness and punctuality are two different things.' A tear of relief rolled down her left cheek. She wiped it, rearranged her hair in the mirror and left. In conclusion, I repeat: No woman admires a man whom she can bully.

'HER INFINITE VARIETY': I have only touched the outer fringe of the iceberg by outlining women's commonest likes and dislikes. 'Which card do I play?' you will naturally ask. There are no set rules for this unique game of love with women. You can only learn by trial and error what your partner wants in sex. But why play a guessing game? Ask her directly but tactfully to tell her preferences. You can begin by telling yours.

I shall conclude this chapter by quoting a passage from the *Kama Sutra*, as translated by B.N. Basu:

'If the man is acting according to the inclination of his wife and so gains her confidence, she, in return, will place her confidence in him and be the willing slave of his love-desire. If she be always too willing to yield to her master's desire, she will be so passive an agent as to be unresponsive; if she be too unwilling, any attempt at physical intimacy will be a failure. Therefore a man should see to it that she co-operates in the sexual act of her own free will and with intense pleasure. She should stand neither in awe nor in fear of her husband. The person who knows the pleasant method of attracting a girl's love by gaining her confidence and intimacy and by increasing her own self-esteem at the same time, is sure to be very dear to women. On the other hand, the man who neglects a girl because of her shyness is considered by her as a fool, ignorant of the ways of a maid and as such despised like a brute. The man who, without caring to understand a girl's psychology, attempts to take or takes possession of her body by force, only succeeds in arousing the fear, horror, concern and hatred of the girl. Deprived of the affection and sympathetic understanding she longs for, she becomes obsessed with anxiety which makes her nervous, uneasy and dejected. She either suddenly becomes a hater of the whole male sex altogether or, hating her own husband, gives herself to other men as a form of revenge.'

Chapter 18

COMMON TOPICS ON WHICH YOU NEED ENLIGHTENMENT

What is the difference between sex and sexuality?

Dr. Masters defines sexuality as a dimension of the personality and sex as a specific physical activity. Sexuality determines the quality of sex. A healthy sexuality ensures normal sex but if the sexuality is warped or repressed because of cultural and social taboos or emotional influences, sexual dysfunction can result.

Are most men monogamous in marriage?

The typical male reply in over 2000 senior executives: 'Men are polygamous by nature.' At least 50 per cent of those senior executives had had sex outside marriage, without their wives knowing about it, yet strongly suspecting it. The other 50 per cent were faithful to their wives upto 10 years after marriage. At least 10 per cent of this second group had had one or more 'extra-marital' experiences after the first 10 years. Here is how one of them put it: 'I love my wife only, but as far as sex is concerned, I need variety. It adds a new dimension to my sex life.' In most cases the marriage remained intact; a few of them had divorced their wives and the majority of this small group had married their secretaries or female executives. The reasons which males usually advanced for their extra-marital affairs were that in most cases their sex lives with their wives had been insufficient for their needs and that it had been boring.

What is the average length of a penis?

I have been criticized at seminars for not stating precisely the average length of the penis. It is not difficult to measure the penises of 2000 or 3000 men and find out the average length of the penis, as has been done in the case of the average height and weight charts. But there is a great pitfall. If I state that the average length happens to be 12.5 centimetres, you will worry yourself that nature has been unkind to you if yours is only 11 centimetres. In extreme cases you may land yourself on a psychiatrist's couch learning to live with your 'small organ'. So I strongly feel that where ignorance is bliss it is folly to be wise—to know the average length of the male organ and be miserable for the rest of your life.

Doctor, is my penis too small to stimulate a woman to orgasm? My friend Hussain's, which I saw in the toilet, is long and thick.

Firstly, you normally see your penis from above, while you observed Hussain's sideways, which always makes it appear longer. Stand sideways in front of the mirror and you won't notice much difference between your friend's and your own penis. Secondly, great variations in penile length occur only among flaccid penises. The large flaccid penis expands only 75 per cent whilst a small penis can expand 100 per cent. The size in erection of most penises is almost the same. Thirdly, the upper two-thirds of the vaginal barrel is insensitive to ordinary touch (except deep penetration): only the lower one-third is sensitive because it has touch fibres. If, say, the distended vagina during intercourse is 15 centimetres, your partner can only feel and enjoy the penis in the last 5 centimetres, that is, the lower one-third portion that is sensitive. Is your penis just over 5 centimetres long, which is the minimum length necessary to satisfy a woman sexually? The answer is universally 'Yes'.

What happens if a male has an unduly long penis, say 20 centimetres?

First and foremost, women do not enjoy long ramrods. They are uncomfortable and can often be painful. Although a long penis may be a great ego-booster to its owner, about 5 centimetres of it remains outside, the next 5 centimetres are gripped by the outer one-third of the sensitive vaginal wall and the remaining half penetrates the insensitive area of the vagina—not a satisfying experience for a male. However, there are a few women who believe that a large penis is more stimulating and exciting. This may be due to their previous sexual conditioning, or belief in the folklore of sex. For the vast majority of women, the length of the penis is unimportant, though it remains the most prized part of the anatomy for a male.

What do I do about my small testes?

Like the size of your penis, the size of the testes does not matter as long as they produce the male hormone testosterone in sufficient quantities. The testes are the glands responsible for your manliness.

Why does my scrotum hang loosely?

The position of the scrotum and the testes is determined by a muscle called the cremaster. When you are anxious, tense and worried and during the hot weather, the scrotum seems to hang loosely. But in cold weather or when you are aroused, the muscle contracts and draws up the testes. The state of the muscle—loose or tight—does not determine your erection or potency.

Are large veins on my penis a sign of oncoming impotence?

You have never complained so far about the prominent veins on your forearms or legs. The veins seem large when your organ is limp. Actually, it is better to have large blood vessels in the penis for a prompt erection, rather than narrow thickened ones.

Is masturbation common amongst Indian males?

Unfortunately, statistics of the prevalence of masturbation in our country are not available, like the Kinsey and Hite Reports in the U.S.A. It is said that 99 per cent of men masturbate, whether they are single or married. The American male usually leads two distinct and definite sex lives simultaneously: 'I have more or less two sex lives, one with my wife and one with myself. I have masturbated for many years,' was one of the typical replies reported in the *Hite Report on Male Sexuality*. In India, however, because of early marriages and the cultural belief still prevalent amongst innumerable males that masturbation is harmful, one can only hazard a guess that the incidence of masturbation amongst males might be on the lower side. However, amongst school and college students and bachelors, I would not be surprised if the incidence matches the U.S.A.

Is masturbation harmful?

Certainly not. We have enough evidence to show that masturbation is not harmful. If, however, it is exclusively preferred to sexual intercourse even when opportunities for heterosexual contacts are available, it should be treated.

How many times can one masturbate safely?

There is no upper limit; it would be totally false to lay down that, for instance, thrice in twenty-four hours is safe while four times is harmful. Formerly the same kind of thing used to be said about sexual intercourse—an upper limit per week was prescribed. Just as you can indulge in as much sex as your horse-power permits you, similarly there is no limit to the number of times you can masturbate.

Why do I feel guilty after masturbating?

A large number of people cannot help their guilt because for generations masturbation was considered to be harmful and many religions have lent their support to this view. It takes a long time to overcome such cultural dogmas.

Which is more pleasurable, masturbation or sex?

Certainly sex with a responding partner.

Is there any difference between orgasm during masturbation and intercourse?

Orgasms during masturbation are the most intense physically. There is no performance pressure, one does it in solitary splendour and the way one wants it. However, the deep emotional and psychological bond with a responding partner is not there and to that extent they are not as satisfying and fulfilling as orgasms during intercourse.

Doctor, I am hooked on masturbation (compulsive masturbation).

If you have become a compulsive masturbator and prefer it even when you have the opportunity for normal sexual intercourse, you certainly need treatment. Consult your doctor.

Will masturbation make me impotent or insane?

Certainly not. It is, on the contrary, healthy in certain circumstances. It provides an escape-valve when the pressure of the sex instinct is unendurable and sex with a partner is not possible.

Are night discharges harmful? What is their normal frequency?

Night discharges are physiological and completely harmless. They usually occur during an erotic dream. There is no norm for 'wet' dreams. They occur when sex with a partner is not possible.

Why do I pass semen every time I urinate?

The whitish discharge in your urine is not semen but phosphate crystals. This condition, called phosphaturia, is quite harmless and usually occurs among vegetarians. Take a sample of your urine to your doctor who will examine it chemically and under a microscope. The report should convince you that the whitish discharge is phosphate crystals and not semen.

How does erection takes place?

My Casanova friend Jacob has a unique answer: 'Doctor, forget about the anatomy, physiology and psychology of erection. It is just a state of mind. With supreme confidence and with the right partner, erection automatically takes place.' However, if you still want a blow-by-blow anatomical account, see Chapter 4.

Why don't I have a rock-like erection?

Your penis is created for penetrating the soft vagina and not for drilling holes in a stone wall! The penis is hardest at the age of 17 to 19, the hardness gradually declining with age. Though a little hardness is necessary for penetration, further hardness is not necessary in order to satisfy your female partner.

Does a man lose his potency when he is fifty?

The popular belief that a man loses his potency at fifty is an absolute myth. Many middle-aged men give up sex and, predictably, become impotent immediately afterwards. The power of erection is present from the cradle to the grave. But physiological changes occur in the penis as part of the normal ageing process. For instance, erection takes a little longer, or the help of the female partner may be needed, or the ejaculation response is delayed.

I am 42 years old and do not become erect instantaneously as I used to when I was twenty. Is this normal?

The erection response at the age of twenty is instantaneous, but gradually declines as we grow older. In the forties it may take a few seconds and in the mid-fifties your partner may have to caress you to produce an erection. Do not panic and think you have an erection problem. It is a normal physiological change which takes place in most men.

Is it true that semen is the most vital body fluid and that 40 drops of blood are needed to manufacture one drop of semen?

Both statements are fallacious. Semen, like saliva or gastric juice or tears, is a body fluid. Saliva and gastric juice are special secretions for digesting food, while tears help to lubricate your eyes. Semen is no more precious than all the other body fluids, the only difference being that it contains sperms, the male gametes for reproduction.

I get a normal erection but my penis becomes limp when I am about to penetrate. Am I becoming impotent?

You certainly have an erection problem due to situational anxiety or worry or distraction. Please refer to Chapter 14, 'Impotence, Its Causes and Treatment', and if the problem persists consult your doctor.

I discharge when I am about to penetrate. What do I do?

You are suffering from a very common disorder called premature ejaculation (see Chapter 15 for Treatment).

I have normal sex and orgasm but no ejaculation. Do I need to consult a doctor?

You are suffering from retrograde ejaculation, where the seminal discharge goes into the urinary bladder instead of coming out through the penile urethra. Your doctor can easily diagnose it for you. Masturbate with a full bladder and after your orgasm, pass some urine. Your voided urine, when it is examined under a microscope, will show sperms. Retrograde ejaculation results from a disorder of the internal sphincter of the bladder, which normally seals off the urethra and blocks the flow of urine during ejaculation. Retrograde ejaculation may also occur after a prostatectomy or if you have diabetes. You should consult your doctor for treatment.

Is it true that a better erection will result in better sex?

No, many studies including the famous Shere Hite report, have shown that the majority of women have denied the current widely prevalent male belief that women are interested in a ramrod-like erection penetrating their vaginas and thrusting vigorously. On the contrary, it hurts their delicate insides, though a majority of them silently suffer the assault by the cavemen. The real Casanovas are not merely the 'Slam-bang-thank-you-ma'am' lovers but artists who know when, where and how to use the lips, the tongue, the hand and the over-rated penis to hold their partners spellbound.

I am twenty-two and at my sexual peak. Is it true, as my friends tell me, that impotence is inevitable as I get older?

Certainly not, as I have repeatedly stated. The power of erection is present from the cradle to the grave. However, the elderly suffer from disease and degeneration of the arteries like atheroma which can result in loss of erection.

Is is true that 'the older the man, the better the sex', asks a twenty-nine-year-old single P.R.O. of a five-star hotel?

Upto a point, if the man is healthy, day by day in every way he gets sexually better as he gets older. He has now graduated in the art of love and is no longer just interested to function as a sprinkler on any and every flower that comes his way!

Is there a good 'aphrodisiac pill' that helps one to get a hard erection?

There is no such pill, though the search has been on since Adam was born.

I am 42 years old and during the last six weeks, my erection has become gradually weaker. What can this mean?

Erectile difficulties of this type are usually due to physical causes. These can be (1) Metabolic, such as the onset of diabetes; (2) Hormonal—deficiency of the male hormone; (3) Liver disorders like amoebic or chronic hepatitis; and (4) Drugs such as tranquillizers, anti-hypertensives or cholinergic drugs of belladonna used in cases of gastric or duodenal ulcers and intestinal colic. Have complete physical check-up, blood profile and hormone profile, especially testicular levels—FSH (Follicle Stimulating Hormone) and LH (Luteinizing Hormone) from the pituitary to ascertain the real physical cause. Your doctor will plan the full investigation profile.

I have been impotent for the last seven years. Would you recommend psychoanalysis?

Psychoanalysis is a long-drawn-out process where the therapist probes deep into your past to ascertain the present cause of your sexual dysfunction. It has a major drawback in that it lasts from three to six years or even longer. Secondly, your female partner is left in the lurch whilst the probing of your psyche is going on. Thirdly, the symptoms do not normally disappear in the order in which they appear and, though you have gained a deep insight into the whys and hows of your mental and emotional make-up, you are unable to reverse your sexual problems. The best therapy for you is sex therapy which is short, begins with the 'here and now problem' and reverses it with the modern Behaviour Therapy. In cases with deep-seated conflicts, the patient is first given a short course of psychotherapy, before starting sex therapy.

Can specific training procedures overcome sexual inadequacies in males and females? Are there any contra-indications for sex therapy?

Sex therapy gives excellent results in most cases. It is contra-indicated if the cause is physical, such as stress, tiredness, early diabetes, a local genital pathology, or a psychiatric disorder like depression or schizophrenia.

Why are most men interested in only penis-vagina intercourse and not any other form of sex? Why do men regard women as a mere piece of 'meat'?

'It is universally assumed—that what men like/want from intercourse is their orgasm,' states Shere Hite in her brilliant and painstaking book, *The Hite Report on Male Sexuality.* 'However what men want from intercourse is something else.' The 7239 men who answered her questionnaire stated that they could easily obtain a more powerful orgasm through masturbation than sexual intercourse. Orgasm was not therefore the be-all and end-all during sex. What men liked most was the close physical contact of the vagina clasping the penis, the ego-boosting effect of being loved and wanted, and, last but not the least, the fact that the thrusting erect penis confirms the male's masculinity.

Is alcohol a sexual stimulant? Does it help cases of impotence?

Alcohol is a depressant, 'a sexual poison', as the noted Bombay sexologist, Dr. Prakash Kothari, calls it. 'It has no place in sexual dysfunction.' Though a little alcohol removes inhibition and stimulates desire, it is difficult to determine when this little becomes too much, especially for the male. It is therefore best to avoid it.

How can I make my partner orgasmic during penis-vagina intercourse? How do I know that my partner is orgasmic during penis-

vagina intercourse? Isn't it very frustrating for her to go on and on without release?

If your partner happens to be in the lucky 30 per cent there is no problem; she can be vaginally orgasmic and your penis will feel the contractions. For the majority of women your best bet is to stimulate her clitorally and let her reach an orgasm, if she so desires. You can then insert your erect organ in the vagina and enjoy carefree sex with her. Secondly, with the woman-on-top position you can have easy access to her clitoris as she moves on your erect penis. Thirdly, she can stimulate herself whilst you are on top and thrusting; most women, are, however, reticent to stimulate themselves in front of the male partner.

It is very important for males to realise that only 30 per cent of women, according to *The Hite Report on Male Sexuality,* reach an orgasm during penis-vagina intercourse—whilst the remaining vast majority (70 per cent) can only be orgasmic during manual clitoral stimulation. The penis, in the man-on-top position, does not come into direct contact with the clitoral area which triggers an orgasm in the female. Besides, the clitoral stimulation orgasms are more intense and localised whilst the vaginal ones are more diffuse and less intense.

It is very difficult for most males to find out whether their partner has had an orgasm or not, especially when the penis does not feel the vaginal contractions.

Besides, females expect their partners to be completely knowledgeable not only about themselves but also about their partners.

What is a fool-proof preventive against venereal disease?

The only effective preventive is to drink a glass of water instead of indulging in sex with a partner you do not know!

If, however, you must have sex:

1. Make sure your partner is well lubricated and has no external sores or ulcers.
2. A comparatively dry vagina causes friction and ardent, vigorous sexual thrusting can break the delicate penile skin, providing an easy entry for a venereal infection.

3. Do not lie around after discharge. Get up and urinate and wash your organs with soap and water.
4. Apply 33 per cent calomel ointment to the penis.

How long should normal intercourse last?

One can never set a time limit as it varies from couple to couple, and according to the psychological and environmental conditions conducive to love-making at the time. However, the sex act should last sufficiently long to provide sexual satisfaction to both partners. Like the length of the penis, the ideal duration for sexual intercourse cannot be defined in minutes and hours.

Isn't it more pleasurable the longer it lasts?

Men have a false notion that if they keep on battering their partner for an hour or more, the greater is her enjoyment. Lengthy intercourse is distasteful and painful for most women, especially if the vagina does not lubricate sufficiently.

How do I know whether my partner is orgasmic during intercourse?

The easiest and surest way for the male to find out is by asking her whether she had an orgasm or not. However, most males are reticent to ask; besides, cultural conditioning has impressed on females that men are not only sexually knowledgeable about themselves but also their partner. Her invariable answer is to remain mum or just say, 'Can't you tell.' Besides, women are born actresses and over the years have learnt to feign an orgasm by moaning and groaning and clasping their husbands tightly, thus making it difficult for him to find out whether she is really orgasmic or only feigning.

However, most men, as Shere Hite rightly points out, are searching for an orgasm in the wrong lane. They have erroneously assumed over the years there is something wrong either with them or their partner, if she cannot reach an orgasm during penis-vagina intercourse. Men all these years have been groping and searching in the dark unfathomed caves of the vagina whilst the clitoris is 'born to blush unseen and waste its sweetness o'er the desert air'. The clitoris is the master-key to unlock the secret of female orgasm. Stimulate her clitoris the right way and enjoy the thrill of her real orgasms, the way nature intended her to explode orgasmically.

What can I do about my small breasts? Don't men like bosomy females?

Most women are hung-up about the size of the breasts just as men are about the length of the penis. There are many treatments like silicon grafting for increasing bust size. But. small-breasted women can respond just as well as their better-endowed sisters. Small can be sexy as it is actually the nipple which is primarily involved in sexual stimulation. However, some men—like some women who cherish long penises—are thrilled by a 'handful' or a 'palmful'.

My husband says that sex should be avoided during a menstrual period as it is unclean and unhealthy. What is the medical thinking about it?

Centuries of cultural conditioning has ingrained in us that sex is forbidden during a period. Sex is not objectionable during a period if both partners desire it, but it is messy and might stain the bed sheets. The heightened female desire and response due to congestion of the genital organs during a period, may even make sex more enjoyable. There are no medical contra-indications, but the vulva and the vagina are more vulnerable to lacerations as well as infection during menstruation. It is also advisable to abstain when the discharge is at its most copious or if the woman has a tendency to haemorrhage.

What about sex during pregnancy?

During the first trimester, sex should be avoided by women with a history of repeated miscarriages and by all women during the expected days of a menstrual period. During the second and third trimester there is no bar to sex until the head descends deeply into the pelvic cavity, lowering the vaginal wall. This happens six weeks before confinement in the first pregnancy and two weeks before confinement in subsequent ones. However, the man-on-top position is very uncomfortable for the pregnant woman and sex should be indulged in the lateral or woman-on-top position. Both partners should practise the utmost cleanliness during coitus as the risk of infection and contagion is greater during pregnancy.

When can sex be resumed after confinement?

Sex can be resumed six weeks after confinement when the uterus returns to its normal non-pregnant state.

Is it normal for a female to have an orgasm every time she has sex?

Orgasm for most women is a five-star luxury not attainable every time she has sex. This is because a woman is not a quick performer like the male who can go bang, bang anytime and anywhere—in the car, in the house or a hotel, on the bed, and ever under it! A woman on the other hand is slow to respond, the orgasm depending on her mood, the environment, atmosphere and adequate sexual stimulation—a combination of factors not easily achieved in the hurry and scurry of the twentieth century. However, Helan Kaplan has described a normal variant of female sexuality in a group of women who do not reach orgasm during sex but are orgasmic during masturbation or when their husbands stimulate them manually or orally. The doctor faces a dilemma in such cases of lack of orgasm. Is the anorgasmia due to pathological inhibition or is it a normal variant of female sexuality? If the initial interview with the couple does not reveal any sexual inhibitions, anxieties or guilt about sex, the doctor should reassure them that the female partner's anorgasmia is a normal variant of female sexuality. If, however, the couple persists that the female partner must become orgasmic, the husband could increase her sexual responsiveness by touching and pleasuring.

Where does orgasm occur in the female?

The argument about the clitoral or vaginal orgasm has been settled by Dr. William Masters. There is neither a pure clitoral nor a pure vaginal orgasm, but pelvic orgasms initiated in the clitoris and accompanied by contractions of the vaginal platform (wall) and the uterus.

What percentage of women reach an orgasm during sex?

Dr. Alfred Kinsey, the pioneer researcher in human sexual behaviour, reported that 75 per cent of women in the sample survey had some orgasmic experience by the end of the first year of married life, and 87 per cent after ten years of married life, while one out of ten never reached an orgasm at all. Though large-scale studies are not available in our country, the proportion of anorgasmic women is much higher.

Is auto-manipulation harmful to women? Is there a difference in the quality of orgasms between auto-manipulation and penis-vagina orgasm?

Self-stimulation to orgasm is not harmful to either sex. Its incidence, however, is higher among men as the sexual urge is more demanding and concentrated in the penis. Shere Hite, the famous model turned sexologist who studied the sexual behaviour of 3000 women for four years and published it in the famous *Hite Report,* states that there is a distinct difference between the auto-manipulative clitoral and the penis-vagina intercourse orgasms. The women answering the Hite Questionnaire reported that the clitoral orgasms during auto-manipulation were sharper and of longer duration, while the penis-vagina orgasms were softer, short and fleeting. The sensation in the former is localised, intense and electrifying, while the latter gave the sensation of a volcanic eruption and a feeling of being shaken. A number of women said they were 100 per cent orgasmic clitorally during auto-manipulation.

How many women masturbate?

The exact figures of women who masturbate are not known. In a study conducted on 67 liberated college girls by a lady researcher on behalf of the author, about 40 per cent admitted to having masturbated. Of the women who replied to the Shere Hite Questionnaire, 82 per cent stated that they masturbated and 95 per cent of them were orgasmic. The remaining 18 per cent denied having ever masturbated. It is quite likely that the percentage of women who masturbate in the general population would be less than 82 per cent as the Hite women were an exclusive set who had no inhibitions about describing their auto-manipulative techniques. The percentage in our country would be much lower because of sexual taboos, guilt and cultural conditioning. Marriages of girls take place at an earlier age than in the USA, the fear of detection is greater in the joint family and the cult of masturbation has not been highlighted here as it has in the USA. 'Masturbation is our primary sex life. It is our sexual base,' writes Betty Dodson in *Liberating Masturbation.* She tells readers that even primates masturbate from early childhood.

'Which is the most satisfying method of auto-manipulation—the clitoris or the vagina or both?' asked a collegian on the telephone without revealing her identity.

Women employ widely different techniques to masturbate and obtain sexual gratification. We have once again to rely on the intensive study by Shere Hite on American women. The majority of the women according to the *Hite Report* use the finger to stimulate the clitoral vulva area, whilst lying on the back, and fantasising or arousing themselves psychically. Initially they stimulate the mons area with their lubricated fingers, then go on to stimulate the side of the clitoris, and end up with rapid jerky stroking of the clitoral body and the glans. Most women masturbated to orgasm in a few minutes. Some hard-pressed for time used a vibrator. A few titillated the clitoris with stroking inside the vagina, while some preferred to simultaneously stimulate their left breast and nipple with their left hand. A few masturbated lying on their stomach, or introducing some object into the vagina. About 30 per cent of women crossed their legs tightly and by strongly tensing and relaxing the upper thigh muscles and the legs became orgasmic.

Should I always have orgasms during intercourse?

Women are not very definite about their feelings during penis-vagina intercourse. Some never have orgasm during coitus but invariably have it during masturbation.

Do women need orgasms for their sexual, physical, mental and emotional health?

Yes. One Hite respondent rightly remarked that 'Whoever said orgasm was not important for a woman must be a man—either a physician or a clergyman.'

When I do not reach an orgasm, I feel tense, irritated and have a congested feeling down under. How do I relieve it?

You should stimulate yourself to orgasm or, better still, your partner should manually or orally stimulate you.

Can just fondling the female genital organs with an erect penis without any penetration result in pregnancy?

Definitely yes. There is usually some pre-ejaculatory fluid from the urethral meatus to lubricate the penis during intercourse which contains a few sperms, and one of them can always fertilise the ovum when pregnancy is not wanted!

Are all women multi-orgasmic?

According to Masters and Johnson, all healthy women have the capacity for multiple orgasms. But these were laboratory findings on electrically or manually stimulated women. It is difficult to find men in today's Stress Century who can last the gruelling multi-orgasmic match during penis-vagina intercourse. The male partner, however, can easily stimulate a woman manually to orgasm a number of times—in fact, as many times as she wants. On an average, women, except in rare circumstances, do not reach more than two or three orgasms. Many of them have to be content without even a single orgasm.

Is mouth stimulation of the penis (fellatio) unhygienic? Do men usually like it?

First and foremost, fellatio is neither unhygienic nor dirty with a man who pays attention to personal cleanliness. If the man has not been circumcised he should retract the foreskin and clean the head of the penis regularly to remove the secretion called smegma which may accumulate and prove slightly offensive.

Most men enjoy fellatio considerably. An ardent lover's mouth is the most potent stimulant to erection. 'Oh doctor, I am in seventh heaven when my beloved sucks me. Alas, it is so rare—only twice in seven years,' observed an ardent fellatio fan. There are a few men who like neither fellatio nor the partner holding them. Women as a rule are reticent not only to hold their partner's penises with their hands but much more to do fellatio on them. They believe that the man will think she is a forward type and that such acts are only indulged in by prostitutes and call girls!

Is oral sex with a woman unhygienic? Are the vulva and vagina full of germs? Do women like it? Can it do any harm to the male?

Oral sex (cunnilingus) with a female partner is perfectly hygienic. It is advisable that both partners should have a bath before they indulge in oral sex with one another. The greatest guru of sexology, Vatsyáyana, 600 years before Christ, recommended this form of sex. Neither oral sex nor intercourse should be indulged in if the woman is suffering from a vaginal infection. The same applies to a male.

Most women are stimulated to seventh heaven by a genital kiss, the most close and intimate expression of love between partners. It is also very exciting and pleasurable for a man to see and feel, with the lips, the torrential love and excitement of the woman.

Cunnilingus is an extremely common love practice in the West; *The Hite Report on Male Sexuality* reports 88 per cent of males enjoyed cunnilingus with a clean woman and 9 per cent did not like it. In India, however, the art of cunnilingus is less common owing to the inbuilt resistance of both partners.

Can a female partner reach her orgasm with oral sex?

The female can easily and quickly reach the most intense orgasm with cunnilingus provided that the male stimulates her clitoral region with his tongue. Many males just kiss the vulva and vagina which, though very excitable and pleasing, may nor result in a climax.

What about anal intercourse?

'Hot, tight and tantalising,' aptly described an anal intercourse fan.
'My partner very rarely permits it but both of us explode.' It may be
that both partners have a strong aversion to anal sex; however, it can
be indulged in when vaginal intercourse is prohibited if the partner is
pregnant or has a fungal infection, or to introduce an element of
variety in humdrum sex. Finally, anal sex can always be used as a form
of birth control; it may also be useful for premarital sex if the woman
is keen to preserve her virginity till she marries. There are certain
disadvantages; penetration, unless it is done after good lubrication
and very gently, can be painful. The position is also not comfortable.
Finally, it is not advisable to resort to vaginal intercourse after an act
of anal intercourse without a proper wash, because there are chances
that the woman may get a B. Coli infection.

What is homosexuality? Is it a sexual perversion?

When a male prefers to make love to a male in preference to a female,
he is said to be homosexual. Homosexuality is wrongly condemned by
society as a perversion, and it is only recently that most societies are
beginning to accept, though very grudgingly, that homosexuality is a
normal variant of male sexuality.

Why do men bottle up their feelings? Does it affect their sexuality?

Boys are always told not to be 'cissies' but to behave like men. They
are told that they should not cry; this is the prerogative of girls. They
should suppress their feelings and no expression should show on their
face. In other words, a man must be a man, every inch a man! Such an
erroneous upbringing has a profound effect on a man's sexuality, so
much so that he may remain inhibited and not get an erection, even
during sex with his partner.

Why does he woo me when he wants my body and why is he a different man once he has had the lollipop—just turns over and snores away?

This is a very common male characteristic and, very rightly, a sore point with most women. A male will go to the ends of the earth to make the woman and then drop her, temporarily at least, like a hot potato, as soon as his ejaculation is over. Men reason that they are slaves of their sexual urges and when sexual tension is mounting, they just want to discharge and get instantaneous relief. In conclusion, as Byron rightly said, 'Men's love of man's life is a thing apart, 'Tis woman's whole existence.'

What is the difference between love and sex?

Love is the most sublime form of emotion whilst sex is merely the act of reproduction. It is physical, with the aim of depositing a sperm from the male into the vagina of a female with the hope that it might meet an ovum and fertilisation will take place.

There can be sex without love, what is popularly called recreational sex. However, the best and most sublime form of sexual union can only take place if love is present as well; and then, as Milton said of Adam and Eve, we may experience the supreme of joy of being 'Imparadised in one another's arms.'

Why is it that during foreplay, I am completely out of bounds for my partner below the navel—that part of my anatomy just does not exist for her?

Men invariably like their penis and testes to be stimulated by their partners. However, women have been subject to centuries of cultural conditioning which has inhibited them to the point that the male organ just did not exist at all for them—it was not to be looked at, not to be touched and never to be caressed.

Gradually, however, more and more women have become aware that their hands and lips caressing the male organ can generate waves of delight. The male partner feels that his partner relishes him totally—every inch of his anatomy and not just above the belly button! See his love for you spring to action.

Except a very few who do not wish their partners to caress their penis, the vast majority are waiting impatiently, to be stimulated. Do not think your partner will consider you forward or a loose woman. On the great clock of time there is only one word—now. Begin today. Don't wait for him to take your hand there.

Chapter 19

INTEGRATING SEX AND LOVE

*When two people love each other, nothing is
more imperative and delightful to them than giving, to give always and everything, one's thoughts,
one's life, one's body and all that one has.*

GUY DE MAUPASSANT

DEAR READERS, we have sailed together in the vast, unfathomed
sea of sexual inadequacies. We soon ran into rough weather and
choppy seas. We drifted hither and thither with every cultural wind
that blew our way. We encountered the innumerable shoals, reefs and
mythical monsters that dwell in this turbulent ocean. The leader of
these monsters was the penis, the king of kings in the kingdom of sex.
Among the monstrous myths you believed were: the bigger it is the
better; it becomes erect instantaneously; it should be as hard as steel;
and it is fail-proof. The second in command was masturbation which
was supposed to make you impotent and mad. Closely behind were
the pair, night discharges and loss of semen mean loss of vitality. The
trio followed; sex is duty; sex is dirty; sex is sinful. The phantoms
haunting women were age and appearance, the size of the breasts, a
sagging bosom and taboo on sex during menstruation.

You started feeling that your sex life was over and you couldn't take
anymore. You were desperate, not knowing what to do or where to
turn for help. You naturally believed that the ship would sink for ever.
You ransacked the vessel fore and aft for a magic solution, a potion to
save you from impending doom. Like a caged tiger you paced to and
fro across the ship, tripping over innumerable obstacles. But nothing
doing. Every moment prolonged your agony till on a dusty, disused
kerosene tin you found the 'pilot'—the navigational guide who would

slowly negotiate your ship of sexuality through choppy seas. You were overjoyed. But initial pleasure gave way to depression. For it is a long, long way to reach the shore of healthy sexuality. 'Isn't there a short cut?' 'Can't I recite a magic mantra or take a magic potion?' you asked. There was none. So in sheer desperation, you sat at the rudder with the pilot to steer your vessel slowly and safely to port with your new knowledge. You skilfully negotiated the obstacles and attacked fatally one by one the mythical monsters. They now lie buried deep in the turbulent sea.

The port of 'Happy Sexuality' is in sight. Our sailing ship is ready to anchor and it is time to say fair winds, clear skies and good sailing to all of you, all your life, in the ever-turbulent ocean of sexuality.

Here is the no-more-anxious adolescent Atul who used to torture himself mentally not to succumb to masturbation (Chapter 1). 'I now know that masturbation is not harmful but is a natural sexual outlet till sex with a female partner is possible,' he said as he jumped springily on the pier. 'Doctor, I now lead two sex lives—one with my wife and the other with myself when I am on my own during tours. Nothing succeeds like success at the sex game.'

'What about you, Dorab?' I asked, as I bade him goodbye (Chapter1). 'I have come down to earth after my fiasco with Diana. I keep away from a woman who wants me to pierce her "like an arrow and keep on piercing her, till she moans, groans and dies in my arms." Everybody cannot be a Casanova,' he concluded philosophically.

'Hold my hand, Sir,' I offered upright old Harry, father of Michael (Chapter 13), as the vessel suddenly swayed. 'Those were the days,' he blurted as he fumbled at the landing with his right foot and mumbled, 'Nobody taught us all this claptrap! One day masturbation is bad, the next day it is good and cures impotence, premature ejaculation and frigidity.' He paused for breath and continued, 'If I had my way I would send Michael and his wife to a desert island for six months. They would jolly well soon be normal sexually, havng nothing else to do! But my old lady dragged me to this cruise, as she does not wish to be away from her son.' Having finished his speech the old man left in a huff. 'Don't mind my husband, Doctor,' his wife whispered softly as I helped her to disembark. 'You know what I have put up with for the last 40 years. I now realise what we have done to Michael. It is not

My parents dinned into me that everything below ⟨wa⟩s dirty and not to be touched, except after ⟨…⟩ during a bath. As for my impossible husband, he ⟨…⟩l, "Women are dirty, deceitful and dangerous. ⟨…⟩ or go near them except when you want a baby!" With a tearful face she continued, 'I can see that we were the cause of Michael's loss of manliness. I admit I was wrong, but my old man will never understand human emotions and psychology.'

Harry perhaps has a point. Modern sex therapy has its critics. Many psychiatrists believed that it merely relieves the symptom—impotence. According to the New York analyst, Natalie Shaines, 'Teaching "push" here and "rub" there is not going to change people.' However, the only alternative prior to Masters and Johnson's two-week intensive therapy was prolonged psychoanalysis which went on for three to six years, treating the remote childhood conflicts while ignoring the immediate causes like fear of failure and spectatoring. It is difficult to evaluate and compare the results of traditional psychotherapy and sex therapy at present. But available reports reveal that traditional psychotherapy is effective in only about 30 per cent of cases of female orgastic disturbances after three to five years, and is ineffective in premature ejaculation. On the other hand Masters and Johnson, Patricia Schiller, the noted founder of the American Association for Sex Education, Helen Singer Kaplan and others have reported a cure rate of over 60 per cent in primary impotence, excellent results with a cooperative partner in secondary impotence, 98 per cent success in cases of premature ejaculation, and 100 per cent success in cases of vaginismus.

Although it is easy to cure sexual dysfunction with sex therapy, there are chances of a relapse, particularly in cases of impotence and premature ejaculation. Masters and Johnson report a relapse rate of five per cent. Recurrence of sexual anxiety produces impotence, often transient, occasionally more lasting. Those cases respond again to sex therapy. 'Hi Derek, you are still in your denims though no longer dejected, I hope,' I asked as he stood patiently to say goodbye. 'Doctor, I have learnt an important fact on this jaunt,' he replied as he shook hands. 'Everything in this universe fails sometime and my penis is no exception. I don't worry myself to death on the days I can't function. I frankly tell my partner that I occasionally suffer from erective failure but that I love her, that I find her very attractive and that my failure has nothing to do with her. I caress her, fondle her and bring her to a climax manually, if she desires. We find it very fulfilling.'

Behind Derek, in a spotless white dhoti, was Ghanshyam (Chapter 1) who had been quick on the trigger and invariably discharged before penetration. Walking at a correct distance behind him was his sari-clad wife, Tuniya. Being a pucca businessman, Ghanshyam described his humiliation and despair about his affliction in monetary terms. 'For four years I was a nervous wreck. I swallowed *churans* and tablets but it got worse with each day. I must have lost at least Rs.8 lakhs of business and spent Rs. 20,000 in treatment. Little did I realise that a few simple sexual tasks for a month would cure me. The cruise has taught me the hard way that there is an easy method to fix up premature ejaculation by relaxation, sensory erotic experiences and stop-start masturbation,' (see Chapter 15). As Tuniya alighted on the pier behind Ghanshyam, she quipped, 'In spite of what you write, Doctor Saheb, about the "Namaste Culture", we Indian women will always do a "Namaskar" with folded hands and not a handshake!'

'Who goes there without even a goodbye to me?' I asked as Sunil shyly tried to slip away. Sixty-year-old Sunil had remarried 35-year-old Rama for companionship and found later that she wanted sex. I beckoned the accountant and told him not to be shy of the young people. Michael said, 'We are all sailing in the same boat,' which encouraged Sunil to confess, 'I believed a man's sex life came to a full-stop at fifty. When I asked my younger, better-informed office friends about sex they retorted, "What do you expect at your age?" My family physician also said the same thing. But now I know that you can enjoy sex at any age if you keep physically fit and accept that erection takes a little longer and may even need your partner's help. The response is less intense and the refractory period is longer. But I have found that the physiological effects of ageing can be offset by a mature mind that enjoys and later fantasizes the experience.'

'I now see with hindsight why men at my age chase young chickens,' said Kapil (Chapter 1) with the seven-year itch. 'It's what you doctors call the male menopause. After my sexual fiasco with willowy

Wandana, I was impotent for two years. But the male hormone shots and therapy have revived my potency and thankfully restored my inner balance.' Next I turn to greet Stella, who said with a brave smile, 'Poor Bruce keeps trying but cannot do a thing (Chapter 1). He then deserts the burning ship without extinguishing the fires of love in me. Formerly, I used to torture myself thinking he did not love me or did not find me attractive enough. I now know his erection problem is due to severe stress at the office. But he loves me and I am content.'

Behind her was petite 22-year-old Sakar who is planning to write a book, *In Praise of Older Men.* With eyes flashing, she said, 'My young, handsome husband ditched me for my best friend. I was bitter and lonely, and to occupy myself began studying German at the Max Mueller Bhavan. Little did I dream I would fall for the studious, frail, 40-year-old Professor Shankar Dayal. Everybody in my class and office made fun of me. How could I tell them what a great lover he is? We will get married as soon as I get my divorce. My former husband just believed in bang-bang-bang every night. He left me unaroused and unfulfilled. But with Shankar it is different. He is so gentle and tender and caressingly sweeps me off my feet until I am fulfilled. He has the three qualities of all great lovers—confidence, maturity and skill, which come with age and experience.' Having made her point, Sakar trotted away on her high heels. Then Michael asked wistfully, 'Doctor, there must be many guys like me who try to bed their newly-wed brides without any knowledge of sexuality and have been brought up to believe that sex is dirty and sinful. How can they get a hard-on?' I explained to Michael that although the 'here and now' immediate causes of his sexual dysfunction were resolved, the remote, deeply embedded childhood conflicts came in the way of a successful outcome. He would need some psychotherapy to resolve his earlier, deeply embedded conflicts.

Michael was born with a clean sexual slate and normal capacity for potency. However, his puritanical and kill-joy parents indoctrinated in Michael from infancy, 'Sex is dirty; sex is sinful. If you want to be a great man have nothing to do with women, keep away from them.' Is it any wonder that Michael's belief system about sexuality was distorted from birth with negative self-images that hampered normal sexual functioning?

'We need to urgently instil knowledge on sex education,' said Dr. Mahinder Watsa, Chairman of the International Council of Sex Education and Parenthood, India, 'to our 100 lakh confused adolescents who will be the parents of tomorrow. At present many suffer from a feeling of guilt and anxiety and are full of sexual myths and misconceptions which are bound to lower their self-esteem and confidence.'

Bringing up the rear, in flowing robes and Arab headgear was Abdulla Shirawi,* the well-known, highly successful business tycoon from Dubai. As stated earlier, his motto is, 'In order to succeed in business, you must first be successful in sex.' Here is the secret of his 'Sex Power'.

'Erection first occurs in the mind and later in the penis. A spontaneous or natural feeling of arousal sets the pace for a sexual encounter. I am an all-or-none man—either I let myself go completely or not at all, if I am not in a mood for sex. *Inshah' Allah Bukhra* (God willing, there is always a tomorrow). After sex, I am naturally invigorated and physically refreshed. Sex Power gives me the supreme confidence to handle any business successfully.'

The twentieth century has been nicknamed the Stress Century. It is also the age of impotence and premature ejaculation. Stress and anxiety are the deadliest enemies of good sex. The new threats to man's healthy sexuality are not from nature, but from the technological monster man has created. Yet the power to combat the sexual ravages of stress and anxiety are within us all. It is not a gift of the gods to a chosen few. *Sex Power is yours.* It is a way of life, unfettered by myths, misconceptions and doubts. And it is a learning process. 'If there is no light anywhere and you have got no one to turn to, this book will lead you out of the darkness and put you together again.' The best aphrodisiac is a sound mind in a healthy body and an interested and interesting partner.

Left alone, I pondered that while the West has swung from sexual taboo and repression to free sexual expression and promiscuity, we in India, 400 years before Christ, never equated sex with puritanism. In

---

* Real name quoted with permission.

fact, Hindu sculptures depicted sexual intercourse as an act of religious significance associated with holy rites. The three objectives of life according to the ancient Hindu sages were *Dharma* (religion), *Artha* (materialism) and *Kama* (pleasure). No less a person than our late Philosopher-President Sarvapalli Radhakrishnan referred to Kama as 'the emotional being of man, his feelings and desires. If a man is denied his emotional life, he becomes a prey to repressive introspection and lives under a continual strain of mortal torture.' This book, which is a blend of East and West, of yesterday and today, is a humble attempt to restore the emotional well-being and inner balance of man through sexual expression and love.

Lady readers will wonder why the most frequently used four-letter word 'love' has never been mentioned in the book. Dr. Prakash Kothari aptly sums up the correlation between love and sex when he says, 'Sex can be the climax of love, but love cannot be the climax of sex.' Very little love is involved in the Indian system of arranged marriages prevalent in over 90 per cent of cases. The parents choose a partner for their son or daughter. A courtship prior to matrimony is almost impossible, so love does not have a chance to bloom. The first intimate expression of the couple is physical and sexual. If sex is right, love may—hopefully—follow. If sex is wrong, the main nourishment for its ripening in an arranged marriage is absent. Hence a knowledge of the art and science of sexuality is vital in both partners for marriage. Closer intimacy naturally permits love to unfold and blossom. Dr. Van de Velde rightly says, 'Only where love is, can the sexual pleasure be at its height, the orgasm ecstatic, the relief complete and the drowsy, dreamy relaxation which follows communication, a perfect peace.'

APPENDIX I

MUSCULAR RELAXATION

MUSCULAR RELAXATION can be done either in the morning or at night just before going to bed. Initially at least, you will need 15 to 20 minutes every day for about a month to learn the correct technique. It is preferable that you lie in bed, eyes closed, with your arms by your side and both legs straight. If you are used to a pillow, it is better to have one. After a few days, you can practise relaxation sitting in a chair with armrests. The room should be darkened and free from undue noise or distractions like the telephone. Do not wear shoes or anything tight around your neck or waist.

(1) The easiest way to learn relaxation is alternately to contract and relax all the muscles of your body. Contract the muscles consciously for about 30 seconds as hard as possible while repeating to yourself mentally, 'Tension.' Learn the feel of tension arising from tight muscles. Relax your muscles naturally while reciting to yourself mentally, 'Relax, relax,' for two minutes. Do not consciously force yourself to relax or concentrate your mind on relaxation, otherwise it will have a contrary effect and make you tense.

(2) Initially, it is better to start with muscular contraction and relaxation of different muscle groups, one by one. Later, you can tense and relax all the muscles simultaneously.

It is easier to memorise and practise relaxation if the muscles of the body are divided into various groups. They are:
   (a) Muscles of the face, scalp, front and back of the neck;
   (b) Both hands, forearms and shoulder girdles;

(c) Chest and abdomen, front and back;

(d) Both lower extremities, including thighs, legs and feet.

(3) You can begin with any group of muscles. Most individuals find relaxation much easier if they start with the upper extremities. Clench both fists tight for about 30 seconds, as hard as you can. Feel, mentally, the taut and tight muscles. Now relax and let go naturally for about a minute. Bend your elbows and contract both biceps muscles as hard as possible, then relax them. Next, extend your elbows, keeping the upper arms straight; tighten all the muscles at the back of your arm and forearm, making them as rigid as possible. Relax and let go. After you have mastered the technique of tightening and relaxing both upper arms with a few minutes of practice, you are ready for the next stage.

Appendix I is from my book, *Rock Around The Clock.*

(4) Frown as hard as you can and contract all the muscles of your face, scalp and lips. Tighten the muscles of the tongue by making them taut and touching the back of the front teeth. Now relax and let go.

(5) Push your head back against the pillow as hard as you can and tighten the muscles at the back of the neck. Relax.

(6) Shrug your shoulders and touch your ears, hold them for a little while and let go.

(7) Breathe in as deeply as you can, hold your breath for a few seconds after inhaling, and then breathe out gently. Repeat 10 to 15 times.

(8) Tighten your abdominal muscles and hold them tight for a few seconds before relaxing. Do this at least 10 times.

(9) Press your back as hard and as long as you can against the bed for 10 to 15 seconds. Let go.

(10) Tighten your thigh muscles and squeeze your buttocks, at the

same time point your feet and toes as far away from your nose as you can. Maintain this posture for a little while and then relax.

(11) Practise tightening all the muscles of your body for about 30 seconds and relax them for a minute or two. Relaxation should come naturally—do not make any conscious effort.

(12) If you are not yet ready to tighten and relax all the muscles of your body simultaneously, you can practise tightening and relaxing the major muscle groups one by one, beginning from the head and neck down to the lower extremities.

(13) Later on, you can give up the initial muscular contraction and start with relaxation of the various muscle groups. You will save your invaluable time!

(14) Finally, practise tightening one group and relaxing the other groups which are not in use. For instance, while walking keep both arms and the mid-torso relaxed. Tighten and relax, alternately, the muscles of the lower extremities which are required for walking.

(15) Tune yourself to relax as soon as tension develops. In the early stages, you have to practise relaxation as a regular exercise; later it will become a habit and come naturally. Many of our patients have mastered the technique. They are no longer jittery and tense. They work hard, day after day, but still have a reserve of nervous energy.

APPENDIX II

EROTIC EXPERIENCES

IN OUR 'Namaste' culture, touching, even if it is non-sexual, is taboo (see Chapter 8). Why is this so? Our society and customs have wrongly associated simple affectionate touching with sex. However, strange as it may seem, we need to be touched all our lives. Even baby chimpanzees who are kept in isolation and deprived of touching, are unable to copulate when they grow up. The same is true of human beings. An individual deprived of sensory experiences is unable to function normally in sex. In other words, in order to be sexual one must always be sensual.

Sexual dysfunction is marked by sensory deprivation resulting from fear of inhibition induced by parents from childhood days. For instance, the mother says, 'Charlie, don't touch the T.V.,' 'Don't touch the clock.' The growing infant needs a lot of sensory experiences, and the 'touch-me-not' training deprives him of proper sensual functioning.

There is, however, a cultural difference between the two sexes. A boy has to be a boy and not a sissy. Our culture does not permit him to touch other boys or girls. Even as a young boy, touching or kissing his mother is taboo. On the other hand, young girls suffer less from sensual deprivation. Society permits them not only to touch their mothers, but other girls as well. They can kiss each other, walk hand in hand or pat the other girl on the shoulder in school and it is accepted as normal. However, it is not so in the case of boys. Modern culture brands him a 'queer' if he pays undue sensual attention to other boys. However, the feeling of being touched or touching the partner can be developed at any age and forms the main plank in the therapy of sexual dysfunction—erectile problems, premature ejaculation and frigidity. It is better if both partners are available. However, they can be done solo as well. Before describing the erotic experience in detail for both groups a few common therapy formats are outlined:

(1) You should not be under stress or worried or over-tired during erotic touching. Practise relaxation for a few minutes (see Appendix 1). You should choose a time when you are not likely to be disturbed by the telephone or by visitors. Undress completely and lie on a comfortable bed in a darkened room. Do this whether you are doing the erotic exercises solo or with a partner.

(2) Intercourse is prohibited. However, some sex therapists, like Dr. Martin Cole in the U.K., do not believe in such a limitation. 'I tell my surrogates that if the client has an erection, then for God's sake move.' Dr. Cole thinks it is a mistake to let a person fail at something for too long. What applies to a surrogate also applies to the female partner.

(3) Pleasuring solo or with a partner should not be performance oriented. For instance, if the female is pleasuring the male, or if he is doing it solo, he should not concentrate on whether he has an erection or not—instead, he should let himself go and enjoy the feeling. Similarly an anorgasmic female should not grit her teeth and want to be orgasmic but instead enjoy the build-up of pleasurable sensations.

(4) In both partners, touching of the breasts or genitals is prohibited for three to seven days.

Exercises: touching yourself
You can do pleasuring with or without a lubricant such as hand or body lotion. The choice is yours. You can touch or stroke yourself as you like—very light touches, either linear or circular—and experience and enjoy the sensations you feel. Can you differentiate between the sensations you feel on the different zones of your body? Discover your particular erotic zones where you feel most pleasurable. Apart from doing this exercise, why not try touching yourself during your day-to-day activities; see, for instance, how it feels whilst shaving or showering or drying yourself with a towel. You should not masturbate

during these exercises at present. The exercises with masturbation are given in the respective chapters. Do the above exercises five or six times till you become aware of and are aroused by your sensations. You may or may not get an erection during this exercise. However, do not focus on your penis at all.

Exercise: pleasuring with a partner

(1) First and foremost, you must be comfortable with your partner and observe the guidelines outlined in sections one to five. It is better if you tell your partner that you are not interested in sex but merely in lying close to her and being caressed by her. Men generally do not realise how often women yearn to lie in close touch with their partner and bask in the nearness of their beloved.

(2) PROHIBIT SEX: The first and foremost instruction to the marital couple is to prohibit sex to remove performance pressure. The male is greatly relieved that he does not have to produce an erection and he can relax and enjoy the sensual pleasure of touching and being touched.

(3) SENSATE FOCUS: Masters and Johnson lay great importance on sensate focus where both partners pleasure each other in turn. In case of male sexual dysfunction it is preferable for the female to start non-demand stroking of the partner's body. It is necessary that the male should communicate his requirements of where and how he likes to be touched. For the first four or five days the breasts and the genitals are not to be touched. It is now the turn of the male to pleasure his female partner in the way she wants. This non-demand sensual touching is a very important step in the restoration of sexual function. Often the male finds that he gets an erection but is prohibited from indulging in intercourse.

(4) The male now fondles the female breasts and vulva; similarly the female partner stimulates the male organs. In this non-performing milieu the male is likely to get an erection. He is, however, warned that even if it dies down he should not worry about it as this is a normal phenomenon even in potent individuals.

(5) After a while when the male confidence is restored, the female partner is advised to mount the male who is lying on his back. She holds the male organ and gently guides it into her vagina. Often, at this point, the erection may die down but the male is assured that the erection will return. If not, he should try on another occasion.

(6) When further confidence is restored after a few attempts in the 'woman-on-top' position, the male now attempts intercourse with him on top. Here it is necessary that the female partner should once again manually guide his penis into the vagina. For 'a woman knows where it goes.'

(7) Most cases of male impotence respond to the removal of the immediate causes, like fear of failure and performance anxiety (like here-and-now causes). Where there is deep psychological conflict psychotherapy may be required, for which a family physician treating such cases will need the help of a psychologist.

Index

FOCUS BOOKS

These books should normally be available at all good bookshops. In case of any difficulty in getting these books they can be ordered from the Publisher. Please indicate the titles required and give your complete name and address including the Pincode.

You could order the books by V.P.P. in which case the current prices of books and the actual postage will be charged to you. Alternatively you may enclose a bank draft or a cheque or a postal order payable to Popular Prakashan Pvt. Ltd. to cover the total price of books ordered and the books will be sent to you post free.

Every effort is made to ensure the accuracy of the price and availability of books but it is sometimes necessary to increase the prices and in these circumstances retail prices may be shown on the covers of books which may differ from the prices shown in this list or elsewhere. This list is not an offer to supply any book.

FOCUS ON HEALTH

Are You Killing Yourself,
Mr. Executive?
by DR. R.H. DASTUR

Sex Power
by DR. R.H. DASTUR

Sex and Diseases
by DR. R.H. DASTUR

What the Doctor says ...
by DR. R. H. DASTUR

Stop Worrying about Backache
by DR. P.S. RAMANI

Integrated Healing Arts
by DR. J.M. JUSSAWALLA

How to Stop Stammering
and Start Living (2nd Ed.)
by DR. AJIT HARISINGHANI

Full Life With Diabetes
by DR. A. S. GODBOLE AND
DR. A. A. GODBOLE

FOCUS ON COOKERY

The Menu Book
by ANJANI NARAVNE

Rasachandrika
by SARASWAT MAHILA SAMAJ

FOCUS ON BUSINESS AND MANAGEMENT

In the Wonderland of Investment
by A.N. SHANBHAG

Tax Planning for You and Me
by B.B. PALEKAR

**Understanding Business Data
Processing Systems**
by ANUPAM BISWAS

Professional Computer Programming
by ANUPAM BISWAS

Computerising Your Business
by ANUPAM BISWAS

How the West Grew Rich
by BIRDZELL & ROSENBERG

GENERAL

Rituals and Festivals of India
by TARA BAPAT

Bhagwad Gita for You and Me
by M.S. PATWARDHAN

Gita and Its Commentators
by S. H. JHABWALA

Helpful Hints
by JYOTI SHENOY

**A Slot Machine, A Broken Test Tube —
An Autobiography**
by S.E. LURIA

WHAT
THE DOCTOR
SAYS...

Dr. R. H. Dastur

- **Does blood transfusion transmit AIDS ?**
- **Can heart attacks be prevented ?**
- **Is there a 'Cancer Personality' ?**
- **How harmful are starvation diets ?**

In his latest book, WHAT THE DOCTOR SAYS..., Dr. R. H. Dastur provides the answers and sheds light on many killer diseases which plague our society, from AIDS to amoebiasis, cancer to cirrhosis, high blood pressure to heart disease, stroke to stress and spondylosis. Based on the author's more than 40 years of extensive medical practice, the book gives up-to-date information and down-to-earth advice on how to safeguard yourself against health hazards and attain a state of complete physical, mental and emotional well-being. Each of the 48 essays is self-contained and can be read independently. Written in the author's distinctive racy, witty and lively style, suitable illustrations of the body's organs and systems enhance the layman's understanding, while R. K. Laxman's inimitable drawings liven up the pages.

"WHAT THE DOCTOR SAYS. . . is an invaluable health guide for every health conscious individual in quest of vibrant health."

-- DR. ALEXANDER P. LANG
Toronto, Canada

FOCUS BOOKS
A Division of
POPULAR PRAKASHAN PVT. LTD.
35-C, Pt. M.M. Malaviya Marg
Tardeo, Bombay 400 034

SEX AND DISEASES

Dr. R. H. Dastur

Focus on Health series has been designed with the conviction that every individual has to play a major role in keeping himself fit. He has, therefore, to be well informed on important aspects of personal health and hygiene.

Promiscuity is the sole cause of sexually transmitted diseases. The secrecy and ignorance have aggravated the spread of the diseases. Medical science has not yet been able to prevent or control the incidence of these diseases. Dr. R.H. Dastur who pioneered Sex education in India by his famous book *Sex Power* has now written companion volume *Sex and Diseases* which should enlighten all those who may be tempted to indulge in sexual aberration so that they may be spared the misery and agony.

"India is one of the worst infected nations in the world. These diseases are most rampant in the age group 16-25. Among the measures for the prevention and control of these diseases, education plays a very important role. Unlike in other countries the subject is hardly ever discussed on the T. V. or Radio here and a publication of this kind should serve a very useful purpose. This book, written by an eminent physician, in his own inimitable style and in simple language conveys to the youngster very useful information on the subject, a book every young person ought to read and digest."

Dr. B. A. Daruvala
Venereologist

FOCUS BOOKS
Division of
POPULAR PRAKASHAN PVT. LTD.
35-C, Pandit Madan Mohan Malaviya Marg
Tardeo, Bombay 400 034